Social Justice and Counseling

Social Justice and Counseling represents the intersection between therapy, counseling, and social justice. The international roster of contributing researchers and practitioners demonstrate how social justice unfolds, utterance by utterance, in conversations that attend to social inequities, power imbalances, systemic discrimination, and more. Beginning with a critical interrogation of the concept of social justice itself, subsequent sections cover training and supervising from a social justice perspective, accessing local knowledge to privilege client voices, justice and gender, and anti-pathologizing and the politics of practice. Each chapter concludes with reflection questions for readers to engage experientially in what authors have offered. Students and practitioners alike will benefit from the postmodern, multicultural perspectives that underline each chapter.

Cristelle Audet, PhD, is an associate professor in counseling psychology at the University of Ottawa. She is past president of the Social Justice Chapter of the Canadian Counselling and Psychotherapy Association (CCPA) and has been involved with CCPA's Ethics Committee since 2010. Dr. Audet has also authored a chapter on social justice for the *Handbook of Counselling and Psychotherapy in Canada* (2016).

David Paré, PhD, is a registered psychologist and a full professor in counseling psychology at the University of Ottawa. In addition, Dr. Paré is director of the Glebe Institute, A Centre for Constructive and Collaborative Practice in Ottawa. He is the author of *The Practice of Collaborative Counselling and Psychotherapy* (2013), and co-editor of *Collaborative Practice in Psychology and Therapy* (2004) and *Furthering Talk: Advances in the Discursive Therapies* (2004).

Social Justice and Counseling

Discourse in Practice

Edited by
Cristelle Audet and David Paré

Routledge
Taylor & Francis Group

NEW YORK AND LONDON

First edition published 2018
by Routledge
711 Third Avenue, New York, NY 10017

and by Routledge
2 Park Square, Milton Park, Abingdon, Oxon, OX14 4RN

Routledge is an imprint of the Taylor & Francis Group, an informa business

© 2018 Taylor & Francis, Inc.

Library of Congress Cataloging-in-Publication Data
Names: Audet, Cristelle, 1970– editor. | Paré, David A., editor.
Title: Social justice and counseling : discourse in practice /
edited by Cristelle Audet and David Paré.
Description: First edition. | New York, NY : Routledge, 2017. |
Includes bibliographical references and index.
Identifiers: LCCN 2017032523 | ISBN 9781138803145 (hardcover : alk. paper) |
ISBN 9781138803138 (pbk. : alk. paper) | ISBN 9781315753751 (e-book)
Subjects: | MESH: Counseling | Psychotherapy | Social Justice | Socioeconomic Factors
Classification: LCC RC480.5 | NLM WM 55 | DDC 616.89/14–dc23
LC record available at https://lccn.loc.gov/2017032523

ISBN: 978-1-138-80314-5 (hbk)
ISBN: 978-1-138-80313-8 (pbk)
ISBN: 978-1-315-75375-1 (ebk)

Typeset in Minion
by Out of House Publishing

To Casey and Liam.
To allies of dignity who seek the voice of others.

Contents

Acknowledgments   x
Notes on Contributors   xii
Preface   xviii

Part I. Interrogating Social Justice as a Guiding Premise

1 **Social Justice Activism and Therapy: Tensions, Points of
   Connection, and Hopeful Scepticism**   3
   Vikki Reynolds and Sekneh Hammoud-Beckett

2 **Counseling and Social Justice: What Are We Working for?**   16
   John Winslade

3 **Challenging Conversations: Deepening Personal and
   Professional Commitment to Culture-Infused and Socially Just
   Counseling Practices**   29
   Sandra Collins and Nancy Arthur

Part II. Training and Supervising from a Social Justice Perspective

4 **Social Justice and Advocacy: Critical Issues in Counselor
   Education**   43
   Nicola Gazzola, Andrea LaMarre, and Olga Smoliak

 5   **Just Supervision: Thinking about Clinical Supervision That
     Moves towards Social Justice**   57
     Karen L. Mackie and Michael Boucher

 6   **Counseling as Post-Colonial Encounter: Hospitality and
     Ethical Relationship**   69
     Kathie Crocket, Elmarie Kotzé, and Rahera Taylor

Part III. Accessing Local Knowledge

 7   **The Therapist as Second Author: Honoring Choices from
     Beyond the Pale**   85
     Gene Combs and Jill Freedman

 8   **Finding Ways Forward: Social Justice for Counselors in the
     Evolution of a Collaborative Practice and Study Group**   98
     Lynn F. Bloom and Noah M. P. Spector

 9   **"Social Justice" as Relational Talk**   111
     Dan Wulff and Sally St. George

10   **Collaborative-Dialogic Practices: A Socially Just Orientation** 124
     Saliha Bava, Rocío Chaveste Gutiérrez, and M. L. Papusa Molina

Part IV. Justice and Gender

11   **Reimagining the Intersection of Gender, Knowledge, and Power
     in Collaborative Therapeutic Conversations with Women and
     Eating Disorders and Men Who Use Violence**   143
     Catrina Brown and Tod Augusta-Scott

12   **Queer Informed Narrative Therapy: Radical Approaches to
     Counseling with Transgender Persons**   159
     David Nylund and Annie Temple

13   **Coming Out: Implications for Sexual and Gender
     Non-Conforming Immigrants and Newcomers**   171
     Mego Nerses and David Paré

Part V. Anti-Pathologizing: The Politics of Practice

14   **Social Justice for Young People in the Youth Justice System**   186
     Donald Baker

15   **DSM Diagnosis and Social Justice: Inviting Counselor
     Reflexivity**   196
     Joaquín Gaete, Olga Smoliak, Shari Couture,
     and Tom Strong

16 **Narrative Practice and the De-Pathologizing of Children's Lives
    at a Walk-In Therapy Clinic: An Opportunity for Socially Just
    Conversations**   212
    Karen Young

17 **Rosie Had Wings They Could Not See: A Consultation with
    Michael White and a Woman Labeled with a Dual Diagnosis**   225
    Jim Duvall and Caroline Tremblay

18 **Creating Safety and Social Justice for Women in the Yukon**   239
    Catherine Richardson/Kinewesquao, Ann Maje Rader,
    Barbara McInerney, and Renée-Claude Carrier

    Index   254

Acknowledgments

David Paré

This volume has afforded the opportunity for sustained dialogues with a wide range of creative and committed colleagues; I'd like to thank all of you for your generosity in sharing your important work, and also your patience in waiting for a book that has been years in the making.

The editorial team at Routledge has seen various changes over the period of the book's incubation, and was always ready at hand with enthusiastic guidance. Thank you to Marta Moldvai, Elizabeth Lotto, Elizabeth Graber, Meira Bienstock, George Zimmar, and Nina Guttapalle; it's been a pleasure to work with you.

And finally, I'd like to thank Cristelle Audet, my steady and unflappable partner who took the lead on this project. Cristelle, I so appreciate how you attended to the big picture throughout, and turned your eagle eye on manuscripts as we moved towards the finished product. Working with you has been one of the most effortless and pleasurable collaborations I've experienced.

Cristelle Audet

While social justice has been a longheld value for me, it is only recently—and through seeing this book come together—that it has crystallized in my professional practice. I have grown tremendously from the amazing colleagues who contributed to this book. I am grateful for the new relationships and allies forged in the process, and furthering collaboration with cherished colleagues with whom I have found a professional home. What I walk away with is an inspiring glimpse into the important work that each one of you does; it seamlessly reminds me just how accessible social justice can be in day-to-day practice with a little intentionality.

I echo David's thanks to the Routledge editorial team. Their patience and tireless support in this project was much appreciated.

David, co-editing this book with you was such a pleasure. You have been gracious in sharing your wisdom along the way. Your postmodern sensibilities have permeated my way of thinking and being, for which I am eternally thankful.

Finally, to my family, my partner Peter, and all those who asked at different points how the book was progressing; your inquiries along the way came from a place of excitement and curiosity that auspiciously kept the wind blowing into the proverbial sails.

Notes on Contributors

Dr. Nancy Arthur is a Professor in Counselling Psychology, the Associate Dean of Research, Werklund School of Education, University of Calgary, and a Registered Psychologist. Nancy co-developed the model of Culture-Infused Counselling with Sandra Collins, which has been adapted for supervision practices and career counseling. Nancy's research focuses on professional education for diversity and social justice, and international learning and work transitions.

Cristelle Audet, PhD, is Associate Professor of Counselling Psychology at the University of Ottawa. She is past president of the Social Justice Chapter of the Canadian Counselling and Psychotherapy Association (CCPA) and involved with the CCPA's Ethics Committee since 2010. She authored a chapter on social justice for the *Handbook of Counselling and Psychotherapy in Canada* (Canadian Counselling and Psychotherapy Association, 2016), and has written about barriers to well-being such as poverty and ageism. She is interested in promoting counseling and psychotherapy practices informed by social justice values, and conducts and supervises research that aims to forefront under-represented voices in counseling.

Tod Augusta-Scott is known internationally for his work with intimate partner violence, narrative therapy, and restorative justice. He works at both the Bridges Institute and the Canadian Armed Forces as a therapist. His most recent projects include co-editing the book *Innovations in Interventions to Address Intimate Partner Violence* (2017) and participating in the documentary film *A Better Man* (2017).

Donald Baker has been working with youth and families for the past 32 years. He currently counsels young offenders who have been detained in the Ottawa area. He is interested in how individuals are often made to feel responsible for institutional and cultural practices.

Saliha Bava, PhD, Associate Professor of Marriage and Family Therapy at Mercy College, Dobbs Ferry, New York, is an advisor at the Taos Institute's doctoral program and on the faculty for Houston Galveston Institute's International Certificate Program in Collaborative-Dialogic Practices (ICCP). As the Director of Research with the International Trauma Studies Program, affiliated with Columbia University, she has researched theater, community resiliency, and psychosocial practices. An American Association for Marriage and Family Therapy approved Supervisor and Clinical Member, she serves on the boards of the American Family Therapy Academy, ICCP, and on the advisory board of Taos Institute. She is the co-founding editor of the *International Journal of Collaborative-Dialogic Practices*. Dr. Bava's scholarship focuses on creative processes for living, hyperlinked identity, cross-cultural relationships, collective trauma and community engagement, digital life, relational leading, research methodology, social justice, and teaching/learning. Currently, she explores the notion of relational play at the intersection of communicative action, anthropology, complexity sciences, performance studies, and design thinking. Visit salihabava.com to learn about her practice and http://thinkplaypartners.com/playlab/ for her research. Twitter: @ThinkPlay

Ms. Lynn F. Bloom, MSW, RSW, is a Registered Clinical Social Worker in private practice and is a Clinical Associate with the Glebe Institute, a group of Ottawa-based mental health counselors who focus on collaborative practice. Ms. Bloom is also an educator, researcher, and community organizer with extensive training in the areas of physical and mental health, and rehabilitation. Ms. Bloom is an Adjunct Professor with the Faculty of Medicine at The University of Ottawa where she is involved in Medicine and Humanities program development, teaching and research.

Michael Boucher works as a Social Worker, Counselor, and Community Worker at St. Joseph's Neighborhood Center—a center for people without health insurance or adequate coverage—in Rochester, New York. He works to explore the intersections of poverty, racism, oppression, resistance, and resiliency in the community as well as in therapeutic practice. He has been engaged in the clinical supervision of interns for more than 20 years.

Dr. Catrina Brown is an Associate Professor and Graduate Coordinator at the School of Social Work and is cross-appointed to Gender and Women' Studies and Nursing at Dalhousie University. Her research and writing focuses on women's health and mental health issues, including eating disorders, substance-use problems, depression, trauma and post-trauma within a feminist postmodern/narrative lens. Her work centers on integrating critical theory into direct critical practice. She is a private practice psychotherapist who uses a feminist, narrative, discursive, and collaborative approach.

Renée-Claude Carrier is the Manager of Kaushee's Place, Yukon Women's Transition Home. She is a feminist activist that has spent all of her working career on improving services and awareness of violence against women. Renée has presented around the world on her work with women and children and is a sought after speaker. She has worked on innovative projects with Watson Lake Youth, RCMP, and local Government.

Rocío Chaveste Gutiérrez, PhD, is Founder, General Director, Professor, and Clinical Supervisor of the Kanankil Institute in Merida, Yucatan, Mexico. Dr. Chaveste is an Adjunct Professor at the Houston Galveston Institute, an associate member of the Taos Institute and a member of the International Research Network of the same institute. She has a PhD in Social Psychology, and three Master's Degrees in Family and Couples Therapy, Organizational Management, Political Communication, and Electoral Marketing. She is the co-author of the book *Prácticas socioconstruccionistas y colaborativas: psicoterapia,* *educación y comunidad* (Unas Letras Industria Editorial, 2010) and editor of *Identidades, y Relaciones: una mirada desde el Socioconstruccionismo y las prácticas colaborativas y dialógicas* (Instituto Kanankil, Investigación y Construcción Social, A.C, 2014). She has also published several articles on Collaborative and Dialogic Practices. She can be reached at: rchaveste@kanankil.edu.mx

Sandra Collins is a Professor in the Graduate Centre for Applied Psychology at Athabasca University. She focuses her research, teaching, and practice in the areas of multicultural counseling and social justice, with particular interest in working with women and members of the LGBTTQI community. As Curriculum Lead in her academic center, she researches and models efficacy and innovation in teaching and learning, including the infusing of multicultural and social justice competencies throughout graduate education.

Shari Couture is a Psychologist in private practice in Calgary, Alberta who specializes in family therapy. She uses discursive research methodologies to study therapeutic processes with the goal of helping practitioners orient to forward moving opportunities in their conversations with their clients.

Kathie Crocket, PhD, is Associate Dean Postgraduate Research at Te Kura Toi Tangata Faculty of Education, University of Waikato. She teaches narrative practice in the Masters of Counselling programme, of which she was Director for 13 years. She is a life member of New Zealand Association of Counsellors.

Jim Duvall is Co-Director and Co-Founder of JST INSTITUTE and Editor of *Journal of Systemic Therapies* (www.jstinstitute.com). He has decades of experience as an educator, researcher, consultant and has authored and co-authored numerous articles, book chapters and books about collaborative and narrative therapy. Jim teaches and consults with organizations internationally throughout Canada, US, Australia, and Asia.

Jill Freedman and **Gene Combs** have led workshops on various aspects of narrative therapy all over the world. Their extensive writings include *Narrative Therapy: The Social Construction of Preferred Realities* (Norton, 2006) and *Narrative Therapy With Couples ... and a Whole Lot More!* (Dulwich Centre Publications, 2002). Jill is the Director of Evanston Family Therapy Center. She has an independent therapy practice in the Chicago area and consults to social service agencies and to schools. Gene is an Associate Professor of Psychiatry in the University of Chicago affiliated Family Medicine residency program at NorthShore University HealthSystem.

Dr. Joaquín Gaete is an Assistant Professor, Clinical Supervisor, and Director of a Clinical Centre (CEAP) at Universidad Adolfo Ibáñez in Viña del Mar, Chile. His research and writing focus on conversational practices fostering self-preferred change in counseling, family therapy, and clinical supervision.

Nicola Gazzola is a Professor of Counseling Psychology in the Faculty of Education at the University of Ottawa. His research interests are in the area of professional issues for counselors, including professional identity of the profession, clinical supervision, and counselor self-doubt. He is a licensed psychologist.

Sekneh Hammoud-Beckett is an Australian Psychologist, colored by her Lebanese-Muslim ancestry. She enjoys the practitioners' space and revels with an innovative and collaborative blend of creativity, social justice activism, and narrative therapy with the people and communities she meets.

Elmarie Kotzé (Ngāti Kaputuhi), D Litt et Phil, Director of the Counsellor Education Programme, Te Oranga, Te Kura Toi Tangata Faculty of Education, University of Waikato, takes great delight in the supervision of doctoral candidates' and MCouns students' research projects. She enjoys the collaboration with colleagues, graduates, and students and has co-authored several articles and book chapters with the professional, research, and teaching communities.

Andrea LaMarre is a PhD candidate in the Department of Family Relations and Applied Nutrition at the University of Guelph. Her work is focused on experiences of embodiment through a critical feminist lens. In her dissertation work, she is using qualitative and arts-based methods to explore eating disorder recovery from the perspective of people in recovery and their supporters.

Karen L. Mackie, PhD, NCC, LMHC, ACS, is a Clinical Faculty Member in Counseling at the University of Rochester's Warner Graduate School of Education and Human Development. A former dancer, she is currently working on integrating intermodal expressive arts for transformation into the training and supervision of mental health and school counselors. She has co-authored previous chapters on social class issues in counseling for McAuliffe and Associates' *Culturally Alert Counseling: A Comprehensive Introduction* (Sage, 2013), currently in its third revision, and presents at national and international conferences on disparities related to social class and aging within counseling and mental health, as well as on collaborative forms of clinical supervision and family counseling intervention.

Barbara McInerney has been the Executive Director of the Yukon Women's Transition Home Society since 2000, and proudly operates Kaushee's Place and Betty's Haven in Whitehorse, Yukon. Barbara coordinates the Yukon Women's Coalition made up of 14 women's groups across Yukon. Barb is a mother and grandmother committed to the advancement of women and girls.

Ann Maje Raider is a Kaska grandmother and a social justice advocate. Following her service as the first democratically elected Chief of the Liard First Nation from 1992–1998, Ann engaged with a small group of Kaska women committed to addressing the legacy of colonialism. They created the Liard Aboriginal Women's Society (LAWS) in 1998. Ann went on to lead the fledgling society, implementing a multi-year healing strategy aimed at responding to the physical and sexual abuse of residential schools, and through the ensuing years, inspiring numerous and innovative social response initiatives related to cultural wellness and social justice. Most recently, the Society unveiled two new multi-year initiatives—the Youth for Safety Project and Women's Advocacy Service. In addition to her pioneering work within her community, Ms. Raider has served on the Yukon Advisory Council on Women's Issues (2006–2016) and the Yukon Aboriginal Women's Circle (2000–2004).

M. L. Papusa Molina, PhD, is Executive Director and Professor of the Kanankil Institute in Merida, Yucatan, Mexico. Dr. Molina has a multidisciplinary doctorate in Public Administration, Chicano Studies and Women Studies, and a Master's degree in Education and Development. She is an Adjunct Professor at the Houston Galveston Institute. She is also an associate member of the Taos Institute and a member of the International Research Network of the same Institute. Her publications and research lines have focused on issues of race, class, gender, and sexuality. More recently she has been exploring inquiry from a relational/dialogic perspective. You can contact her at: mlmolina@kanankil.edu.mx

Mego Nerses, MEd, RP, is a Registered Psychotherapist and a Canadian Certified Counsellor. He has a Master's degree in Counselling. Mego provides psychotherapy in English, Armenian, and Arabic. His clinical work is focused on sexual issues, refugees, and trauma. He is the recipient of the 2017 Humanitarian Award by the Canadian Counselling and Psychotherapy Association (CCPA) for his contributions to the well-being of LGBTQ+ refugees and asylum seekers to Canada.

David Nylund, LCSW, PhD, is a Professor of Social Work at California State University, Sacramento and the Clinical Director of the Gender Health Center. David Nylund is also a faculty member of the Vancouver School for Narrative Therapy. He is the author of many books and articles on Narrative Therapy.

David Paré, PhD, is a Registered Psychologist and a Full Professor in Counselling Psychology at the University of Ottawa. In addition, David is director of the *Glebe Institute, A Centre for Constructive and Collaborative Practice* in Ottawa. David has written widely and presented internationally on the subject of narrative and collaborative therapies, as well as offering training and supervision in these areas. He is the author of *The Practice of Collaborative Counselling and Psychotherapy* (Sage, 2013), and co-editor of *Collaborative Practice in Psychology and Therapy* (Haworth Press, 2004) and *Furthering Talk: Advances in the Discursive Therapies* (Kluwer Academic/Plenum Press, 2004).

Vikki Reynolds, PhD RCC, has a deep commitment to social justice and her work is based on an anti-oppression and decolonizing framework. She plays a leading role in building communities in a spirit of solidarity, putting ethics at the forefront. Vikki Reynolds is a Consultant, Instructor and Supervisor specializing in Team Development, Resisting Burnout and Organizational Change. Her work addresses addiction, substance misuse, diversity, homelessness, trauma, and violence. As a Clinical Supervisor and Therapeutic Supervisor Vikki is informed by narrative therapy and collaborative therapy, and provides individual and group clinical supervision to therapists and community workers. Vikki's articles and talks are available for free on her website: www.vikkireynolds.ca

Dr. Catherine Richardson/Kinewasquao is a Metis/Cree woman, scholar, counselor, and activist working in the School of Social Work at the University of Montreal. She studies responses to violence as well as practices of cultural safety, dignity, resistance, and recovery for victims. She is a co-founder of the Centre for Response-Based Practice focused on ending structural and interpersonal violence, and specializes in addressing interpersonal and state violence and reforming child welfare practice.

Noah M. P. Spector, MSW, PhD, RSW, holds a Master's of Social Work degree from McGill University and a doctorate in Educational Counselling at the University of Ottawa. His research focuses on young people and their families' experiences of mental health treatment. Noah currently works as an Emergency Room Crisis Intervention Worker and teaches family therapy at the Children's Hospital of Eastern Ontario.

Sally St. George, PhD, is Professor in the Faculty of Social Work at the University of Calgary and a Family Therapist and Clinical Supervisor at the Calgary Family Therapy Centre. She conducts workshops on family therapy and qualitative inquiry. Sally serves on the Boards of Directors for the Taos Institute, an organization dedicated to developing social constructionist practices worldwide, and the Global Partnership for Transformative Social Work, which involves co-developing transformative practices in social work education. For the last 20 years, Sally has worked on *The Qualitative Report* and is currently Senior Editor for this online journal.

Tom Strong is a Professor, Couple and Family Therapist, and Counselor-Educator at the University of Calgary who researches and writes on the collaborative, critically informed, and practical potentials of discursive approaches to psychotherapy. For more details on Tom and his research please consult: www.ucalgary.ca/strong

Olga Smoliak's main areas of research are family therapy and discourse analysis. She uses discursive methods of inquiry (e.g., conversation analysis, discursive psychology, membership categorization analysis) to examine interactions in therapy. She also conducts research in the field of gender and language and explores how the broader sociocultural context influences well-being and how therapists can promote social inclusion and justice.

Rahera Taylor (Ngāti Maniapoto), MCouns, has worked in a range of community settings, and more recently as a School Guidance Counsellor, after an earlier career in the Probation Service. She hosts the annual week-long *noho marae* at Maniaroa, for the University of Waikato's counselor education programme. Rahera is married to Leo, who is of Te Atiawa iwi. They have four adult children, and a whangai granddaughter, Danielle, who with her partner Simon, has given Rahera and Leo two beautiful whangai great grandchildren, Maia and Malakai.

Annie Temple is a Licensed Clinical Social Worker in Sacramento, California. She currently works as a Mental Health Therapist at a community health agency that specializes in treating people living with HIV/AIDS. Her clinical interests include narrative therapy, acceptance and commitment therapy, and dialectical behavior therapy. Annie strives to have a social justice informed practice.

Caroline Tremblay is Co-Director and Co-Founder of JST INSTITUTE. She has over 25 years of rich and diverse experience working with people across the lifespan, from youth in crisis to adults and families. She has provided services in crisis intervention centres, medical and psychiatric organizations, EAP companies, school settings, as well as in private practice. She is currently working at the University of Texas Medical Branch in Galveston as a Kidney/Pancreas Transplant Social Worker.

John Winslade is a Professor of Counseling at California State University, San Bernardino. He was previously Associate Dean there in the College of Education and Coordinator of the Counseling and Guidance Program. He is interested in social constructionist ideas and narrative practice and has co-authored 11 books in this field along with numerous articles.

Dan Wulff, PhD, is Professor in the Faculty of Social Work at the University of Calgary and served as a Family Therapist and Clinical Supervisor at the Calgary Family Therapy Centre for the past 10 years. Dan also serves on the Boards of Directors for the Taos Institute and the Global Partnership for Transformative Social Work as well as serving as a Co-Editor of *The Qualitative Report*. Dan teaches graduate-level social work practice and research courses and has taught post-structural family therapy at Blue Quills College and Grande Prairie Regional College, both in northern Alberta.

Karen Young, MSW, RSW, is the Director of Windz Institute (www.windzinstitute.com) operated by Reach Out Centre for Kids in Oakville, Ontario, Canada. She teaches workshops and certificate programs, provides supervision, and oversees research in brief and narrative therapy. Karen has published about brief and narrative practices and walk-in counselling in numerous journal articles, four book chapters, an E-learning course, and co-authored a policy paper for the Ontario government on brief and walk-in services.

Preface

Stand in a forest amid a cathedral of trees, or by the sea where the swell breaks on the shore, and take in the scene before you. Look long and closely at the details of the panorama and you will notice that each color you tag with a single label is more complex than that, composed of subtle variations of shade and hue. Turn your attention to the various shapes and contours. Nowhere is a straight line to be found sharply defining a border. Even the seam where water meets sky reveals a subtle curve on closer perusal. The ecosystem that envelopes us delights us in its infinite variation, its seemingly innate resistance to sharp-edged classification. We are inspired by the promise it offers of revealing yet another unimagined shape or texture—a plant or creature never yet seen or conceived—and we are quick to rise up in defence of the biological diversity that is emblematic of nature's wonder.

It is a curious thing that the diversity we celebrate in nature more broadly is most often met with unease in the social realm. Variations in race, religion, gender, language, ability, and sexual orientation tap deep veins of fear and hostility. Heterogeneity, seen as a threat to public order, is curtailed by exclusionary social policy, targeted by violence on the streets and battlegrounds. These are the realities of the lives of a large proportion of people who seek mental health services. Many of the challenges they face are intertwined with injustices and inequities that form the backdrop to counseling and psychotherapy conversations. And yet the individualistic outlook of mainstream mental health practice has not historically illuminated this struggle over difference that is the landscape for so many lives. Indeed, rather than understanding psychological distress in reference to social justice, the helping professions have demonstrated a historical preoccupation with documenting and classifying deviance from the norm.

The chapters assembled here seek to bring an alternate view forward. They describe practice premised on the assumption that much of what is "wrong" in the lives of people seeking help is located not in their craniums, but in the contexts they inhabit, where justice and injustice are played out on a daily basis. This premise shows up not only in the attention paid to injustice in the wider social sphere, but also in the vigilance paid to the language exchanged in what Rachel Hare-Mustin has called the "mirrored room" where therapists may inadvertently duplicate oppressive practices in therapeutic conversations.

Social justice is now being described as a "fifth force" in counseling and psychotherapy, with calls for social justice values and principles to be integrated into our training, research, and practice. The discourse of social justice in counseling stands on the shoulders of feminism, multiculturalism, critical psychology, and postmodernism, bringing forth a crucial shift in how we have come to understand problems that lead individuals to seek help. Practice oriented to social justice celebrates diversity and adopts a position of advocacy alongside people in the face of the many social forces that seek to constrain or erase it. This calls for a widening of our gaze. Amid an individualistic tradition of "locating the problem within the person," counseling and psychotherapy informed by social justice consider ways in which societies are structured and how systems and policies contribute to and impede well-being.

Though there have been calls to promote a social justice perspective, we have noticed much of the counseling and psychotherapy literature devoted to the topic remains theoretical at this point. Most often, social justice discourse urges counselors to adopt an advocacy role, challenging the status quo and becoming agents of social change. While a much needed endeavor to counter oppression and marginalization, we have often heard from practitioners that they subscribe to social justice values but either don't know how to enact them in their day-to-day work with clients or else feel somewhat intimidated by the magnitude of a task such as "changing society." The result is an experience of powerlessness in their practice.

We hope this volume will help to address those challenges. It brings together the voices of multiple practitioners who share reflections and practice-based anecdotes on the myriad ways that social justice is enacted utterance by utterance in their work, whether with students, supervisees, or clients. It is now widely acknowledged that stigmatization perpetuates dignitary harm and has negative ramifications for mental health. How we talk *about* and *to* people makes a very big difference. The helping professions in effect control access to various possible versions of identity available to people by virtue of the credibility and prestige assigned to professional discourse. This book adopts the view that all of this is a matter of social justice; it is premised on the notion that talk is action, and therefore justice and injustice are played out in all of our professional conversations.

Practitioners and counselor educators ourselves, we are invested in this topic at multiple levels. As white cisgender female (CA) and male (DP) middle-class professionals, we have been spared most of the social injustices that many of our clients and some of our students face on a daily basis. This book represents our attempt to keep those injustices visible in gathering together accounts of practice informed by an understanding that there is no neutral place to stand in the world. Nevertheless, there are various ways to approach the challenge of keeping context in the foreground of practice. And so we do not offer a singular model or framework of social justice counseling, nor an all-encompassing depiction of the ever-changing landscape of social justice. Rather we celebrate the diversity of responses from a wide range of practitioners who share first-hand accounts of their efforts to uphold, protect, and promote social justice in their interactions with the people they serve.

The volume is comprised of 18 chapters organized into 5 parts: (1) interrogating social justice as a guiding premise; (2) training and supervising from a social justice perspective; (3) accessing local knowledge; (4) justice and gender; and (5) anti-pathologizing/the politics of practice. The parts are preceded by introductions that provide an overview of the part theme and a glimpse of the content of the chapters therein. Each chapter concludes with reflection questions for the readers to engage experientially in what authors have offered.

No doubt readers will discern themes between these covers that speak most to their own interests and perspectives; nevertheless, we would like to alert you to some key threads woven throughout the book. All just conversations involve *challenging status quo thinking*, inviting critical reflection—even on the construct of "social justice" itself—in order to avoid the inadvertent duplication of dominant discourses and practices. Also key is *promoting a broadened vision for counseling* that makes sense of problems as challenges that can be linked to social inequities, power imbalances, and systemic discrimination, rather than manifestations of individual pathology or deficit. This expanded view includes an *emphasis on context*, which foregrounds people's agency, values, and competence in the face of the challenges they are up against. Finally, the theme of *promoting collaborative practice* may be the most distinct of the book's threads. It entails an analysis of the role of power in therapeutic conversations and the importance of practitioner reflexivity. It embodies "working with" rather than "working on," understanding that therapeutic conversations are a venue for social justice, appreciating that in addition to advocating for clients *between* sessions, the face-to-face encounter is a critical site for performing "just talk."

Compiling these writings has been an enlightening and rewarding process for us. We hope that you will also find among these chapters novel alternatives to the individualism that too often pervades counseling and psychotherapy, attributing individual distress to client deficits, and obscuring the many inspiring initiatives people take in the face of social inequities.

PART I

Interrogating Social Justice
as a Guiding Premise

In the spirit of the critical orientation to entrenched discourses and practices that pervades this book, we open with a section devoted to interrogating the very construct around which the chapters are organized. The term "social justice" rolls off the tongue easily, but means many things to many people. And the practice of social justice entails far more than a referral to a non-profit organization or phone call to a local legislator.

This opening section begins with a piece that provides many more questions than answers. In Chapter 1, Social Justice Activism and Therapy: Tensions, Points of Connection, and Hopeful Scepticism, Vikki Reynolds and Sekneh Hammoud-Beckett take on the big picture, writing about what they call the "strained relationship" between activism and therapy. Assuming an activist stance from within a profession calls for a vigilance of insidious invitations to assume forms of purported expertise or neutrality—stances that ultimately contribute to the very injustices they may seek to address. Vikki and Sekneh remind us that our work always happens in larger contexts—economic, political, historic. Those contexts are the ubiquitous backdrop to all interactions between practitioners and the persons who consult them. Their response to this complexity is to situate ethics at the heart of all dialogic exchanges—not the individualizing ethics of codes and standards, but a collective ethics that seeks justice by attending to historical legacies and systemic inequities.

John Winslade takes on the topic of social justice in Chapter 2, Counseling and Social Justice: What Are We Working For?, by pondering the very nature of the enterprise itself. While he is quick to point to formative life experiences that have fueled a career of passionate commitment to social justice in counseling and psychotherapy, John urges readers to slow down and unpack the terminology associated with social justice. Citing examples of aspirations to "put an end" to injustice, he observes that social justice is an ongoing process rather than a final destination; there will always be new forms of injustice to address. Perhaps more ominously, he reminds us that history has shown that those who revolt against oppression are at risk of becoming oppressors themselves without ongoing reflexive vigilance. Words like "emancipation" and "progress" have an uplifting ring to them; and yet it is worth asking what protections for the vulnerable are being jettisoned in the act of emancipation, and progress on whose terms and at whose expense? Like Vikki Reynolds and Sekneh Hammoud-Beckett, John gravitates to ethics as a key facet of social justice. And he reminds readers that ethics permeate every moment of a dialogic exchange: social justice is enacted utterance by utterance in our professional conversations.

Chapter 3, Challenging Conversations: Deepening Personal and Professional Commitment to Culture-Infused and Socially Just Counseling Practice, makes a compelling case that issues of social justice can only be grasped by turning the mirror on one's own social location. Sandra Collins and Nancy Arthur describe the dawning realization of social inequities experienced by many practitioners as they deepen their exploration of their own privilege. They observe that the barriers to social justice that people face are not merely in external contingencies, but unacknowledged power differentials between practitioners and the persons they serve. Their conclusion, that "enacting social justice begins with relinquishing our urge to privilege our own perspectives," is a call to rigorous and sometimes painful self-examination en route to socially just practice.

CHAPTER 1

Social Justice Activism and Therapy: Tensions, Points of Connection, and Hopeful Scepticism

Vikki Reynolds and Sekneh Hammoud-Beckett

This writing invites a critique of the tenuous, strained, yet hopeful relationship between social justice activism and therapy (Reynolds & Hammoud-Beckett, 2012). It addresses the tensions of therapy replicating oppressive practices, and invites a critique of our practice with an aim to move us more in line with our collective ethics for justice-doing (Reynolds, 2009; Reynolds & polanco, 2012). This critique entails addressing our positioning in relation to power, privilege, and disadvantage; resisting neutrality and taking overt positions for justice-doing; naming and beginning to respond to white supremacy and colonialism in our traditions of practice; problematizing our relationship to social control and social change in our work; and resisting competition as affronts to our solidarity. A critical engagement with reflective practice will be offered (Freire, 1970; Tomm, 1985), inviting a hopeful scepticism (Kvale, 1996; Ricoeur, 1970) about our practice enacting the ethics we espouse. Our hope is to breathe life into our ethical engagement with practice, and move towards justice-doing in our work.

Our analysis occurs on the shoulders of women of color feminism (Smith, 2006), critical race theory (Crenshaw, Gotanda, Peller, & Thomas, 1995), queer theory (Butler, 1990), critical trans theory (Spade, 2011), decolonizing practice (Fanon, 1961; Lawrence & Dua, 2005; Walia, 2012, 2013), and anti-authoritarian social justice activism (Buechler, 2005; Chomsky, 2005; Shantz, 2011). Our hope is to contribute to the rich histories of scholarship and activism regarding the precarious relationship of justice-doing and the helping professions (Razack, 2002; Rodriguez, 2007; Rossiter, 2006).

Sekneh is a woman of color from a Muslim background with a family experience of migration to Australia. Vikki is a working-class woman and a Canadian-born white settler, whose people migrated to Canada from Ireland, England, and Newfoundland. The analysis that follows is the basis for all of our therapeutic work, not only work with people from oppressed locations. For example, all of our praxis addressing colonization is relevant and required in all of our work on Indigenous territories, whether we are working with Indigenous people or settlers.

We offer reflection questions in each section with the hope of unsettling our complicity and re-newing our ongoing commitment to work with intention and

3

accountability. We invite you to take a moment and identify a social issue you have encountered in your work that you would like to explore through a lens of justice-doing. We expect that not all questions can be readily answered, but we see such instances as an opportunity for readers to identify areas for further reflection and action.

Addressing Power and Privilege

To enact a decolonizing anti-oppression stance we need to reflect, as Sontag (2003) says, on how the suffering of others is systemically mapped onto the privileges we hold as helping professionals. These privileges are often made invisible by the obscuring of power. Kvale (1996) warns that an investigation into our practice, and our ability to enact the ethics we espouse, might reveal transgressions we neither intended nor accepted responsibility for.

Addressing our privilege foments discomfort that is both predictable and necessary (Kumashiro, 2004) in terms of unsettling our relationships to power and opening us up to accountability. These reflexive questions, that can never be fully answered, provide a frame for beginning to address our access to power and responding accountably in relationships of power:

- What are the intersections (Crenshaw, 1995; Truth, 1851) of my own power and privilege with the locations of my disadvantage? How am I accountable for unearned privileges?
- How do I resist positioning myself in my locations of disadvantage when serving suffering others? That is, when we are in the power position of therapist, how do we resist positioning ourselves as the oppressed person in the relationship due to some other site of disadvantage? How do we get our own sites of disadvantage out of the way if they are not useful?
- How am I responding to power both moment to moment and contextually in this interaction?
- How am I resisting righteousness, posturing, and the double comfort (Heron, 2005) of naming privilege righteously, but doing nothing to mitigate it—such as naming white privilege, and then dominating the space?
- How can I invite, embrace, and hold the discomfort required to accountably address my access to power?
- Who is in solidarity to shoulder me/us/our organizations up in making space for discomfort, accountability, and repair of power relations? What ideas, practices, and lived experience helps me/us in doing this?
- How are we holding ourselves as professionals, as well as holding our teams, organizations, and professions, to account for transgressions of power? How are clients invited in safe and trustworthy enough ways to name transgressions? What structures and practices are in place to make this naming possible and useful consistently and predictably across time?

Resisting Neutrality and Taking Overt Positions for Justice-Doing

A stance for justice-doing creates a position for therapists to respond to our work alongside suffering others (Sanders, 2007) as activists and to work for socially just structural change. In activism, it is the duty of the witness to do more than respond to suffering, and to take up the project of resisting and transforming the structures in society that create the conditions for oppression and exploitation.

This requires a critical resistance towards neutrality and objectivity (Cushman, 1995; Dyer, 2002) within the helping professions. As therapists there is a risk that we can participate in deconstructing and naming transgressions of power without taking on the social project of transforming the societies in which we live. As Maori researcher Linda Tuhiwai Smith (1999) says in *De-Colonizing Methodologies*, deconstruction is a useful practice, "but it does not prevent someone from dying" (p. 3).

Simultaneously, as practitioners, we must be careful and critical of how our well-intentioned activism can be used to justify and strengthen the structures that we oppose (Smith, 2006; Spade, 2011). For example, feminist activism against a rape culture (Buchwald, Fletcher, & Roth, 1993) has been used in some contexts to shift more resources to police, nominally for women's safety, in the face of widespread cuts to feminist-based programs, such as shelters, counseling, and court advocacy. We also need to be cautious of using the rhetoric of social justice (Wade, personal communication) to engage in competition, appropriate cultural knowledges, and enact empty posturing.

These questions invite a questioning of our relationship to objectivity, neutrality, and being silent in the face of oppression:

- Despite our overt ethical stances for justice-doing, what positions are we *not* taking or are being silent about? What promotes this silence: ignorance, tiredness, discomfort, lack of moral courage, not knowing what to say and how to say it so it can be heard as critique and not attack, concern for career or advancement? Or is silence promoted by histories of being unsupported, victims of backlash, lack of allies, precarious employment, lack of safety as opposed to discomfort, lack of privilege, power, and solidarity? Conversely, when can we take up silence as resistance (Hammoud-Beckett, 2007a) to oppression? How can we discern when it is safe-enough and we are required to speak, and when we need to build more solidarity as a tactic to make effective change?
- How are the politics of neutrality and objectivity mapped onto the legacies of white supremacy and colonization in the helping professions? How are professional objectivity and neutrality connected to other sites of oppression and exclusion; such as homophobia, transphobia, ableism, and stigma against mental illness?
- How do we resist the particular discourses of professionalism that are barriers to justice-doing and maintain our required and useful connections within these disciplines?

- Harlene Anderson teaches that we invented our professions and their codes of ethics, and when they are not just it is our obligation to challenge and transform them (Everett, MacFarlane, Reynolds, & Anderson, 2013). Who is alongside us, and what organizations and communities are in solidarity with us when we challenge, resist, and transform our professional bodies?
- How do we hold these positions against neutrality and for justice-doing alongside requirements from funding bodies that side with and maintain structural oppressions?

Naming and Responding to White Supremacy and Colonization

European and Anglo-colonialism in Canada and Australia (and elsewhere) originated in political violence against Indigenous peoples in attempts to steal and exploit Indigenous land, wealth, resources, and children and place Indigenous peoples into a class of servitude. Words such as "torture," "genocide," "racism," and "white supremacy" are omitted from the discourse used to describe this deliberate violence against Indigenous people (Chrisjohn & Young, 1997; Logan, 2001; Richardson & Reynolds, 2014).

Indigenous warrior Gord Hill (2010) describes colonialism as comprised of invasion, occupation, genocide, and assimilation. "Residential schools" in Canada worked to violently assimilate the children whose families survived genocide. Between 48 percent and 70 percent of the children were sexually abused (Feldthusen, 2007). In some schools this figure was as high as 100 percent. The non-sexual physical abuse was often barbaric and indicates that the violence was systemic and deliberate, that those in charge were aware and acted with impunity (Feldthusen, 2007). In Australia, the "Stolen Generations" (Read, 1981) refers to the government kidnapping of between 1 in 10 and 1 in 3 Aboriginal children who were taken to missions or adopted to white families (Knightley, 2000).

In response to the Truth and Reconciliation process in Canada, and the "non-apology" of the federal government (Coates & Wade, 2009) that failed to take full responsibility and did not offer repair, non-Indigenous academic Paulette Regan (2010) asks what it would mean in concrete terms for the settler majority to shoulder the collective burden of the history and legacy of residential schools.

The helping professions are inextricably linked with these violent histories and current oppressions, and practice within contexts of colonization. Indigenous people are often pathologized and described by professionals as mentally ill, traumatized, and addicted, as opposed to seeing their behavior as resistance and naming that they are more often oppressed than depressed. A decolonizing ethical stance requires an inquiry into the relationship of therapy and community work and white supremacy (Akinyela, 2002; Smith, 2006). It also calls for an examination of the professions' (and professionals') participation in colonization (Gergen, 2005; Hammoud-Beckett, 2007b), what Todd and Wade (1994) name as "psycholonization" and McCarthy (1995) describes as "benevolent colonization."

Sekneh and Vikki have different migration paths and therefore connected but different accountabilities to the Indigenous peoples whose territories we live on. We struggle with how we collectively decolonize ourselves, our families, communities, and organizations from our specific migration histories. Accountability for land theft, and histories of atrocities against Indigenous people, is complex. We struggle:

- What accountabilities can we enact in order to ethically identify as more than settlers and migrants?
- As settlers and migrants, how can we embrace our nuanced experiences of identity, honoring our histories of migration and honoring our ancestors, and the precarious journeys they embarked on?
- How can we resist centering our own migration experiences, or alternately resist the paralysis of guilt? How, instead, can we intentionally center accountability, openness, and responsibility to address colonialism?

Practitioners who identify as white are further required to examine the interconnectedness of colonialism, euro-centrism (Said, 1979), and white supremacy (Said, 1993; Smith, 2007), and to resist and dismantle these oppressions. The following questions offer a frame for therapists who are non-Indigenous to begin to investigate their relationships to colonization and accountable responses to it:

- How am I positioning myself, individually and collectively, on Indigenous territories? How might I act in accord with protocols of the Indigenous communities whose land I live and work on?
- How might I hold all of my work accountable to colonialism, keeping such accountability at the forefront consistently rather than sporadically or not at all—even when working with other non-Indigenous people?
- How might we (as individual practitioners, organizations, and professions) address the colonialism entrenched in the traditions of therapeutic and community practice?
- How might we be directed by and accountable to Indigenous people in our work?
- What can we do to actually enact inclusivity (Sin & Yan, 2003) and authentic partnerships and not tokenism in including Indigenous people?
- How might we strategically name and resist colonialism in interactions with funders and governing bodies? What is our role and ethical obligation as non-Indigenous workers in resisting, dismantling, and transforming systemic oppressions that make space for our voices at tables with funders/government/academia at the expense of Indigenous people and voices?
- How are we (as practitioners, organizations, and professions) participating, overtly, covertly, unintentionally, or with ethical blindness, in the psycholonization of Indigenous people? How might we be doing this in ways that perpetrate colonialism and oppression and construct Indigenous people, families, and communities as unwell, broken, and incapable?

Problematizing Our Relationship with Social Control and Doing Social Change Work

Social justice educator and activist Paul Kivel's (2007) excellent and troubling chapter "Social service or social change" poses foundational questions for workers and non-profit organizations regarding the ethical stance for our work. Are we taking up the project of resisting oppressions and transforming societies, or are we "serving" people who are oppressed and exploited, possibly accommodating them to oppression? As Andrea Smith (2011), a member of the Women of Color Collective says, "You can't heal your way out of patriarchy." For example, we need to see women who have experienced sexual assault individually in therapy to assist with their personal recovery and simultaneously engage the wider community in the social project of resisting and transforming a rape culture. We need to both walk alongside people who are working to change their relationships to suffering, and work with them for social change directly related to the systemic oppressions that are the root of suffering.

Practitioners who are not working in non-profit organizations or government agencies are not outside of these struggles, but also need to reflect on their role in making social change, and on the accessibility of their services. We need to be strategic about the parts of our work where funding restrains and directs us in ways that replicate the structures of inequity we are responding to and trying to dismantle. Addressing funding needs accountably requires that we navigate complex terrains. Non-profit organizations struggle with the diverse implications of funding and ethical obligations to maintain funding to keep their doors open to people who need them.

We acknowledge that we hold this critical analysis along with accountability for our community work being inextricably linked to these tensions. The following reflexive questions invite an inquiry into the ethical stance of our social service work and its connection to the project of social change and transformation of our unjust societies:

- Are we accommodating people to individual lives of suffering, or are we taking on the project of changing the social structures that promote oppression?
- Are we rigorously questioning our possible role (as workers, teams, and organizations) in maintaining social control and increasing surveillance that fall on "over policed and under protected" (Kushnick, 1999) people and communities?
- How can we establish trustworthiness that we are not acting as agents of state control and additional surveillance of our society's most disadvantaged people? (For example, how do we protect migrant people without status who need our care but who do not trust any government-funded agency not to report them to governments who attack and transgress their human rights to refuge?)
- How are we, our teams, and agencies taking on the task of resisting and transforming oppressive social structures within our organizations and government

agencies that create and uphold the suffering of the people we aim to serve? (For example, how are we working to take on rape culture, hire people from minoritized and marginalized locations?)

- Are we holding accountability to funding sources higher than accountability to the people we aim to serve? If so, how can we resist this, and what people/ communities/organizations can help us get our practices more aligned with our ethics?
- How can workers and non-profit organizations participate in accountable ways with funding bodies, especially as funders may restrict critiques of governments and social policies?
- How can we, as communities of workers and non-profit organizations, stay in strained relationships of solidarity when we are set up for financial competition against each other for scarce resources? How do we decline invitations to division and competition and shoulder each other up in order to collectively take up the project of changing society and responding to the suffering of the people we work with?
- How can we sustain ourselves as workers, organizations, and movements in these messy terrains? What points of connection give us enough wiggle room to be in these spaces of capitalism and social control and maintain our ability to do dignity, and enact our collective ethics?
- While we hold onto and work for our shared vision of a just society in the future, how do we continue to enact ethics within flawed systems? How can we know we are not being co-opted or complicit? How do we resist cynicism and continue our struggles to transform the organizations and government structures we work with and in?

Resisting Competition as an Affront to Our Solidarity

The capitalist context of our work requires that we are in competition with each other, as individual workers and organizations, for resources. Some 30 years of Western democracies' relationship to neo-liberalism and the dismantling of the social net has left people with precarious lives (Butler, 2004; Walia, 2013) and also placed workers in the context of a scarcity of resources amid an abundance of need. This scarcity of resources is of course a myth (Rosenthal, 1999), as evidenced by limited government funding of social work as opposed to seemingly limitless funding to aid corporations (Klein, 2007), militarization (Dawson, 2014), and the prison industrial complex (Davis, 1998; Rodriguez, 2007). Workers and organizations are pitted against each other like dogs fighting over bones.

As workers we are not immune to this competition, despite our explicit claims to the ethics of collaboration and solidarity. We are recruited into the ideas and practices of competition, often replicating the competitive discourse of the sporting realm, whereby the other is positioned as an opponent who can be vanquished through domination and superior strength and skill. If our mandates and collective ethics espouse the desire to change society towards justice-doing, this competition is counter-productive: We know that we need each other in order to resist and transform the structural oppressions that promote people's suffering.

For example, in work against the violence of men, competition invites comparisons and negative judgments of this work as vying for the same resources as work supporting women who have suffered men's violence. But we know we have to take on oppression on all fronts, and that work with people who use violence and people who are victimized are interconnected. Resisting and transforming a rape culture requires we work with all women, men, and gender-variant people suffering from and performing violence (Reynolds, 2014a). As bell hooks (2000) teaches, "Feminism is for everyone." A useful line of questions might include:

- How can we resist competition and enact solidarity in our work with both people who have used violence and people who have experienced violence?
- What practices can we create to hold all of this work accountable to people who have suffered from violence (Hammoud-Beckett, 2007a)?
- How can the safety of people subjected to violence be held at the center of all of this work?

Our solidarity is required for our collective liberation. Australian feminist Elspeth Probyn (1993) addresses the challenges to feminist solidarity and the power differences that exist between white feminists and women of color feminists. She acknowledges the moral courage required for women of color to speak of racism, and names this act "speaking with attitude" (p. 140). This is not the act of speaking about oneself or the other, rather it is "speaking within the space between myself and another self" (p. 140). Because feminism is a movement, not an individual project, she reminds us to recognize that "without her I am nothing" (p. 163).

Here are some questions to frame an inquiry into our complicity with competition and to make our solidarity more intentional and public:

- How can we hold onto a believed-in respect for the work of others, based on an understanding of our collective ethics? How can we create dignifying relationships of respect across organizations and domains of practice with an aim to be of use to people we aim to serve?
- How can we resist competition related to funding? How can we prioritize promoting social change, holding the needs of the people we aim to serve at the center? What collaborations or solidarity can we offer to other workers and organizations as we resist disrespectful competition that requires we denigrate their work and reputations, and specifically their ability to be of use?

Conclusion

We hope that this critical investigation into our ethical stances for justice-doing in our collective work unsettles our complicity and renews our ongoing commitment to work with intention and accountability. We want to unsettle a sense of normalcy or "professional competency," and embrace the discomfort necessary for an ongoing invitation to a hopeful scepticism that invites us to rigorously critique the claims to ethics we hold (Reynolds, 2014b). As we have not delivered on a just society we cannot envision what doing justice would fully look like in practice (Chomsky, 2005), and we join other activists, practitioners, and community members in the hard work required to develop authentic and believable ethical stances that are both decolonizing and anti-oppressive.

We are shouldered up in this project by Arab writer Joumana Haddad (2012), who challenges patriarchy and a myriad of intersecting oppressions. In solidarity, we honor her acknowledgment of the multiplicity of silenced and uninvited voices, and we commit to carving out spaces for these people and voices in our classrooms, organizations, supervision, and societies, and to ongoing resistance against their erasure (Namaste, 2000) and disappearance:

> I owe all these anonymous women and men [sic] a great debt of gratitude. I keep on hearing their beautiful, hijacked voices echoing in my head, inspiring me and pushing me beyond my limits day after day, word after word. You deserve to hear them too … I am neither a lonely voice in the wilderness, nor an extraordinary exception. My microphone simply works, theirs is broken. But one day it will be fixed. And oh how will they roar when that day finally comes.
>
> (Haddad, 2012, p. 157)

Dedication

For Cheryl White and David Denborough, who brought us together, and continue to create spaces that inspire and challenge us in the doing and questioning of just practice in community work. For the people and voices shut out and missing from our teams, organizations, and classrooms: We acknowledge our complicity in these disappearances.

This work and writing occurred on Indigenous territories on Turtle Island (which includes North America) and Australia.

Acknowledgments

This work is truly collaborative. We acknowledge the moral courage and intelligence of our many teachers, most especially students, supervisees, activists, and people we have consulted with who chose to gift us with their critique, questioning, and sometimes just anger, to our benefit, at their cost, across huge divides of privilege. Katy Batha, Riel Dupuis-Rossi, and Aaron Munro, our cultural consultants, contributed to the usefulness of this chapter. Mr. Peaslee helped again.

References

Akinyela, M. (2002). De-colonizing our lives: Divining a post-colonial therapy. *The International Journal of Narrative Therapy and Community Work, 2,* 32–43.

Buchwald, E., Fletcher, P., & Roth, M. (1993). *Transforming a rape culture.* Minneapolis, MN: Milkweed Editions.

Buechler, S. (2005). New social movement theories. *Sociological Quarterly, 36*(3), 441–464. doi: 10.1111/j.1533–8525.1995.tb00447.x

Butler, J. (1990). *Gender trouble: Feminism and the subversion of identity.* New York, NY: Routledge.

Butler, J. (2004). *Precarious life: The powers of mourning and violence.* London: Verso.

Chomsky, N. (2005). *Chomsky on anarchism.* B. Pateman (Ed.). Edinburgh: AK Press.

Chrisjohn, R., & Young, S. (1997). *The circle game: Shadow and substance in the residential school experience in Canada.* Penticton, BC: Theytus Books.

Coates, L., & Wade, A. (2009, August). "For this we are sorry": A brief review of Canada's most recent non-apology to Aboriginal Peoples. Presented at Under the Volcano Festival of Art and Social Change Program. Vancouver, BC.

Crenshaw, K. (1995). Mapping the margins: Intersectionality, identity politics, and violence against women of color. In K. Crenshaw, G. Gotanda, G. Peller, & K. Thomas (Eds.), *Critical race theory: The key writings that formed the movement* (pp. 357–383). New York, NY: The New Press.

Crenshaw, K., Gotanda, G., Peller, G., & Thomas, K. (Eds.), *Critical race theory: The key writings that formed the movement.* New York, NY: The New Press.

Cushman, P. (1995). *Constructing the self, constructing America: A cultural history of psychotherapy.* Reading, MA: Addison Wesley.

Davis, A. (1998, September 10). Masked racism: Reflections on the prison-industrial complex. Color Lines. Retrieved from www.colorlines.com

Dawson, T. (2014, August 19). Military policing in Canada under scrutiny following Ferguson protests. *Edmonton Journal.* Retrieved from http://edmontonjournal.com

Dyer, R. (2002). The matter of whiteness. In P. S. Rothenberg (Ed.), *White privilege: Essential readings on the other side of racism* (pp. 9–14). New York, NY: Worth.

Everett, B., MacFarlane D., Reynolds, V., & Anderson, H. (2013). Not on our backs: Supporting counsellors in navigating the ethics of multiple relationships within queer, Two Spirit, and/or trans communities. *Canadian Journal of Counselling and Psychotherapy, 47*(1), 14–28. Retrieved from http://cjc-rcc.ucalgary.ca

Fanon, F. (1961). *The wretched of the earth.* New York, NY: Grove Weidenfeld.

Feldthusen, B. (2007). Civil liability for sexual assault in Aboriginal residential schools: The baker did it. *Canadian Journal of Law and Society, 22*(1), 61–91. doi: 10.1017/ S0829320100009121

Freire, P. (1970). *Pedagogy of the oppressed.* New York, NY: Continuum.

Gergen, K. (2005). *An invitation to social construction.* Thousand Oaks, CA: Sage.

Haddad, J. (2012). *Superman is an Arab: On God, marriage, macho men and other disastrous interventions.* London: Westbourne Press.

Hammoud-Beckett, S. (2007a). Nurturing resistance and refusing to separate gender, culture and religion: Responding to gendered violence in Muslim Australian communities. In C. White & A. Yuen (Eds.), *Conversations about gender, culture, violence and narrative practice*. (pp. 43–51). Adelaide, Australia: Dulwich Centre Publications.

Hammoud-Beckett, S. (2007b). Azima ila Hayati-An invitation in to my life: Narrative conversations about sexual identity. *The International Journal of Narrative Therapy & Community Work*, *1*, 29–39. Retrieved from http://dulwichcentre.com.au/international-journal-of-narrative-therapy-and-community-work

Heron, B. (2005). Self-reflection in critical social work practice: Subjectivities and the possibilities of resistance. *Journal of Reflective Practice*, *6*(3), 341–351. doi: 10.1080/14623940500220095

Hill, G. (2010). *500 years of Indigenous resistance*. Vancouver, BC: Arsenal Pulp Press.

hooks, b. (2000). *Feminism is for everybody: Passionate politics*. Cambridge, England: South End Press.

Kivel, P. (2007). Social service or social change? In INITE! Women of color against violence (Eds.). *The Revolution will not be funded: Beyond the non-profit industrial complex*. (pp. 129–150). Cambridge, MA: South End Press.

Klein, N. (2007). *The shock doctrine: The rise of disaster capitalism*. Toronto, ON: Knopf Canada.

Knightley, P. (2000). *Australia: A biography of a nation*. New York, NY: Vintage.

Kumashiro, K. (2004). *Against common-sense: Teaching and learning towards social justice*. New York, NY: Routledge.

Kushnick, L. (1999). "Over policed and under protected": Stephen Lawrence, institutional and police practices. *Sociological Research Online*, *4*(1). Retrieved from www.socresonline.org.uk/home.html

Kvale, S. (1996). *Inter-views: An introduction to qualitative research interviewing*. London: Sage.

Lawrence, B., & Dua, E. (2005). Decolonizing antiracism. *Social Justice*, *32*(4), 120–143.

Logan, T. (2001). *The lost generations: The silent Métis of the residential school system*. Winnipeg, MB: Southwest Region Manitoba Métis Federation.

McCarthy, I. (1995). Serving those in poverty: A benevolent colonisation? In J. van Lawick & M. Sanders (Eds.), *Gender and beyond*. Amsterdam, Netherlands: L.S. Books.

Namaste, V. (2000). *Invisible lives: The erasure of trans-sexual and transgendered people*. Chicago, IL: University of Chicago Press.

Probyn, E. (1993). *Sexing the self: Gendered positions in cultural studies*. London: Routledge.

Razack, N. (2002). *Transforming the field: Critical antiracist and anti-oppressive perspectives for the human service practicum*. Halifax, NS: Fernwood.

Read, P. (1981). *The stolen generations: The removal of Aboriginal children in New South Wales 1883 to 1969*. Department of Aboriginal Affairs (New South Wales government). Retrieved from http://dmsweb.daa.asn.au/files/Recognition_of_Overseas/Reading%207_StolenGenerations.pdf

Regan, P. (2010). *Unsettling the settler within: Indian residential schools, truth telling, and reconciliation in Canada*. Vancouver, BC: UBC Press.

Reynolds, V. (2009, December). Collective ethics as a path to resisting burnout. *Insights: The Clinical Counsellor's Magazine & News*, 6–7.

Reynolds, V. (2014a). Resisting and transforming rape culture: An activist stance for therapeutic work with men who have used violence. *Ending Men's Violence against Women and Children: The No to Violence Journal*, Spring, 29–49.

Reynolds, V. (2014b). Centering ethics in therapeutic supervision: Fostering cultures of critique and structuring safety. *The International Journal of Narrative Therapy and Community Work, 1*, 1–13. Retrieved from http://dulwichcentre.com.au/international-journal-of-narrative-therapy-and-community-work

Reynolds, V., & Hammoud-Beckett, S. (2012). Bridging the worlds of therapy and activism: Intersections, tensions and affinities. *International Journal of Narrative Therapy & Community Work, 4*, 57–61. Retrieved from http://dulwichcentre.com.au/international-journal-of-narrative-therapy-and-community-work

Reynolds, V., & polanco, m. (2012). An ethical stance for justice-doing in community work and therapy. *Journal of Systemic Therapies, 31*(4) 18–33. doi: 10.1521/jsyt.2012.31.4.18

Richardson/Kianewesquao, C., & Reynolds, V. (2014). Structuring safety in therapeutic work alongside Indigenous survivors of residential schools. *The Canadian Journal of Native Studies, 34*(2), 147–164. Retrieved from www.brandonu.ca/native-studies/cjns

Ricoeur, P. (1970). *Freud and philosophy: An essay on interpretation.* New Haven, CT: Yale University Press.

Rossiter, A. (2006, October). Innocence lost and suspicion found: Do we educate for or against social work? *Critical Social Work, 2*(1). Retrieved from www1.uwindsor.ca/criticalsocialwork

Rodriguez, D. (2007). The political logic of the non-profit industrial complex. In INCITE! Women of Color against Violence, (Eds.), *The revolution will not be funded: Beyond the non-profit industrial complex* (pp. 21–40). Cambridge, MA: South End Press.

Rosenthal, S. (1999, January 1). The myth of scarcity. Retrieved from www.susanrosenthal.com

Said, E. (1979). *Orientalism.* New York, NY: Vintage Books.

Said, E. (1993). *Culture and imperialism.* New York, NY: Vintage Books.

Sanders, C. J. (2007). A poetics of resistance: Compassionate practice in substance misuse therapy. In C. Brown & T. Augusta-Scott (Eds.), *Narrative therapy: Making meaning, making lives* (pp. 59–77). London: Sage.

Shantz, J. (2011). *Against all authority: Anarchism and the literary imagination.* Exeter, UK: Imprint Academic.

Sin, R., & Yan, M. (2003). Margins as centres: A theory of social inclusion in anti-oppression social work. In W. Shera (Ed.), *Emerging perspectives on anti-oppression social work* (pp. 25–41). Toronto, ON: Canadian Scholar's Press.

Smith, A. L. (2006). Heteropatriarchy and the three pillars of white supremacy: Rethinking women of color organizing. In INCITE! Women of Color against Violence (Eds.), *Color of Violence: The INCITE! Anthology* (pp. 66–73). Cambridge, MA: South End Press.

Smith, A. L. (2011). Andrea Smith at Women's World 2011. Retrieved from www.youtube.com/watch?v=eCZY78dbiD0

Smith, C. (2007). *The cost of privilege: Taking on the system of white supremacy and racism.* Fayetteville, NC: Camino Press.

Sontag, S. (2003). *Regarding the pain of others.* New York, NY: Picador.

Spade, D. (2011). *Normal life: Administrative violence, critical trans politics, and the limits of law.* Brooklyn, NY: South End Press.

Todd, N., & Wade, A. (1994). Domination, deficiency and psychotherapy. *The Calgary Participator*, 37–46.

Tomm, K. (1985). Circular interviewing: A multifaceted clinical tool. In D. Campbell & R. Draper (Eds.), *Applications in systemic therapy: The Milan approach.* London: Grune & Stratton.

Truth, S. (1851). *Ain't I a woman? Civil rights and conflict in the United States: Selected speeches* (Lit2Go Edition). Retrieved from http://etc.usf.edu/lit2go

Tuhiwai Smith, L. (1999). *Decolonizing methodologies: Research and Indigenous peoples.* London: Zed Books.

Walia, H. (2012, January 1). Decolonizing together: Moving beyond a politics of solidarity toward a practice of decolonization. *Briarpatch Magazine.* Retrieved from http://briar-patchmagazine.com

Walia, H. (2013). *Undoing border imperialism.* Oakland, CA: AK Press.

CHAPTER *2*

Counseling and Social Justice: What Are We Working For?

John Winslade

It is only fair that I speak to how I was moved toward the influences that I shall speak of here in this chapter. In the 1970s, the Vietnam War and the anti-Apartheid movement in New Zealand awakened in me a concern about how power and politics are made manifest. Then the Maori critique of the colonizing influences in humanistic counseling disturbed my interest in this field of practice. Little did I know at that time that later my grandchildren would be members of the Ngati Awa iwi (a Maori tribe). I was drawn to narrative therapy in the 1990s because of its (post-structuralist) emphasis on power relations and the valuing of culture as politically implicated in human "nature." I became increasingly interested as a result in post-structuralist ideas, which considerably complicate the conventional North American sectional perspective on social justice. Accordingly I speak in this chapter to a slightly different emphasis.

Beneath the enthusiasm for social justice lie some conceptual problems that need to be carefully thought through. They are not just of intellectual interest, because they lead to different emphases in practice. In this chapter I shall pose some dilemmas for how we might think about social justice in order to sharpen thinking about what it means, and to avoid uncritically associating it with every practice that is vaguely "good." Social justice can become a consciously chosen path of commitment, but I propose that counselors eschew a millenarian view of social justice (explained below) and recognize social justice as a principle of interpretation and a guide to practice, rather than as a destination of history. I shall also argue that counselors should embrace social justice afresh in the practice of counseling itself, not just by taking up advocacy outside of counseling practice.

"Social Justice" or Simply "Justice"?

As Brian Barry (2005) explains, "Until about a century and a half ago, justice was standardly understood as a virtue not of societies but of individuals" (p. 4). Individual justice, often called "liberal justice," aims to ensure that individuals do not cheat or steal from each other and honor contracts. Social justice, in the

16

words of John Rawls (1991), is about "fairness" from the point of view of the wider social good and applies more to institutions than individuals. It was first applied to relations between employers and employees, and has been extended to providing social services (beginning with education and health care) equally to all citizens.

When laws and social institutions actively prohibit groups of people from access to such rights, opportunities, and resources, social justice has often aimed at "emancipation" from unfair treatment or unjust restrictions. Social movements have, therefore, sought equality of legal rights (such as the right to vote) for a series of social groups (racial minorities, women, LGBT persons).

The struggle to create a modern democratic state in which ordinary people were freed from the domination of feudal aristocratic rule fueled the English Civil War and Revolution, the French Revolution, and the American Revolution. In the nineteenth century, after the Industrial Revolution had invented new ways to exploit the working class, the cause of emancipation was taken up by trade unions and developed into Marxist ideology, which fueled the Russian revolution and also gave rise to the welfare state, universal education, old age pensions, health care, Roosevelt's New Deal, and Johnson's Great Society. Social justice causes also included various progressive movements with emancipatory goals, such as the abolitionist movement, the civil rights movement, the suffragette movement, the modern feminist movement, and campaigns against child labor and for LGBT rights, disability rights, and prison reform.

A dilemma lies in what precisely is meant by emancipation. The aspirational orientation of social justice is toward a future, a world in which new forms of emancipation arrive, rather than on the immediacy of the present. Derrida (De Cauter, 2004) therefore talks about justice to come (*à venir* or *avenir*, meaning the future). Social justice is thus about creating a world that does not yet exist. As Deleuze would say, it is about actualizing what is virtual within the present (Deleuze & Parnet, 1987). The concept of freedom has thus been expressed in a virtual form in important documents, such as the American Constitution or the United Nations Declaration of Human Rights, but often needs to be actualized in specific contexts of living. The concept of emancipation always turns our attention toward the future—towards creating a better world.

Cautions about Emancipation

It is also necessary to view emancipatory causes with caution. As much as the emancipatory impulse in many social movements can be appreciated, it pays to remember that those who were emancipated often protected their own emancipation from encroachment by others. In the great revolutions, for example, those emancipated had to be property owners, white and male. The catchcry of the French Revolution, for example, was "Liberty! Fraternity! Equality!" There was no "sorority." Nor in the American Revolution did emancipation extend to slaves, Native Americans, or Mexicans (nor later to Chinese immigrants). Not all has been pretty in these social movements. Often emancipation for some has happened at someone else's expense.

For example, in the contemporary North American context, concerns have been expressed that feminist campaigns for the emancipation of women have benefited white middle-class women at the expense of women of color or working-class women. The campaign for same-sex marriage, too, has been criticized for advancing the cause of middle-class gay and lesbian persons at the expense of, say, transgender persons.

Historically, there have been groups who have sought emancipation for themselves, only to turn against others. For example, the English Civil war led to Cromwell's bloodthirsty attack on the Irish. The French Revolution led to the reign of terror and Napoleon's imperialism. The Russian and Chinese Revolutions led to the cruelties of Stalin and Mao. And the American Revolution led to various genocides against Native Americans, the perpetuation of slavery, and is still felt in the power of the National Rifle Association to prevent restrictions on access to guns, with the result that children in schools continue to be shot in the name of "freedom" for gun owners. In other words, emancipation has sometimes had a spotty history. The promise of emancipation has not been always matched by what its zealous advocates have done. They have too often engaged in acts of oppression of others.

We also need to be cautious of automatic assumptions about social progress. Jean-François Lyotard (1984) argued that progress is a modern grand narrative and it can fool us into assuming that every emancipatory step is an irreversible advance toward greater social justice. History is not that simple. Romantic ideas about progress have been coming under considerable pressure by the insights of postmodernism, by the gathering ecological and climate change crisis, by the continuing threat of nuclear annihilation, by economic boom and bust cycles, and by encountering the limits of scientific methods. If these limits apply to technological progress, they can also apply to social progress.

What is more, social forces often pull in different directions and sometimes pit themselves against emancipatory change. When a significant victory toward social progress is won, these forces do not suddenly disappear. They often regroup and invent new forms of injustice or clever ways to undermine social justice causes. We therefore need to treat campaigns for emancipation and social progress with discernment, rather than assuming that they always represent the cause of social justice.

Emancipation Should Not Be Abandoned

Should we therefore reject the values of emancipation and of social progress? No. On ethical grounds we should resist falling into a cynical perspective that risks emphasizing the failures of every progressive movement and de-emphasizing their achievements. It is important to be vigilant about the risks of emancipatory movements perpetrating new forms of injustice, but every social movement that resists the inevitability of the present or the status quo still deserves recognition for opening a counter story. It is worth remembering the possibilities for living that the call for emancipation has opened up for many people.

To address new forms of injustice, a sense of what social justice might look like is needed to animate resistance to injustice. Without an evolving analysis of the process by which injustices are produced, it would be difficult to articulate something different. We still need to deconstruct the ways in which people in many contexts are alienated from possibilities of living. The constant renewal of the analysis of injustice is thus an ongoing task. At the same time, people are constantly working creatively to formulate expressions of greater justice. As Foucault (2000) teaches, every expression of power generates forms of resistance that contain within them seeds of a new social assemblage. Let me now turn to the ways in which conventional thinking about social justice might be modified.

Ethical Principle or Millenarian Goal?

Simon Glendinning (2011) in his introduction to Derrida's metaphysical project showed how a sense of justice (Derrida proclaims the importance of justice, such that it lies beyond the reach of deconstruction) needs to be freed from an automatic view of social progress. In particular, Glendinning notes the baggage imported into our "images of thought" (Deleuze, 1994, p. 129) from the long history of millenarian thinking in the Western tradition. It often appears as barely questioned assumptions about social justice.

In a millenarian vision, social justice represents a promised land, a heaven on earth, a state of social nirvana, a final plateau that progressive practice is working toward. All will be well when we finally get there. The word millenarian literally suggests a thousand years of freedom. Social justice is sometimes imagined as a steady march led by messianic figures onward and upward toward a better future. With each step forward, more and more people will throw off their shackles and emancipate themselves. This millenarian or messianic tradition can be detected in stated goals such as the "elimination" of racism, poverty, homophobia, sexism, and so on, as if achieving social justice will one day soon bring an end to history and we can all relax. By way of example, the American Counseling Association's (ACA) Counselors for Social Justice (CSJ) Code of Ethics on social justice calls for counselors to "promote equity and an end to oppression and injustice in communities, schools, workplaces, governments, and other social and institutional systems." As a sentiment it is laudable but, as a goal, it is flawed and risks frustration and cynicism.

Social injustice, moreover, never stands still. It continues to invent new mechanisms with which to disconnect people from their sense of vitality and their dreams for their lives. Thus every advance must expect a regrouping of the forces of injustice that produce new forms of oppression, and new ways to alienate people from having a say in their own lives.

Let me list a few examples. Capitalism continually evolves new forms of exploit-ation, such as the outsourcing of jobs. The internet has benefited large corpora-tions more than small local businesses. Social media have provided new tools with which to target and control people. In some places, prenatal scanning has led to increases in the abortion rate for girl babies. Closed circuit TV and computerized databases made the tools of surveillance that Foucault (2000) analyzed as the basis for modern power more widely available. Asymmetric violent conflict between governments and "terrorist" groups (often claiming the name of social justice) has killed many innocent people. Therefore, if new forms of injustice are constantly being invented, so too do new forms of protest and new visions of social justice also constantly need to be invented.

In contrast with millenarian hope, social justice causes at different times move forwards or backwards. Taking a longer view of history might afford us a sense of civilizations progressing forward at times and regressing backwards at others. The direction of social movements is not uniformly progressive. For example, the sexual abuse of children has been through "several cycles of awareness and denial" (Enns, 1996, p. 361) in the last hundred years. As Robert Whitaker (2002) shows, the treatment of the mentally ill in America was more humane in the nineteenth century than after the rise of eugenics in the twentieth century and is still probably not as socially just as it was 150 years ago.

The cause of social justice, therefore, will never be complete. This is not a pes-simistic statement but a recognition of the complexity of social change. We have to be in it for the long haul, because we are unlikely to reach the promised land (much as Martin Luther King foresaw before he died) and, even if we did, we would need to protect it against new forms of injustice and against the return of old ones. The cause of social justice demands constant vigilance.

So how might counselors conceptualize social justice, if not in millenarian terms? I would suggest holding the principles of social justice like an ethical prism through which to view events. This prism can help notice the nuances and sub-tleties of injustice under our noses. Social justice actually needs to be constantly reinvented in the light of changing social circumstances.

This focus might include analysis of new mechanisms that produce injustice. They might also include celebration of the myriad of little ways through which people evade oppression, laugh at it, construct workarounds, gather together to combat alienation, creatively express protest, and win small victories against oppressive forces. Counseling clients are engaged every day in such actions. Staying open to inspiration from these sources, and finding joy and vitality in each moment of them, requires rejecting the postponement of such joy until a revolu-tion happens. The pursuit of social justice need not postpone celebration until a final destination is reached.

The distinction here might be between social justice as a state of being or a project of becoming. Rather than achieving a final state of emancipation for each identity group, social justice might better pursue the never-ending task of becom-ing, which is the expression of constant differentiation. In becoming other than who they have been told they can be, people invent new ways of living. This is an ongoing activity, based on the expression of ethical principles, constantly in need of renewal, more than it is a journey to a promised land.

Is Social Justice a Goal for Counseling Itself or Does It Lie Outside of Counseling?

The counseling field needs to sort out what its most useful role might be in the cause of social justice. In some texts, concern for social justice sounds like a call to diminish the importance of individual counseling in favor of action on a larger social scale. Counseling individuals is represented as too small in scope to make a big enough difference (Chung & Bemak, 2012; D'Andrea, 2002). The real action lies in working on behalf of larger groups or communities. The counselor starts to sound like a professional social activist whose most important counseling role turns towards advocacy in wider social arenas on behalf of clients.

I believe an exclusive focus on advocacy is not always the best use of a counselor's skills. The CSJ website lists advocacy at the top of the list of its "competencies" (itself a term that derives from a neoliberal educational agenda) for counselors to learn. Counselors, however, should also pay attention to counseling itself. Counseling clients need help to make sense of the forces of injustice affecting their lives, leading to the problems they are experiencing. This does not have to be a "band aid" approach (Chung & Bemak, 2012). The choice is not just between working with individuals or with larger sociopolitical contexts. It is also a choice between counseling approaches that flow between the personal and the sociopolitical or that keep these things separate as either/or alternatives. Clients need counseling to help them identify counter stories that inspire them to take significant steps toward social justice.

Good counseling helps make sense of the social formations that produce relations of oppression and of how injustice becomes internalized as forms of consciousness through processes of subjectivation (Lazzarato, 2014). It is a complex task that counselors are better trained than other professionals to address. Every oppression and injustice tries to convince people to swallow its message about what to expect from life. It adjusts persons to take their place in an unjust social world without complaining (and often enlists counseling for this purpose). People are encouraged to construct identities that fit neatly into the neoliberal modern world and to blame themselves for any failure to do so. The CSJ website rightly encourages counselors to recognize signs of "internalized oppression." This emphasis is important since "internalized oppression" is a manifestation of all injustices. People are routinely produced as docile citizens (Foucault, 2000) and convinced that injustice is the natural order and there must be something wrong with them if they do not accept it.

For this reason, one cannot be concerned about social justice without also being concerned about the steady encroachment of normalizing judgment (Foucault,

1999) further into our lives. The latest version of the *Diagnostic and Statistical Manual of Mental Disorders* (American Psychiatric Association, 2013) is evidence of this, but the warnings were also sounded by Carl Rogers (1961) a long time ago (Winslade, 2013). Michael White (2002) has correctly analyzed the experience of personal failure, and therefore of depression, as indicative of social injustice, more than of individual deficits produced by brain chemicals.

An important job for counselors is to help people understand personal struggles as connected with forces of social injustice. Economic recession, for example, produces pain unequally for those with few economic resources and produces depression, anxiety, and personality problems. Helping people link social forces and personal distress should not be neglected by counselors who are busy as social advocates and activists. As Paré (2014) points out, we usually think of social justice work as about action, but conversation, including therapeutic conversation, is also action. Through conversation, people construct lives, identities, relationships, and communities in more just or less just formats. Feminist approaches to counseling first embodied this principle in the slogan, "The personal is political!"

Feminist therapists have been joined by others who have embraced social justice and taken it seriously enough to generate new theoretical positions. Narrative therapy (White, 2007; White & Epston, 1990) attracted my interest because it built social justice concerns into the center of theory and practice, rather than as an afterthought. The same can be said for the "Just Therapy" of Waldegrave, Tamasese, Tuhaka and Campbell (2003), Davies' and Neal's (1996) "pink therapy," Guattari's (Deleuze & Guattari, 1977) schizoanalysis, Jenkins' (2009) invitational practice, and Wade's (1997) response-based counseling. And there are many others.

People also respond to what they internalize. When they encounter injustice, they may swallow some aspects but they also express resistance to what is done to them. I remember the 13-year-old boy who told his school counselor, "I'm ADHD, but I don't believe it." This statement includes both recognition of internalization that he cannot avoid, and also an expression of resistance. Counselors, when they hear such statements, have a choice. They can "train students and clients in self-advocacy skills" (CSJ Code of Ethics, 2011) or help them identify what they are *already* doing to protest their situation and invite them to grow that resistance. The former approach risks colonizing the client with the counselor's knowledge. The latter is more likely to generate agency and effect internal and external change simultaneously, because it is based in the client's cultural world.

What Are We Working For?

Counseling for social justice should not, therefore, be limited to analyzing and making sense of injustice. Its express aim should also be the promotion of the counter forces to injustice that have many names. One of the weakest of these, but still important, is the word equality. As Lazzarato (2014) points out, equality is necessary, but not sufficient, for producing lives in accord with social justice. Equality has been written into many laws around the world, but powerful forces that work against social justice have learned to use it to their own advantage. Take, for example, how the "Citizens United" Supreme Court decision in the United States twisted the meaning of equality to constitute powerful corporations as citizens with the right to the same provisions of political equality as any individual (Kairys, 2010).

Nevertheless, equality is important when legal inequality has been institutionalized, for example, under Jim Crow laws in the American South, or under apartheid laws in South Africa prior to 1994. Once legal equality is achieved, however, there is still no guarantee of social justice, because people recreate injustice behind the back of the law. For example, racially segregated housing is no longer legal in the United States, but has effectively been recreated through the development of inner city ghettoes and gated communities. It is no longer a legal barrier, but it still structures people's experience.

The concept of "equity" is often a better candidate than "equality" for what social justice might promote. It recognizes equality of *outcomes* as more important than equal *rights* before the law. It thus allows for experiences of living to be targeted that go beyond legal rights. Affirmative action programs are examples of mechanisms based more on equity than equality (a distinction not understood by those who think affirmative action refers to quotas). Equitable provision of counseling services, for example, might not always be strictly equal. It might expand provisions for those whose needs are greater as a result of inequity elsewhere in the social system.

But even equity has limits. It does not help us deal with the ways in which some are treated as "other" or with the internalized psychological consequences of such othering. Take, for example, how transgender people are often not granted legitimate places from which to participate in social exchange. Social exchange, conversation, and personal recognition are beyond the reach of laws and of economic provisions. Hence, other concepts have been developed to address them (see below).

Moreover, like equality, equity is limited by its aims of producing the same for all, whether we are talking about equality of inputs or equity of outcomes. The problem is that personal needs and desires are different and people's lives take multiple shapes. Providing everyone with the same service would not address such multiplicity, just as a hospital that treated everyone on Tuesday mornings for heart disease might provide equality of services but not help all patients appropriately.

"Inclusion" is another candidate for what to work for. It has been used extensively in relation to disability and has served as a rallying point for the disability movement. But achievements in the name of inclusion have not always turned back the process of othering, because persons with disabilities are still often engaged through the lens of disability first, and expected to be grateful for "charity" from others.

A more promising concept has been advanced by Derrida (Derrida & Dufourmantelle, 2000). He advocates "hospitality toward the other." "Hospitality" suggests a strong sense of welcoming and valuing those who are different. It conveys a sense of obligation to form positive relations with others. It implies not just tolerating others' right to exist, nor just refraining from discrimination against them, or avoiding stereotypes, but actively engaging and inviting them into our world as full participants. For Derrida, a corollary of such hospitality is that it needs to be hospitality for the other "as other." In other words, hospitality should not be contingent upon a person fitting what "we" would expect. Hospitality toward the other is a promising ethical value on which social justice counseling might be practiced.

Redistribution or Subjectivation?

Many social movements that target social justice have focused on restructuring socioeconomic arrangements to make it possible for groups of people to leap over barriers preventing them from pursuing their dreams. Clearly, economic redistribution can enable the taking up of agency. The social imaginary (Taylor, 2004) that has driven many social justice campaigns can be expressed in the famous slogan, "From each according to his [sic] ability; to each according to his need" (popularized, but not invented, by Marx, 1875). It expresses a vision of a society to come in which the values of the golden rule and aspirations of democracy are institutionalized.

Redistribution of economic resources is inimical to the values of competitive capitalism and has been under constant attack from the dominant neoliberal political ideology of the last 40 years. Despite this opposition, calls for redistribution of wealth have been a frequent refrain of social justice movements. The "Occupy" movement was a recent example.

For counseling, however, economic redistribution has limited value. Apart from their own services, counselors do not have much to distribute, let alone redistribute. When it comes to other economic resources, counselors usually have little say in how these are distributed. If a client is unemployed, counseling might be helpful with unpacking personal meanings about the situation but cannot provide a job. True to its Marxist origins, the concept of redistribution is largely focused on economics as the base on which other aspects of living are built. However, the assumption that everything flows from an economic base and that subjective experience is an epiphenomenon of this flow reduces counseling to a trivial activity. I think we can do better.

The idea of social justice as delivered largely by economic redistribution needs to be expanded to address the ways in which economic and social forces are intimately connected with forms of subjectivity. The analyses of Foucault, Deleuze, and Guattari have shown how subjectivity is actively produced by forces of governmentality (Foucault, 2010) in forms that fit with economic and social forces. As Lazzarato (2014) explains, the production of subjectivity is central to the forces of injustice. Lazzarato describes the work of large social machines that shape people's lives in two principal ways.

The first is the process of "social subjection" in which individuals are subjectivated or assigned forms of identity to live within: male and female genders, social classes, racial categories, nationalities, identities as students, pensioners, the sick and disabled, consumers, and nuclear family members. These identities are produced by discourses of the self, by disciplinary knowledge systems, by schooling, by the circulation of social norms, and by social practices of everyday life (De Certeau, 1984). Recent nuanced shifts in these processes of assigning people ready-made subjectivities have seen many people transformed from salaried laborers into entrepreneurs of the self. For many with few resources to sell on the labor market, the result is the production of "precarious" lives (Standing, 2011).

Second, there are also, according to Lazarrato, parallel and complementary processes of desubjectivation that undermine agency in people, even as they are being produced by such forces. Lazarrato pinpoints how human beings are increasingly constituted as components in machines of production of modern life, with little chance to speak as individuals. Examples of machines are the television machine, the military industrial complex, the internet machine, processes of surveillance, and the advertising machine. In these machinic processes, people lose key parts of free citizenship; they experience the crushing of the ability to speak (Deleuze, calls this the "crushing of enunciation," cited by Lazzarato, 2007); they are less individuals than they are "dividuals" (Deleuze, 1992); they are lumped together into statistical existence as populations; and their personal desires are torn away from them. Instead, they have to perform their function in the machine (as employee, consumer, or television viewer).

What does this mean for social justice and for counseling? First, this analysis adds to the complexity of forces that diminish people's ability to create lives on their own terms. It is a much more complex task than that of removing structural "barriers," because the forces that produce injustice have learned how to get around barriers. Modern social machines work much more directly to produce forms of subjectivity than used to be the case. As well as equal rights, people need internal freedom from forces of subjectivation and desubjectivation. It is not as simple as it used to be to mount a struggle for emancipation, because the forces of subjectivation and desubjectivation that produce injustice are operating inside people's heads and bodies, more than just through external repression.

The task of countering these processes has, therefore, also changed. Rather than just struggles for emancipation and rights, the pursuit of social justice now also involves freeing people from an inner sense of assigned identity and from alienated positions in social machines. Emancipation entails developing a sense of agency through creative responses that are necessarily often more singular than collective. It entails people differentiating their identities from those assigned to them and recreating the agency that is split asunder by the desubjectivation produced by social machines. If modern lines of force crush the possibility of enunciation, then counseling is an important venue where such enunciation might become possible again.

The difficulty of these tasks is magnified, because the contemporary scene is so complex. It is not always easy to see what to do. Creating greater freedom is not the same for everyone. Counseling can play an important role in helping people figure out how they are being both subjectivated and de-subjectivated. Counselors are skilled at talking with people about internalizing processes and this is precisely what is needed, now more than ever. Counseling theory, however, needs to explicitly address the deconstruction of forces of subjection and de-subjection. Older approaches based in empathy, and even empowerment, are no longer sufficient.

My contention is that counselors who embrace social justice as an ethical principle can do more than just advocate for the redistribution of economic resources or legal rights. These things are still necessary, but they have become insufficient responses to the forces of injustice. Instead, counselors might embrace a unique role for counseling itself in the production of lives, through helping people recognize complex forces that shape how they are produced and seek to articulate places of difference.

Not all counseling is focused on social justice. Counselors can practice counseling that assists in the production of people to fit tidily into assigned categories and adjusts their desires for their lives to fit with unjust social systems. Without a concern for social justice, counselors can respond to the production of personal distress in completely individualistic terms, with little concern for the damage done by pathologizing discourses. Such counseling acquiesces in the face of injustice without challenging it. The cause of social justice requires us to examine such practices and to reconstitute them for more valuable purposes.

Counselors alert to social justice concerns can make ethical distinctions between exposing work done by social machines and obscuring it. Social justice needs to be articulated as an ethical principle to guide practice, more than as a destination of history. It involves providing clients with the experience of recognition for what they seek to enunciate and with encouragement to differentiate their lives in creative ways. These ways may not be the same for everyone and, therefore, social justice counseling needs to theorize the production of nuanced differentiation, rather than group belonging. This need is particularly salient where people are rendered invisible, or lumped into categories of personhood that can be manipulated. If social forces are at work as much inside people's heads as in laws and structural arrangements of the social world, then counseling has an important role in helping people articulate a life that is not so limited by thoughts they have been recruited into. This task will never end but, even though the promised land is not reached, people can achieve local and particular emancipatory goals. Indeed, it is often at the local level that emancipation occurs. A thousand tiny victories, rather than one big revolutionary structural shift, can be celebrated. That, I believe, is something worth working for in counseling.

Reflection Questions

1. What are examples of the struggles against power relations that clients present to you in counseling?
2. How are people constructed in these struggles?
3. What values assist you to help people sort through how they will position themselves in relation to these struggles?
4. Which social movements do your clients find provide helpful resources in emancipating themselves from injustice?
5. How does your favored counseling approach theoretically support social justice work?

References

American Psychiatric Association. (2013). *Diagnostic and statistical manual of mental disorders* (5th ed.). Washington, DC: Author.

Barry, B. (2005). *Why social justice matters.* Cambridge, UK: Polity Press.

Chung, R. C. -Y., & Bemak, F. (2012). *Social justice counseling: The next steps beyond multiculturalism.* Thousand Oaks, CA: Sage.

Counselors for social justice (2011). The Counselors for Social Justice (CSJ) Code of Ethics. *Journal for Social Action in Counseling and Psychology, 3*(2), 1–21. Retrieved from http://jsacp.tumblr.com

D'Andrea, M. (2002). Counselors for social justice: A revolutionary and liberating force in the counseling profession. *Counselors for Social Justice Newsletter, 2*(2), 24–29. Retrieved from https://counseling-csj.org

Davies, D., & Neal, C. (Eds.) (1996). *Pink therapy.* Maidenhead, UK: Open University Press.

De Cauter, L. (2004). For a justice to come: An interview with Jacques Derrida. Retrieved from http://archive.indymedia.be/news/2004/04/83123.html

De Certeau, M. (1984). *The practice of everyday life* (S. Rendall, Trans.). Berkeley, CA and Los Angeles, CA: University of California Press.

Deleuze, G. (1992). Postscript on societies of control. *October, 59,* 3–7.

Deleuze, G. (1994). *Difference and repetition* (P. Patton, Trans.) New York, NY: University of Columbia Press.

Deleuze, G., & Guattari, F. (1977). *Anti-Oedipus: Capitalism and schizophrenia.* London: Penguin.

Deleuze, G., & Parnet, C. (1987). The actual and the virtual (E. R. Albert, Trans.). In *Dialogues II* (pp. 148–152). New York, NY: Columbia University Press.

Derrida, J., & Dufourmantelle, A. (2000). *Of hospitality (cultural memory in the present)* (R. Bowlby, Trans.). Palo Alto, CA: Stanford University Press.

Enns, C. Z. (1996). Counselors and the backlash: "Rape hype" and "false memory syndrome." *Journal of Counseling and Development, 74*(4), 358–368. doi: 10.1002/j.1556–6676.1996.tb01880.x

Foucault, M. (1999). *Abnormal: Lectures at the Collège de France 1974–1975* (V. Marchetti & A. Salomoni, Eds., G. Burchell, Trans.). New York, NY: Picador.

Foucault, M. (2000). *Power: Essential works of Foucault, 1954–1984 (Vol. 3).* J. Faubion, Ed., R. Hurley, Trans.). New York, NY: New Press.

Foucault, M. (2010). *The government of self and others: Lectures at the Collège de France 1982–1983*. New York, NY: Palgrave Macmillan.

Glendinning, S. (2011). *Derrida: A very short introduction*. New York, NY: Oxford University Press.

Jenkins, A. (2009). *Becoming ethical: A parallel, political journey with men who have abused*. Lyme Regis, UK: Russell House.

Kairys, D. (2010). Money isn't speech and corporations aren't people. Slate. Retrieved from www.slate.com/articles/news_and_politics/jurisprudence/2010/01/money_isnt_speech_and_corporations_arent_people.html

Lazzarato, M. (2007). Semiotic capitalism: Social subjection and machinic enslavement. Retrieved from http://automatist.net/deptofreading/wiki/pmwiki.php/Semiotic Capitalism

Lazzarato, M. (2014). *Signs, machines, subjectivities*. Sao Pãolo, Brazil: n-1 Publications.

Lyotard, J. -F. (1984). *The postmodern condition: A report on knowledge* (G. Bennington & B. Massumi, Trans.). Minneapolis, MN: University of Minnesota Press.

Marx, K. (1875). Critique of the Gotha Program. In *Marx/Engels selected works, vol 3* (pp. 13–30). Moscow: Progressive Publishers.

Paré, D. (2014). Social justice and the word: Keeping diversity alive in therapeutic conversations. *Canadian Journal of Counseling and Psychotherapy, 48*(3), 206–217. Retrieved from http://cjc-rcc.ucalgary.ca

Rawls, J. (1991). *A theory of justice* (Revised ed.). Cambridge, MA: Harvard University Press.

Rogers, C. R. (1961). *On becoming a person: A therapist's view of psychotherapy*. Boston, MA: Houghton Mifflin.

Standing, G. (2011). *The precariat: The new dangerous class*. London: Bloomsbury.

Taylor, C. (2004). *Modern social imaginaries*. Durham, NC: Duke University Press.

Wade, A. (1997). Small acts of living: Everyday resistance to violence and other forms of oppression. *Contemporary Family Therapy, 19*(1), 23–39. doi: 10.1023/A:1026154215299

Waldegrave, C., Tamasese, K., Tuhaka, F., & Campbell, W. (2003) *Just Therapy—a journey: A collection of papers from the Just Therapy Team, New Zealand*. Adelaide, Australia: Dulwich Centre Publications.

Whitaker, R. (2002). *Mad in America: Bad science, bad medicine, and the enduring mistreatment of the mentally ill*. Philadelphia, PA: Perseus.

White, M. (2002). Addressing personal failure. *International Journal of Narrative Therapy and Community Work, 3*, 33–76. Retrieved from http://dulwichcentre.com.au/international-journal-of-narrative-therapy-and-community-work

White, M. (2007). *Maps of narrative practice*. New York, NY: Norton.

White, M., & Epston, D. (1990). *Narrative means to therapeutic ends*. New York, NY: Norton.

Winslade, J. M. (2013). From being non-judgemental to deconstructing normalising judgement, *British Journal of Guidance & Counselling, 41*(5), 518–529. doi: 10.1080/0306988 5.2013.771772

Challenging Conversations: Deepening Personal and Professional Commitment to Culture-Infused and Socially Just Counseling Practices

Sandra Collins and Nancy Arthur

Most counselors and counseling students likely agree with the basic principles of social justice: (1) cultural responsiveness in practice, (2) equity and accessibility of counseling services, (3) recognition of systemic barriers and sources of oppression that lead to client distress, (4) importance of remediation of social inequities, and (5) advocacy for clients' full inclusion and participation in society (Collins, Arthur, McMahon, & Bisson, 2015; Ginsberg & Sinacore, 2015). However, to fully engage in culturally responsive and socially just counseling practices, we must move beyond a surface understanding of social justice to a deep appreciation of the multiple dimensions and concepts that underpin our vision of *Culture-Infused Counseling* (Arthur & Collins, 2010). We must examine our cultural selves, the worldviews and cultural identities of our clients, and our relative positioning of power and privilege within society. As we dig deeper into the meaning of these concepts, we are likely to encounter values conflicts, denial and resistance, unconscious *isms*, or other personal and professional barriers.

In this chapter, we explore several challenges that have emerged from our research, counselor educator, and counselor roles. Our knowledge in this area derives from our interactions with students, clients, and other professionals in the field. We believe that professional education needs to be informed by the realities faced by both clients and those who work directly with them and vice versa. We draw on our own practice examples to illustrate principles and processes for culture-infused, socially just counseling. We quote students, counselors, and practicum supervisors to bring the ideas to life, drawing from our research into how to best teach principles of multicultural counseling and social justice (Arthur & Collins, 2012). We provide guidance for the challenging conversations essential to moving through more subtle barriers to socially just practice.

Embracing the Complexity and Situatedness of Privilege—We Are Products of Our Socio-Cultural Positioning

The last half-century has evidenced dramatic shifts in defining and enacting human rights policies and standards (Pettifor, 2010). These changes impact us both personally and professionally. I (SC) am aware of how much I am privileged through the hard-fought battles of others before me. Yet, I hold a gut-level unease, as a woman and as a lesbian, within professional environments, shifting political climates in Canada, and escalating international crises. I observe both subtle and more blatant erosion of the basic rights for women, as well LGBTQ[1] populations. I am simultaneously aware of my own privilege through education, socioeconomic status, and the whiteness of my skin. I empathize deeply with the cultural oppression experienced by the young, unemployed, transgendered client I am working with—yet, hold in conscious awareness my relative positioning of privilege.

Privilege is defined as an unearned advantage, embedded in social status or position, which brings with it benefits or resources not available to others (Singh et al., 2010). Social, economic, and political privilege typically rests outside of our individual and collective awareness. White privilege affords me (NA) many opportunities in daily life, both in Canada and in my work/travel abroad. Access to education has exposed me to information and ways of understanding the world that I strive not to take for granted or impose on others. I struggle with the blatant and subtle ways that women are positioned in our society, with the burden of generations of inequities. I am acutely aware of the negative attributions towards my single-parent status, although many do not fit my privileged position. I am reminded of the social responsibility placed on mothers for the well-being of children and care-taking of others, without equitably distributed social and economic resources or recognition of social and relational work (Richardson, 2012).

Individuals and groups encumbered by social, cultural, economic, or political barriers are acutely aware of various forms of cultural oppression. They see it played out around them on a daily basis. They encounter prejudice and discrimination based on visible or invisible markers of cultural identities or social locations (Arthur & Collins, 2014). People from non-dominant groups often monitor their daily interactions for cues of risk, marginalization, or hostility. For example, a young woman in a wheelchair sits quietly as her new counselor addresses questions to the caretaker who accompanies her, mirroring the invisibility she often experiences in society. The hyper-vigilance towards subtle and blatant forms of discrimination is often cognitively and emotionally draining, leading individuals to adjust, minimize, or hide aspects of their cultural identities to *fit in*. The pain and trauma resulting from ongoing social exclusion and daily experiences of discrimination can manifest in serious mental health concerns (Birrell & Freyd, 2006).

As counselor educators, we center teaching and learning in personal narratives to support students to connect with the concepts of social justice and privilege (Patrick & Connolly, 2013). We have challenging conversations with graduate students about positioning themselves consciously on the shifting landscape of privilege and oppression. Many may not have fully examined the impact on their position of privilege of gender, ethnicity, sexual orientation, ability, age, socio-economic status, language, or religion (Collins, 2010). A student in our research (Arthur & Collins, 2012) commented:

> Prior to starting my [graduate] program, I did not think of myself as privileged, as I am female, I did not grow up with money, and I have had to work very hard. Although this has an effect on me, I now have an appreciation of the privilege of being born in Canada, being of average physical attractiveness, being white and having an opportunity to further my education that are far from the realities of many others. I am now more aware that I have a voice that is needed by others.

It is easy to slip into the myth that hard work, persistence, and good choices inevitably lead to success, as these assumptions are embedded in theories and models of counseling (Flores, 2009). For example, we might inadvertently blame a client who has low income for what we consider to be unhealthy choices, because we misperceive poverty as a consequence, rather than a precursor, to poor health (Lavell, 2014). Alternatively, we may fail to critically analyze relative power and privilege in our negotiation of a sliding scale fee, leaving our client disempowered, with a sense of indebtedness that undermines the counseling process. We might *privilege* our personal or professional knowledge, perception, or language, over our client's expertise, through leading questions, un-tentative inferences, or culture-bound hypotheses.

We encourage you to talk openly about privilege with colleagues and clients, beginning with conscious awareness of those aspects of your personal cultural identity that tend to go unexamined (Collins & Arthur, 2010). Another student noted (Arthur & Collins, 2012):

> Before my graduate school experience, I had never thought much about what it meant to be … born with the color of skin, gender, sexual orientation, and social status I was … was eye-opening and heartbreaking at the same time: I had to face some ugly truths about privileges and injustices woven into my life.

To avoid inadvertently playing out privilege and power in your relationships with clients, it is important to apply a critical lens to case conceptualization, attending to the social determinants of health and the influence of contextual factors on client problems and preferred outcomes (Vera & Speight, 2003). This opens space for client knowledge to be prioritized and for clients to become active collaborators in change processes that mirror their unique perspectives and lived experiences (Paré, 2014).

Grappling with the Reality of Cultural Oppression—It Is Not About *Me* ... , But It Is All About *Me*!

Injustice is hard wired into the stratified nature of our society, our profession, and our world (Fox, Prilleltensky, & Austin, 2009). It is also inescapably embedded in history. One of the most difficult conversations we have with students relates to positioning themselves relative to the past and present cultural oppression of Indigenous Peoples in Canada (Stewart & Marshall, 2015). For example, a counseling student reacts strongly to the experience of rejection by an Indigenous client who told her that the student could not understand her experience and does not return for counseling. The student was left wondering about her personal responsibility for historical oppression as a member of the dominant population. It is often challenging to recognize responsibilities for the historical legacy of oppression and navigate its impact on contemporary practices. However, the *professional is political*, and we must look at how professional practices implicitly or actively support either the status quo or social change (Arthur & Collins, 2014).

Acknowledging privilege requires more than simply recognizing your current socio-cultural positioning; it also demands recognition of the implications of cultural group affiliation, past and present, on the cultural oppression of others, and how difference is defined and acted upon. Look beyond the presenting symptoms of clients to consider the processes through which people are positioned as more or less powerful, how their presenting concerns might be related to the ways that people are valued or devalued, and who has access to social resources, such as education, employment, and quality health/mental health care (Arthur & Collins, 2015a).

Many students struggle to own their inter-connectedness with cultural oppression. As instructors, we tread carefully to avoid student disempowerment, denial, and backlash (Todd & Abrams, 2011); however, consciousness-raising sometimes provokes strong emotional reactions (Arthur & Collins, 2012):

> A lesson on white privilege ... talked about how white people are more privileged than other populations. I am tired of being only seen for the color of my skin. It seemed like a lesson in hypocrisy, that no matter how culturally sensitive I am, how multiculturally competent I become, my knowledge and experiences, values and beliefs—I will always be a white oppressor ... Stop shaming white people. I am more than my skin color.

As counselor educators, we strive to create an environment for students to safely wrestle with these emotions and to reconcile their relative position of privilege, within themselves and within their personal and professional lives. It is sometimes a profound challenge for counselors to invite dialogue about social inequities and to hold the space for our clients to express their rage, grief, and sometimes hostility about their profound experiences of cultural oppression, in the face of our own connections, as members of dominant populations, to these injustices. Dismissing this lived reality, either overtly or covertly, silences them and risks perpetuating social injustices, essentially colonizing our clients to our view of the world. The legacy of the residential school system, for example, must be borne by many of us, because of our ethnicity, our religion, and our heritage as colonialists. We must be willing to grapple with our own grief and anger about the bequest of both responsibility and privilege.

When confronted with such significant impacts of relative privilege, it is human nature to deny, minimize, and rationalize. To be effective and ethical in our work with members of non-dominant populations, we are called instead to *lean into* our discomfort, to set aside our need to be absolved of collective responsibility, and to find a path to justice, alongside our clients. Compassion and cultural empathy are only possible if we willingly accept our positioning within the landscape of privilege and work to restructure society with and on behalf of our clients. Coming to terms with our own privilege opens us to a deeper understanding of our clients' lived experience; invites critical reflection on the systemic influences, past and present, on our clients' problems; and infuses conscious awareness and open dialogue about culture and social justice into our work.

Navigating Complex Values Conflicts—Challenging the Myth of Neutrality

Counseling has historically laid claim to being value neutral. However, the illusion of value-free practice leads to inadvertent cultural blindness and supports an oppressive status quo, both within the profession and within society (Mintz et al., 2009). As holders of positions of power and privilege, we have an ethical and social responsibility to clearly define our values and to honestly grapple with conflicts between our own values, the values of the profession, and the values of our clients. There is also a growing consensus that we must broaden our roles and responsibilities to actively advocate, with and on behalf of clients, for changes in the unjust systems that negatively influences their lives (Chang, Crethar, & Ratts, 2010). It is impossible to orient towards advocacy and hold to a value-neutral or apolitical positioning.

Social justice values are embedded within our codes of ethics, to guide us through complex values conflicts. We are called to employ cultural awareness and respect for diversity to promote the best interests of our clients (beneficence), to do no harm (nonmaleficence), and to respect clients' rights to self-determination (autonomy). At the same time, we are expected to think beyond the individual client–counselor relationship to foster the dignity and just treatment of all people (justice) and be responsible to our society (societal interest) (Canadian Counselling and Psychotherapy Association, 2007). Do our codes of ethics go far enough to mobilize action between awareness and sensitivity, to actively address the injustices faced by many people due to the ways that their cultural identities and diversity position them in non-dominant roles along with unequal social standing (Arthur & Collins, 2015b)?

Many clients hold multiple, fluid, and intersecting identities that are expressed in different ways based on social locations (Collins, 2010). Values conflicts and cultural oppression can occur within and across various groups. Transgender and sexual minorities, for example, may face increased discrimination from within their non-dominant ethnic communities and struggle with difficult choices related to costs of embracing gender and/or sexual identities. The rights of women to self-determination and ownership over their own bodies may come into conflict with the religious tenants of more fundamentalist elements of dominant religions. The voices of Aboriginal populations may be marginalized within discourses about women's or LGBTIQ issues. As advocates of social justice, we must wade into these deep waters, by grappling with our own biases and preferred worldviews and by navigating values conflicts in our work with clients. We suggest three key principles to guide professional reflection about values conflicts (Mintz et al., 2009; Vera, 2009).

First, cultural sensitivity, although absolutely core to ethical and competent practice, is secondary to respect for basic human rights (as defined by both national and international bodies). In other words, to embody the ethical principles of *justice* and *social interest*, counselors cannot endorse or engage in the oppression of one group under the guise of respect for another. As counselor educators, we sometimes encounter students who hold discriminatory attitudes, justified through religious beliefs. We are obliged to come alongside our students and actively challenge the slippery slope of *tolerance of intolerance*. Over time, the focus of ethnocentric bias has shifted—from gender, to ethnicity, to disability, to sexual orientation and gender identity, to religion (Arthur & Collins, 2010)—and it will likely shift again in the future. We invite students to carefully consider the *othering* that happens in any dichotomy of *us* and *them* and to carefully examine the processes that position groups in our society to experience social inequities. We challenge students to carefully examine the alignment of their beliefs with professional values. We invite them to actively co-construct higher order values, such as social justice, that may provide a bridge to reconciling personal biases, maintaining empathy, and motivating action in working directly with and on behalf of clients to address social inequities that adversely impact their health and well-being (Kennedy & Arthur, 2014; Mintz et al., 2009). To reiterate, respect for human rights is primary in considering the contextual and situational influences experienced by individuals and groups in our society that are relevant for exploring oppression.

The second principle for guiding professional reflection about values conflicts is that *counseling is about clients*—they are the sole reason for our existence as a profession. It is our privilege, not our right, to witness their lives and support them in meeting their unique and idiosyncratic goals. Each of the principles from the code of ethics (beneficence, nonmaleficence, autonomy, and societal interest) reflects the counselor's professional *responsibility to others*. Although it is not always possible, we strive to support all students to reconcile their positions of privilege; examine biases that have been embraced as if they are *truths*, as opposed to social constructions (Paré, 2014); and to restructure their thinking in a way that reflects the values of the profession. Ultimately, our responsibility is to the profession, to society, and to future clients. In correspondence with the second principles, we advocate for a client-centered approach to understanding and resolving values conflicts.

Third, in an effort to resolve values conflicts, counselors must distinguish between prejudicial perspectives (e.g., negative and unfounded judgments based solely on an individual's cultural identity—gender, sexual orientation, ethnicity, etc.) and values conflicts (e.g., differences in worldview or assumptions about healthy/unhealthy functioning). We are each responsible for addressing personal prejudice through consultation, supervision, continuing education, etc. Discrimination has no place in our counseling practices. Values conflicts, on the other hand, are likely to arise for all of us. As individuals in positions of power, we must recognize the risk of imposing our values on our clients (e.g., compromising their *autonomy*) and thoughtfully assess if, when, and how to explore differences in values (either our own or those of the profession) with our clients, remembering the principles of *beneficence* (best interests of the client) and *nonmaleficence* (do no harm).

I (SC) reflect on my work with a client involved in the illegal drug trade as an illustration of how these principles might play out in practice. I built safety and rapport by viewing him as a whole (i.e., not defined by this one aspect of his identity) and finding points of connection (e.g., using characters from the *Breaking Bad* series to enhance shared understanding of his worldview and experiences). My stance of openness and curiosity about his life built a foundation of trust to collaboratively negotiate values differences in setting counseling goals. I critically reflected on where I could ally with this client and where to draw professional boundaries, based on the values of *justice* and *social interest* for both the client, for me as a professional, and for society. I used humor and transparency to engage my client in exploring the similarities and contrasts between these values and co-creating a change agenda. We agreed that it would be inappropriate for me to help him avoid being arrested; however, we could work together on managing his anger with individuals he worked with and career planning, specifically, a long-term exit plan. I felt no personal angst in working with this client; my role was to position the work to benefit him and, simultaneously, to reflect the social justice values of the profession. Counselors must wade willingly, but critically, into these grey zones.

Re-Defining Boundaries and Ethical Responsibilities—Enacting Social Justice

A practicum supervisor summed up the social justice imperative of the profession eloquently (Arthur & Collins, 2012):

[I]f social justice and multiculturalism is not the core of what counseling should be about, then what is it? ... I believe our job is to help people find ways to live according to their preferred ways; to me that is not possible if social injustice is part of the equation; if a client is marginalized, how would that be their preferred way of going about life, and how would counseling be successful if there were no changes in that regard?

Engagement in social justice action necessarily leads us past the narrow, intra-psychic focus of traditional counseling models. It demands that we both critically observe and take action beyond our own office walls, and it pushes the boundaries of our comfort zones and professional identity (Kennedy & Arthur, 2014).

One of the most challenging aspects of this social justice journey is letting go of what we think we know and, instead, forefronting the client's knowledge and lived experiences. A counselor reflected on a professional training experience (Arthur & Collins, 2012) in which social context was

systematically downplayed ... Every example of context was systematically countered through "empirically-validated" justification for personalizing and pathologizing. To experience the lack of insight and reflexivity in trusted pro-fessionals taught me how I, myself, had been a believer in the professional as expert.

Another counselor noted (Arthur & Collins, 2012): "counselors can easily fall into the 'I know what's best for you' category, and be a part of the system that we are try-ing to change." Viewing our clients in context and as the experts in their own lives opens possibilities for different approaches, roles, and relationships as counselors.

We invite readers to broaden the boundaries of how they define their counselor roles. Embracing a broader mandate of social action necessitates critical thinking and ethical decision-making that takes into account social location and experi-ences of cultural injustice (Fox et al., 2009). What might this actually look like in practice? Here are some examples from our own work with and on behalf of our clients: We invite clients to shift their assumption of personal *fault* and to recog-nize their symptoms as reactions to a bigger life picture. We meet with clients with disabilities in their homes or via Skype to ensure access to counseling services. We use our networks to locate resources for clients when they have faced barri-ers. We offer services free of charge for clients in financial crises. We invite clients to take action—to take steps to stand up and address social/systemic change. We function as advocates and allies for clients in navigating various organizational systems, write letters on their behalf, or simply accompany them to meetings with other individuals or organizations. We note patterns across clients and raise issues of inequity with employers, human resources managers, and employee assis-tance providers. We speak out against policy decisions that compromise access to employment or educational opportunities, questioning whose interests are being served.

Each of these activities requires carefully negotiated, context-specific, and shared understanding of the implications of imbalances of power and privilege, the nature and purpose of the client–counselor relationship, the relative voices of counselor and client, and the boundaries of counselor roles and responsibilities. We invite you to examine the structures, explicit and implicit rules about how counseling services are delivered, and to consider who is well served and whose voices are excluded (Moodley, 2009). The structures and policies of organizations may be limited by funding mandates, budgetary constraints, and social/political agendas. Making change happen within counseling agencies is a political act that takes time and energy, and it often requires the support of colleagues, supervisors, and managers (Arthur, Collins, McMahon, & Marshall, 2009). It may require us to relinquish certain aspects of our positions of privilege (our time, our resources, and sometimes our revenue) or use our privilege strategically. We believe there is a role for every counselor in social transformation, starting with small steps in how we view our clients and our day-to-day practices. We advocate for the integration of these roles into counseling in all practice settings, as part of our professional job description. In the words of wisdom of one of our students (Arthur & Collins, 2012):

> You're reading about people and they're organizing marches with a thousand people or they're fundraising to get the ten thousand dollars to the lawyer, which is social justice … But there's littler social justices along the way. You know behind the scenes stuff … this is also social justice. It's not always the big, glamorous things … I can do that.

Enacting social justice begins with relinquishing our urge to privilege our own perspective (Arthur & Collins, 2012):

> [I]n every step, every turn in our conversations with clients, we have the opportunity to engage in a kind of social justice conversation. For example, in not engaging in conversational violence, a way of imposing our views or discourses on clients' meaning making processes. So, even at the micro-level, I think something can be done.

Conclusion

Over the past several decades, there has been great success in educating counselors about cultural diversity and contextual influences on client well-being. It is time to move beyond awareness of cultural diversity to purposeful and systematic redressing of social injustices and cultural oppression within our practices, our professions, our society, and ourselves. There is a call within the literature for the integration of social justice values at all levels of counseling programs, from organizational structures to program policies to learning processes (Mintz et al., 2009). Addressing systemic oppression or inequities within our own professional contexts is a starting place for freeing ourselves up and creating collective momentum to address social injustices more broadly. To a large degree, our careers as counselors, academics, and/or researchers are built upon the backs of the socially oppressed. In other words, if we lived in a just world, there would be less work for us to do! For us that is the ultimate in professional privilege. If for no other reason than that we make our living, in large part, on the consequences of social oppression, we are obliged to act with and on behalf of our clients to enact social justice.

As counselors, we are uniquely positioned with the communication, mediation, and program planning and evaluation skills to engage in education, consciousness raising, advocacy, and consultation to enhance our professional practice environments. A practicum supervisor noted the importance of joining together to promote social justice at all levels (Arthur & Collins, 2012):

> We ... need to be aware of oppressions, underprivileged experience and to promote solidarity and care for others ... some of our clients have a "diagnosis" not found in DSM-IV—"born without luck." Unfortunately to have substantial change in the society we need to have more than things we do in our offices ... We need to advocate for the less privileged ... outside of therapy, promoting social values and changes toward universal human rights.

We leave you with a challenge to take one step forward today for social justice. As Audre Lorde so aptly stated: "I realize that if I wait until I am no longer afraid to act, write, speak, be, I'll be sending messages on an Ouija board, cryptic complaints from the other side!" (Lorde, 2004, p. 66).

Reflection Questions

1. How might you inadvertently play out privilege and power in your relationships with clients, your case conceptualizations, or your preferred change processes?
2. How might you set aside your own urge for validation, your desire to be liked, or your need to be right in order to fully *lean into connection* with your clients?
3. How might you *hold the space* for clients to express their legitimate rage over historical cultural oppression—even when that rage is directed at you or what you represent?
4. How might you use your position of relative privilege to advocate on behalf of clients or facilitate systems-level change to reduce socio-cultural injustices that negatively impact client well-being?
5. How might you expand the parameters of your counseling roles and/or practices in small ways to incorporate social justice?

Note

1 LGBTIQ refers to lesbian, gay, bisexual, transgender, intersex, and questioning.

References

Arthur, N., & Collins, S. (2010). *Culture-infused counselling*. Calgary, AB: Counselling Concepts.

Arthur, N., & Collins, S. (2012, June). *Facilitating culture-infused conversations and therapeutic processes*. Workshop presentation at the Winds of Change 5 Conference, Conversations on the Margins: Therapeutic Change, Social Change, Social Justice, Ottawa, Ontario.

Arthur, N., & Collins, S. (2014). Counsellors, counselling, and social justice: The professional is political. *Canadian Journal of Counselling and Psychotherapy, 48*(3), 171–185. Retrieved from http://cjc-rcc.ucalgary.ca

Arthur, N., & Collins, S. (2015a). Multicultural counselling in Canada: Education, supervision, and research. In A. Sinacore & F. Ginsberg (Eds.), *Canadian Counselling and Psychology in the 21st century* (pp. 42–67). Montreal, QC: McGill-Queen's University Press.

Arthur, N., & Collins, S. (2015b). Culture-infused counselling and psychotherapy. In L. Martin & B. Shepard (Eds.), *Canadian counselling and psychotherapy experience: Ethics-based issues and cases*. Ottawa, ON: Canadian Counselling and Psychotherapy Association.

Arthur, N., Collins, S., McMahon, M., & Marshall, C. (2009). Career practitioners' views of social justice and barriers for practice. *Canadian Journal of Career Development, 8*, 22–31. Retrieved from http://cjcdonline.ca

Birrell, P. J., & Freyd, J. J. (2006). Betrayal and trauma: Relational models of harm and healing. *Journal of Trauma Practice, 5*(1), 49–63. doi: 10.1300/J189v05n01_04

Canadian Counselling and Psychotherapy Association. (2007). *Code of Ethics*. Retrieved from www.ccpa-accp.ca

Chang, C. Y., Crethar, H. C., & Ratts, M. J. (2010). Social justice: A national imperative for counselor education and supervision. *Counselor Education & Supervision, 50*(2), 82–87. doi: 10.1002/j.1556–6978.2010.tb00110.x

Collins, S. (2010). The complexity of identity: Appreciating multiplicity and intersectionality. In N. Arthur & S. Collins (Eds.), *Culture-infused counselling* (2nd ed., pp. 247–258). Calgary, AB: Counselling Concepts.

Collins, S., & Arthur, N. (2010). Self-awareness and awareness of client cultural identities. In N. Arthur & S. Collins (Eds.), *Culture-infused counselling* (2nd ed., pp. 67–102). Calgary, AB: Counselling Concepts.

Collins, C., Arthur, N., McMahon, M., & Bisson, S. (2015). Assessing the multicultural and social justice competencies of career development practitioners. *The Canadian Journal of Career Development, 14*(1), 4–16. Retrieved from http://cjcdonline.ca

Flores, L. (2009). Empowering life choices: Career counseling in the contexts of race and class. In N. Gysbers, M. Heppner, & J. Johnson (Eds.), *Career counseling: Contexts, processes, and techniques* (pp. 49–74). Alexandria, VA: American Counselling Association.

Fox, D., Prilleltensky, I., & Austin, S. (2009). Critical psychology for social justice: Concerns and dilemmas. In D. Fox, I. Prilleltensky, & S. Austin (Eds.), *Critical psychology: An introduction* (2nd ed., pp. 3–19). Thousand Oaks, CA: Sage.

Ginsberg, F., & Sinacore, A. (2015). Articulating a social justice agenda for Canadian counselling and counselling psychology. In A. Sinacore & F. Ginsberg (Eds.), *Canadian counselling and psychology in the 21st century* (pp. 254–272). Montreal, QC: McGill-Queen's University Press.

Kennedy, B., & Arthur, N. (2014). Social justice and counselling psychology: Recommitment through action. *Canadian Journal of Counselling and Psychotherapy*, *48*(3), 186–205. Retrieved from http://cjc-rcc.ucalgary.ca

Lavell, E. F. (2014). Beyond charity: Social class and classism in counselling. *Canadian Journal of Counselling and Psychotherapy*, *48*(3), 231–250. Retrieved from http://cjc-rcc.ucalgary.ca

Lorde, A. (2004). From the cancer journals. In M. Sewell (Ed.), *Breaking free: Women of spirit at midlife and beyond* (pp. 61–68). Boston, MA: Beacon Press.

Mintz, L., Jackson, A., Neville, H., Illfelder-Kaye, J., Winterowd, C., & Loewy, M. (2009). The need for a counseling psychology model training values statement addressing diversity. *The Counseling Psychologist*, *37*(5), 644–675. doi: 10.1177/0011000009331931

Moodley, R. (2009). Multi(ple) cultural voices speaking "outside the sentence" of counseling and psychotherapy. *Counseling Psychology Quarterly*, *22*(3), 297–307. doi: 10.1080/09515070903302364

Paré, D. (2014). Social justice and the word: Keeping diversity alive in therapeutic conversations. *Canadian Journal of Counselling and Psychotherapy*, *48*(3), 206–217. Retrieved from http://cjc-rcc.ucalgary.ca

Patrick, S., & Connolly, C. M. (2013). The privilege project: A narrative approach for teaching social justice and multicultural awareness. *Journal of Systemic Therapies*, *23*(1), 70–86. doi: 10.1521/jsyt.2013.32.1.70

Pettifor, J. (2010). Ethics, diversity, and respect in multicultural counselling. In N. Arthur & S. Collins (Eds.), *Culture-infused counselling* (2nd ed., pp. 167–188). Calgary, AB: Counselling Concepts.

Richardson, M. (2012). Counseling for work and for relationship. *The Counseling Psychologist*, *40*(2), 190–242. doi: 10.1177/0011000011406452

Singh, A. A., Hofsess, C., Boyer, E., Kwong, A., Lau, A., McLain, M., & Haggins, K. L. (2010). Social justice and counseling psychology: Listening to the voices of doctoral trainees. *The Counseling Psychologist*, *38*(6), 766–795. doi: 10.1177/0011000010362559

Stewart, S., & Marshall, A. (2015). Counselling Indigenous people in Canada. In A. Sinacore & F. Ginsberg (Eds.), *Canadian counselling and psychology in the 21st century* (pp. 68–89). Montreal, QC: McGill-Queen's University Press.

Todd, N. R., & Abrams, E. M. (2011). White dialectics: A new framework for theory, research, and practice with White students. *The Counseling Psychologist*, *39*(3), 353–395. doi: 10.1177/0011000010377665

Vera, E. (2009). When human rights and cultural values collide: What do we value? *The Counseling Psychologist*, *37*(5), 744–751. doi: 10.1177/0011000009333985

Vera, E. M., & Speight, S. L. (2003). Multicultural competence, social justice, and counseling psychology: Expanding our roles. *The Counseling Psychologist*, *31*(3), 253–272. doi: 10. 1177/0011000003031003001

Training and Supervising from a Social Justice Perspective

Reviewing the literature on counselor training and supervision over recent decades, a trajectory can be discerned—an individualistic view of persons dominates in earlier years, with a steady rise in attention to social context as the decades advance. The humanist worldview personified in the seminal writings of Carl Rogers, for instance, characterized the process of counseling and psychotherapy as one of personal growth. Rogers' legacy endures in the emphasis on the centrality of empathy to the therapeutic process. At the same time, wider public discourse is increasingly preoccupied with controversy surrounding the politics of identity, as attention tilts towards the social dimension of lived experience. This is reflected in the growth of literature on multicultural and social justice practice, work that trains a spotlight on issues such as power relations and cultural meaning obscured by a perspective focused on individual growth. A wider domain of practice demands an expanded skill set—a refrain threaded through this section's chapters on counselor training and supervision.

In Chapter 4, Social Justice and Advocacy: Critical Issues in Counselor Education, Nicola Gazzola, Andrea LaMarre, and Olga Smoliak make a strong case for counselor education programs to adapt to an evolving social/relational outlook evident both within the field and in society more broadly. Nicola and colleagues take it as a given that sociopolitical inequities are ubiquitous, arguing that empowerment both within counseling relationships and society more broadly begins with acknowledging these disparities. In the realm of counselor education, this includes examining the intersectional aspect of identities—the way that persons may experience both privilege and marginalization in different contexts of their lives. The authors cite the individualistic perspective that dominates the discipline of psychology as a barrier to infusing counselor education with the sort of critical, reflexive perspective that foregrounds the operations of power within counseling. They recommend a pedagogy that situates educators and students in their social locations. Achieving this involves creating a safe learning environment where vulnerability is embraced; unpacking identities involves "getting personal," and can be a cause for discomfort if it entails discovering unearned privilege or passive collusion with marginalizing practices. This inherently systemic view attends to counselor education across a variety of levels, calling for a revamping of not just classroom practices, but hiring practices and admission standards.

In Chapter 5, Just Supervision: Thinking About Clinical Supervision that Moves Towards Social Justice, Karen Mackie and Michael Boucher point to growing income inequality as a bellwether of injustices across society that directly impact mental health and well-being. Karen and Michael lament the relative lack of attention paid to social inequity within the counseling literature as they describe their efforts to build a community of practice around the intersections of clinical supervision and social justice. From a familiar refrain of "I want to help people and make a difference," supervisees are invited to develop a more fine-grained version of that picture anchored in their values, leading to examination of unjust social, political, and economic factors that contribute to the problems that people face. Drawing on case studies from their work, Karen and Michael demonstrate how supervision can be extended to activism that reaches beyond individuals and helps to connect people to the resources and communities that resonate with their causes.

The section concludes with an account of hospitality as a metaphor to understand the ethical responsibilities of counseling and counselor education in a postcolonial nation. The setting for Chapter 6, Counseling as Post-Colonial Encounter: Hospitality and Ethical Relationship, is counselor education at the University of Waikato, Aotearoa New Zealand. The place, vividly described by counselor educators Kathie Crocket, Elmarie Kotzé, and Rahera Taylor, is Maniaroa marae, a Māori First Nation venue where hospitality makes possible radical forms of learning and teaching. The chapter describes in some detail how hospitality produces learning and teaching in this particular place. It shows how, in responding to the hospitality offered in this place, students and staff experience a call to engage deeply with the implications of colonization, which includes locating themselves in historical, social, and political relations. Three student stories illustrate these processes playing out, expressing social justice in action in the offering and witnessing of accounts that produce ethical subjectivity.

CHAPTER 4

Social Justice and Advocacy: Critical Issues in Counselor Education

Nicola Gazzola, Andrea LaMarre, and Olga Smoliak

The elimination of social and institutional practices that foster and maintain domination or oppression is of central concern to those taking a social justice perspective (Young, 1990). This perspective can also be found historically in certain strands of counseling and counseling psychology theory (Kennedy & Arthur, 2014; Kiselica & Robinson, 2001). Two of the major roots of contemporary counseling are firmly planted in social justice and advocacy: (a) seeing the provision of mental health counseling for persons with mental illness in the 1700s as a *moral imperative* (see Brooks & Weikel, 1996) and (b) Parson's work with unemployed youth sparking the vocational guidance movement (Myers, Sweeney, & White, 2002). Over the last quarter century, counselors and counseling psychologists have begun infusing social justice concerns into existing counseling approaches, developing practices distinctly rooted in social justice values and premises (Crethar, Rivera, & Nash, 2008).

While there have been calls to similarly integrate social justice principles into counselor education and training (cf. Brubaker, Puig, Reese, & Young, 2010; Constantine, Hage, Kindaichi, & Bryant, 2007), movement on this front has been slower. The literature has been eloquent in articulating the importance of social justice issues, but has less to say about how to re-imagine counselor education programs to address social justice concerns (Brubaker et al., 2010; Vera & Speight, 2003). This is particularly concerning in light of the increasingly diverse clientèle for whom social justice is far more than a theoretical topic, and more of a daily reality. Counselor educators must therefore continue to develop and refine ideas and guidelines for practice and education in order to adequately and ethically address issues of social justice (Hargrove, Creagh, & Kelly, 2003).

As we write this chapter, we draw from our backgrounds and experiences as counselor educators (NG and OS) and as a graduate student (AL) from graduate counseling and family relations programs at two different universities in the province of Ontario in Canada. We believe counselors need to keep step with the expanded attention to social justice in the field and be prepared through their foundational training to work with clients whose presenting concerns are intertwined with sociopolitical inequities. More than simply keeping up with the increasing diversity of counseling clientèle, however, this call for social justice coincides with our personal experiences of dominant power structures in society. Though we are relatively advantaged socially and economically as academics with light-skin privilege, we have felt the constraints of gender roles, assumptions about sexuality, ethnicity, and more as we have moved through our lives and worked with clients. Our own spaces of social belonging also bump up against those of our clients in ways that can constrain understanding and limit the scope of our academic and clinical work. In this chapter, we review the counselor education literature from the United States and Canada, describing how a social justice perspective is currently broached in counselor education, identifying challenges associated with infusing social justice into pedagogy, and offering suggestions for systematically integrating social justice principles into training to help bridge theory and practice.

Situating Social Justice within Counselor Education

Within counseling, taking a social justice approach means moving beyond recognizing and appreciating cultural differences, which is the focus of multicultural counseling, toward advocacy or actively working through social inequities (Vera & Speight, 2003). Building on Pedersen's (1999) description of multiculturalism as the fourth force in counseling psychology, we agree with the conceptualization of social justice as a fifth force, with an emphasis on how systemic inequities shape clients' concerns, the therapeutic alliance, and the supervisor–trainee relationship (Chung & Bemak, 2012). Social justice counseling entails moving beyond the intrapsychic realm to focus on how attention to sociopolitical inequities might facilitate client empowerment not only in the therapeutic encounter but also in society more broadly (Kiselica & Robinson, 2001). Training the next generation of social justice counselors means fostering an affective, intellectual, and pragmatic orientation to social justice among trainees (Vera & Speight, 2003).

Promoting a social justice orientation among trainees entails deliberate action on the part of counselor educators dedicated to social justice principles. To enact social justice training, many educators have turned to critical pedagogy, encouraging the development of critical consciousness and awareness about social, political, and economic oppressions (Freire, 1970). Critical pedagogy-informed educators encourage students to question the "neutrality" of knowledge (Nylund & Tilsen, 2006) and invite an exploration of systemic contributors to clients' distress by encouraging critical self-reflexivity (i.e., reflecting on one's social location and role in practice) and fostering a supportive generative learning community (hooks, 1994). While counselor education models and frameworks oriented to social justice have relied upon critical pedagogy, trainees are also encouraged to move beyond mere critical consciousness toward enacting social change through advocacy (Reynaga-Abiko, 2010). In order for students to be able to do so, however, there is a need for counselor educators and supervisors to actively work to create a collaborative environment in which no one person holds all the power in the relationship, sometimes referred to as "de-centering" (Reynolds, 2013).

Counselor education rooted in intersectional feminist, postmodern, and/or post-colonial perspectives can help to generate collaborative training environ-ments that are foundational to fostering social justice practice. These perspec-tives foreground diversity and offer viable alternatives to "essentialist" accounts of gender, race, class, and other social identities along the lines of which people have been oppressed. While there is some movement toward adopting social justice principles and premises in counselor education, bringing this theoretical and philosophical commitment to bear on practice is not without challenges. Appreciating entrenched barriers is an important first step. In the next section, we introduce some of those barriers as a precursor to offering suggestions for inte-grating a social justice perspective into counselor education.

Challenges to Integrating Social Justice in Counselor Education

The socially dominant assumptions we hold that permeate our actions—including our counseling practices—can be almost invisible and easy to overlook. By virtue of their dominance, many of those assumptions reflect a privileged perspective that ignores the inequities that have very real consequences for non-dominant groups. This poses challenges for counselor education along several dimensions. For starters, counselors need to identify the ethnocentrism reflected in many of their attitudes and featured in the traditional canons of counseling and profes-sional psychology. An interrogation of these taken-for-granted views can involve challenging self-examination. It also calls for engagement with a range of theory and methods thinly represented in mainstream counselor education. But a change of orientation towards social justice involves more than a theoretical revision or the adoption of a skill or competency; it is something closer to a shift in one's gen-eral orientation to life.

Ethnocentricity and the Challenge of Getting Personal

The ethnocentric perspectives of Western counselors and counselor educators can be obstacles to adopting a diversity-oriented and anti-discriminatory agenda foundational to social justice work (Marsella & Pedersen, 2004). Whiteness and other privileges are often "invisibilized" in counseling and counselor education, leading to a perpetuation of Eurocentric, White, hetero-normative, middle-class accounts of human action and experience or "see[ing] the world from one per-spective" (Sue, 2004, p. 762). While counseling students may be exposed to knowl-edge *about* minority groups, they are less often encouraged to explore how their own spaces of belonging intersect with those of their future clients (Richardson & Molinaro, 1996). This selective teaching, even when done with the best of inten-tions, may lead to the reinforcement of cultural stereotypes and misunderstanding of diverse clients' and students' experiences (Marecek & Hare-Mustin, 2009).

To move beyond a view of minorities as the "other" involves getting personal in the sense of inviting critical self-reflection. In a counselor education setting, collective self-examination inevitably uncovers power divides and inequities within the classroom itself. This can promote discomfort and resistance among majority counselors, and among counselor educators themselves who may be reluctant to acknowledge their own privilege. The interrogation of social disparities within the classroom, and the invitation to recount histories of marginalization or privilege, pose additional challenges for counselor educators because the ensuing discussions require delicate facilitation to ensure participants can share experiences in a respectful and productive manner.

Minimal Educational Opportunities in Critical Perspectives

The relative marginalization of a critical, reflexive perspective in the wider society with respect to issues of privilege and marginalization is mirrored in the counseling profession itself. Counselors have not generally been taught to see political concerns and aims—in the sense of issues related to power and privilege, social inclusion, and access to resources and opportunities—as central to their practice (Prilleltensky & Nelson, 2002). Rather, counseling and professional psychology have traditionally adopted a neutral, objective, and apolitical stance (Speight & Vera, 2004). For example, the context of clients' concerns tend to be downplayed in favor of focusing on the intrapsychic realm, particularly in cognitive and psychodynamic approaches (Silverstein & Brooks, 2010). This relates to social justice because when counselors overemphasize individual factors, they may inadvertently collude with and reinforce oppression (Prilleltensky, 1997); for example, attributing blame for relational distress to a female partner in a heterosexual relationship for lacking assertiveness skills and self-esteem, rather than considering how macho discourses contribute to men being socialized to use aggression in relationships.

Critical perspectives—including those stemming from feminism, postmodernism, critical psychology, social constructionism, hermeneutics, and interpretive social science—invite counselors to consider contextual and political issues in making sense of people's lives and of the therapeutic process. Many counselor educators have had little or no exposure to these perspectives and methods of inquiry, in part because mainstream psychology has historically maintained strict disciplinary boundaries, only marginally accessing and contributing to these theoretical and methodological developments (Gergen, 2001; Yeh & Inman, 2007). Counselor educators wishing to further develop a social justice orientation may benefit from seeking education in these critical perspectives and fostering interdisciplinarity in research, practice, and training (Speight & Vera, 2004). Among possible resources, we recommend exploring Prilleltensky (1997, 2002) for the role of values and assumptions in counseling, Foucault (1979) for the role of discourse in shaping/being shaped by social interaction, and Freire (1970, 1978) on critical pedagogy. These resources might, together, help to orient trainee counselors and counselor educators alike to the critical value of integrating an acknowledgment of social positionality into counseling practice.

Conceptualizing a social justice orientation as a distinct stance (e.g., reflexive, collaborative, transparent, curious) is part of integrating critical content into the curriculum, but tweaking the curriculum alone is insufficient for transitioning to a social justice orientation in counselor education. Readiness to embrace a social justice agenda means transforming not only the content of the teaching but, more importantly, the *person* of the educator or counselor. As Lee (2007) remarked, counseling for social justice "is more than a professional obligation; it is about living one's life in a manner that is dedicated to promoting access and equity" (p. 1). This process starts with examining one's beliefs, values, and assumptions— determining where one stands in the world. There is no place to stand outside of the arena where social justice and injustice play out on a daily basis. This extends to counseling theories, which adhere to certain assumptions and values and represent the interests of certain social groups (i.e., have political implications). Counselors' reluctance to take an explicit political stance can be conceptualized as a political stance of its own (Hare-Mustin, 2003). A key aspect of helping counselors adopt a critical perspective therefore involves assisting them in identifying and acknowledging how their worldviews feature in their lives and practice. In the next section we will provide ideas about shaping counselor education programs to accomplish these various aims by infusing them with an orientation to social justice.

Incorporating Social Justice in Counselor Education Programs

The integration of social justice into a counselor education program can happen at several levels, from broad domains related to counselor accreditation and program admission standards, to specific instructor–student or student–student interactions. Clearly, the scope of possibility is beyond the space allotted here; however, in the next section we will touch on a number of domains, offering a preliminary look at possibilities for infusing social justice into counselor education programs.

Social Justice and Professional Standards

Recent years have seen a range of welcomed initiatives with regards to social justice at the level of ethics codes and counselor and counseling program accreditation. Accrediting bodies and professional associations in the United States and Canada have moved towards adopting anti-oppressive, anti-discriminatory, and inclusive accreditation and ethical standards (e.g., Commission on Accreditation for Marriage and Family Therapy Education (COAMFTE); American Psychological Association; Canadian Psychological Association; Council for Accreditation of Counseling and Related Educational Programs (CACREP)). Accrediting bodies themselves adopt various orientations toward social justice, diversity, and multiculturalism. For example, the most recent version of the AAMFT accreditation standards emphasizes that programs should strive for diversity, inclusion, and anti-oppression (COAMFTE, 2014). CACREP similarly names "multicultural counseling, cultural identity development, and social justice and advocacy" as one of the core curricular areas that cumulatively comprise the foundational knowledge of the counseling profession; social justice is also among the CACREP standards for leadership development for doctoral-level trainees. The CACREP standards gesture toward an orientation we share with others (e.g., Arthur & Collins, 2010; Kiselica & Robinson, 2001; Speight & Vera, 2004) who conceptualize social justice as more than recognizing diversity, but advocating for anti-oppression.

The extent to which counselor education programs reflect the changes in accreditation standards varies considerably and depends on specific faculty, program, and geographic location (Goodrich & Silverstein, 2005; Toporek & McNally, 2006). Generally, programs infuse diversity considerations more than social justice concerns (Pieterse, Evans, Risner-Butner, Collins, & Mason, 2009). Though trainees may credit their graduate education with raising their awareness of diversity (McDowell, 2004), more work is needed to clarify how issues of social justice and diversity—and associated educational goals, outcomes, and practices—overlap and are distinct (Pieterse et al., 2009).

Equitable Representation Among Students and Educators

Another key concern for those interested in infusing social justice into counseling programs is how to attract diverse students and faculty. Besides "walking the talk" by addressing inequities, the promotion of diversity improves the learning experience in relation to social justice. A diverse faculty offers a multiplicity of perspectives, protecting against the projection of a narrow worldview that earlier characterized much counseling and psychology theory. A diverse student body makes it possible for students to learn about issues through embodied personal anecdotes directly shared with one another.

When programs reach a "critical mass" (i.e., 30 percent minority representation among staff, faculty, and students), minority individuals are more likely to feel comfortable on predominantly White campuses (Ponterotto, Alexander, & Grieger, 1995). Program admission procedures and standards may operate systematically to disadvantage applicants from minority backgrounds (Davis, 2002); significant changes are required to facilitate access for marginalized individuals. Programs have accordingly been advised to involve diverse faculty and students in the recruitment process, offer financial aid to diversity students, revise recruitment materials, establish links between academic programs and historical institutions of color, and foster personal contact between diverse faculty members and prospective students (e.g., Ponterotto et al., 1995; Shin, 2008).

Despite this call to recruit, admit, and retain more diversity faculty, staff, and students, programs have had only limited success in achieving diversity (McDowell, Fang, Brownlee, Young, & Khanna, 2002; Wilson & Stith, 1993). Minority individuals continue to be underrepresented in graduate psychology programs across the United States and comprise only 22 percent of master's students, 27 percent of doctoral students, and less than 20 percent of faculty (Kohout, Pate II, & Maton, 2014). Importantly, achieving diversity is about more than "meeting the diversity quota" (McDowell et al., 2002, p. 180). Without ideological and cultural change toward social justice, diversification efforts may yield further alienation among socially marginalized faculty and students, rather than facilitating social justice through building diversity (McDowell et al., 2002).

Social Justice as Policy and Mission

There are various ways a counselor education program can be modified to lean towards social justice concerns. These include introducing standalone courses in diversity and multiculturalism, making the topic mandatory, prescribing social justice as an area of concentration, or establishing practica with a social justice focus (Toporek & McNally, 2006). Boston College, George Mason, Penn State, Marquette, Ball State, and Loyola universities have opted to infuse social justice throughout their counseling programs, a practice that is encouraged (Henriksen & Trusty, 2005) but relatively unexplored in the research literature on social justice training (Toporek & McNally, 2006).

In our (OS and AL) Couple and Family Therapy graduate (master's level) program at the University of Guelph, a commitment to multiculturalism and social justice is reflected in a mission statement that includes: striving for diverse student enrollment; spreading the reach of the profession to under-serviced communities and geographic areas; and maintaining commitment to inclusive clinical services that are affordable, accessible, and culturally appropriate. The program has five educational goals, one of which is "social context and power relations" concerned with developing an understanding of how systemic marginalization and discrimination may impact clients' lives. The educational goals are infused throughout the curriculum, and student progress is tracked by periodic monitoring of specific learning outcomes.

Developing a Social Justice Curriculum

There is no single most effective approach to designing and developing a liberatory, emancipatory, and empowering social justice curriculum or course of study in counseling (Harley, Alston, & Turner-Whittaker, 2008; Palmer & Parish, 2008). As mentioned, some programs use standalone courses to teach social justice (Filkowski, Storm, York, & Brandon, 2001), while others find that spreading the focus centralizing across the overall curriculum facilitates significant changes in students' awareness, skills, and knowledge (Chung & Bemak, 2012; Goodrich & Silverstein, 2005). From our perspective, distributing social justice considerations across the entire curriculum *and* offering at least one single course in these issues is a pragmatic approach to addressing some of the barriers to integrating social justice identified above: a separate course can cover social justice issues in depth, while other practice-oriented elements (e.g., supervision, practica, areas of specialization, clinical placements) provide opportunities for students to integrate and apply their knowledge and skills. This blend combines conceptual knowledge and awareness of social inequities and injustices (Capper, Theoharis, & Sebastian, 2006) with skill development focused on social justice concerns (O'Brian, Patel, Hensler-McGinnis, & Kaplan, 2006).

Pedagogical Positioning

Because social justice is concerned with issues such as power inequities in relationships, identity construction, "voice," the politics of representation, and so on, the integration of social justice into a counselor education program involves far more than the substitution of didactic content. The initiative calls for a wholesale overhaul of pedagogical process (Alvarez & Miville, 2003). Alvarez and Miville (2003) suggest that educators clarify their assumptions about the learning process and preferred pedagogical stance with students, as these determine the content, structure, and process of teaching. To do this, they could ask themselves a series of questions around three areas: the process of learning, the role of teachers, and the role of students (e.g., teaching as predominantly content or process oriented, instructor as social justice expert versus facilitator, learner as active versus passive). Answers to these questions help determine instructional method, for example, deciding to use primarily didactic instructional methods (i.e., knowledge transmitted from instructor to learner), interactive ones (i.e., dialogue and experiential, active learning), or a blend of these. For instance, when thinking about the process of learning, educators might ask themselves what their definition of learning is (Is it a unilateral knowledge transmission? Is it a collaborative generation of knowledge?). In exploring the role of teachers and students, they might consider: Do I see myself as someone who is socially situated and has lived experience of social inequities or as someone standing outside of the socio-cultural dynamics of power? If the former, how might my social positioning shape my teaching and interactions with specific students? How do I invite students to reflect on their experiences with power and privilege?

Arguably, the incorporation of a social justice focus entails adjustments aimed at creating more space for student voices and perspectives as a counterbalance to the prevailing dominance—at the wider social level and in academia—of "expert" perspectives. For Alvarez and Miville (2003), the *processes of sharing, reflecting, and relating* in the classroom become the main instructional tools. The instructor's role in this context is not to display their expertise in social justice but to create an environment for a respectful and generative exchange of ideas and experiences. Much of the learning happens "sideways": as *all* participants in the classroom community are socially situated, their lived experiences provide vivid illustrations of the social structures that generate privileges and oppressions.

Managing the Conversation

An exploration of social justice among counselors inescapably involves group dialogue and the challenges of managing complex and emotion-laden conversations. Social justice-oriented educators embody an openness to learning and being transparent about their own social positioning and experiences with power, privilege, and oppression (Mitchell, 2007) as a precursor to inviting students to do the same. Witnessing their teachers processing issues has demonstrated impacts on student outcomes, including greater awareness, skills, and knowledge of social justice issues (Peterson, Cross, Johnson, & Howell, 2000).

A personal account of one's own (typically uneven) journey toward self-reflexivity and a sensitivity to social justice might include accounts of unexamined privilege and racism. Inviting students to do the same, including exploring their intersectionality (cf. Cheshire, 2013; Parks, Hughes, & Matthews, 2004; Tilsen, 2013) is invariably eye-opening for most participants. It helps them to appreciate the complex intersection of multiple identities, moving beyond singular (stereotypical) categories of gender, race, age, sexual orientation, disability, and so forth. As a consequence, the collective analysis does not gravitate to simple dichotomies that fail to reflect the complexity of the issues at hand. Inviting students to discuss their own social positioning as it relates to that of clients helps them anticipate the multiplicity of scenarios they will soon confront in their practices (Alvarez & Miville, 2003; Mitchell, 2007). Much of the learning happens via interaction, which Brown (2004) discovered leads to greater social justice and diversity awareness and sensitivity than didactic environments (Brown, 2004).

Facilitating student discussion around the dynamics of marginalization and oppression in and outside of the classroom is a critical aspect of teaching a social justice course. Such a course necessarily entails working through emotionally charged topics (e.g., sexual orientation, gender, race); students need to be supported in managing possible interpersonal conflicts or turmoil that such topics may bring up. It helps to collectively establish clear ground rules for sharing both face-to-face and online. The process of examining risks invites students to anticipate the possible fallout of ill-considered comments and promotes a culture of accountability among classmates. In addition to shedding light on the experience of diverse others, the process of talking through difference contributes to developing cross-cultural communication and conflict resolution skills that may generalize to professional practice and other aspects of students' lives.

Social justice education involves far more than simply learning a new theory or a set of competencies. It is a challenging and provocative process, but is also emancipatory and empowering (hooks, 1994). Classroom interactions around power and privilege invite participants to reflect deeply on the consequences of social location and help them better understand themselves and their clients.

Conclusion

Although the literature indicates that counselors have embraced the idea of integrating social justice and advocacy in their work with clients, there exists a considerable divide in concretely applying social justice practices (Speight & Vera, 2008). This may be due, in part, to the lack of systematic integration of social justice practices within counselor education programs. Indeed, many counselor education programs have yet to devise ways of providing students with opportunities to move beyond an ideological engagement with diversity toward the development of practical skills for counseling in a socially just way. When social justice is not integrated into counselor education programs, students may remain unaware of how their interactions with clients can either perpetuate or mitigate oppression (Brubaker et al., 2010; Vera & Speight, 2003).

The unevenness of social justice integration across training programs may be ascribed to a tension between theoretical and philosophical positions embracing social justice on the one hand, and the real-world pressures of delivering counseling in the individually oriented way expected in society and much of the counseling profession on the other. Counselor educators are sometimes compromised in their efforts to expand their teaching into social justice territory. They experience pressure to maintain credibility within a field that encourages the acquisition of static "competencies," but are sometimes reticent to engage in a reflexive self-examination that would show how attending to social justice transcends the mere expansion of skill sets. The integration of a social justice orientation to counseling practice and to counselor education is about more than acquiring a new set of competencies, as we hope this chapter has demonstrated. When all interactions, whether with clients or students, are understood as inescapably unfolding within a social justice domain, we will likely see a tightening of the gap between social justice counseling theory and the practice of counselor education.

Reflection Questions

1. How can I practice and teach in a way that implicates my own lived experiences and social location without over-emphasizing my own experiences or making assumptions about clients' and students' experiences based on their social location?
2. What are some of the incompatible concepts between how I was trained in counseling and a social justice orientation?
3. How can I incorporate social justice in my practice while still embracing my core counseling values?
4. What are some of the biggest facilitators and challenges that I personally experience when envisioning myself as a social justice counseling practitioner?
5. What are some institutional barriers in the setting where I work or study to infusing a social justice orientation into counseling practice or education?

References

Alvarez, A. N., & Miville, M. L. (2003). Walking a tightrope: Strategies for teaching undergraduate multicultural counseling courses. In D. Pope-Davis, W. Liu, & R. Toporek, *Handbook of multicultural competencies in counseling and psychology* (pp. 528–547). Thousand Oaks, CA: Sage.

Arthur, N., & Collins, S. (2010). *Culture-infused counselling* (2nd ed.). Calgary, AB: Counselling Concepts.

Brooks, D. K., & Weikel, W. J. (1996). Mental health counseling: The first twenty years. In W. J. Weikel & A. J. Palmo (Eds.), *Foundations of mental health counseling* (pp. 5–29). Springfield, IL: Thomas.

Brown, E. L. (2004). What precipitates change in cultural diversity awareness during a multicultural course: The message or the method? *Journal of Teacher Education, 55*, 325–340. doi: 10.1177/0022487104266746

Brubaker, M. D., Puig, A., Reese, R. F., & Young, J. (2010). Integrating social justice into counseling theories pedagogy: A case example. *Counselor Education and Supervision, 50*, 88–102. doi: 10.1002/j.1556-6978.2010.tb00111.x

Capper, C. A., Theoharis, G., & Sebastian, J. (2006). Toward a framework for preparing leaders for social justice. *Journal of Educational Administration, 44*, 209–224. doi: 10.1108/09578230610664814

Cheshire, L. C. (2013). Reconsidering sexual identities: Intersectionality theory and the implications for educating counsellors. *Canadian Journal of Counselling and Psychotherapy, 47*(1), 4–13. Retrieved from http://cjc-rcc.ucalgary.ca

Chung, R. C., & Bemak, F. (2012). *Social justice counseling the next steps beyond multiculturalism*. London: Sage.

Commission on Accreditation for Marriage and Family Therapy Education (2014). *Accreditation standards: Graduate & post-graduate marriage and family therapy training programs*. Retrieved from www.aamft.org/imis15/Documents/COAMFTE/COAMFTE_Accreditation_Standards_Version_12.pdf

Constantine, M. G., Hage, S. M., Kindaichi, M. M., & Bryant, R. M. (2007). Social justice and multicultural issues: Implications for practice and training of counselors and counseling psychologists. *Journal of Counseling & Development, 85*, 24–29. doi: 10.1002/j.1556-6678.2007.tb00440.x

Crethar, H., Rivera, E. T., & Nash, S. (2008). In search of common threads: Linking multicultural, feminist, and social justice paradigms. *Journal of Counseling & Development, 86*, 269–278. doi: 10.1002/j.1556-6678.2008.tb00509.x

Davis, L. R. (2002). Racial diversity in higher education: Ingredients for success and failure. *Journal of Applied Behavioral Science, 38*, 137–155. doi: 10.1177/00286302038002001

Filkowski, M. B., Storm, C. L., York, C. D., & Brandon, A. D. (2001). Approaches to the study of gender in marriage and family curricula. *Journal of Marital and Family Therapy, 27*, 117–122. doi: 10.1111/j.1752-0606.2001.tb01144.x

Foucault, M. (1979). *Discipline and punish: The birth of the prison*. New York, NY: Vintage Books.

Freire, P. (1970). *Pedagogy of the oppressed*. New York, NY: Continuum.

Freire, P. (1978). *Pedagogy in process: The letters to Guinea-Bissau*. New York, NY: Seabury Press.

Gergen, K. J. (2001). Psychological science in a postmodern context. *American Psychologist, 56*, 803–813. doi: 10.1037/0003-066X.56.10.803

Goodrich, T. J., & Silverstein, L. B. (2005). Now you see it, now you don't: Feminist training in family therapy. *Family Process, 44*, 267–281. doi: 10.1111/j.1545-5300.2005.00059.x

Hare-Mustin, R. T. (2003). Foreword. In L. B. Silverstein & T. J. Goodrich (Eds.), *Feminist family therapy: Empowerment in social context* (pp. xiii–xiv). Washington, DC: American Psychological Association Books.

Hargrove, B. K., Creagh, M. G., & Kelly, D. B. (2003). Multicultural competencies in career counseling. In D. B. Pope-Davis, H. L. K. Coleman, W. M. Liu, & R. L. Toporek (Eds.), *Handbook of multicultural competencies in counseling and psychology* (pp. 392–405). Thousand Oaks, CA: Sage.

Harley, D. A., Alston, R. J., & Turner-Whittaker, T. (2008). Social justice and cultural diversity issues. *Rehabilitation Education, 22,* 237–248. doi: 10.1891/088970108805059264

Henriksen, R. C. Jr., & Trusty, J. (2005). Ethics and values as major factors related to multicultural aspects of counselor preparation. *Counseling and Values, 49,* 180–192. doi: 10.1002/j.2161-007X.2005.tb01021.x

hooks, b. (1994). *Teaching to transgress: Education as the practice of freedom.* London: Routledge.

Kennedy, B. A., & Arthur, N. (2014). Social justice and counseling psychology: Recommitment through action. *Canadian Journal of Counseling and Psychotherapy, 48*(3), 186–205. Retrieved from http://cjc-rcc.ucalgary.ca

Kiselica, M. S., & Robinson, M. (2001). Bringing advocacy counseling to life: The history, issues, and human dramas of social justice work in counseling. *Journal of Counseling & Development, 79,* 387–397. doi: 10.1002/j.1556-6676.2001.tb01985.x

Kohout, J. L., Pate, W. E., II, & Maton, K. I. (2014). An updated profile of ethnic minority psychology: A pipeline perspective. In F. T. L. Leong (Ed.), *APA handbook of multicultural psychology, Vol. 1: Theory and research* (pp. 19–42). Washington, DC: American Psychological Association.

Lee, C. C. (2007). *Social justice: A moral imperative for counselors* (ACAPCD-07). *Professional Counseling Digest.* Alexandria, VA: American Counseling Association.

McDowell, T. (2004). Listening to the racial experiences of graduate trainees: A critical race theory perspective. *The American Journal of Family Therapy, 32,* 305–324. doi: 10.1080/01926180490454791

McDowell, T., Fang, S., Brownlee, K., Young, C. G., & Khanna, A. (2002). Transforming an MFT program: A model for enhancing diversity. *Journal of Marital and Family Therapy, 28,* 179–191. doi: 10.1111/j.1752-0606.2002.tb00355.x

Marecek, J., & Hare-Mustin, R. T. (2009). Clinical psychology: The politics of madness. In D. Fox, I. Prilleltensky, & S. Austin (Eds.), *Critical psychology: An introduction* (2nd ed., pp. 75–92). London: Sage.

Marsella, A. J., & Pedersen, P. (2004). Internationalizing the counseling psychology curriculum: Toward new values, competencies, and directions. *Counseling Psychology Quarterly, 17,* 413–423. doi: 10.1080/09515070412331331246

Mitchell, T. D. (2007). Critical service-learning as social justice education: A case study of the Citizen Scholars Program. *Equity & Excellence in Education, 40,* 101–112. doi: 10.1080/10665680701228797

Myers, J. E., Sweeney, T. J., & White, V. E. (2002). Advocacy for counseling and counselors: A professional imperative. *Journal of Counseling & Development, 80,* 394–402. doi: 10.1002/j.1556-6678.2002.tb00205.x

Nylund, D., & Tilsen, J. (2006). Pedagogy and praxis: Postmodern spirit in the classroom. *Journal of Systemic Therapies, 25,* 21–31. doi: 10.1521/jsyt.2006.25.4.21

O'Brian, K. M., Patel, S., Hensler-McGinnis, N., & Kaplan, J. (2006). Empowering undergraduate students to be agents of social change: An innovative service learning course in counseling psychology. In R. L. Toporek, L. H. Gerstein, N. A. Fouad, G. Roysircar, & T. Israel (Eds.), *Handbook for social justice in counseling psychology: Leadership, vision, and action* (pp. 59–72). London: Sage.

Palmer, A., & Parish, J. (2008). Social justice and counseling psychology: Situating the role of graduate student research, education, and training. *Canadian Journal of Counseling*, *42*, 278–292. Retrieved from http://cjc-rcc.ucalgary.ca

Parks, C. A., Hughes, T. L., & Matthews, A. K. (2004). Race/ethnicity and sexual orientation: Intersecting identities. *Cultural Diversity and Ethnic Minority Psychology*, *10*(3), 241–254. doi: 10.1037/1099-9809.10.3.241

Pederson, P. (1999). *Multiculturalism as a fourth force*. Philadelphia, PA: Taylor & Francis.

Peterson, K. M., Cross, L. F., Johnson, E. J., & Howell, G. L. (2000). Diversity education for preservice teachers: Strategies and attitude outcomes. *Action in Teacher Education*, *22*, 33–38. doi: 10.1080/01626620.2000.10463003

Pieterse, A. L., Evans, S. A., Risner-Butner, A., Collins, N. M., & Mason, L. B. (2009). Multicultural competence and social justice training in counseling psychology and counselor education: A review and analysis of a sample of multicultural course syllabi. *Counseling Psychologist*, *37*, 93–115. doi: 10.1177/0011000008319986

Ponterotto, J. G., Alexander, C. M., & Grieger, I. (1995). A multicultural competency checklist for counseling psychology programs. *Journal of Multicultural Counseling and Development*, *23*, 11–20. doi: 10.1002/j.2161-1912.1995.tb00262.x

Prilleltensky, I. (1997). Values, assumptions, and practices: Assessing the moral implications of psychological discourse and action. *American Psychologist*, *52*, 517–535. doi: 10.1037/0003-066X.52.5.517

Prilleltensky, I., & Nelson, G. (2002). *Doing psychology critically: Making a difference in diverse settings*. New York, NY: Palgrave Macmillan.

Reynaga-Abiko, G. (2010). Opportunity amidst challenge: Reflections of a Latina supervisor. *Training and Education in Professional Psychology*, *4*, 19–25. doi: 10.1037/a0017052

Reynolds, V. (2013). Centering ethics in group supervision: Fostering cultures of critique & structuring safety. *The International Journal of Narrative Therapy and Community Work*, *4*, 1–13. Retrieved from http://dulwichcentre.com.au/international-journal-of-narrative-therapy-and-community-work

Richardson, T. Q., & Molinaro, K. J. (1996). White counselor self-awareness: A prerequisite for developing multicultural competence. *Journal of Counseling & Development*, *74*(3), 238–242. doi: 10.1002/j.1556-6676.1996.tb01859.x

Shin, R. Q. (2008). Advocating for social justice in academia through recruitment, retention, admissions, and professional survival. *Journal of Multicultural Counseling and Development*, *36*, 180–192. doi: 10.1002/j.2161-1912.2008.tb00081.x

Silverstein, L. B., & Brooks, G. R. (2010). Gender issues in family therapy and couples counseling. In J. C. Chrisler & D. R. McCreary (Eds.), *Handbook of gender research in psychology, Volume 2: Gender research in social and applied psychology* (pp. 253–277). Verlag, NY: Springer.

Speight, S. L., & Vera, E. M. (2004). A social justice agenda: Ready or not? *The Counseling Psychologist*, *32*, 109–118. doi: 10.1177/0011000003260005

Speight, S. L., & Vera, E. M. (2008). Social justice and counseling psychology: A challenge to the specialty. In S. D. Brown & R. Lent (Eds.), *The handbook of counseling psychology* (4th ed., pp. 54–67). New York, NY: Wiley.

Sue, D. W. (2004). Whiteness and ethnocentric monoculturalism: Making the "invisible" visible. *American Psychologist*, *59*, 759–769. doi: 10.1037/0003-066X.59.8.761

Tilsen, J. (2013). *Therapeutic conversations with queer youth: Transcending homonormativity and constructing preferred identities*. New York, NY: Jason Aronson.

Toporek, R. L., & McNally, C. J. (2006). Social justice training in counseling psychology. In R. L. Toporek, L. H. Gerstein, N. A. Fouad, G. Roysircar, & T. Israel (Eds.), *Handbook for social justice in counseling psychology: Leadership, vision, and action* (pp. 37–44). London: Sage.

Vera, E. M., & Speight, S. L. (2003). Multicultural competence, social justice, and counseling psychology: Expanding our roles. *The Counseling Psychologist, 31*, 253–271. doi: 10.1 177/0011000003031003001

Wilson, L. L., & Stith, S. M. (1993). The voices of African-American MFT students: Suggestions for improving recruitment and retention. *Journal of Marital and Family Therapy, 19*, 17–30. doi: 10.1111/j.1752-0606.1993.tb00962.x

Yeh, C. J., & Inman, A. G. (2007). Qualitative data analysis and interpretation in counseling psychology: Strategies for best practices. *Counseling Psychologist, 35*, 369–403. doi: 10.1177/0011000006292596

Young, I. M. (1990). *Justice and the politics of difference.* Princeton, NJ: Princeton University Press.

CHAPTER 5

Just Supervision: Thinking about Clinical Supervision That Moves towards Social Justice

Karen L. Mackie and Michael Boucher

Any counselor in training who is coming through an American graduate counselor education program in 2017 is doing so during a time in which income inequality is greater than it has been since the Great Depression (Matthews, 2014; Mishel, Bivens, Gould, & Shierholtz, 2012). Paul Kivel (2000) breaks this down a little more and reminds us that in the US, 1 percent of the population controls about 47 percent of the net financial wealth of the country, and the next 19 percent of the population controls another 44 percent. Thus 80 percent of the population tries to gain their share of just 9 percent of the wealth.

This is no small matter. Wilkinson and Pickett (2009) in their groundbreaking book, *The Spirit Level*, demonstrated what many counselors have witnessed: that as income inequality rises, so do a whole host of other social ills with roots in social-structural inequalities—organized in relation to race, gender, ability, and age—that directly impact mental health and well-being. These ills include increases in the rates and intensities of substance misuse, incarceration, obesity, violence, and experiences of unemployment, along with decreases in educational performance—to name just a few (Paul & Moser, 2009; Tate, Fallon, Casquarelli, & Marks, 2014).

In such a context, it would seem vital that counselor training address issues of inequality and social justice as a foundational concept in addressing mental health. Our experience has shown otherwise, however. Few of the current paradigms of counseling and/or clinical supervision appear well equipped to help counselors and counseling trainees connect with and integrate the rich history of social justice and activism from other disciplines into their work as counselors or therapists, even as these professional frameworks broadly consider notions of cultural diversity, cultural competence and, more recently, counselor humility (Tervalon & Murray-Garcia, 1998) in training standards. Only in recent years have explicit efforts to bring a social justice orientation to the counseling and counseling psychology professions begun to take hold at the center of the profession itself (D'Andrea & Daniels, 2009; Ratts, Singh, Nassar-McMillan, Butler, & McCullough, 2016; Toporek, Dodge, Tripp, & Alarcon, 2009).

Being Deliberate

It is our firm belief that, as historian and activist Howard Zinn (2002) once said in his memoir of the same name, "You cannot be neutral on a moving train." Many of us who are counselors would likely be located in the affluent top 20 percent of people living in this country, giving us substantial assets that provide security, social benefit, and access to social capital, education, leisure, and so forth. As such, we must be aware of the privileges of our own social location and clearly name where we stand within the structures of power. If, in addition, we find ourselves involved in counselor education as faculty instructors or clinical supervisors, we may increasingly see it as our ethical responsibility to directly engage these issues of social justice and social inequality in our own work, and to help students and interns engage and address these ideas as well (ACA, 2014).

We also recognize that, within our roles as supervisors and educators, we face an ongoing challenge to think and act differently in order to better meet the demands of educating for social justice in a global world. Attempting to rise to this challenge has invited us into more intentional reflection and experimentation with the language and the activities that comprise clinical supervision and its intersections with social justice. This chapter will look more closely at the kind of work that supervision with trainees entails in order to develop heightened consciousness/praxis with respect to enacting social justice. Our hope is to more ably engage in a "deliberate practice" of supervision; one that reflects a grounding in the value base of the novice counselor, one that reflects a greater awareness of the social location of that counselor, and one that works to address the context of social inequality in which we all find ourselves (see Chow et al., 2015).

Setting the Context: Ours and the Location of this Story

Before we go any further, it is important for us to situate ourselves with respect to our own social location. I (MB) am a white, heterosexual, college-educated male who came from a working-class French-Canadian family in New Hampshire—currently living in a relatively affluent suburb of Rochester, New York. I have been working in a professional capacity as a social worker and counselor for about 20 years. For the past 18 years, I have been primarily working at St. Joseph's Neighborhood Center, a neighborhood health center sponsored by the Sisters of St. Joseph that serves the under- and un-insured in relation to accessing health care services. Much of my work has been focused on working with people who are living in poverty and thinking about the intersections of poverty, racism, oppression, resistance, and resiliency in the lives of the people who consult us. I have been a clinical supervisor for students for more than 10 years.

I (KM) am a white, heterosexual, college-educated immigrant to the US, who came from an aspiring working-class family in the UK and, like my colleague (MB), currently live in a relatively affluent village just outside Rochester, New York. I have been a professional counselor for over 30 years and a full-time counselor educator and clinical supervisor for the last 15 of these. The Warner Graduate School at the University of Rochester assumes that the purpose of education is to support human development and learning in service of making the world more just and humane. In our counselor education programs, we explicitly aim to develop practitioners and researchers who see themselves as capable and caring therapists and also as agents of social change, helping to improve the systems and contexts in which people live their lives.

The collaboration that we speak of in this chapter emerges out of the professional relationship that the Warner Graduate School has with St. Joseph's Neighborhood Center, one of its supervision sites. Students have the option of being considered for placement at this site during their year-long internship in counseling practice and, in recent years, tend to select this option if they have a strong interest in integrative models of health care delivery. Both of our institutions hold social justice to be a primary value, and it is out of this shared commitment that we began to think more pointedly about what practices help in the development of a social justice perspective among trainee therapists. In working together over the last five years, we have been striving to build a community of practice (Lave & Wenger, 1991; Wenger-Trayner & Wenger-Trayner, 2015) around the intersections of clinical supervision and social justice—one that embodies a genuine understanding that race, class, gender expression, and other forms of social privilege limit what can be known or attempted without widening our social net and listening closely to what differently positioned others have to say.

Starting Out: Exploring Values

Almost every graduate student intern that we have supervised in our mental health counseling training partnership has said a version of the following in response to a question about why they entered this field. "I just want to help people and make a difference in the world." What is more, most of the students who say this have an awareness of social inequality that is tied to their desire to be of service to the world. One idea that has been highly salient in developing our recent thinking in response to what our students are saying is Kathie Crocket's (2004, 2007) premise that clinical supervision is a site for the production of a professional self-story. If a supervisee wishes to develop a professional identity as someone "who makes a difference in the world" in relation and tension with helping to improve the individual life of a client, we will likely need to reflect this aim in our supervision practices. Jane Speedy (2000), a British supervisor in the narrative tradition, claims that the process of supervision is multi-storied, so even as we produce new understandings of it, there is no need for us to abandon all previous paradigmatic understandings of supervisory relationships and practices. We do contend, however, that these understandings will need to be held in tension with innovations of practice that come closer to serving socially emancipatory ends, if we wish to enable our trainees to more effectively make a social justice difference for and with their clients.

To this purpose, a significant portion of the early work that I (MB) do with students relates to exploring their own histories of becoming counselors and how they find themselves in this endeavor and not in, say, biology, literature, or global studies. These conversations often include telling significant stories and sharing events around the issues of justice (or injustice) in the life of the trainee, whether personal experience or something they witnessed. By engaging the student in conversations around these experiences and their prior life choices, we clarify their values and do at least three additional things. First, by highlighting the values that drew them into the work to begin with, we are more able to then draw specific connections between their values and values related to the pursuit of social justice. Second, we help to frame the work that they engage in as a means to further their ability to enact fairness, healing, justice, and whatever other values they might hold. Finally, these conversations open the possibility for us to speak of work towards social justice in terms of movement work and activism across time.

Taken together, these conversations about values lessen the likelihood that our social justice work is an imposed agenda and instead is one that flows more from trainees' commitments than anything else. Once a trainee has already said that these are important values in their work, the supervisor, whether university or site based, can continue to follow up on these conversations throughout the course of the counseling internship. This approach also acknowledges that this work is about the trainee, but it is also about so much more. The hopes and dreams of this particular trainee are linked to countless others who have gone before (and exist elsewhere) who are trying to embody similar values and ideals. In this respect, there is the beginning of a convergence between a social justice perspective on clinical supervision and what Michael Carroll (2001) has termed "the spirituality of supervision" practice in which a connected way of being self-reflective changes supervision from being a functional activity into a way of living as "an interior person" in both life and professional work. Greater capacity for spiritual interiority tends to ground a trainee's (or supervisor's) commitments to act from a place of deep values and connections to others in the wider world and allows for sustainable action.

To illustrate, I (MB) often ask students within the first few supervision sessions if it would be OK if I posed a few questions about their histories of choosing this field, and their specific graduate program and placement site. I might start with general questions like:

- Can you say a little bit about what brought you to decide to become a counselor? How did you choose the Warner School as your graduate school or St. Joseph's as your placement site? What about this work resonated with you?
- What's one story that you could tell that would give me a sense of how becoming a counselor enables you to make a difference? What kind of difference do you want to make in the world?

Then I move to more specific questions like:

- Can you tell me a story about an injustice that you witnessed or experienced that may have influenced the work that you have decided to do?
- Who are the people you look to as models in this work? What, specifically, do you look to about their lives or witness?

Once we have explored the value system of the trainee, we move to explore the many other social identities embodied in a trainee.

Social Justice Praxis

Because social justice praxis is a newly emerging understanding in the profession of counseling, there are not yet a lot of resources available to help supervisors and trainees. In a recent article outlining what combined multicultural and social justice competencies might look like for the counseling profession, Ratts et al. (2016) contend that a primary developmental domain in counseling practice is counselor self-awareness. Their view is that multicultural and social justice competency must begin "internally with the counselor" (p. 37). They go on to say that "becoming aware of one's attitudes and beliefs is an important precursor to understanding social group identities, marginalized and privileged group statuses, power and privilege, limitations, strengths, assumptions, values and beliefs" (p. 38). A counselor's self-understanding thus stands at the core of social justice competencies for, without a solid understanding of the power and privilege we may possess as supervisors or as trainees, we risk perpetuating injustice.

For example, one student that I (MB) was working with was reviewing an audiotape of a session she had with a client. The client that she was counseling was an African-American woman in her twenties who had recently been fired from a low-wage nursing home job. The counselor was a white woman also in her twenties. At one point in the session, the client said, "They just up and fired me. For nothing!" After a brief silence, the counselor responded, "People usually don't just get fired for nothing." As we unpacked this brief exchange, I asked the counselor if I could ask her questions about her own life and experiences. She had never been terminated from a job, nor had she had any kind of employment challenges in her life. Every job she held, she excelled at and was well liked. She had also always worked in majority white settings and had almost no experience with the stories of discrimination that many people of color speak of in employment settings. In short, people had always been fair, reasonable, and supportive to her and she assumed that this was true for everyone. Her privilege was invisible to her.

As she reflected further, she became aware of how an assumption like this could effectively silence a story of injustice in the life of her client because her question carried with it some not so subtle blame that the client must have done *something* to get fired. The counselor felt embarrassed that her question could have had that impact, and so we brainstormed what other questions the counselor might ask to try to open up some space for inquiry into the client's experience. During the next session with the client, the counselor told the client that she was uncomfortable with the line of questioning that she had used and said she would like to ask a bit more about the firing. The client appreciated the chance to say more about the situation and the counselor found out that her client was the fourth woman of color to be fired from this job (under the same supervisor) in the last few years. After hearing this, I (MB) recommended that the client speak to a local labor attorney who helps low-income workers in situations such as these.

In their article, Ratts et al. (2016) develop a very useful framework that we have begun to apply in our work with students. This framework holds multicultural and social justice praxis at the core of therapeutic work and then uses a quadrant approach based on the degree of marginalization or privilege experienced by both counselor and client across developmental domains, to help counselors think about needed knowledge, skills, dispositions, and actions. Using this framework, we might ask counselors in training questions like:

- In what quadrant would you locate this current client encounter?
- How might your power and privilege be playing out with respect to the power and privilege of the client?
- What factors would help you decide whether to provide counseling or social justice advocacy (or both) in this client situation?

Bridging Therapy and Activism

In recent years, our work at St. Joseph's and at the Warner School has also been influenced by the thinking of Canadian therapist, activist, and supervisor Vikki Reynolds who, with Australian therapist Sekneh Hammoud-Beckett, has articulated the challenges of bringing the worlds of therapy and activism together. In their article titled "Bridging the Worlds of Therapy and Activism: Intersections, Tensions and Affinities," Reynolds and Hammoud-Beckett (2012) say that "psychotherapy has much to answer for in terms of siding with oppression, and serving as a tool for social control that maintains oppressive structures of power—both state power and interpersonal power" (p. 58). In working with our students at the very beginning of the internship, we have them read this article and then ask some questions like:

- What caught your attention from the article? Why do you think that caught your attention?
- What do you think about the authors' statement? What resonates with you? What questions does it raise for you?
- What might this statement mean for your individual work with clients?
- What might this statement mean for our agency or your graduate program?

Our purpose in introducing the ideas of activism within therapy is to take seriously that not all counseling work, in and of itself, is about social justice. Just because we "think" we are making a difference does not mean that our work is addressing social inequality. We agree with Reynolds and Hammoud-Beckett when they say that "therapy and activism are very different projects" and that "it's important to acknowledge the limitations of therapy as an act of justice doing" (p. 58).

Our hope, however, is to invite emerging therapists into a broader understanding of the problems that they hear about in private sessions. This broader understanding might require actions other than those routinely practiced within therapy. Therapy has its place in the healing of the world, but by itself does little, if anything, to fundamentally address the social-structural problems that undergird so much of what our clients face in their everyday lives. Other kinds of action may be needed and counselors may need to learn how to engage some of these.

The Just Therapy team from New Zealand picks up on similar themes and forms another philosophical pillar of our approach. Charles Waldegrave and his colleagues (2003) suggest that "when people come to therapists depressed and in bad housing, and their clinical or social problems are treated within the conventional clinical boundaries, they are simply made to feel a little better in poverty" (p. 268). While some may find this a harsh critique of the therapeutic endeavor, we find that there is much truth in this statement. Developing these ideas further with trainees in supervision seems to be a critical step in cultivating a social justice perspective. Our work tries to help trainees notice and name unjust social, political, and economic factors that contribute to the problems that people face. To this end, we might directly ask trainees questions like:

- What would you see as larger social forces that support the problems that your client is speaking about with you?
- Do you talk to your clients about what connections they might see between social injustice that they face and the problems that show up in their life?
- How do you think your clients resist the oppression that might otherwise overwhelm them?

By asking direct questions like this, we encourage trainees to notice that individual problems are often supported and sustained by oppression in the form of racism, sexism, ableism, heterosexism, or economic inequality, for example. This kind of dialogue circles back around to the trainee's own personal social location and privilege, encouraging reflection on how the trainee's life and the client's life might be connected by oppression or injustice. Finally, such questions help a trainee to see that clients are also agents in their own lives, resisting hardship and oppression every day (even if they cannot stop it).

Waldegrave (2009) also suggests that therapists and trainees—because of their direct access to stories of pain and hardship in individuals and communities—are uniquely poised (and they suggest have a responsibility) to "identify, quantify, and describe the severity and causes" (p. 96) of social pain and step into the public debate around these issues. He and the Just Therapy team also suggest that therapists need to think about ways to link the lives of the oppressed and marginalized so that, somehow, even within the boundaries of appropriate confidentiality, they might find solidarity with each other and begin to develop collective means to address the problems that they face.

In our work, we reflect on ways that therapists-in-training might think more broadly about "interventions" that could enable multiple clients to become part of a larger project that seeks to address some of what they are collectively facing. We find ourselves asking questions such as:

- Are there social movements or activist groups in Rochester, New York or nationally that might be connected to the issues that your client is facing? If you are not aware, where might you go (or who might you consult) to find out? Have you asked your clients if they are aware of any?
- Are you connected to any larger movements that are actively engaged in trying to counter some of what your clients face? If so, how did you get connected to those? What is important to you about your connection to them?
- Have you spoken to your clients about if they would want to speak with others who might be facing similar stressors?

Putting the Pieces Together

Developing supervisory practices that lean into conversations related to social justice remains a developing field. What we have tried to provide here are some thoughts on how we might operationalize what we do so that other supervisors might think more broadly about their work with trainees. It is worth noting, however, that this is not meant to be an individualized process. There is a great deal that can be done collectively with trainees and that, in fact, *needs* to be done collectively. In our assessment, there are so many more conversations that need to be developed regarding this topic—conversations around spirituality, ethics, and hermeneutics to name just a few. Below we provide two case examples that we think help to clarify actions that a supervisor might take as he or she seeks to support a social justice perspective with a trainee.

Case Example 1: Amy

One powerful example that I (KM) can share about how a supervision practice can have a larger recursive social justice impact is to relate the experience of a student, Amy, and her mother. Amy had interned at St. Joseph's Neighborhood Center and, as part of her site supervision process, had shared her verbal responses to some of the questions posed in this chapter. She had also recounted the story of how she felt about her mother's challenges with mental illness while she was growing up and how she disliked how others subsequently positioned her as a "survivor" of sorts when she shared her history. Narrative letter writing—a common practice used in narrative approaches to therapy that helps to document alternative and preferred story lines spoken of in the therapeutic encounter—can also be applied in supervision. Michael (MB) often writes a narrative letter to interns as they near the end of their supervision with him, which usually includes a summary of the student's work in the internship—highlighting the insights and progress that the student has identified over the course of time; only this time he targeted the letter not to Amy, but instead to Amy's mother.

At the university, in peer group supervision, Amy spoke of how much this act had touched her in that the contribution Amy's mother had actually made to her becoming the kind of therapist she was had finally been recognized in non-sympathetic and non-reductionist ways. I asked Amy if she and her mother would give consent for me to share Michael's letter with our much wider community of supervisors as an example of what social justice supervision might contribute to a trainee; that is, how a supervisor with an eye towards social justice can use his or her own power to surface a submerged story of love and capacity that defies the ramifications of being considered a mentally ill person in society. In so doing, Amy and her mother got to experience being honored for what they knew about maintaining a bond that could help Amy launch a career as a new therapist, despite their earlier severe challenges together. Amy shared in group supervision with me that she identified how many other women are judged incapable of being good mothers when they receive a diagnosis of mental illness. She said this pained her because not only did it dishonor the mothers, but it led to characterizations of people like her as "exceptional" and having succeeded "despite" their mothers instead of "because" of them. A narrative that re-positioned and re-wrote this story of relationship through suffering empowered both Amy and her mom, and connected their personal experience to the plight of women and others without social power or voice, who live in the margins. The supervision activity in this example had social justice effects that went beyond supervision's usual narrow professional purposes, and contributed indirectly to justice-doing (Reynolds & Hammoud-Beckett, 2012) by telling a more generative story that can stand against stories of pathology.

Case Example 2: Nick

In another example, one of the supervisees that I (MB) supervised a few years ago was working with a woman who was at risk of losing her home due to bank foreclosure. This led to supervisory conversations with all of the interns I oversee about asking their clients a little more about their housing situations. We found that two other clients were having similar issues. A local grassroots group in Rochester called Take Back the Land (TBTL) had been quite active (and successful) in helping to stop housing foreclosure through advocacy efforts, but also by blockading houses with TBTL members and allies so that sheriff deputies could not (or decided not to) enforce the confiscation of the property. We informed all of the clients with foreclosure issues about an upcoming demonstration that they could attend to hear more from TBTL members and also from other families who had had their foreclosure stopped. I accompanied one intern and met two of the clients at the demonstration. The clients could not believe that an organization like TBTL existed and became more involved in housing rights activity in Rochester. The student wrote about the experience in a reflection paper and shared this with his peers who were very moved by the whole account and reported back to the student that they had found that it challenged them to see their work differently. Specifically, students in his class had not thought that they could do things like this in their work and began to think of clients in their own contexts who might benefit from connection to other people facing similar social problems.

Conclusion

As we mentioned in our introduction, the context of inequality in which we find ourselves as a nation raises serious concerns. Counselors in training are coming into this mix preparing to be "front-line" witnesses to diverse stories of social breakdown, yet are often unprepared to make necessary connections between what they witness and the traditions of social justice and activism that might help to address the social problems that contribute to client problems. If supervisors are not attuned to this dimension of practice, they remain complicit (intentionally or not) with the power structures that perpetuate these problems.

Our intent in this chapter has been to share our own evolving steps toward being non-complicit as we construct a more relational, responsive, formative, and just stance in how we inhabit our roles as clinical supervisors and instructors. We know we have a long way to go, but find that centering our focus on how supervision itself can embrace an ethos of justice-doing has added an enlivening, purposeful energy to our training efforts. We invite readers to develop their own thoughts about what we have written as we, too, continue to develop our perspective on doing justice as counseling supervisors.

Reflection Questions

1. What fundamentally does supervision as a practice do? Can it contribute directly to justice-making? In what ways?
2. Can a supervision process that centers on the cultivation of an inner philosophical commitment to social justice better help trainees embrace questions of justice, ethics, and care as internally derived rather than externally apprenticed via their supervisor?
3. On what can or should clinical supervisors themselves reflect to foster justice-doing?

4. Does it seem that a consideration of supervision as a formation process, as much as a monitoring, developmental, or gatekeeping process, could support greater engagement with social justice activism within counseling? How might this align with or contrast with other models of supervision connected to professional identity and monitoring?
5. What pros and cons can you identify related to the dominant language of "supervisor/supervisee"?

References

American Counseling Association (2014). *ACA Code of Ethics*. Alexandria, VA: Author.

Carroll, M. (2001). The spirituality of supervision. In M. Carroll & M. Tholstrup (Eds.), *Integrative approaches to supervision* (pp. 76–89). London: Jessica Kingsley.

Chow, D. L., Miller, S. D., Seidel, J. A., Karen, R. T., Thornton, J. A., & Andrews, W. P. (2015). The role of deliberate practice in the development of highly effective psychotherapists. *Psychotherapy, 52*(3), 337–345. doi: 10.1037/pst0000015

Crocket, K. (2004). Storying counselors: Producing professional selves in supervision. In D. Paré and G. Larner (Eds.), *Collaborative practice in psychology and psychotherapy* (pp. 171–182). New York, NY: Haworth Press.

Crocket, K. (2007). Counselling supervision and the production of professional selves. *Counselling and Psychotherapy Research, 7*(1), 19–25. doi: 10.1080/14733140601140402

D'Andrea, M., & Daniels, J. (2009). Promoting multiculturalism, democracy and social justice in organizational settings: A case study. In J. G. Ponterotto, J. M. Casas, L. A. Suzuki, & C. M. Alexander (Eds.), *Handbook of multicultural counseling* (pp. 591–602). Thousand Oaks, CA: Sage.

Kivel, P. (2000). Social service or social change: Who benefits from your work? Retrieved from www.paulkivel.com

Lave, J., & Wenger, E. (1991). *Situated learning: Legitimate peripheral participation*. Cambridge, UK: Cambridge University Press.

Matthews, C. (2014, October 31). Wealth inequality in America: It's worse than you think. *Fortune Magazine*. Retrieved from http://fortune.com

Mishel, L., Bivens, J., Gould, E., & Shierholtz, H. (2012). *The state of working America* (12th ed.). Ithaca, NY: Cornell University Press.

Paul, K. I., & Moser, K. (2009). Unemployment impairs mental health: Meta-analyses. *Journal of Vocational Behavior, 74*(3), 264–282. doi: 10.1016/j.jvb.2009.01.001

Ratts, M. J., Singh, A. A., Nassar-McMillan, S., Butler, S. K., & McCullough, J. R. (2016). Multicultural and social justice counseling competencies: Guidelines for the counseling profession. *Journal of Multicultural Counseling and Development 44*(1), 28–48. doi: 10.1002/jmcd.12035

Reynolds, V., & Hammoud-Beckett, S. (2012). Bridging the worlds of therapy and activism: Intersections, tensions and affinities. *International Journal of Narrative Therapy & Community Work, 4*, 57–61. Retrieved from http://dulwichcentre.com.au

Speedy, J. (2000). Consulting with gargoyles: Applying narrative ideas and practices in counselling and supervision. *European Journal of Psychotherapy and Counselling, 3*(3). 419–431. doi: 10.1080/13642530010012057

Tate, K. A., Fallon, K. M., Casquarelli, E. J., & Marks, L. R. (2014). Opportunities for action: Traditionally marginalized populations and the economic crisis. *The Professional Counselor*, 4(4), 285–302. doi: 10.15241/kat.4.4.285

Tervalon, M., & Murray-Garcia, J. (1998). Cultural humility versus cultural competence: A critical distinction in defining physician training outcomes in multicultural education. *Journal of Healthcare for the Poor and Underserved*, 9(2), 117–125. doi: 10.1353/hpu/2010-0233

Toporek, R., Dodge, D., Tripp, F., & Alarcon, L. (2009). Social justice and community engagement: Developing relationships beyond the university. In J. G. Ponterrotto, J. M. Casas, L. A. Suzuki, & C. M. Alexander (Eds.), *Handbook of multicultural counseling* (pp. 603–618). Thousand Oaks, CA: Sage.

Waldegrave, C. (2009). Cultural, gender, and socioeconomic contexts in therapeutic and social policy work. *Family Process*, 48(1), 85–101. doi: 10.1111/j.1545-5300.2009.01269.x

Waldegrave, C., Tamasese, K., Tuhaka, F., & Campbell, W. (2003). *Just Therapy—a journey: A collection of papers from the Just Therapy team New Zealand*. Adelaide, South Australia: Dulwich Centre Publications.

Wenger-Trayner, E., & Wenger-Trayner, B. (2015). Communities of practice: A brief introduction. Retrieved from http://wenger-trayner.com/introduction-to-communities-of-practice

Wilkinson, R., & Pickett, K. (2009). *The spirit level: Why greater equality makes societies stronger*. New York, NY: Bloomsbury Press.

Zinn, H. (2002). *You can't be neutral on a moving train: A personal history of our times*. Boston, MA: Beacon Press.

CHAPTER 6

Counseling as Post-Colonial Encounter: Hospitality and Ethical Relationship

Kathie Crocket, Elmarie Kotzé, and Rahera Taylor

This chapter explores the metaphor of hospitality for counseling and counselor education, as a move towards possibilities for social justice in a post-colonial nation. In Aotearoa New Zealand the status of Māori as *tangata whenua*[1], First Nation people, is acknowledged through an emphasis on bi-culturalism, at the same time as ongoing immigration produces a multicultural society. Hospitality as practice and metaphor derives from and is lived by the host *tangata whenua* culture. It is also articulated within the Western philosophical traditions that we employ to theorize and practice counseling ethics. The relationship between *tangata whenua*, the descendants of the colonizers, and more recent migrants is clearly dependent on ongoing negotiation and clarification of the terms of hospitality, just as any counseling relationship is based in agreed forms of professional hospitality. This chapter describes and theorizes a particular aspect of counselor education where the program staff and students experience *tangata whenua* hospitality—for its contribution to possibilities for just and ethical counseling practice. These possibilities emerge, we suggest, when in response to hospitality students and staff are called to give an account of ourselves, an account that locates us within the landscapes and relationships that have emerged out of this country's colonial history.

Arriving and Being Welcomed

Our group gathers beside the parked cars. We have travelled long distances to this rural, coastal setting. We are staff and students in the Master of Counseling program, arriving to stay for a five-day teaching block at Maniaroa, 150 kilometres from our university. This is a noho marae, where we live together, eating, talking, sleeping, learning, in this sacred place where we will experience aspects of the Māori world—and learn about ourselves. We are here as part of a compulsory MCouns theory course. Committed to narrative therapy practice and putting post-structuralist theory and inquiry to work, our MCouns program is shaped by questions of social justice, one expression of which is to make ourselves available to learn in this culturally specific space.

For the welcome we are dressed in black, women in skirts, submitting ourselves to the custom of the occasion. A man is identified to speak on behalf of
our group. We have prepared to sing together once he has spoken. Readying
ourselves for this encounter of welcome, we become a collective, an assemblage of visitors. We are Māori, Pākehā, and more recent migrants, in this
moment all visitors presenting ourselves to be welcomed. We signal our readiness by standing together quietly by the open gate. The silence is broken by
the call of welcome, inviting us forward, signalling hospitality. Ahead, the
doors of the *wharenui*, the meeting house, are open. Whaea Hinekahukura
Aranui stands on the porch, her voice ringing out in welcome across the space
between us.

This moment is particular to place, to Aotearoa New Zealand, where an imperial-
colonial history precedes any encounter, including in teaching or counseling,
that we may wish to call post-colonial. The pedagogy of the week is of this place,[2]
this rural, seaside marae and its people, and of this nation and its peoples. It is
a pedagogy informed by a professional Code of Ethics that refers to both social
justice and the Treaty of Waitangi, the founding document of this country signed
by the iwi and the British Crown in 1840: "Counsellors shall seek to be informed
about the meaning and implications of the Treaty of Waitangi for their work.
They shall understand the principles of protection, participation and partnership with Māori" (New Zealand Association of Counsellors, 2002, Introduction,
para. 4).

Three decades ago the Just Therapy team (Waldegrave, 1985, 1990) placed social
justice at the center of social service practice in New Zealand; and Māori psychiatrist Sir Mason Durie (1989, 2001, for example) showed the limitations of the
versions of personhood and well-being produced by a Western worldview, arguing
that the psy-professions must engage with Māori understandings. In counselor
education at our university, this call was made by Hinekahukura Aranui, now a
respected elder who has hosted many *noho marae* to prepare counselors to work
with her people. Here learning goes beyond particular cultural competencies (see
Crocket & Kotzé, 2010; Monk, Winslade, & Sinclair, 2008), to robust investigation
of the discourses that constitute life for us and for clients. The immersion of a five-
day *noho marae* sets the scene to encounter learning at what Jones and Jenkins
(2008) term the colonizer-indigene hyphen. This is the kind of radical learning
that calls us into giving accounts of ourselves (see Butler, 2005), that is, to locate
ourselves within historical, social and political relations—social justice at work.
Offering and witnessing such accounts, in this marae context, prepares students
for performing social justice in counseling practice.

While we are welcomed unconditionally, we experience a series of tensions.
There is the tension of learning the protocol of the encounter: remembering to
pause at the appropriate moment to acknowledge those who have passed on, for
example; or of all that is unfamiliar for those students for whom this is a first marae
visit. But even if we have been welcomed before, we cannot know what is ahead.

Entering the *wharenui*, for the speeches of welcome and encounter, the tension of a gender-specific seating arrangement, men in the front and women behind, may need to be managed. For the men there may be the tension of sitting exposed on the speakers' bench, sweat forming in anticipation of the responsibility of standing to speak in response to the welcome, but without fluency in the Māori language.

Writing about New Zealand's post-colonial context, Jones and Jenkins (2008) point to the ethical necessity of living out such tensions if we are to learn *"from* the Other, rather than learning *about* the Other" (p. 471):

> What I learn is not about you, but I learn from you about *difference*. This, of course, returns us to the hyphen, that stroke that both enforces difference and makes the link between.
>
> (Jones & Jenkins, 2008, p. 482)

> ...
>
> The desire for engagement must lead colonizer scholars to a deeper understanding of our own settler culture, society, and history as deeply embedded in a relationship with the culture, society, and history of indigenous people. Such an orientation to the hyphen invites colonizer peoples to seek to know ourselves in the relationship with Others, to locate ourselves in the "between"—to develop a stronger sense of how our Selves are and have been formed in the troubled engagement with indigenous people and their lands and spaces.
>
> (Jones & Jenkins, 2008, p. 482)

If there is such a thing as social justice, then, we suggest, it is to be found in the tensions of small moments of encounter. In such moments, steps towards troubling privilege, learning about difference, and understanding inequity become possible. These are critical steps in counselor formation.

Before We Arrived

Perhaps the terms "hospitality" and "Māori" are synonymous. Māori are known for making people welcome. *Manaaki* or *manaakitanga*, the words that most closely align with hospitality, have many meanings: help, hospitality, generosity, openheartedness, courtesy, looking after, caring for, behaving kindly and with good intention. *Manaaki* and *manaakitanga* are strengths of her people, suggests Rahera, at the same time acknowledging that big-heartedness is sometimes exploited.

As host for the *noho marae*, Rahera[3] has looked forward to this week, excited and challenged by the responsibilities she carries. She is interested in where the students come from, the stories they bring. She considers the fears and anxieties some may have about living a communal life. How can she make their stay easier, their fears and anxieties less? She wonders how many recent migrants there will be, where they will be from, how long have they been in Aotearoa, what languages they speak. She thinks about her responsibilities. How does she raise awareness of her people as *tangata whenua*, their place in the recent history of Aotearoa, their ways of being, the effects of colonization and struggles that ensue? What can we learn about what the fallout from colonization requires of counselors as we work towards social justice in counseling?

There is practical preparation for the group's arrival. Rahera travels from her home, 80 kilometers south. Her first stop, near Maniaroa, is to check in with her advisor, Aunty Tuti (Hinekahukura Aranui). A legacy of childhood remains strong, the need to consult an elder. Arriving at Maniaroa, Rahera and Larry Crow, the male elder, prepare to receive us as guests.

Larry turns on water and power, while Rahera opens the *wharenui*, greeting the ancestors who will watch over and care for us at Maniaroa. Rahera looks at the carved figure of Waiwaia—her people's *taniwha*, a water spirit, who lives in the Waipa River where Rahera spent hours as a youngster, swimming and eeling. Waiwaia is a friendly *taniwha*: Rahera knows that Elmarie and Kathie always sleep under this carving during our *noho*. She knows, too, that Elmarie is drawn to the carving on the wall opposite. This carving is of Maniapoto, the ancestor of Rahera's *iwi*, inside a cave protecting a small child.

Rahera goes to the gate when the first cars arrive. The lessons begin immediately: she greets each person in Māori—*"tēnā koe"*—offering a *hongi*, a pressing of noses in greeting. If there is no woman student to lead the group, Rahera undertakes the role of responding to the welcoming call. By moving forward together in response to the call, we three—Rahera, Elmarie, and Kathie—again become a close teaching team who will support the students and each other through this week. Elmarie and Kathie (full-time MCouns staff) depend upon Rahera's cultural knowledge and guidance as together we produce a place-responsive pedagogy. Rahera offers us the gift of learning and teaching together at the indigene-colonizer hyphen.

Settling In: Guests Invited to Make Ourselves at Home

> Our cars are unpacked. Food is stored in the kitchen. Tables are set up and covered in red tablecloths at one end of the large dining hall, and AV equipment set up at the other end. Mattresses are arranged around the edges of the wharenui, covered with the bedding we have each brought. We store our belongings neatly alongside each mattress. Gentle guidance has been offered about how we use space, for ourselves, and for the material things we bring. While we three [authors] prepare the first shared meal, the students explore the marae buildings, or the immediate outdoors overlooking the Tasman Sea. We take up the offer of hospitality: responding to the call, we are beginning to make ourselves at home.

Our own histories shape how we take up the invitation to make ourselves at home. Brent, one of the students, sits in the sun, looking at Mount Taranaki in the distance. He breathes the air, and slowly shifts his gaze to the iron-rich sand of the beach, and to the sea. "Tangaroa [the sea] speaks differently

here on the west coast," he says. "This maunga [Taranaki] speaks to our East
Coast maunga": relationships extend beyond people to landscapes. "And it's different here. The carvings of the *wharenui* are different from where I come from."
Brent is Ngāti Porou; he has lived beside the Pacific Ocean on the East Coast.
The *marae*—but not *this marae*—is a familiar setting for him. He engages with
the familiarity and the unfamiliarity of this welcome, this place, this land, this
mountain, and Tangaroa.

Encountering *Mana Whenua* in Rahera's Invitation to Explore

Lunch is over, the kitchen chores completed. We sit on our mattresses in the
wharenui, as the afternoon session begins. Rahera stands to speak. Her *karakia* (blessing) shapes the space. She invites the students to move beyond the
marae gates, to climb the hills behind, to explore the river or beach below. She
asks that students return with three objects, to be returned later to the places
they were found. She suggests students take time while outdoors to connect
with the surroundings and imagine life here in this rural coastal setting as it
might have been long ago, before colonization.

Rahera's assignment can be read through the lens of a Māori view of *time-space* as
one: "the Māori word for time and space is the same," writes Smith (1999, p. 50).
Particularly for new migrants for whom this landscape is unfamiliar, but also for
us all, this is an opportunity to consider and enter into different dimensions of
time-space: "different orientations towards time and space, different positioning
within time and space, and different systems of language for making space and
time … underpin notions of past and present, of place and of relationships to the
land" (Smith, 1999, p. 55). Invited to explore the land and the beach, we experience
the *mana whenua* of the local people whose ancestors knew this land intimately.
We experience at once contemporary hospitality alongside acknowledgment of
the loss of land for Māori as a consequence of colonization. Out on the hills or
on the beach, in our moving and stopping, our looking, listening, smelling, and
touching, we experience hospitality and its reciprocal call to us as guests, in ways
particular to this place-time.

Hospitality gives to the other with all the aporetics of the "gift," for gifts likewise bind the other to me in gratitude and a need to reciprocate. What is true
of hospitality is true, too, of the gift, and of deconstruction itself: it does not
come down to knowing anything, but to doing something.

(Caputo, 1997, p. 112)

The students have been asked to find objects meaningful to them, to bring these
objects back and sit together in the *wharenui*, to each speak the connection

between this object and their own lived experience. In speaking together and making connections to place and time, we all find ourselves *doing something*, acting in response to the hospitality that is extended to us. As staff and students in a university entangled in Western systems of knowledge, we have been invited to learn and teach on other terms:

> The arguments of different indigenous peoples based on spiritual relationships to the universe, to the landscape and to stones, rocks, insects and other things, seen and unseen, have been difficult arguments for Western systems of knowledge to deal with or accept. These arguments give a partial indication of the different worldviews and alternative ways of coming to know, and of being, which still endure within the indigenous world.
>
> (Smith, 1999, p. 74)

We have prepared for this encounter. During our first class, on campus, students were welcomed onto the University's *marae*, Te Kohinga Mārama, along with hundreds of students beginning study in our Faculty. As a class we stayed together overnight in the university's *wharenui*, where our colleague Cheri Waititi taught about its meanings. One splendid carving there is of *Manaakitanga*. This word, *manaakitanga*, we might translate into English as *care*, or any of the words Rahera offered above. But what gets lost in translation? Is it possible for Pākehā to understand the hospitality that *manaakitanga* carries? Such questions have stayed with us in the weeks between the two *noho marae*, sustained by readings provided for online discussion. Together students have grappled with post-structural theory that also questions the foundations of Western Enlightenment thinking. They have read post-colonial literature that calls us to understand unearned privilege, and the colonial history of our country. In online discussions students have made links between this literature and their own lives. Now, here at Maniaroa, beneath the rafters of the *wharenui*, in the embrace of *manākitanga*, we are called to respond to the gift of hospitality.

The Embrace of the *Wharenui*: Our First Evening

After dinner we gather in the *wharenui*. The invitation is to learn and immerse ourselves in things Māori: the *mauri*, life force, of the *wharenui*, the histories told on decorated rafters, woven panels, and exquisite carvings. We experience *manaakitanga* in ways that have potential for transformation in becoming counselors.

Emphasizing Maori values as holding respect for place and honoring family and ancestors, O'Connor and MacFarlane (2002) explain: "when meeting new friends, Maori identify themselves by naming their home region's mountain(s) river(s), lake(s) and other topographical features. They also identify their parents and ancestors. Such traditions are in stark contrast to individual-centered identification" (p. 224). One by one we stand and further introduce ourselves, many of us making an effort, however stumbling, to use some Māori language. We link to the places we come from. Rahera and Hinekahukura, as hosts, often offer particular welcomes to recent migrants, and to Māori from other parts of the country. Māori students are not an homogenous group: some have rich links to their own *marae* and history, while for others their time at Maniaroa gives a first opportunity to purposefully identify as Māori. We learn contemporary Māori songs that we sing throughout the week. We learn about the stories the *wharenui* holds, told through the art on the roof and walls. While the beauty of the material world—for example, the wooden carving depicting an ancestor—is readily seen, for many of us it is harder to grasp the conceptual and spiritual, that this *wharenui* is experienced as alive and breathing, that it is indeed an ancestor. Whatever we understand of this metaphysical world, we are generously taken on a journey that traverses the history of the *tangata whenua*, and beyond: we learn about a scoundrel who deceived his own brother, as well as about revered, courageous and wise leaders. Stories and song still echoing, we sleep beneath the ribs of the house as it embraces us.

A knock on the wall of the *wharenui*, and a gentle blessing giving thanks for the night's sleep, wake us the following morning.

Day 2: Student Presentations and Responses to Each Other

In response to hospitality, in preparation for discussions about culture and gender—indeed in preparation for socially just professional practice in counseling—this course requires students to prepare a short presentation using post-structural theory to give an account of an aspect of their own lives (see Crocket & Kotzé, 2010). This *marae* week has many objectives—including connecting with others, the land and the people of the land; and interacting with personal stories and stories of colonization. Throughout the teaching and learning of counseling practice, we emphasize the importance of giving accounts of ourselves. Giving an account of oneself (Butler, 2005) is more than telling a story. It involves the ongoing production of the self as an ethical subject, situated in historical, social, and political relations. In giving an account at Maniaroa, it is not possible to ignore the colonial history where land was taken, including through war and confiscation, with consequent benefits for Pākehā and ongoing losses for Māori. This history provides a ground for accountability, the study of oneself in ethical relation in order to account for one's part in historical, social, and political relations: "I become an object to myself at the moment in which I am accountable to an Other" (Butler in Olson & Worsham, 2000, p. 749). Further, Butler suggests that we cannot assume to know what the Other invites of us: the voice of the Other within oneself "*is* and *is not* the Other" (Olson & Worsham, 2000, p. 749). If our responsibility is—as we have suggested above—to *do something*, a further step in *doing* is to account for ourselves in ways that show the shaping discourses of our own lives. If such a thing as social justice is possible, then a step towards this possibility arises from a desire to not unwittingly replicate operations of power/knowledge. As teachers, our hope is that by accounting for aspects of their own historical, social, and political location, and by witnessing each other's accounts, student counselors' repertoire of ethical responses will be extended (Crocket, Kotzé, & Flintoff, 2007).

Some students stand before their peers to speak as *tangata whenua*, descendants of the people who landed on the shores of this part of Aotearoa many years ago. Other Māori students have tribal affiliations in other parts of the country; and then there are those Māori for whom the *noho marae* is a complicated and painful engagement with a heritage lost. There are new migrants to Aotearoa New Zealand, from Asia, Europe, Africa, and North America; others have clear links, still, with other parts of the world; there are students from the Pacific who will return to practice in their home countries; and then there are the descendants of the white colonial settlers. To illustrate this accounting-for-ourselves practice, we re-present below brief moments from presentations given by three students, Huia, Brent—both Māori—and Adri, a more recent migrant.

Huia

It is evening as we gather in the *wharenui*. The lighting is muted, setting the mood for the sacred story we hear. Huia tells of learning that her 16-month-old first-born son was to lose his eye to surgery, because of cancer. The family had travelled to the city for medical intervention, with wider family—*whānau*—also gathering in support of the parents and their young one, far from home.[4]

> We wanted the surgery for our boy. We could see the effect of the diseased eye on his daily life. But Western medical science did not grasp the significance to our *whānau* of this body part, however diseased, however unrecognisable it might become after dissection. For the surgeon and the pathologist the eye became just pathological tissue: for our *whānau* the eye, even diseased and dissected, was inseparable from whakapapa, his ancestral line. Care for the child and our shared *whakapapa* meant that we fiercely advocated for an understanding of the inseparability of body, spirit, and *whānau*. This eye was not just human tissue to be discarded after surgical removal, but was still part of what made our child our child. The eye was something that we could still talk to, acknowledging its *mauri*, its life essence.
>
> There was sadness for us that our boy had to be separated from the eye, but in our grief and loss we also knew that the diseased eye was matter that the *whānau* had a sacred responsibility to return to Papatūānuku, the earth of our boy's ancestors. We had a responsibility to return it to where it belonged, to the earth where he was from. We advocated for the eye to be returned to us after relevant tests, our sense of connection to this diseased tissue not readily understood or accepted by the team who had successfully removed what the medical world classified as diseased tissue to be disposed of. Their goal was the separation of healthy and unhealthy tissue while for us there remained—and remains—a sense of connectedness to the eye. We

are thankful that the eye was returned to us, and we were able to return it to the earth of our boy's ancestors.

Huia's story is a gift. In this *wharenui*, on this night, in the presence of the ancestors, we are called to the threshold of the indigene-colonizer hyphen. In efforts to learn about difference, the word "worldview" is often used. In this moment "worldview" loses its clichéd status, its abstraction. Worldview becomes a matter of human tissue, a mother's pain, *whānau* care, disease, earth, and metaphysical connectedness. In the sacred silence of the gift, we are invited into transformation, the effect of which we cannot foresee.

Brent

Brent asks that his presentation take place on the *marae atea*—the space in front of the *wharenui*, structured for the possibility of contestation and active engagement with the other. It allows for expression of pain, anger, hope and *tino rangatiratanga* (sovereignty). At Maniaroa the sea can be seen, heard, and addressed from here. Brent begins his presentation with a *karakia*, a blessing on us all gathered here and on the story he tells of the pollution of the waters of his home. Here, on the west coast, he tells of an east coast council discharging sewage directly into the sea, which Brent's people had long fished and lived alongside.

> I thought my friend, the community leader, understood the relationship between Māori and Tangaroa. I thought our friendship had taught him something of the sacredness of Tangaroa, that he understood that the sea is not there to be polluted by a city's untreated sewage. To go surfing or fishing amidst waste pumped into the waters of our city beach filled me with disgust and anger.
>
> The community joined together in protest. I was right there alongside, protesting to stop the pollution of our kapata kai and continued desecration of Tangaroa. Standing together to make a difference for future generations, for the mokopuna of us all. The protest got a lot of publicity. I got publicity for the stand I was taking. My participation in protesting was in care of the environment, of Tangaroa, of God's creation. However, my actions were met with fierce resistance and criticism within the Christian church where I was a priest. Some senior Pākehā church members reprimanded me. Reprimanded for caring about God's creation, for my sense of responsibility for guardianship of Tangaroa, for standing with my people and exposing the effects of decisions made by those in power.

Brent's tears flow as he speaks. Our tears flow with his. We have the sense of the tears of the ancestors mixing with ours. As we sit with the sea in our vision, the betrayal becomes something in which we are all implicated. We all share in the desecration of the earth. We are brought face-to-face with our own complicity, and our failures of responsibility for ecological justice.

Adri

Adri uses the small screen in the dining room to project images of landscapes, people, art, words, and family. She weaves between stories of many losses: of lives, relationship, country, identity, and migration, as she presents "mourning as becoming": "perhaps mourning has to do with agreeing to undergo a transformation (perhaps one should say submitting to transformation) the full result of which one cannot know in advance" (Butler, 2006a, p. 21).

On the screen Adri projects a photo, introducing her family's arrival in Aotearoa.

> Here is the moment. The ship Waterman arrives in Lyttelton Harbour, New Zealand. It is 1956. My parents arrived six months apart. My father arrived first, alone with only one suitcase. They left their parents in the land of their birth.
>
> Immigration disrupts the sense of belonging to a land, a language, a people and a culture. By speaking my name and connecting it to my ancestors I speak myself into existence, making visible the absence of my heritage and people. I stand with all people who suffer vast population transfers that Butler (2006b) associates with the diaspora. Butler quotes Said (2003, p. 53) who wrote of the "unresolved cosmopolitan consciousness of someone who is both inside and outside their community." I live outside of the land of my ancestors. This is the place from where I speak.

Alongside her own dislocation from the land of her ancestors, Adri speaks the pain of knowing that New Zealand's white immigration policy afforded her parents entitlements at the expense of Māori displacement. Her parents were unwittingly part of a specific selection to ensure White domination, policies denying Māori their *tangata whenua* status.

For Rahera this is an important point for new migrants and all non-Māori to understand, that the hospitality that *tangata whenua* offer to newcomers is a welcome that arises out of First Nation status: as *tangata whenua* Māori are not merely one of a number of ethnic groups who occupy Aotearoa. Adri's migration story, together with Rahera's teaching, has us all reconsider the privilege and responsibilities of calling Aotearoa home.

Ako: Reciprocal Learning

Bishop and Glynn (1999) suggest that *ako*, the Māori word that means both to teach and to learn, promotes "learning of knowledge-in-action" (p. 170). Throughout the week at Maniaroa, learning arises from constant processes of knowledge-in-action. Rahera and others prepared for our coming, welcoming us with generous hearts, shaping knowledge for our learning encounters. In the welcoming call and speeches, the singing, and the *hongi* with which students were greeted; in the shared work in the kitchen; in walking, laughing, and singing together; in the rich cultural stories told in the *wharenui*; in the student presentations, our learning is of and for knowledge-in-action. The actions of these moments of this week are knowledge-in-action at the indigene-colonizer hyphen. We have encountered the privilege "to know ourselves in relationship with Others, to locate ourselves in the 'between'—to develop a stronger sense of how our selves are and have been formed in the troubled engagement with indigenous peoples and their lands and spaces" (Jones & Jenkins, 2008, p. 482). And the actions are also anticipated actions as we together foresee our ethical responsibilities towards socially just practice in counseling.

> *Toia te waka matauranga*
> *Ma wai e to? Maku e to, mau e to*
> *Ma te whakaranga ake e to*
> Haul forth the canoe of education
> Who should haul it? I should, you should
> All within calling distance should haul the canoe
> (See Macfarlane, 2007, p. 161)

Reflection Questions

1. What most captures your attention in this chapter in terms of doing social justice?
2. What links do you make with your own commitments to social justice?
3. Having read our account, what possibilities for counselor education might you anticipate in your context?

Glossary

ako—to learn/teach
Aotearoa—New Zealand
hongi—press noses in greeting
iwi—tribe
kapata kai—food cupboard/source
karakia—blessing
manaaki—to care for, respect
manaakitanga—care, hospitality
mana whenua—prestige, history, knowledge and practices associated tribal land
Māori—indigenous person of Aotearoa/New Zealand
marae atea—open area in front of the meeting house
mauri—life principle
mokopuna—grandchildren, descendants

Ngāti Kapatuhi; Ngāti Maniapoto; Ngāti Porou—tribal names
noho marae—education experience with overnight stay, at traditional tribal place
Pākehā—non-Maori, European—descendants of settlers
Papatūānuku—Mother Earth
Tangaroa—[guardian of] the sea
tangata whenua—local people/people of the land
taniwha—water spirit
Te Kohinga Mārama—*marae* at the University of Waikato
tēnā koe—greeting
tino rangitiratanga—Māori sovereignty
whaea—respected older woman ("aunty")
whakapapa—genealogy
whānau—family
wharenui—meeting house

Notes

1   Where possible we provide an immediate in-text translation of Maori language, comple-menting the glossary at the end of the chapter.
2   On Google maps, Awakino Heads Road, Awakino 4376, offers a view of this location. The satellite view shows the marae buildings, with red roof, opposite the southern end of Awakino Heads Road.
3   Rahera, a graduate of the MCouns program, has been assigned hosting responsibilities by her people.
4   The introductions to these first-person accounts have been written by Kathie and Elmarie, in consultation with each student. The first-person accounts are from each student's own writing.

References

Bishop, R., & Glynn, T. (1999). *Culture counts: Changing power relations in education.* Palmerston North, New Zealand: Dunmore.
Butler, J. (2005). *Giving an account of oneself.* New York, NY: Fordham University Press.
Butler, J. (2006a). *Precarious life: The powers of mourning and violence.* London: Verso.
Butler, J. (2006b). *Primo Levi for the present.* [Video file]. Retrieved from www.youtube.com/watch?v=UBNIYA9MCfs
Caputo, J. (Ed.). (1997). *Deconstruction in a nutshell: A conversation with Jacques Derrida.* New York, NY: Fordham University Press.
Crocket, K., & Kotzé, E. (2010). Narrative/postmodern perspectives on counselor education. In G. McAuliffe & K. Eriksen (Eds.), *Handbook of counselor preparation: Constructivist, developmental, and experiential approaches* (pp. 393–406). Thousand Oaks, CA: Sage.
Crocket, K., Kotzé, E., & Flintoff, V. (2007). Reflections on shaping the ethics of our teaching practice. *Journal of Systemic Therapies, 26*(3), 29–42. doi: 10.1521/jsyt.2007.26.3.29
Durie, M. (1989). A move that's well overdue: Shaping counselling to meet the needs of Maori people. *New Zealand Counselling and Guidance Association Journal, 2*(1), 13–23.

Durie, M. (2001). *Mauri ora: The dynamics of Maori health*. Melbourne, Australia: Oxford University Press.

Jones, A., & Jenkins, K. (2008). Rethinking collaboration: Working the indigene-colonizer hyphen. In N. Denzin, Y. Lincoln, & L. Smith (Eds.), *Handbook of critical indigenous methodologies* (pp. 471–486). Thousand Oaks, CA: Sage.

Macfarlane, A. H. (2007). *Discipline, democracy and diversity: Working with students with behaviour difficulties*. Wellington, New Zealand: NZCER Press.

Monk, G., Winslade, J., & Sinclair, S. (2008). *New horizons in multicultural counseling: New directions for working with diversity*. Thousand Oaks, CA: Sage.

New Zealand Association of Counsellors. (2002). *Code of ethics*. Hamilton, New Zealand: Author.

O'Connor, M., & Macfarlane, A. (2002). New Zealand Maori stories and symbols: Family value lessons for Western counsellors. *International Journal for the Advancement of Counselling, 24*(4), 223–237. doi: 10.1023/A:1023368729169

Olson, G., & Worsham, L. (2000). Changing the subject: Judith Butler's politics of radical resignification. *JAC: Journal of Rhetoric Culture and Politics, 20*(4), 727–765. Retrieved from http://jaconlinejournal.com

Said, E. W. (2003). *Freud and the non-European*. London: Verso.

Smith, L. T. (1999). *Decolonising methodologies: Research and indigenous peoples*. Dunedin, New Zealand: University of Otago Press.

Waldegrave, C. (1985). Mono-cultural, mono-class, and so called non-political family therapy. *Australian and New Zealand Journal of Family Therapy, 6*(4), 197–200. doi: 10.1002/j.1467–8438.1985.tb01141.x

Waldegrave, C. (1990). Just therapy. *Dulwich Centre Newsletter, 1*, 5–47. Retrieved from http://dulwichcentre.com.au

PART III

Accessing Local Knowledge

The anthropologist Clifford Geertz coined the term "local knowledge" to capture the intimate familiarity with the particularities of a culture that only insiders themselves possess. The phrase is resonant with therapeutic practice that leans in to social justice concerns because it speaks of privileging the voices of clients. Achieving that through collaborative dialogue involves helping people notice and separate from dominant discourses that mute their purposes, while being mindful of how therapy itself can inadvertently collude in that muting by imposing normative standards for "growth," "change," "health," and so on. The chapters in Part III approach this challenge from a variety of perspectives, exploring the empowering consequences of a tenacious curiosity about local knowledge.

In Chapter 7, The Therapist as Second Author: Honoring Choices from Beyond the Pale, Gene Combs and Jill Freedman capture the spirit of attending to local knowledge by characterizing the therapist as a second author. The chapter shows how a narrative therapist's job is to help people supplant, subvert, and question the domination of normative judgments; to recognize, celebrate, and spread the news of meaningful lives lived beyond the pale of the dominant culture. Inspired by the writings of Michel Foucault, narrative therapists assist in bringing forth and witnessing stories of nonstandard lives—lives lived meaningfully and fulfillingly in response to unjust norms. Drawing on a mix of personal anecdotes and clinical examples, the chapter describes some of the subtleties of taking what Michael White called a "decentered but influential" therapist stance.

In Chapter 8, Finding Ways Forward: Social Justice for Counselors in the Evolution of a Collaborative Practice and Study Group, Lynn Bloom and Noah Spector tell the intriguing story of the evolution of a peer supervision group as the group strives to find a balance between maintaining homogeneity of practice while being open to diverse voices within its membership. The chapter introduces the Narrative Therapy Study Group, whose initial mandate was to create a venue for learning and practicing narrative therapy. Narrative's attention to the politics of voice encouraged members to reflect on how issues of social justice are always at play in relationships, whether the conversations between counselors and clients, or the collective conversations among colleagues. As members articulated their various learning preferences, the study group's focus became more eclectic, though it remained committed to core values of respect and collaboration that brought members together in the first place. The chapter is a demonstration of how an ethic of social justice plays out among counselors in a collective process of co-creating a study group uniquely suited to the needs of its members.

Chapter 9, "Social Justice" as Relational Talk, cautions against the insidious potential of therapy to be a colonizing force that nudges clients in the direction of socially sanctioned ways of being. After presenting illustrations of how this routinely and inadvertently occurs, Dan Wulff and Sally St. George present examples of "walking the talk" of social justice by inviting families to critique and analyze social discourses from within therapeutic conversations. The practice is founded on questions that unpack what are too often characterized as people's "personal troubles" in order to see them as relational creations frequently fed by social inequities. Examples include encouraging an exploration of comments by clients about unfairness, as well as collaborative interrogations of taken-for-granted "shoulds" and other entrenched assumptions about normative ways of being that operate on individuals and families but are not always subject to critical evaluation. Wulff and St. George argue that to overlook these influences is to conspire in keeping them hidden. Instead, they propose an unmasking of what they call the "daily injustices" to open new possibilities for addressing individual and family distress.

The section ends with Chapter 10, Collaborative-Dialogic Practices: A Socially Just Orientation, a case illustration by Saliha Bava, Rocío Chaveste Gutiérrez, and Papusa Molina, which demonstrates an intriguing perspective on local knowledge, characterizing it as a relational process arising in responsive dialogue. Their chapter tracks the identity transformation of a former gang member in Merida, Mexico. The story is told through a series of encounters between gang members and a community worker, and serves to illustrate key principles of Collaborative-Dialogic Practices (CDP). Distinct from the metaphor of "treating" a client, CDP is characterized by a "not-knowing" stance on the part of practitioners, who engage in mutual inquiry with the persons who consult them. Working this way, power is decentralized; a key skill comprises the ability to avoid assuming the role of the expert who labels problems and proposes solutions. The focus is on creating language expressive of the particular social interaction without imposing a singular language which risks privileging a "helper's" interpretation. The chapter recounts the transformation of gang member Vanilla who, over the course of a series of interactions with community workers, eventually reclaims his given name Manuel when he leaves the street life and takes on a job in community development.

CHAPTER 7

The Therapist as Second Author: Honoring Choices from Beyond the Pale

Gene Combs and Jill Freedman

We find the metaphor of "the pale," as used in the phrase "beyond the pale," useful in maintaining a commitment to social justice in our work. "Pale" (from the Latin word *palus*) originally referred to a stake of the sort that is used to make a fence. The term has generalized so that it applies to the real or imagined fences that demarcate the boundaries of a given culture. Thus, under Catherine the Great, "the Pale of Settlement" referred to the area on the Western border of Russia where Jews were allowed to live. Conversely, in Ireland, The Pale of Dublin marked the boundary of English Imperial culture. Irish peasants living beyond the pale were not protected by The Crown. Thus beyond the pale has come to mean "outside the bounds of civilization" or "outrageous."

Several authors (e.g., De La Torre & Floyd-Thomas, 2011; MacMullan, 2005; Sanneh, 2010) have taken the pale a step farther, using it as a deadly serious pun meaning "beyond whiteness" in works that examine the bounds of privilege set by racism. Because we are both white, we find this extension of the metaphor helps us keep that privilege in mind as we work for social justice.

Although they may not think about it this way, most people who come to therapy do so because they or someone influential in their lives has concluded that they are living in ways that are beyond the pale of contemporary culture. Standards of what is good and proper in terms of class, wealth, gender, race, beauty, academic achievement, athletic ability, or psychological functioning set up idealized versions of accomplishment and success that function as societal fences, allowing only some of us to live inside the pale of polite society, while keeping others marginalized. As therapists who wish to support social justice (Combs & Freedman, 2012), we think it is our job to create a space that allows people to live meaningful lives—perhaps even to celebrate their "nonstandard" lives—when circumstances or their preferences place them beyond the pale of societal norms. We approach social justice work as the promotion of an "insurrection of subjugated knowledges." This phrase, from the work of Michel Foucault (1980, p. 81), refers not to replacing one narrow set of standards with another, more just, set of narrow standards, but to giving voice and legitimacy to a wide range of knowledges and practices that have previously been disqualified. Foucault (1980, p. 82) says:

I also believe that it is through the re-emergence of these low-ranking knowledges, these unqualified, even directly disqualified knowledges ... a particular, local, regional knowledge, a differential knowledge incapable of unanimity and which owes its force only to the harshness with which it is opposed by everything surrounding it—that it is through the re-appearance of this knowledge of these local popular knowledges, these disqualified knowledges, that criticism performs its work.

The standard discourses of traditional psychotherapy can all too easily constitute a set of restrictive norms that narrowly define healthy, well-functioning individuals and families. In therapy guided by these standard, normative discourses (such as DSM diagnoses and structuralist ideas of healthy families), a therapist's job becomes one of helping people to meet or exceed the dominant norms. A narrative therapist's job, as we construe it, is different. We want to help people question the domination of normative judgments; to have the possibility of recognizing, celebrating, and spreading the news of meaningful lives lived beyond the pale of the dominant culture.

David Paré (1995, p. 7) has reminded us that this mindset applies not just to narrative therapy, but to all therapies based in social constructionism:

A social constructionist epistemology, which construes knowledge as embedded in language and arising from culture, inevitably must call into question any accepted clinical wisdom regarding appropriate hierarchies and boundaries, any normative prescriptions for what constitutes a "healthy" family. When our gaze extends beyond the Western cultures that gave rise to mainstream family therapy, we discover that our fundamental conceptions of the child, of mothers' love, of the self, and of countless other constructs are widely differentiated across contemporary societies.

We are aware that working from within this mindset can be more challenging in some contexts than others. One of us (JF) works in a private practice in which there is relative freedom to develop and flow with non-standard desires and values. The other (GC) works in a large University/Corporate hospital system where the combined kingdoms of the medical model and corporate capitalism stake out more circumscribed boundaries. Although the contexts of our daily work are different, we are both guided by a narrative, post-structuralist, social-justice-focused way of working and of experiencing the world.

Overview

We once saw Michael White do a consultation interview with a man who, in looking back on his history of repeatedly hurting women in relationships, had decided to remain single. For this man, the choice was an act of personal accountability. He could imagine a more satisfying future in following the choice; he liked the person he would be in taking that path. However, the interview included a reflecting team, and during the team's reflections, a participant expressed sorrow at the man's choice, saying she saw relationships as the most wonderful way to embrace life. She said it made her sad to think of the man never participating in that. When the time came to reflect on the reflections, Michael was adamant in honoring the man's choice; he took great care not to let it get overshadowed by the woman's sadness. This experience caught our attention, and as we have remembered it and discussed it through time, it has become a symbol for the seductive pull of dominant discourses and norms, and of the ethical questions surrounding the power therapists wield over how people's choices are responded to. We want people to be the privileged authors, the "first authors," of their life narratives, and we want those narratives to find support, audience, and sustenance when they are being lived out in territory beyond the pale of dominant norms.

This experience was particularly helpful to us personally when we were embarking on the journey to adoption. Although no one officially judges whether people are fit to become parents when they form their families biologically, it is very different for parents who want to adopt. There are interviews, home inspections, reference checks, and classes that are required of people hoping to adopt. The instructor began the first class we attended with these words: "All adoption is born of grief." We, in fact, were thrilled to be adopting and have continued to be thrilled with the entire experience. If we could go back in time and become biological parents instead, we would not take that choice. But, in order for our dreams to come true, we had to be "approved" by the agency whose representative was telling us that we should grieve and that our plan was made in sadness, with the implication that this way of creating a family was second best. We are not suggesting that our daughter's birth parents may not have experienced grief or that her separation from them may not have included grief for her. We are suggesting that the person who evaluated us as potential parents was in a position of power from which, guided by the dominant idea that adoptive parents have "issues" with grief, she could have diminished our joy. Instead, our narrative, Foucauldian worldview let us form our happy family outside the pale of grief.

We can't completely separate ourselves from our cultures of origin. Few of us would want to give up all our biases, nor should we. What is required is a commitment to understanding as many of our biases as we can and to reviewing the effects of those biases. Our job is much more to ask questions than to answer them; and, as Rachel Hare-Mustin (1994) reminded us more than 20 years ago, it is our job to ask questions that invite people to reflect on the discourses that are shaping their desires, their intentions, and their ideas about what is possible. If we think of therapy as taking place in a mirrored room, if we only reflect standard cultural discourses, those will be the ones through which we understand the lives and relationships of the people we work with. If we don't challenge the discourses in the mirrored room of therapy, it may be that no one will. Often this involves noticing discourses that are absent from the room and making space for them in the therapeutic conversation. We want and need to be influential in this process, but we strive to stay in the position of second authors. We want to be "influential but de-centered" (White, 2005, p. 9).

Adrienne Rich (1986, p. 99) reminds us:

> When those who have the power to name and to socially construct reality choose not to see you or hear you … when someone with the authority of a teacher, say, describes the world and you are not in it, there is a moment of psychic disequilibrium, as if you looked in the mirror and saw nothing. It takes some strength of soul—and not just individual strength but collective understanding—to resist this void, this non-being, into which you are thrust, and to stand up, demanding to be seen and heard.

We do not think it is just to expect people coming for help to "resist this void" and "demand … to be seen and heard" with no support or encouragement. We think it is more appropriately the responsibility of the therapist (who, like it or not, is in a more powerful position) to help socially construct a reality that honors the circumstances and preferences of people who are struggling with the effects of marginalization. We set the context. We get paid. We talk about the other people's difficulties and potentially embarrassing circumstances, not our own. As Vikki Reynolds (2011) writes, "Our work can replicate the kinds of dominance we hope to alleviate, accommodating people to lives of poverty, and participating in social control" (p. 35).

Supporting a person's choice, helping him or her stand up and be heard or even helping someone to hear their own voice speaking their own preferences, is a demanding task. Without even recognizing it, we can make people feel invisible and unheard, so we strive to really listen, and to understand people's preferences, hopes, and values. At the same time, we recognize that people don't always choose well; what first comes out of their mouths as statements of their desire or intention can be problems talking through them. For example, I (JF) worked with a young person who wanted to drop out of high school. In a slow, careful unpacking of his conclusion that dropping out would be the best choice, it became apparent that some unfortunate experiences at school had convinced him that he didn't have what it took to make it as a student. When I asked questions that helped him consider other ways he might look at those experiences, it became clear that he had hopes and dreams that he could best meet by staying in school, and that he had the makings of a good-enough student. He is currently doing well in his second year of college.

Conversations in which we honor people as the privileged authors of their own stories are by necessity exploratory and tentative. We need to stay open to supporting a young person's choice to (for instance) not pursue education, but we want to make sure it is really his considered choice. We, like the reflecting team member in the example of Michael White's consulting interview, can be blind to the pull of cultural discourses. We can all too easily assume that the boundaries set by normative stories constitute the universe—that anything outside their pale is too outrageous or too dangerous to be considered. It is important that we strive to carefully understand and honor the non-standard choices people are drawn to, and to stay out of the "first author" position as we help them examine the effects of their choices. Thinking of ourselves as second authors—paraphrasing, questioning, reflecting, offering (but not imposing) editorial comments—helps us keep our balance as we question the influence of discourses and unpack people's positions so that both they and we are clearer about what supports and what undermines their preferences and the possibilities they perceive for their lives.

The most important thing we do to bring forth people's marginalized, but cherished, desires and dreams is to go *slowly*. This gives us a chance to unpack and understand people's thinking and preferences and makes us less likely to lead with our assumptions. I (GC) work with an immigrant from Mexico who had a debilitating injury from an accident at work and was lied to and cheated by his employer and the doctors who worked for the employer's disability insurer. He had previously seen several therapists, all of whom had urged him to be satisfied with his disability payments and to move on, not to focus his life on the accident and the unjust treatment. In slow, careful conversations I listened and asked small questions, intending to unpack his experience. Together, we came to the conclusion that what was most important to him was "having his day in court"; having an official societal audience to the injustices he had suffered. He didn't care about the money he might or might not get. He did care about speaking out about what happened to him and how particular privileged, prejudiced people had humiliated him and brought pain to his life. Even though colleagues might have thought it was not in this man's best interest to help him maintain his focus on speaking out—that it would be better to help him let go and move on—he found it very meaningful to speak his desire and have it heard. He has gone through several lawyers, all of whom have ended up urging him to accept an out of court settlement. He has taught himself more law than I will ever know. But the lopsidedness of power in our courts has blocked him again and again. Never losing the thread of the accident, his rage at mistreatment, and his hunger for a day in court, our conversations over time have come to include other contexts in which he can speak out and stand for justice. He has involved himself in local politics, especially with helping sponsor and promote a group for undocumented young people. He is still seeking his day in court, but he is also finding joy and fulfillment in helping young people stand up for recognition and fair treatment. He has learned to tell the story of his ongoing struggle for justice in a way that is inspiring for members of his marginalized community and that sustains him in the struggle. He has said that this therapy has supported what he cares about, rather than getting him to adapt to what others think best.

One thing that makes the conversations we are focusing on here tricky is that discourses are generally simple and absolute in their definitions and requirements, but people's lives are complex. I (JF) worked with one family in which the father struggled with alcoholism. He had been absent at important times and violent at others. Different communities, with their different sets of valued norms and assumptions, would tend to assume different things about this man, and fit him into different pigeonholes—"abuser," "alcoholic," "sexist"—but my focus was on assisting family members in telling their own stories of their particular struggles according to their values. At one point in our conversations, his adult daughter told a story of times that he had told her she could be whatever she wanted to be. She said that this message had supported her throughout her life. "You are a good father," she told him. The good father story was true and meaningful, but it lay outside the pale of standard assumptions about men who have been (at times) violent, drunk, and absent. In our work as second authors, rather than insisting that people shape their experience into something universal, simple, and consistent, we try to support the "truth" in narratives that have complex meanings that don't fit neatly together. Dickerson (2014) describes this as "utilizing the poststructuralist position/belief in multiple identities or multiple versions of self" (p. 407).

The prevailing discourses about therapy can lead us to expect that therapists will share their wisdom and determine the direction of therapy based on their professional knowledge. But this sort of centered, therapist-as-first-author help can only ever give legitimacy to "expert" stories; stories from within the pale of the very norms and values that have already pathologized and excluded the people we are sitting with. We want to help people; we don't want to withhold useful information when we have it, but we want to be very careful not to impose unnecessary limits on people or to judge them by unjust or overly limiting standards. The balance necessary for staying influential but decentered takes near-constant practice and reflection. Michael White (1997) provided a list of practices that he recommended as useful in this tricky balancing act. Our paraphrase of his list is as follows:

- Keep the knowledge, skills, and preferences of the person(s) seeking help at the center.
- Maintain awareness of, and reflection on, the power relationships at play in the therapy itself.
- Maintain awareness of, and reflection on, the power relations of everyday life and how they provide the context for the problems that bring people to therapy.
- Monitor and take responsibility for the effects of our actions on the lives and relationships of the people who consult with us.

Narrative Practices

The most important aspect of honoring stories from beyond the pale is the narrative, post-structuralist worldview that helps us see legitimacy in lives lived outside of dominant discourses. This worldview colors all of our practices. We would like to discuss the way just a few narrative practices help us bring forth, hear, and support marginalized, non-standard stories while staying in the position of second author.

Externalization

Narrative therapy is probably best known for its central practice of externalizing problems. When we externalize a problem, we usually seek to locate it in a discourse rather than in the person or persons affected by the discourse. For instance, when a person speaks of their problem as "depression," instead of asking what it feels like to be depressed, we begin an inquiry into the effects of depression (which we hold in our own minds as an external, objectified entity) on his or her life. If they name, for example, feelings of worthlessness as an effect, we may inquire about what standards they are measuring their worth by. We can then ask about who sets those standards and whether those are the people and institutions they want to be in charge of their lives. In doing so, we are deconstructing the problem by showing how it is a construction linked to a discourse. This allows us to help people remember and reflect on their own knowledge in a different light, outside the shadow of the pathologizing discourse. This questioning of the boundaries drawn by the dominant culture supports a way of working that offers the possibility of valuing and building on stories from beyond the pale. We do this unpacking through small questions in tentative steps so that we can maximize chances for people to find their own way rather than having their path dictated by us.

Mapping a Statement of Position

Mapping a "statement of position" (White, 2005) is a highly structured process that we sometimes follow in helping people clarify and more fully describe where they stand in relation to a problem. Once people have clearly stated their position, documented it, and had it witnessed by a therapist (and perhaps others), they can decide in a step-by-step way the path they want to follow in maintaining that position.

There are four steps in mapping a statement of position:

1. *Negotiate a name for, and description of, the problem.* We seek descriptions that are in people's language, not expert language, and that fit closely with their experience. This very first step is based on the assumption that expert categories are not sufficient to identify problems and that the person in relationship with the problem is the more appropriate namer. Rather than therapists naming a problem "depression," for example, a person coming for consultation may, with careful, patient questioning, name it "the heavy hand of hopelessness." When we follow this step we immediately put people in the position of first author.

2. *Map the effects of the problem.* Rather than following a generalized list of the way problems work, we ask people about the particular effects of a problem in their lives and relationships. We could think of this step as bringing forth the story of what the problem has done so far. In suggesting that the story be told in terms of effects, we are exerting influence; but in naming which effects are important to him or her, the person stays in first author position.

3. *Ask the person to evaluate the effects that have been named.* Our role in this step is not to counter the effects or to suggest ways to resist them, it is only to ask questions that invite people to evaluate the effects of the problem in their lives and relationships. The practice we describe here is a radical departure from more expert approaches in which therapists evaluate the people who seek their help. We ask people to evaluate for themselves each of the effects they have described, according to their own values and standards. We facilitate their evaluation with questions such as:
   - Do you think this is helpful or not helpful?
   - Is this what you want for your life or would you prefer something else?
   - What is it like for the problem to be causing this effect in your life?
4. *Ask people to justify the evaluations they have made in the third step.* These two steps are actually paired, so that after we ask, "Do you think this is helpful or not helpful?" we might ask, "Why is this not helpful?' or after asking, "Is this what you want for your life or would you prefer something else?" we might ask, "Can you tell me what you would prefer and why that would be preferable?" Many therapists learning this practice wonder about asking people to justify an evaluation they have made, because the answer often seems obvious. Through this practice we have learned that although things may seem obvious, the "obviousness" is an effect of assumptions that are so popular, so much a part of standard discourse, that we are blind and deaf to them. This step invites people to truly be in the first author position; it allows room for them to name purposes, intentions, and preferences that may not have occurred to the therapist at all.

While we don't always fully and formally map a statement of position, we find that practice with this way of thinking and working helps us give shape and direction to our interactions with the people who come to us for help, and it helps us "lead from behind," staying in the second author position.

Situating

Michael White (1995, p. 69) writes:

> If I make a comment that comes across as a strong opinion … it only leaves the person or the family with the choice of either submitting to my opinion or railing against it. If, however, I have the opportunity to situate this comment within the context of my personal experience, imagination, and intentional states, then persons can determine for themselves how they might take the comment. This opens many possibilities for dialogue and for the consideration of alternative views and opinions.

From the very first time we meet, we ask people if they have questions they would like to ask us. We say something like, "You are deciding whether to open your life to me. There may be some things important for you to know in doing that." This question both exposes the power difference in our positions in the therapy context and offers a suggestion about one way to justly respond to that difference. Some people respond and ask questions as we are negotiating a therapy relationship. But even if they do not, we suggest that as we go along, if they have questions about why we asked a particular question or said a particular thing that we welcome their questions. This practice is meant as a way to be clear that we are speaking as particular people rather than as experts speaking with the disembodied voice of Psychology. We want it to be very clear that we are open to discussing our experience in relation to a specific question or comment so that those working with us can decide for themselves how to take what we have said. This practice also helps us cultivate an ongoing awareness of our privilege, and of the fact that as white, economically advantaged, cis-gendered people with advanced degrees we have easy access to many things that are much less available to the people who have come to us for help.

Taking It Back Practices

One way we can respond to the power difference built into therapy relationships is to recognize and acknowledge that these relationships are not one-way and that we are always affected by them. By letting someone know that their experience taught us something, moved us in some way or influenced the ideas we bring to other therapy relationships, we are recognizing the contribution people make to our own lives and to the lives of others, even though the focus is on their particular difficulties and desires. Michael White (1997, p. 146) says:

> Taking it back practices are not a formula for the production of a form of therapist-centeredness, but are an antidote to this … the expressions and the agenda of the persons seeking consultation remain at the center of the work.

"Taking it back" might be as simple as saying, "The way you described what it meant to you to be able to buy an ice cream cone for your grand-daughter came back to me as I was sharing ice cream with my daughter; it made the moment richer." Or it might involve ongoing discussions, such as the ones we described earlier in this chapter with the Mexican immigrant seeking his day in court. A recurring theme in my (GC) conversations with that man was my acknowledgment of what he was teaching me about the subtleties of anti-immigrant prejudice and the pervasiveness of its influence in his community.

Therapist Roles

While we find "second author" to be a useful guiding metaphor for our role in approaching therapy as a project of social justice in which we seek to support an insurrection of subjugated knowledges, there are other, related, role descriptions that we also find helpful.

Interviewer

As a partner in conversation we primarily ask questions. Although asking questions is influential, in that each question proposes a specific, limited domain for conversation, people can answer in many ways, including not answering at all or asking a question in return. Thinking of our main role as one of asking questions keeps us out of first author position. It leaves more space for people to be the primary authors of their own life narratives.

Recording Secretary

We take notes during our conversations, striving to accurately record the words and images people use. In asking for permission to take notes we often say, "If I try to remember what you say, it will be my story of your story, but if I write down your words, it will be your story." We give family members copies of our notes if they would like to have them, and we keep copies so that we can track preferred stories as they develop in people's own words. In my (GC) hospital-based work, I take delight in keeping my notes as free of medical jargon as possible and in making it clear that I am keeping something more like a journal of people's personal, particular hopes, dreams, and accomplishments, than a generalized record in medical-ese of their pathology, faults, and flaws.

Archivist

We not only record and keep notes; we also collect and save videos, drawings, transcripts, and the like as part of an archive of insider knowledge that, with permission, we can share with others who are struggling with similar problems. This sharing of insider knowledge helps keep us decentered while helping to foster a community in which marginalized people support each other in living vibrant, meaningful, non-standard lives. For a rich example of this sort of archival work, see the anti-anorexia work of David Epston and various colleagues (Epston et al., 2000–2013; Maisel, Epston, & Borden, 2004).

Documentarian

Besides our notes, we regularly make documents that can take the form of memos, letters, certificates, or proclamations as a way of recognizing, thickening and circulating knowledge of people's accomplishments, stands, and turning points. In documenting particular, local knowledge and accomplishments, which often occur outside the pale, we increase their legitimacy and memorability. This could be as simple as a handwritten post-it note that says "Timmy is against bullying."

Or it might be a formally printed and framed declaration of an important new project such as one we made for a woman named Pat, titled "Pat's Stand on Living and Dying," which lists 12 different reasons, in her own words, that Pat was now choosing to resist the effects of abuse and claim the right to live a full and happy life.

Audience

We contribute to people's experience of the meaningfulness and memorability of their stories by listening and responding. It can be particularly important for a person's audience to include someone who acknowledges the meaning of stories that the larger culture marginalizes or suppresses. For many people, a therapist might be the only attentive, supportive listener available.

Editor

In a practice that Michael White (2007, p. 46) called "editorializing," we need to be at our most mindful to avoid centering ourselves. In editorializing, we summarize what we are hearing and recording as our conversations unfold. This is our opportunity to check our understandings and get guidance about whether we are hearing what people want us to hear, and whether we are using images and words that closely track their experience. What we hear, record, and re-tell is unavoidably selective, and our selection is guided by particular intentions. We select externalized descriptions of what is problematic. We emphasize moments that stand outside the problematic narrative, and we seek out details of the stories that support what's useful to remember from those moments. But, to the extent that it is possible, we want to avoid imposing our own values, prejudices, or assumptions. Our editorial summaries are always probing for richer, thicker, more hope-filled descriptions, but those descriptions must, if we are true to our intentions, fit closely with the desires and dreams of the people who have come to us for help.

Spreader of News

Since we are more interested in local knowledge than professional knowledge, we can support marginalized stories by linking the lives of those who live out these stories to the lives of other people who share the purposes, intentions and values that infuse the stories. When we do this we help people join together in a sense of community in which their purposes are recognized, rather than marginalized. For example, I (JF) worked with a heterosexual couple who first described the problem as their married daughter and her two young children living in their basement. Their daughter's marital arrangement seemed to be erratic and not financially sound, but the daughter was committed to this relationship. The parents first described wanting to help re-launch the daughter through "tough love." But, after several conversations in which they declared their intentions without following through, I slowed down the process to carefully deconstruct their description and learn about their hopes and intentions. I learned that friends and family were urging them to stop lending their daughter their car, stop providing a home for her and their grandchildren, and stop making it possible for her not to work outside the home. Their friends and family had them thinking they must be co-dependent and failing as parents. But in our careful, slow conversation it emerged that it was important to these particular parents that their children, no matter how old, knew that they had a home. They, in fact, delighted in being present every day in the lives of their grandchildren. The problem was what *other* people thought, not what they were experiencing. By reaching out to our local therapy community, I was able to find another therapist working with a couple whose adult children also lived with them. My colleague asked if that couple might write down some of what sustained them in feeling good about their choice to do this. When I shared the short document with the couple I was seeing, they reported a sense of not being alone and said this feeling helped them hold on to their values when friends and family offered unsolicited advice.

Conclusion

A number of things are important in honoring choices from beyond the pale. At the top of the list is thinking about problems as located in discourses, rather than in people. Without this basic aspect of the narrative worldview, it is difficult to recognize possibilities that lie outside of dominant norms. Social justice aspects of the narrative worldview are reflected in many of the practices of narrative therapy, including asking questions so that the people coming for consultation provide their own answers, rather than the therapist offering answers through statements. It is important that we recognize the power imbalance inherent in therapy relationships and do our best to address that imbalance through practices such as carefully situating our responses. Being a second author is built into narrative therapy practices, but it is an ongoing responsibility, and a central tenet of social justice work, to recognize, thicken, support, and circulate the knowledge, skills and values that are carried in stories of people living on the margins of society.

Reflection Questions

1. Can you identify practices in your work that put you in the position of first author? If so, do you have ideas about how you could adapt these practices to position the persons you work with as first authors?
2. What assumptions that you make about those you work with might stand in the way of honoring their preferences and values?
3. Do you have thoughts about when in your work it would be most useful to situate what you are saying?
4. How can we be more accountable for our privilege as therapists?

References

Combs, G., & Freedman, J. (2012). Narrative, poststructuralism, and social justice: Current practices in narrative therapy. *The Counseling Psychologist, 40*, 1033–1060. doi: 10.1177/0011000012460662

De La Torre, M. A., & Floyd-Thomas, S. M. (2011). *Beyond the pale: Reading theology from the margins*. Louisville, KY: Westminster John Knox Press.

Dickerson, V. (2014). The advance of poststructuralism and its influence on family therapy. *Family Process, 53*, 401–414. doi: 10.1111/famp.12087

Epston, D., et al. (2000–2013). The archive of resistance: Anti-anorexia/anti-bulimia. Retrieved from www.narrativeapproaches.com/?page_id=42

Foucault, M. (C. Gordon, Ed.) (1980). *Power/knowledge: Selected interviews and other writings, 1972–1977*. New York, NY: Pantheon Books.

Hare-Mustin, R. (1994). Discourses in the mirrored room: A postmodern analysis of therapy. *Family Process, 33*(1), 19–35. doi: 10.1111/j.1545-5300.1994.00019.x

MacMullan, T. (2005). Beyond the pale: A pragmatist approach to whiteness studies. *Philosophy Social Criticism, 31*, 267–292. doi: 10.1177/0191453705051706

Maisel, R., Epston, D., & Borden, A. (2004). *Biting the hand that starves you*. New York, NY: Norton.

Paré, D. A. (1995). Of families and other cultures: The shifting paradigm of family therapy. *Family Process, 34*, 1–19. doi: 10.1111/j.1545-5300.1995.00001.x

Reynolds, V. (2011). Resisting burnout with justice-doing. *The International Journal of Narrative Therapy and Community Work, 4*, 27–45. Retrieved from http://dulwichcentre.com.au/international-journal-of-narrative-therapy-and-community-work

Rich, A. (1986). *Blood, bread, and poetry: Selected prose 1975–1989*. New York, NY: Norton.

Sanneh, K. (2010, April 12). Beyond the pale: Is white the new black? *The New Yorker*. Retrieved from www.newyorker.com/magazine/2010/04/12/beyond-the-pale-4

White, M. (1995). *Re-authoring lives: Interviews and essays*. Adelaide, Australia: Dulwich Centre Publications.

White, M. (1997). *Narratives of therapists' lives*. Adelaide, Australia: Dulwich Centre Publications.

White, M. (2005). Michael White workshop notes. Retrieved from www.dulwichcentre.com.au/michael-white-workshop-notes.pdf

White, M. (2007). *Maps of narrative therapy*. New York, NY: Norton.

CHAPTER 8

Finding Ways Forward: Social Justice for Counselors in the Evolution of a Collaborative Practice and Study Group

Lynn F. Bloom and Noah M. P. Spector

Within pressured work environments, collaborative practice groups have been shown to reduce isolation for mental health counselors (Paré, 2009, 2013), and to provide a place for connection and revitalization. Such peer-facilitated groups of counselors and mental health workers who get together to reflect on their practice have historically fulfilled multiple mandates, including supervision, peer support, interagency networking, knowledge exchange between university and community (Paré, 2009), and continuing education (Bloom et al., 2014).

This chapter recounts the story of the Narrative Therapy Study Group, or NTSG, a unique collaborative practice group that began in 2008 in Ottawa, Ontario. Comprised of frontline mental health counselors and social workers outside the boundaries of any formal institution, NTSG is a study and peer support group that operates independently without any external organizational funding or mandate. NTSG follows a strong tradition in the Ottawa area of collaborative practice groups, although it remains unique in character and design. Members of the group choose to participate outside of their regular work hours, selecting topics for group discussion that interest and inspire them. NTSG is grounded in post-modern or social constructionist ideas, in which reality and meanings are understood as co-constructed through dialogue (Haley, 2002) and individual identity is seen as impacted by powerful social and cultural forces (Paré, 2014).

The name "NTSG" attests to the group's origins as a study group dedicated to the acquisition of narrative therapy concepts and practices (White & Epston, 1990), which include: centering clients as experts, viewing problems as separate from people, and considering the social and cultural contexts in which problems thrive—concepts that we see as complementary to social justice aims. As the reader will see, NTSG has moved well beyond its original purpose of teaching narrative therapy, while still identifying with the social justice ideals and peer support intentions that inspired its members at the outset.

Traditionally, social justice is understood as an approach whereby counselors seek to minimize oppression and domination by social structures or organizations, and to ensure that their clients have fair access to resources and opportunities (Kennedy & Arthur, 2014). Part of this practice involves counselors reflecting on their own position of privilege and authority in relation to clients, and how they may incorporate client and systemic advocacy within a socially and politically informed practice (Kennedy & Arthur, 2014; Paré, 2014; Reynolds, 2011; Vera & Speight, 2003).

While counselors generally see social justice activities as applying to their work with clients, it is sometimes challenging for them to turn the spotlight on themselves. This chapter demonstrates how counselors' own communities of practice can also be affected by unequal power relationships that emerge in group communication with peers. It details a challenge that the NTSG encountered when its commitment to encouraging self-expression conflicted with its mandate to adhere strictly to the study of narrative therapy; ironically the group, which originally chose to study narrative therapy because of its alignment with non-oppressive practices, began imposing restrictions on which topics and ideas were acceptable for discussion. We recount how the group resolved this conflict by reflecting on the social justice values of promoting within-group diversity (Paré, 2014) and group inclusivity (Shapiro, 2003). The group decided to privilege these values over the mandate to adhere strictly to one proscribed theoretical lens. Ultimately, this decision generated vibrant discussions among members and enriched the counseling approaches of individual participants—even those whose primary theoretical orientation differed from a narrative therapy approach. By studying the resolution of this conflict, we show how a social justice approach can promote non-hierarchical interactions among peer support groups like NTSG.

By way of introduction, we (LB and NS) have been co-facilitators of NTSG for the past five years. In addition to sharing a social work background, with its foundational ethics of social justice and client autonomy, we also share a Jewish heritage, where issues of racism and oppression inform our identity and inspire our commitment to inclusivity and mutual respect. After more than 20 years as a hospital-based rehabilitation social worker, Lynn is currently in private practice in Ottawa, Ontario, and is a clinical and training associate at The Glebe Institute (a group of mental health practitioners in Ottawa who share a social constructionist practice orientation). Noah is a crisis intervention worker in a children's hospital emergency department and has a PhD in Educational Counseling. NTSG is comprised of mental health counselors from a variety of educational and personal backgrounds. Members of the group work in direct practice with a broad range of clients, in both private settings and within large institutions (i.e., hospitals and community centers). They come from diverse ethnic and socio-economic backgrounds and, as we have learned over our many group conversations, their personal and familial histories of discrimination and displacement have informed their work with marginalized populations. While the majority of group members have a stated preference for narrative therapy and related social constructionist approaches, they remain open to engaging and learning from a variety of theoretical perspectives, considering the extent to which these perspectives enrich their own skills and represent non-oppressive approaches to practice.

Statements from NTSG members who we interviewed for this chapter are included periodically so that their voices may be heard directly. Pseudonyms have been used to respect their confidentiality. In the first section, the early days of NTSG are recalled, when founding members gathered to learn the fundamentals of narrative therapy. The reader will be given a sense of what it was like to participate at the beginning, when members first discovered a supportive community of like-minded counselors. These early years of NTSG will then be contrasted with a subsequent period of tension during which NTSG changed its leadership style and welcomed new members with a more varied professional background and orientation. The origin of these tensions will be considered and examples provided of how they were resolved. The theme of social justice for participants figures prominently, relating to how NTSG opened up to the voices of all group members, even those whose original training and orientation diverge from a social constructionist perspective.

The chapter then goes on to consider NTSG as it is today, describing how the group is currently structured, and how it has evolved to a place where the expertise and knowledge of individual group members is honored and respected. The egalitarian space where group members gather for collaborative learning is described in some detail, and the authors provide an example of a peer-led session highlighting the career accomplishments of a group member. Finally, in the chapter's conclusion, we present a metaphor generated by NTSG group members to describe how they envision their place within the collaborative practice community from which they have emerged, a community that continues to inspire and sustain them.

NTSG Origins and Evolution

NTSG was co-founded by two counselors trained in narrative therapy as an eight-week, community-based study group for social workers and other mental health counselors. At the time of NTSG's inception in 2008, there were few opportunities for the focused study of narrative therapy within the Ottawa area. There were, however, local collaborative practice groups from which NTSG could draw inspiration and knowledge (Paré, 2009, 2011). Narrative therapy, as developed by Michael White and David Epston (1990), appealed to the original members because of its egalitarian, non-authoritarian approach to practice, its respect of client and worker competence, and its attention to social and cultural influences. Group participants were, from the outset and continue to be, committed to a social justice perspective that contextualizes counseling practice in this broader way.

The group of (usually) eight practicing social workers and mental health counselors met after work hours in a small, warmly lit counseling space rented to us for the evening by a local therapist. Much like NTSG today, most original members worked as front-line counselors and were accustomed to very little or no peer support within their work settings. As an original member of the group, I (LB) recall that the collaborative style of learning and the focus on reflective practice seemed startlingly original next to traditional, hierarchical forms of individual supervision where managers or senior clinicians adopted a more expert, evaluative stance.

These first NTSG sessions involved an explanatory lecture followed by an experiential component in which group members explored some of the practices of narrative therapy (White, 2007). NTSG co-leaders also posted "maps" of externalizing, remembering, and re-authoring on the walls of the room, so that participants could follow these ideas and learn to ask questions in a narrative manner. These "maps," or sequential questions, were intended to guide conversations away from problematic stories, to preferred stories connected to people's hopes, strengths, purposes, values, and intentions (Morgan, 2000).

A second part of the study group session involved an interview with a participant around a practice issue or personal issue impacting practice. The experiential component was structured using a reflecting team format following Michael White's description of definitional ceremony (Morgan, 2000; White, 1995).

I (LB) remember how powerful I found a re-authoring conversation when I was centered in such an interview. The co-leader asked me to name the thing that was holding me back from going to an international conference to speak on a narrative topic. I remember how she subsequently helped me to externalize my fear as "The Voice of Caution" and then to consider what skills I had already demonstrated in standing up to this fear. I remember this experience as transformational, marking a turning point in my career and freeing me to do many future public presentations.

During the interview, the co-leader asked me questions about the social and cultural forces that might support the hesitancy of women to speak in a public arena. This example helped bring forth, for me, the power of deconstructive questions, linking individual problems to cultural forces and power relationships in society (White, 1993). As a consequence, I have been able to ask my clients similar, empowering questions: what were the social and cultural forces in their lives that may have contributed to problems they might have viewed as self-generated?

Over the two years of NTSG's initial phase, many of the group members gained confidence in their understanding of narrative therapy ideas, and in their skills and abilities in applying these ideas to their counseling. I recall group participants expressing a passionate interest in this approach, and a desire to share their new learning with colleagues and clients outside the group setting. However, alongside a commitment to egalitarian values, I (LB) noticed that group members were corrected at times when expressing their unique viewpoints. Upon reflection, I recall being interrupted when, as a reflecting team participant, I expressed an idea that the co-leader explained was "interpretative"—that is, not grounded in my own experience. I further noted that the pressure to formulate discussion questions in a manner congruent with narrative practices occasionally led to the constriction of free-flowing dialogue. In other words, constraints upon dialogue, more evident as the group matured, were sometimes apparent even in these early training sessions.

In his writings, Michael White (2007) distanced himself from what he calls a "policing" (p. 5) of conversations in which narrative metaphors and maps might pre-determine or direct conversations. He expressed the hope that therapeutic conversations would open avenues of possibility rather than imposing ideas or templates. It would be inaccurate to state that the occasional correction of non-narrative formulations in the early NTSG group ever amounted to a totalitarian "policing" of conversations. However, constraints on dialogue, resembling the "policing" to which White (2007) refers, did emerge in a more problematic form in the group's second phase. It was then that tensions surrounding the theoretical "correctness" of participants' comments started impacting group dynamics more significantly. New group members were subtly discouraged from raising divergent ideas, and we began to struggle with issues of "voice" (whose ideas would be granted attention) and "hierarchy" (who would define our orientation and principles). Social justice for group members ultimately demanded an opening of space for dialogue, a process to be considered in the following section on NTSG's transitional phase of development.

Resisting Constraints—NTSG in Transition

NTSG entered a second phase in its evolution when the original co-leaders were no longer able to continue. The group, which wished to remain together, was in agreement when we stepped forward to become peer facilitators. NTSG thus became a peer-led group rather than one led by experts. This move entailed a re-distribution of power into the hands of group members, who were now engaged and accountable in determining the group's focus and future direction. As the new co-facilitators, we recall that at the time we felt a responsibility to uphold a social constructionist orientation and to focus on skill building in narrative therapy. Coincidentally, several new group members joined NTSG with the expressed desire to learn from narrative therapy but with foundational knowledge and training that diverged from NTSG's preferred orientation. The challenge was to incorporate these new members and orient them to narrative therapy, while not alienating them in the process.

As co-facilitators, we were wary of exploring concepts like "transference" or "attachment," which were periodically offered up by newer group members to explain phenomena observed during counseling conversations. When these ideas were raised, we initially told participants that a narrative therapy approach was not compatible with understandings of clients' thoughts and behaviors based on psychoanalytic ideas or other non-narrative conceptions. Ensuing discussions in the group regarding how transference and attachment could be reconfigured in narrative terms still did not resolve a tense atmosphere in sessions when these ideas were brought forward.

In reflecting on that time, I (LB) believe that my tone might have been too authoritative, and might have seemed offensive or dismissive. Following several reflective discussions, as facilitators, we came to realize that we were privileging our own ideas above those of the group members. We observed that this practice ironically went counter to the value of honoring each member's contributions. We felt that we were inadvertently exercising power over individual group members, thus contravening our guiding social justice principle of resistance to domination and oppression (Kennedy & Arthur, 2014; Young, 1990).

In our desire to respect all members' ideas, we began to question our well-intentioned but restrictive style of facilitation. Upon reflection, we wondered whether as group facilitators we were trying to keep a focus on narrative therapy training while, on a collective level, the group was resisting what many members identified as imposed constraints on spontaneous dialogue. The constraints were about the "policing" of dialogue, about which ideas were privileged and which were rejected, and about the suppression of ideas that did not fit what we understood to be the group's narrative therapy orientation. As co-facilitators, we recognized that the right to speak and the question of what can be spoken about are issues of power and voice, not only in the counseling relationship (Hare-Mustin, 1994) but in collaborative practice groups as well.

While in conversation with me (LB), one group member, Elaine, reflected on these issues:

> There was one instance, where, with a newer group member who had an opinion that was different, we did have an issue ... I think people were particularly passionate about how this did not agree with narrative, and maybe we came across as being a bit forceful. But it was reflected on and discussed. I think the fact that it was "caught" and reflected upon was a good thing.

Another group member, Geoff, reflected on one instance where his comments may not have been appreciated:

> Well, I remember on one occasion making a suggestion about something from psychodynamic therapy and it did not get a terribly strong support from the group so I thought to myself, "Maybe I did not express it very well, or maybe we were trying to focus on something else." But I think this was a one-off event. Generally, I think the group is quite open. Everyone listens.

Geoff indicated that his understanding of narrative ideas has evolved during his years in the group. Many of the ideas and skills of narrative therapy have informed his practice. For example, he has found the narrative idea of externalizing (i.e., considering problems as separate from people) particularly useful in his work. Rather than having left the group because of not feeling heard, he remains an important and valued group member.

As the group matured, NTSG members developed relationships of trust and mutual respect. Theoretical correctness became less important than creating a space where everyone felt comfortable sharing their ideas. As new facilitators, we were learning how to engage with members of different theoretical orientations in a more open and inclusive manner. The group was correspondingly engaged in a process of collective reflection, in which values of inclusivity and mutual support were re-shaping how dialogue would take place.

The work of Glen Larner (2011) was influential to us as co-facilitators at the time. Larner (2011), a clinician who worked for many years in mainstream mental health services, acknowledges the areas of shared language between post-modern and other approaches. He critiques postmodern approaches that reject competing paradigms, suggesting that such positions promote a potential intolerance of other perspectives and a turning away from available knowledge that might be helpful to clients. We felt that Larner's (2011) advice to be hospitable to other approaches fits well with our interest in the diverse views of group members and our increasing concern as facilitators that people were not feeling free to express themselves within the group. In cultivating an awareness and reflexivity in relation to the right to speak, we were hoping that power could be shared equally among the members, providing each member with unimpeded space for personal expression.

This hospitality to diverse approaches resonated with group members, who upheld the social justice value of respecting the right of every person to participate in conversations that concern them (Crethar, Rivera, & Nash, 2008). We were all conscious that relaxed, free-flowing dialogue could not occur in an environment where participants were not able to say what they thought without worries about being criticized.

As group members and co-facilitators engaged in this process of re-invention, we inevitably found ourselves departing to some extent from some founding premises of the group. While not evident at the time, it is now clear that the group was reflexively extending the boundaries of its mandate.

Despite a certain directional confusion, group members were clear that they wished to make space in the room for the consideration of other theories and practices that might be compatible with a narrative therapy approach. Concurrently, co-facilitators and most group members agreed on their commitment to a social constructionist orientation—towards non-oppressive practices, respect of individual diversity, and dialogic negotiation of meaning (Anderson, 2005; Gergen, 1991; Hoffman, 2000; Paré, 2014; Strong, 2000).

At this time, the group decided to invite guest speakers from non-narrative traditions into conversation. They were curious about how such theories and practices could inform their work, and to what degree these traditions incorporated ethics of egalitarian and client-centered practice. Examples of training sessions the group found compatible with narrative therapy included: mindfulness (Gehart & Paré, 2008), strengths-based CBT (Padesky & Mooney, 2012), sand tray (Preston-Dillon, 2009), narrative medicine (Charon, 2001), and letter writing (Shilts, Liscio, & Rambo, 2008). Rachel's comment below illustrates this open approach to other viewpoints:

I am all about learning from different perspectives. And it's narrative and CBT or narrative and emotion-focused therapy. Comparing and contrasting. It is interesting to learn about a new idea and to bring in the narrative piece. When you practice from a narrative perspective, it's a philosophical position. People are their own experts. I have trouble working from a pathology model but if people come from a place where they see clients as their own best experts, that's fine.

The Narrative Therapy Study Group in 2016

Today, NTSG is no longer solely dedicated to the mastery of narrative therapy skills, but identifies itself as an advanced practice study group with broader learning and peer support objectives. NTSG now requires new members to have a prerequisite introduction to narrative therapy and social constructionist ideas, as these ideas are considered foundational. Over time, NTSG group members, and we as co-facilitators, have become more comfortable when non-narrative ideas are brought forward during discussion. The present group atmosphere is more relaxed and we have noticed that members contribute to conversations in a more spontaneous manner.

NTSG continues to meet in Ottawa, in the private home office of two group members. At the beginning of each year, members contribute a fixed sum, which is used throughout the year to pay guest speakers. Eight, two-hour evening sessions are offered monthly from September to May. Members of NTSG who wish to facilitate a session are reimbursed for their work and have the opportunity of recouping almost the full amount of their yearly fees in the process. This financial remuneration makes NTSG more equitable and accessible to counselors who otherwise might have difficulty funding their own attendance. By encouraging members to facilitate sessions, NTSG adheres to a social justice perspective of focusing on practices that emerge from within communities and encouraging action outside of these communities (Helms, 2003; Paré, 2014). In the case of NTSG, participants are encouraged to inform themselves about a particular topic and teach this topic to the group. This process allows members to teach one another and to bring the knowledge gained in their preparation and presentation within NTSG to their practice outside the group.

NTSG's physical meeting space is small but intimate with paintings on the walls, stuffed animals perched along the top of a well-worn couch, and a diverse assortment of chairs offering seating for the (usually) 10 members. The group has created a welcoming environment as described by Rachel:

> I think our group is a space where people can be themselves and where they can be supported in how they are in practice. We don't talk about personal things but it is a supportive space, not an aversive space. Where the vibes are good. I go because I want to learn and grow. I never feel shut down.

Rachel's characterization of the NTSG environment as "supportive" and "non-aversive" evokes Kathy Weingarten's (1991) depiction of "intimate" or safe space, a generative place where connection and change can happen in counseling. A place of relaxation is also described by Griffith and Griffith (1994) as a space where sufficient relaxation allows for reflective, attentive, generative conversation between people. This kind of space stands in contrast to the hurried, competitive, and hierarchical environments within which many of the group members function on a daily basis. The space is an important feature of the group's mandate to support, nurture, and empower its members, as a form of social action countering the stress and isolation of practice.

Centering the Knowledge of Group Members

The current phase of NTSG is characterized by a collective awareness that the diverse "local knowledge" (Geertz, 1974) of individual group members is of as much value to the group as the opinion of outside experts. This awareness is reflected in the invitation to group members to lead sessions based on their own areas of specialization and to consider how the ideas and practices they discuss connect with narrative therapy and related social constructionist ideas.

Recently a group member chose to facilitate an NTSG session on resilience. Leanne, a social worker with many years of experience with survivors of breast cancer, focused the session on both her own resilience and that of her clients. She opened the session with a theoretical discussion of Padesky and Mooney's (2012) strengths-based CBT model, comparing this model to a narrative therapy approach. In the second part of the session, I (LB) interviewed Leanne around the theme of her own resilience, and group members subsequently reflected on Leanne's story (Andersen, 1987; White, 1999). Leanne indicated that her clients' responses to their own personal challenges were the biggest source of inspiration to her. The group had a chance to hear a rich description of Leanne's early influences, the factors behind her dedication to social justice and advocacy, her creative efforts in producing a book for families of breast cancer survivors, and her future hopes and aspirations.

A third part of the session involved an exercise in which group members worked in pairs, and were asked to share with their partner recollections of a difficult situation, challenge, or loss. Reflective questions were provided so that participants could practice asking the types of questions that focused on how people had responded to challenging life situations (Wade, 1997). Although Leanne had been in the group for six years, this was the first time she chose to facilitate a session. The reflections by NTSG group members reinforced for Leanne the story of her own fortitude over a long and successful social work career. Leanne was sustained over the years by her clients' strength in the face of breast cancer.

This interview is illustrative of how NTSG has provided space for the "not strictly narrative" idea of resilience to be considered. Rather than conceiving of resilience as a quality or personality "trait," Leanne, together with group members, reflected on how personal agency, family bonds, and social relationships bolstered her clients and herself in times of challenge or adversity. Resilience could then be understood as a response to hard times—a response supported by a community of family, friends, and counselors. Many group members present that evening were inspired by Leanne's account of her early influences, her mentors, and her enduring enthusiasm for her work.

Conclusion

This chapter focused on how NTSG responded to social justice issues of "voice" and "power" that emerged during its development. In fact, it was around these issues that the group coalesced as it struggled to define its identity. Our collective experience has taught us that when counselors reflect on their dialogue with peers, issues of power and hierarchy within the group process may influence how they relate to each other. Tensions and power dynamics within an ever-changing group ultimately will arise, and there will be an ongoing need to address these dynamics overtly. During its evolution NTSG has maintained an open and "safe space" for participants to support one another, and to share ideas, thoughts, and experiences. NTSG has learned to value the experience and knowledge of group members, and to create opportunities for members to lead sessions where they can highlight their individual expertise.

In June of 2014, NTSG created a collaborative poster that summarized its composition, orienting ideas, and practices (Bloom et al., 2014). The creation of this project was a consolidation of the group's emerging identity, and the presentation of this work was the first public recounting of its development. The group chose to put a bridge on the poster as a visual metaphor to describe itself. The bridge connects NTSG members to one another, to other orientations and perspectives, and to all those who wish to hear its story.

While the next phase in NTSG's evolution may be unclear, we hope that the members of NTSG will continue to support one another and to work in solidarity with their clients and the surrounding community. As co-facilitators of NTSG, we would like to end on a note of wondering about the group and where it will evolve, and of appreciation for all that has come before. We may be stepping onto the bridge without a clear destination, but we are confident of finding ways forward, together.

Reflection Questions

1.   What are the pros and cons of facilitating a group focused on counseling practice while adhering steadfastly to a single theory?
2.   The authors speak of a social justice issue that emerged within NTSG related to whose ideas were accepted and valued within the group. Can you think of a similar situation, either in a counseling supervision or peer support group, where you have noticed that someone's voice or opinion was not being

acknowledged? How did this impact the group process? What effects, if any, did it have on that individual's subsequent participation?

3. How did you respond to the authors' discovery that, even among experienced practitioners, there was a tendency to defer to experts? Do you find some of your own clients deferring to experts, for better or for worse?
4. What counseling practices do you engage in to ensure clients' voices are heard? Can you name some ways of creating dialogues with the people who consult you that make it less likely that your clients/consultees will defer to you as "the expert"?

References

Andersen, T. (1987). The reflecting team: dialogue and meta-dialogue in clinical work. *Family Process, 26*(4), 415–428. doi: 10.1111/j.1545-5300.1987.00415.x

Anderson, H. (2005). Myths about "not-knowing." *Family Process, 44*(4), 497–504. doi: 10.1111/j.1545-5300.2005.00074.x/full

Bloom, L. F., Spector, N. M. P., Corsini, L. J., Munt, G. W. G., Studd, A. W., Elliott, B., … Rishwain, M. (2014, April). Outside the boundaries of the institution: Development of a narrative therapy study group for the continued education of health professionals. Poster session presented at Creating Space IV Symposium of the Medical/Health Humanities.

Charon, R. (2001). Narrative medicine: Form, function, and ethics. *Annals of Internal Medicine, 134*(1), 83–87. doi: 10.7326/0003-4819-134-1-200101020-00024

Crethar, H. C., Rivera, E. T., & Nash, S. (2008). In search of common threads: Linking multicultural, feminist and social justice counseling paradigms. *Journal of Counseling and Development, 86*, 226–278. doi: 10.1002/j.1556–6678.2008.tb00509.x

Geertz, C. (1974). "From the native's point of view": On the nature of anthropological understanding. *Bulletin of the American Academy of Arts and Sciences, 28*(1), 26–45. doi: 10.2307/3822971

Gehart, D., & Paré, D. (2008). Suffering and the relationship with the problem in postmodern therapies: A Buddhist re-visioning. *Journal of Family Psychotherapy, 19*(4), 299–319. doi: 10.1080/08975350802475049

Gergen, K. J. (1991). Emerging challenges for theory and psychology. *Theory & Psychology, 1*(1), 13–35. doi: 10.1177/0959354391011002

Griffith, J., & Griffith, M. (1994). *The body speaks*. New York, NY: Basic Books.

Haley, T. (2002). The fit between reflecting teams and a social constructionist approach. *Journal of Systemic Therapies, 21*(1), 20–40. doi: 10.1521/jsyt.21.1.20.23095

Hare-Mustin, R. (1994). Discourses in the mirrored room: A postmodern analysis of therapy. *Family Process, 33*(1), 19–35. doi: 10.1111/j.1545-5300.1994.00019.x

Helms, J. E. (2003). A pragmatic view of social justice. *The Counseling Psychologist, 31*(3), 305–313. doi: 10.1177/0011000003031003006

Hoffman, L. (2000). A communal perspective for relational therapies. *Journal of Feminist Family Therapy, 11*(4), 5–17. doi: 10.1300/J086v11n04_02

Kennedy, B. A., & Arthur, N. (2014). Social justice and counseling psychology: Recommitment through action. *Canadian Journal of Counseling and Psychotherapy, 48*(3), 186–205. Retrieved from http://cjc-rcc.ucalgary.ca

Larner, G. (2011). Deconstructing theory: Towards an ethical therapy. *Theory & Psychology*, *21*(6), 821–839. doi: 10.1177/0959354310395061

Morgan, A. (2000). *What is narrative therapy? An easy-to-read introduction*. Adelaide, Australia: Dulwich Centre.

Padesky, C. A., & Mooney, K. A. (2012). Strengths-based cognitive–behavioural therapy: A four-step model to build resilience. *Clinical Psychology & Psychotherapy*, *19*(4), 283–290. doi: 10.1002/cpp.1795

Paré, D. A. (2009). Notes from the basement: Developing therapist communities through collaborative practice groups. *Journal of Systemic Therapies*, *28*(3), 1–20. doi: 10.1521/jsyt.2009.28.3.89

Paré, D. A. (2011). Reflective learning through collaborative practice groups. *International Journal of Collaborative-Dialogical Practices*, *2*(10), 24–35. Retrieved from https://collaborative-practices.com

Paré, D. A. (2013). *The practice of collaborative counseling and psychotherapy: Developing skills in culturally mindful helping*. Thousand Oaks, CA: Sage.

Paré, D. A. (2014). Social justice and the word: Keeping diversity alive in therapeutic conversations. *Canadian Journal of Counselling and Psychotherapy*, *48*(3), 206–217. Retrieved from http://cjc-rcc.ucalgary.ca

Preston-Dillon, D. (2009). Narrative approaches in sand therapy: Transformative journeys for counselor and client. Paper presented at the American Counseling Association Annual Conference and Exposition, Charlotte, NC.

Reynolds, V. (2011). Resisting burnout with justice-doing. *International Journal of Narrative Therapy & Community Work*, *4*, 27–45. Retrieved from http://dulwichcentre.com.au/publications/international-journal-narrative-therapy

Shapiro, B. Z. (2003). Social justice and social work with groups. In N. Sullivan, L. Mitchell, D. Goodman, N. C. Lang, & E. S. Mesbur. (Eds.), *Social work with groups: social justice through personal, community and societal change*. New York, NY: Haworth Press.

Shilts, A. S., Liscio, L., & Rambo, M. A. (2008). Return to sender: Letter writing to bring hope to both client and team. *Journal of Systemic Therapies*, *27*(1), 59–66. doi: 10.1521/jsyt.2008.27.1.59

Strong, T. (2000). Six orienting ideas for collaborative counsellors. *European Journal of Psychotherapy & Counselling*, *3*(1), 25–42. doi: 10.1080/13642530050078547

Vera, E., & Speight, S. (2003). Multicultural competence, social justice, and counseling psychology: Expanding our roles. *The Counseling Psychologist*, *31*(3), 253–272. doi: 10.1177/0011000002250634

Wade, A. (1997). Small acts of living: Everyday resistance to violence and other forms of oppression. *Contemporary Family Therapy*, *19*(1), 23–39. doi: 10.1023/A:1026154215299

Weingarten, K. (1991). The discourses of intimacy: Adding a social constructionist and feminist view. *Family Process*, *30*(3), 285–305. doi: 10.1111/j.1545-5300.1991.00285.x

White, M. (1993). Deconstruction and therapy. In S. Gilligan & R. Price (Eds.), *Therapeutic conversations* (pp. 22–61). New York, NY: Norton.

White, M. (1995). *Re-authoring lives: Interviews and essays*. Adelaide, Australia: Dulwich Centre.

White, M. (1999). Reflecting-team work as definitional ceremony revisited. *Gecko: A Journal of Deconstruction and Narrative Ideas in Therapeutic Practice*, *2*, 55–82.

White, M. (2007). *Maps of narrative practice.* New York, NY: Norton.

White, M., & Epston, D. (1990). *Narrative means to therapeutic ends.* New York, NY: Norton.

Young, I. (1990). *Justice and the politics of difference.* Princeton, NJ: Princeton University Press.

CHAPTER 9

"Social Justice" as Relational Talk

Dan Wulff and Sally St. George

We often hear authors, professors, and practitioners champion attention to social justice in clinical work. We include ourselves among this lot. But manifesting this intention by what one specifically says and does with clients is very challenging (Doherty, 2012). *Asserting* that one does social justice work is not the same as *doing* it in one's everyday practice and life—as they say, "walking your talk" is the challenge.

Despite years of experience of seeing client families, as well as supervising practicum students and teaching therapeutic listening and conversational skills, we are quite aware that our own interviewing skills and those of our students are lacking when it comes to including social justice issues into our clinical interviews and supervision. We are trying to develop ways to work with individuals and families that deliberately recognize the larger system influences on individual behavior—not every therapeutic problem can be reduced to a consequence of intra-family dynamics or intra-psychic mis-alignment (Paré, 2014). We have long known that material circumstances in a person's life impact his/her relationships and behaviors in profound ways. Distribution of wealth and opportunities have serious consequences for individuals and how they relate to their worlds. The aphorism that says that people should just "pull themselves up by their bootstraps" is now widely seen as reflective of a position that downplays or hides privilege (Rios, 2015).

We are social work academics and practitioners who are privileged in many ways. Our early practice careers in home-based therapy work and inner-city school counseling sensitized us to the connections between the "lack of privilege" and limited opportunities, few possibilities/alternatives, and despair. We try to use our academic voices and positions to invite fellow professionals to work more diligently and courageously to understand and speak to the troubles that client families face as intimately connected to the social contexts they inhabit rather than to the more prevalent view that examines individual failings.

We utilize our social constructionist leanings to help us consider the quality of our work with clients and remain particularly alert for the ways that we inadvertently participate in ignoring or sidestepping unfairnesses that clients face. In this chapter, we reflect on some ideas that might facilitate efforts to become a more "socially just therapist" with individuals, families, or groups. We will begin by discussing the tendency for therapy to colonize clients into dominant ways of thinking and acting (Whitaker, 2010) and then we will follow up with some suggestions/strategies of how to build practices that "walk the talk" of social justice work in therapy.

Social Justice Challenges in Clinical Work: Therapy as Colonizing

Depending on the theory chosen, practitioners can conceptualize human behaviors as individual in origin and in expression or as a response to others within a nexus of interactions (Gergen, 2009). If conceptualized in a relational way, individual behavior is understood as a response that is contextually located and contextually integrated. From this vantage point, this so-called "individual" behavior is more a manifestation of interactions. An individual's action is akin to a note in a melody or a frame in a movie—while it provides a picture or a glimpse, if de-contextualized, it is absent of clarifying meaning. For example, seeing children in the school classroom will likely reveal a variety of behavioral performances that will differ somewhat from the ways they behave at home, with their peers on the playground, an overnight stay at a friend's house, or in the therapist's office. While the children each remain individuals, their expression of who they are is variable depending on context and who they are with. Persons story themselves in various ways depending upon their relationships, and the stories therapists attend to and develop with clients are a function of where they focus their attention and questions.

Yet in many of our field's current preferred patterns of helping, helpers often de-contextualize people's behaviors, imagining their clients as free-standing autonomous beings. It is a common practice to consider ourselves as independent beings from one another and capable of solo thoughts and actions, unimpeded and uninfluenced by others. These notions of accountability and responsibility are built on this individualistic idea that each of us owns our ideas and our behaviors. We think there are more helpful and generative alternatives to this view. Rather than seeing ourselves as separate and independent, we believe it is more helpful to understand persons as unique collections of affiliations, participants in shared communities of understanding and location. While the individualizing of therapy, perhaps simpler to efficiently manage and monitor, is very widespread, we think there is a significant risk for this way of working to contribute to the further colonization of clients—we subtly or not-so-subtly impose our preferred understandings and the consequent minimization or usurpation of their preferred ways of seeing themselves. While those prescriptive practices occur at the community and broader social levels, "the risk of reperpetrating the injustices ... is always there at the micro level, utterance by utterance, in therapeutic conversations" (Paré, 2014, p. 207).

Among those who have provided critiques of social work, Margolin (1997) describes how counseling and therapy may be sites where well-intentioned helping professionals may encourage conformity to societal norms/practices and institutional priorities as the primary orientation to offering help. If a client has been labeled or otherwise identified as a "behavior problem" or risk, the general approach is to encourage the client to modify her/his behavior to fit better within whatever standard of conduct she/he was "out of step." The logic operating is that a client who has violated rules or standards of conduct will achieve a better quality of life by ceasing to violate those standards. If the client can remove the behaviors that activated others to see that client as troubled or disturbed, then the client can escape the harmful and limiting consequences that they are experiencing.

Initiatives to help people change to be more in accordance with societal expectations or norms (while a case could be legitimately made that those expectations/ norms should themselves be changed) may well be considered an injustice to the person (Foucault, 1995; White, 1990). Therapists would be well advised to reflect upon their efforts to effect change with clients, examining the degree to which they are pursuing solutions aimed at having clients adjust to circumstances versus seeing the larger systems as culpable and in need of change. The level of change-making is mis-aligned—a societal condition or expectation is misunderstood to be a personal shortcoming. In our view, to modify the individual in such an instance is to attempt a solution at the wrong level of solution-making, not only reducing the chances of successful intervention but also unfairly asking an individual to address changes that are more appropriately the domain of the larger system (Ryan, 1971).

For example, consider the situation of a child in elementary school who is reported by his teacher to be a troublemaker and will be suspended unless he becomes more cooperative. Looking into the matter with other parents and teachers reveals the boy's teacher to be in power struggles with many of the students in his class and unwilling to adapt her teaching style to better maintain a learning environment. We could see the problem as the individuals involved or we could look into the pressures, evaluations, and expected solutions that both teacher and student might experience as overwhelming. Denborough (2008), Munro, Reynolds, and Plamondon (2013), and Bracho (2013) each remind us that larger-scale societal problems (e.g., domestic violence, lack of housing, poor health care) are not simply the result of faulty decision-making on the part of clients or practitioners. Locating responsibility for change solely in individuals misses the structural or societal contribution and accountability for the troubles individuals or families face.

Another illustration of locating societal issues in individual performances is the tendency to look at men's violence toward women as a purely individual act. This view easily misses the influences of the dominant culture in laying the groundwork (and support) for such acts. Efforts to mitigate male violence that are solely focused on individuals are less effective and tend to mask the roles played by larger influences (Denborough, 2008). An effective approach to the problem of violence must take into account the larger context that supports and encourages the individual performances of violence.

Another example of an individualizing view is societal pressure on parents to "control" their children, which sometimes leads to excessive attempts—including physical force—at gaining compliance. This leads to understanding the parents' actions as expressions of personality flaws, with no consideration of how their actions reflect an attempt to live up to society's expectations of parents as authority figures. A relational perspective renders visible the pressure on parents to force compliance from their children. Our analysis here does not condone the use of violence; rather we acknowledge the societal pressure to force compliance that can incite violent parental responses. Our recommendation would be to offer support to the parents to find other ways to guide children without subscribing to violence.

Yet another example of re-examining our conceptualization about the locus of persons' problems is the call by Munro et al. (2013) to re-examine how we provide shelter for persons on the street by looking at the structural issues of homelessness: "We believe people are responsible for their choices, but only those choices they have the power to make ... Who is housed or homeless is greatly informed by access to individual power and privilege" (p. 63). Persons with access to sufficient money, significant "connections" within the housing authority, and resources to create successful applications to the housing deciders are able to stave off homelessness. Persons without these types of resources are at a serious disadvantage in their efforts to achieve housing.

A final example of what becomes visible when the influence of larger societal levels is considered involves population health outcomes. These can be understood as the consequence of insufficient medical facilities, complicated forms or eligibility criteria, or lack of trained staff to relate to the patients in their own language (Bracho, 2013), rather than a consequence of poor personal health habits of members of that population. The lack of facilities and resources for persons who need them reflects a lack of justice of the community/society toward its individual citizens. Not taking care of all citizens is more a fault of the governing body than personal failings of those who need or request help. Seeing poor health as an individual failing of the patient obscures the failings of a public health system that does not sufficiently meet the needs of its population.

In the context of family therapy, focusing on how clients do not live up to external standards of behavior also misses the chance to attend to the family's local knowledge and expertise in living. The family's understanding of their life context and history can easily become jettisoned in favor of the dominant prescriptions for behavior, undermining the family's abilities and worth (Paré, 2014). This raises a serious future concern about the family abdicating their own judgments and insights for external, expert-presented standards. This may unfortunately erode the family's self-efficacy and sense that they can "make it" in the world. This can become another form of repression or oppression offered in the name of helping.

Social Justice as Relationally Nested

Social justice work can be seen in any relational arena. Relationships between individuals or groups of people potentially produce imbalances, burdens, unfairnesses, or injustices (Mullaly, 2010; Reisch, 2014). We will illustrate various examples of social injustice. These illustrations are not exhaustive nor meant to be the most pervasive.

Governments are in relation to their citizenry and organizations are in relation with their employees and customers/clients. Distribution of services and the decisions that are involved in selecting what is to be done and for whom necessitate choices that will undoubtedly please some and displease others. Power and privilege gravitate toward leaders or upper management, raising questions as to how decisions, goods, and services are shared. Social justice work in this arena examines who is included and who is excluded in these decisions.

Social justice work can also be taken up by a therapist, teacher, neighbor, or friend responding deliberately to assist when he/she observes an egregious action or mistreatment of another. This can take the form of calling the police, physically defending someone, writing a letter of support, or any other way of supporting/ defending someone who is under threat or attack. This approach to social justice work requires that we notice such incidents and willingly step forward to take some sort of corrective or supportive action in response. This is not merely an individual act—this is an individual or small group responding to an interpersonal or social condition of another that recognizes the shared community that we live within. Those societal conditions also impact us and we are implicated in the rules and practices involved in our communities.

Therapists also may dedicate their practice to work with persons who come for therapy to recover from abuse by another (e.g., domestic violence, physical or sexual abuse of children). One develops practices to restore the person harmed to a successful life by providing support and resources that are especially tailored to the problem the client group has been facing. While the restoration may involve some direct advocacy and defending to protect clients from the person(s) who harmed them, the majority of the focus is on offering direct therapeutic help in ways that individually assist the client to "recover" her/his previous level of functioning.

Working on daily injustices/insults that are "under the radar" refers to addressing the injustices/insults of underemployment, not having enough money to send one's child to camp, having to work extra hours or jobs because of unfair salaries or lack of job security, unavailability of proper medical care, school classifications that deny children access to needed services/supports. In this version of working for social justice, we see people's troubles as resulting from many injustices that are part of their everyday lives. These injustices become integrated into clients' daily lives because of their pervasiveness in the daily fabric of their lives. Taken collectively, these unfairnesses or injustices are likely not distinguishable by clients as factors implicated in the troubles of their lives—they are largely "off the radar." But daily injustice is the location of our efforts to surface the role it can have in the troubles families in therapy face. This is the primary focus of our chapter.

Building Social Justice into Therapeutic Conversations

Based upon our experience working with families, we would like to discuss some ways that a practitioner might invite attention to social justice issues that are of the variety of the fourth location of social justice listed above—those everyday injustices or insults that families face. What follows are four slightly different ways to build social justice talk into conversations with clients:

- When families voluntarily invoke justice or fairness language (e.g., "It is not right," "I shouldn't have to worry about him," "She betrayed me," "He violated our agreement"), the therapist joins that conversational thread, asking to hear more of the story to learn how families came to such conclusions as well as the effects and implications.
- Asking about the burdens (K. Tamasese, personal communication, March 26, 2014) of their lives and how balanced those burdens are (e.g., "What responsibilities do you bear in your family?" "How do you feel about the load of responsibilities you are carrying?" "Who else is carrying some of the load?").
- Directly asking families about the influence of the "isms" of the world in their lives (e.g., "What role do you see racism playing in the problems your daughter is having at school?" "Do you think your son would face the same questions that your daughter is facing if he was in the situation she is in?").
- Asking families about the impact of influential societal discourses in asserting "ways they *should* be" (e.g., "What would your mother say about the situation you are having with your children if she were here?" "To what degree would others approve if you changed your ways of getting along? Who would approve? Who would disapprove?").

Following Up On Justice/Injustice Language

In therapy, we might hear about injustices in the stories that people tell about their lives. Important events in their stories can reveal moments and situations in which they were mistreated, subjected to unfairnesses, or disrespected in ways that "should not have been." These injustices need only to be felt by the person him/herself and they do not need to be verified as factually true. If they are felt as true, they are organizing and impactful for the person.

As we take more notice of these declarations of unfairness within family interactions, we have begun asking more questions in our conversations with families. Some examples follow.

- You have mentioned several times about how unfairly your parents have treated you—especially compared to your brother and sister. Could we take a look at your family's ideas about fairness in living together? How would you each describe your family's stand/stance on what fair treatment is? Who are in positions to determine what is fair and unfair? How would you know if there has been an unfairness? Does unfairness belong to one person or to all of you? What would others outside of your family notice and describe as this family's position on fairness?

- Is this your first experience with judging another person's response to you as "not right" or undeserved by you? What do you see as common between past experiences that were "not right" and the one we were just talking about?
- This might be a hard question, but often when we feel like we have been treated wrongly or unjustly, we resist, sending out messages to let others know things are wrong. It may be with words, but it does not have to be with words. What are the ways you communicate your resistance to being mistreated? How do you think these messages are received?

Asking about Burdens

We can notice injustices by listening to the daily routines of people's lives, attending specifically for who is carrying the burdens and the degree of balance and reciprocity in carrying those burdens (T. K. Tamasese, personal communication, March 26, 2014). Acknowledging the loads that people carry gives credit to those persons for that work while simultaneously foregrounding those burdens—not as shortcomings or weaknesses, but rather as life work and responsibilities. We think that approaching therapy in this way is more appreciative of persons while at the same time addressing the challenges of their lives.

The questions might even seem routine to experienced clinicians. "Who does what work in the family? Who carries what responsibilities? How did these responsibilities get divided up? When was the last time you looked at the distribution of duties and assessed their effectiveness?" In this way, we can examine the injustices that family members might feel from within their family and the arrangements for taking care of their families. Introducing the metaphor of injustice/justice in all its manifestations may provide a means to discuss ways that interpersonal arrangements and conflicts may be traced to larger system expectations and discourses that may themselves harbor elements of unfairness and injustice. Such talk directs attention away from individual failings or weaknesses and instead encourages talk about reciprocities within the family and between the family and larger systems.

The value of the "carrying burdens" metaphor as applied to the troubles occurring within a family is in emphasizing the relational nature of our lives and the troubles we face. The language of burdens makes space to discuss inequities and unfairnesses as they contribute to problems in living. Carrying burdens is an alternative way of describing or taking responsibility for bearing the weight and stress of others and can oftentimes occur because of expectations circulating in the worlds in which we live.

Discussing the "Isms"

We think that it is important to look for the larger injustices and discriminations that are grounded within cultural traditions and that could be implicated in the troubles that bring families to therapy. Through experience, we have found that cultural conversations in therapy can quickly slip sideways and inadvertently re-inscribe the very hurts, pressures, and oppressions that our clients already feel. When we sense that any of the "isms" may be in play (mentioned explicitly or implicitly), we ask about the "ism" as a matter of degree. For example, if we suspect that "classism" may be a player in the problem of experiences of bullying at school or work, we might ask, "To what degree do you think that the differences in social class (e.g., how much money you make, the neighborhood you live in) has to do with this constant harassment you experience from this other group of people?" The same kind of question could be used for the consequences of racial discrimination, sexism, ageism, or homophobia.

Exploring the Influence of Societal Discourses

We have conducted several research projects on our practices using what we call research as daily practice (St. George & Wulff, 2014; St. George, Wulff, & Strong, 2014; St. George, Wulff, & Tomm, 2015a; St. George, Wulff, & Tomm, 2015b; Wulff, St. George, Tomm, Doyle, & Sesma, 2015). In these projects, we have examined societal discourses in relation to the problematic patterns that families seem to get trapped into and that produce ongoing distress. Below are some examples of how societal discourses could be considered as implicated in family troubles and ways we may begin to include these discourses into our therapeutic conversations.

Sibling rivalry could be based upon a belief that life should be fair and equal (K. Tomm, personal communication, May 11, 2015). Children and adults who believe this usually must then engage in steady monitoring and accounting. Any perceived inequity is grounds for protesting through disruptive behaviors (which could also look like individual selfishness from the outside).

- It sounds as though you might have different meanings or understandings for "all of our children are treated the same or equally." Could we talk about this idea for a bit, where it came from, what you (parents) are trying to convey when you say it, and what you understand when you hear it (children)?

Stealing may be based upon a belief that material "ownership" is not valid—one does not have exclusive dominion over property. Another related fairness idea is that it is "unjust" when some people have disproportionate amounts of property or access to privileges. As long as inequalities exist in the world of ownership and possessions, ownership claims can and will be challenged. Unequal or unjust distribution of goods and services could provide a rationale for stealing.

- Most people would think of stealing as a moral issue. Can you explain what messages you want understood by the different views this family holds on stealing?

Fighting is a counterpoint to the idea of "playing by the rules" (i.e., not fighting) because playing by the rules oftentimes is not effective in achieving fairness or equity. Fairness is such a strong value that its absence or subversion may lead persons to threaten or carry out verbal or physical violence in response. There may be some situations or circumstances that are unfair to some and if the current set of rules supports the status quo, fighting (or breaking established rules) may make a strong statement of commitment to a principled position of seeking justice.

- Fighting is disagreeable and yet very common in our society. Some explain that under certain circumstances, fighting is justified and necessary. What are you trying to accomplish by fighting that other attempts you have used have not been successful?

Focus on individual desires/wants more than collective interests can be seen as a logical extension of our cultural value of individualism. Our societal institutions privilege individual performance and accumulation of power, prestige, and wealth. The balancing of the societal expectations around individual performance along with the value of living cooperatively within a family, social groups, and communities poses difficult challenges: when do we place individual wants/needs over the wants/needs of our collective lives (families and communities)? With competition for schools, jobs, and other economic opportunities being so intense, electing to focus on our individual selves first seems to hold the greatest attraction for us, even though the trade-off is oftentimes a diminishing satisfaction in family life.

- We live in a society that encourages persons to be successful in many different ways, including professional and material success. How far should we go to achieve success? Are there times and places we should not work so hard to get ahead? Where is the line we draw to privilege our relational lives over individual performances? And who gets to decide?

Doing poorly in school highlights the over-reliance of education in the life situations of some individuals. Compulsory education has long been accepted within our Western societies to the point that it has become an unquestioned value for all children. The promise of education (good jobs, monetary success, and elite status) is oftentimes not realized and students' lack of focus at school may serve as an acknowledgment that the extensive focus on education in a child's life is many times overdone.

- There are so many messages about school that come at us every day—in the news in the neighborhood, through advertising, from school personnel. For example, one of the big ideas that we all are aware of is the only way to get ahead is to have an education. To what extent do you think this is true?

Psychiatric diagnoses given to persons could alternatively be seen as judgments of those who do not fit the societal specifications of what a person should be, do, or say. Maintaining one's behaviors in spite of these labeling processes could be seen as protesting normative prescriptions of a community. The diagnostic label marks them as different from others in ways that uphold and confirm normative standards while simultaneously marginalizing them as deviant (Whitaker, 2010). For example, persons who are labeled "bipolar" are so labeled because they do not conform to the consistency, dependability, stability, and predictability expected of persons in our society. Another plausible understanding of the behaviors exhibited by a person labeled as bipolar could be of a person adopting more fluid and change-able behaviors that could lead to a more satisfying way of life. A person diagnosed with ADHD may be rebelling against conformity to pre-set standards or protocols of learning and behaving. This could be a protest against being subservient to adult wishes and scripts of conduct. We want to emphasize that the characterizations above represent alternative understandings from the dominant understandings presented by our society and, as such, they are only possibilities. Entertaining such alternative understandings is a way for therapists to invite or offer new ways of looking at diagnoses; they are not meant to be imposed on a client (as for some, the current understandings of diagnoses are acceptable and useful for clients).

- Diagnostic language seems to fill the media airwaves. I am wondering about what you all think about having someone of your family being labeled this way. I ask because I have had many families who had mixed opinions and beliefs about the usefulness or fairness of these labels.

Drinking alcohol has become a societal focus that is not altogether coherent. On the one hand, consumption of alcohol is big business and strongly promoted in the media and in relationship to sporting events. Consuming alcohol is part of what many consider to be "manly" behavior—to drink (and at times, heavily) is tied up with what men think helps to define their masculinity. On the other hand, drinking while driving or when angry many times leads to death and destruction. The consumption of alcohol represents the twin positions society simultaneously holds that provides the context for many mismatches between the dominant soci-etal position and individual actions. Alcohol consumption (to excess) is often-times associated with persons who are facing extreme pain or trouble—it serves as a way to numb the pain, albeit temporarily. In some situations, it becomes a statement of how bad one's life has become. Only focusing on the physical/chem-ical dependency aspects misses the person's life context and situation that supports drinking alcohol.

- I have been interested in the conflicting messages that are out in our society—it is acceptable to drink; drinking is not acceptable; only certain people have the right to drink; alcoholism is a biological problem; alcoholism is a psychological problem; drinking is sexy, manly, and so on. Before we go on in our conversation, could we take a moment to find out where each of you stands on this issue, and what the expectations are for your family with regard to this issue?

Conclusion

As we asserted at the outset of this chapter, therapists are well placed to see how individuals and families are impacted by societal conditions and discourses. To not see these influences is to risk imposing/colonizing "the way things are" on our clients, and in effect, hiding these relational influences. Not seeing how these influences shape the troubles in individual and family life does not mean that those influences are not involved. As therapists turn their attention to deliberately examining larger societal influences on the everyday stresses and difficulties that individuals and families face, they can open new and innovative ways of addressing personal troubles. To not attend to these influences is to conspire to keep them hidden, in effect, to allow us to be "status quotitians" (Wood & Tully, 2006, p. 21). Hopefully, more therapists will take up the challenge to re-examine the ways in which therapists and clients conceptualize "personal troubles" and to look for ways in which these personal troubles can be re-contextualized to seeing them as relational creations, providing a way for us to see societal and structural influences as implicated in creating and sustaining family distress.

Reflection Questions

1. How does one compare the relative degree of individual self-agency with the influence of the larger systems and discourses when assessing how behaviors are enacted?
2. How do you ethically proceed if clients prefer to receive traditional mental conceptualizations of individual pathology while you, as a family therapist, prefer to factor in the larger systems/discourses? Do you simply make a referral to another therapist who subscribes to individual pathology? Do you modify your approach?
3. What case could be made that social justice ideas have no business in family therapy?
4. How would family therapy change if we saw the troubled family dynamics that present in therapy as derivative of the external factors that stress families? Could we imagine external forces as the triggers that lead families into failed attempts to address those external conditions?
5. What therapeutic practices have you already been exposed to, or have you generated yourself, that attend to social justice issues in persons' lives?

References

Bracho, A. (2013). Community leaders promote local health [TEDMED talk]. Retrieved from www.youtube.com/watch?v=jxCG6d4LiGQ

Denborough, D. (2008). *Collective narrative practice: Responding to individuals, groups, and communities who have experienced trauma*. Adelaide, Australia: Dulwich Centre Publications.

Doherty, W. (2012). Therapy as craft: Healing clients one brick at a time. *Psychotherapy Networker, 36*(5), 22–29. Retrieved from www.psychotherapynetworker.org

Foucault, M. (1995). *Discipline & punish: The birth of the prison*. New York, NY: Vintage.

Gergen, K. J. (2009). *Relational being: Beyond self and community*. Oxford, UK: Oxford University Press.

Margolin, L. (1997). *Under the cover of kindness: The invention of social work*. Charlottesville, VA: University of Virginia Press.

Mullaly, B. (2010). *Challenging oppression and confronting privilege* (2nd ed.). Don Mills, ON: Oxford University Press.

Munro, A., Reynolds, V., & Plamondon, R. (2013). Lessons from self-organizing shelter communities: "We were already a community and you put a roof over us." *The International Journal of Narrative Therapy and Community Work, 2*, 61–78. Retrieved from http://dulwichcentre.com.au/international-journal-of-narrative-therapy-and-community-work

Paré, D. (2014). Social justice and the word: Keeping diversity alive in therapeutic conversations. *Canadian Journal of Counselling and Psychotherapy, 48*(3), 206–217. Retrieved from http://cjc-rcc.ucalgary.ca

Reisch, M. (2014). Introduction. In M. Reisch (Ed.), *The Routledge international handbook of social justice* (pp. 1–5). London: Routledge.

Rios, C. (2015, May 17). Debunking the "pull yourself up by your bootstraps" myth. Retrieved from http://everydayfeminism.com/2015/05/debunking-bootstraps-myth/

Ryan, W. (1971). *Blaming the victim*. New York, NY: Pantheon.

St. George, S., & Wulff, D. (2014). Braiding socio-cultural interpersonal patterns into therapy. In K. Tomm, S. St. George, D. Wulff, & T. Strong (Eds.), *Patterns in interpersonal interactions: Inviting relational understandings for therapeutic change* (pp. 124–142). New York, NY: Routledge.

St. George, S., Wulff, D., & Strong, T. (2014). Researching interpersonal patterns. In K. Tomm, S. St. George, D. Wulff, & T. Strong (Eds.), *Patterns in interpersonal interactions: Inviting relational understandings for therapeutic change* (pp. 210–228). New York, NY: Routledge.

St. George, S., Wulff, D., & Tomm, K. (2015a). Societal discourses that help in family therapy: A modified situational analysis of the relationships between societal expectations and healing patterns in parent-child conflict. *Journal of Systemic Therapies, 34*(2), 31–44. doi: 10.1521/jsyt.2015.34.2.15

St. George, S., Wulff, D., & Tomm, K. (2015b). Talking societal discourses into family therapy: A situational analysis of the relationships between societal expectations and parent-child conflict. *Journal of Systemic Therapies, 34*(2), 15–30. doi: 10.1521/jsyt.2015.34.2.15

Whitaker, R. (2010). *Anatomy of an epidemic: Magic bullets, psychiatric drugs, and the astonishing rise of mental illness in America*. New York, NY: Broadway Paperbacks.

White, M. (1990). *Narrative means to therapeutic ends*. New York, NY: Norton.

Wood, G. G., & Tully, C. T. (2006). *The structural approach to direct practice in social work: A social constructionist perspective* (3rd ed.). New York, NY: Columbia University Press.

Wulff, D., & St. George, S. (2014). Research as daily practice. In G. Simon & A. Chard (Eds.), *Systemic inquiry: Innovations in reflexive practitioner research* (pp. 292–308). London: Everything is Connected Press.

Wulff, D., St. George, S., Tomm, K., Doyle, E., & Sesma, M. (2015). Unpacking the PIPs to HIPs curiosity: A narrative study. *Journal of Systemic Therapies, 34*(2), 45–58. doi: 10.1521/jsyt.2015.34.2.45

CHAPTER 10

Collaborative-Dialogic Practices: A Socially Just Orientation

Saliha Bava, Rocío Chaveste Gutiérrez, and M. L. Papusa Molina[1]

When I become involved in the study of aerography, I release what I have here [he touches his chest]; nobody is going to fool me, I have already lived it all, the coke, jail, I have walked the streets without a shirt, all of the wild life, I know, no one can tell me anything, I try to lend a hand to the people who are there now, I was one of the "clika,"[2] I know all about the "onda de la 13,"[3] I know there have been a lot of street fights, when the gangs started, when we would get together, it was cool because in the south of town all of us "clikas" would get together to talk, everything swirled together like graffiti, we invited guys from Cancun, Mexico City, cool graffiti painters, we would meet people from other places but with no fighting, without anything.

(Chaveste, 2014, p. 15; translated from Spanish)

Manuel talks without smiling or meeting Rocío's eyes. The movement of his arms accompanies the words with rhythm, creating a language with his hands. He is wearing a shirt buttoned up to the collar; on the outside, he has a pink scapulary of the Virgin of Guadalupe and a silver chain with a pendant that says *Vanilla*—the name that 10 years ago he decided to leave behind, the name he was known by and respected as a gang leader in Yucatan, Mexico.

What happens when a young man, self-defined as a "gang guy," decides to set aside his name "Vanilla" and call himself Manuel?[4] How do we look at the change that takes place, from belonging to a gang to later working in a municipal office, without being focused on predetermined "outcomes" of our work with Manuel? In this chapter, we elaborate on Collaborative-Dialogic Practices (CDP) as a socially just practice by reflecting on the above questions.

Locating Ourselves and Our Writing

Rocío, Saliha, and Papusa met in the context of the network of Collaborative and Dialogic Practitioners via the Houston Galveston Institute, the founding home for CDP. Papusa and Rocío work together at the Kanankil Institute in Yucatan, Mexico, and Saliha, originally from India, has been living and working in the United States since 1995 and is a professor at Mercy College in New York. This chapter started as a conversation, among participants, at the International Summer Institute (ISI),[5] Mexico 2013 (Bava, McDonough, Chaveste, & Molina, 2013).

The story we use to illustrate the application of CDP emerges from a project Rocío coordinated when she was the Director of Social Development from 2001 to 2004 for the city of Merida in Yucatan. We share the story from the "relational hermeneutics" (Anderson, 2007a, p. 13) view of CDP rather than "explain" the transformation that occurs in Vanilla/Manuel's identity. Relational hermeneutics foregrounds understanding as an interpretive process that occurs in dialogue and relationship. Interpretations are contextual since they are situated in history, culture, and tradition (Anderson, 2007a). This chapter itself is also an interpretation, a retelling informed by our reflections on the event to be recounted. We believe all understanding is interpretational and relational. In your reading of the story, you might notice "gaps" in the narrative. They occur due to the hermeneutic process— that is, due to a plurality of interpretations. In addition, the lack of a linear narrative potentially raises questions that we want you to raise as part of your reflective experience of an ongoing dialogic process. As practitioners, we step into an ongoing dialogic process when people invite us into their lives by seeking "help." Due to the discursive nature of therapeutic processes (McNamee, 2004), our account is nonlinear and interpretive, open to multiple ways of understanding and narrating. People often fill the gaps in their understanding of what is happening in the stories with "theories," which we, as authors, resist in our practice and in this writing. We invite you to notice how your interpretations fill in the gaps in our story and writing.

My Name Is No Longer Vanilla, My Name is Manuel

Vanilla was one of the gang leaders in an impoverished zone of Merida, and everyone respected him highly. Rocío remembers the first time she saw him and his friends, in a "town meeting." The expressions on their faces, when they felt listened to, surprised her. She was there to have conversations with people of the community about their needs. The reunion took place in a church. The women there were talking about being afraid of the gangs and concerned that their younger sons would get recruited into them. The youth were talking about how the police were coming around and harassing them when they were hanging out. This meeting, looking back, was the kickoff to a community collaboration.

Vanilla came to Rocío's office sometime after Fernando, one of the community workers trained in CDP, started working with the "gang." He told her that he would like to have a steady job. He said he needed to do something to feel useful and wanted to do something different. Rocío helped Vanilla get a job at the Social Development Office. When she met him on his first day of work and said, "Hello Vanilla, welcome," he responded, "From now on my name is no longer Vanilla. My name is Manuel."

The "gang project" emerged from the ongoing conversations between Fernando and Vanilla/Manuel; the relationship they constructed, as they shared time, spaces, and ideas, not only transformed their identities but also generated a different set of community relations. This story of shifting identity from Vanilla to Manuel illustrates how CDP goes beyond the zones traditionally set for psychotherapy: one-on-one conversations, private office, and so forth. The CDP approach to change can be equated with a stance, a way of being, rather than as prescriptive or procedural steps. In this chapter, we weave together parts of Vanilla/Manuel's story and the "gang project" as we share the assumptions of this CDP stance. Subsequently, we will epistemologically explore social justice from a CDP perspective. We believe that looking at social justice as a process invites us to avoid hegemony both in our practices and also in our conceptualization. It questions what is the dominant discourse and according to whom? And who does it serve? In a similar vein, the conceptualization and framing of social justice needs to be part of our discursive practices, in constant fluid motion—an ongoing practice of coordination rather than a set of colonizing or hegemonic concepts or practices.

Collaborative-Dialogic Practices: A Philosophical Stance

Collaborative-Dialogic Practices (Anderson, 1997; Anderson & Gehart, 2007) (aka Collaborative Practices and Collaborative Language Systems) is an emergent philosophically based approach to engaging people in clinical, community, organizational, learning, and research contexts. Originally developed in the 1970s by Harry Goolishian and Harlene Anderson at the Houston Galveston Institute within a therapeutic context, the stance has evolved as language practices have shifted over time; however, the practices continue to be embedded in hermeneutics, dialogue, and social construction epistemologies (Anderson, 2007a; Anderson & Goolishian, 1988). In her historical reconstruction of CDP, Anderson (2007b) outlines the shift from the social systems metaphor to the metaphor of "linguistic systems—as fluid, evolving communicating systems that exist in language" (p. 30).

Collaborative-Dialogic Practices (CDP) proposes an epistemological shift in our conception of knowledge and language and their production in conversations and relationships. Drawing on philosophers Wittgenstein and Bakhtin, both knowledge and language production are viewed as relational dialogical activities that are ongoing and never-ending collaborative practices of making up our social world (Anderson, 2007a; Gergen, 2009; Pearce, 2007). Knowledge, then, is a process rather than a product; a dynamic phenomenon that is performative (Bava, 2014; Levin & Bava, 2012) and enacted, rather than stored and then retrieved from some space "in the mind."

Drawing on the Vanilla/Manuel story, we illustrate the use of seven interconnected features of the CDP stance: not-knowing, mutual inquiry, the "client" as the expert, being public, being spontaneous and living with uncertainty, mutually transforming, and orienting towards everyday ordinary life (Anderson, 1997, 2007c, 2012).

One of the pillars of CDP is the *not-knowing* position (Anderson, 1997, 2007c). By adopting a not-knowing stance, we attempt to flatten the hierarchy within which we are participating by positioning what the client brings at the center of the conversation. Most clients position practitioners as experts by the mere fact that they are seen as the facilitator of practice, whether psychotherapy, education, or research. Through the process of *mutual inquiry* and curiosity, we learn how clients view us, what they seek from us and how to relate in ways that have the potential to lower hierarchy. Not-knowing, a value that informs a process orientation to knowledge construction as a dialogical act, positions one to focus on the collective construction of shared meanings and local language by the conversational partners. From this perspective, power is decentralized—seen to be located in the relationship rather than in a position or person.

As part of the gang project, Fernando, one of the community workers trained in CDP, started spending nights in the community in south Merida where Vanilla/Manuel lived. First, he would sit in his van and observe and let the gang members observe him. He then started to come out from inside the van, staying next to his vehicle, occasionally smoking. Eventually, the day came when he went to buy some refreshments and asked gang members, Vanilla/Manuel among them, if they would like to talk with him. This tentative approach allowed all of them to be engaged in a series of coordinated actions—observe and be observed, share a smoke and a drink—that eventually led them to have a conversation. Fernando adopted a not-knowing position with the gang members; he was being *spontaneously responsive* and *engaging in uncertainty*. He had no idea where those conversations would lead him or how his relationship with the "gang members" would develop.

Almost as a consequence of the "not-knowing" position, tentativity[6] emerges as a way of presenting to clients, and community members, ideas that have been generated in other interactions—with colleagues, texts, people in our daily life, and other clients—debunking certainty and the notion of "truth." In a presentation at ISI, communication theorist John Shotter (personal communication, June 17, 2014) proposed that uncertainty is not just to be tolerated, but embraced as part of the way we relate to each other, thus having ethical and political implications. The conversational process is not about convincing and finding who is right, but tentatively inviting the other to participate in a give and take towards the construction of a "local language" where all discourses are invited into the conversation if they are useful to the client. Fernando did not judge the "gang youth" about their drug use but became curious to learn more. He sought to learn about their views:

> I talked with one of the guys, and we achieved a strong contact. When I found him, he was doing drugs, smoking crack at that very moment. We sat down to talk. The key moment was when we began to talk about what was happening

in the area, about why they were there. Under the effects of the drug, he began talking about his family and what all had happened to him. I remember that I bought some sodas since I had read that when you come down from a drug trip, you want something sweet: chocolate or sodas. So I went to buy one and when the others saw this, little by little they drew closer. We talked about addictions, diseases, sex, and really, the information they had was incredibly good: they know how to take care of themselves, protect themselves and had a really cool story.

(Chaveste, 2014, p. 20, translated)

Fernando focused on the discourse of the person he was talking with rather than being informed by addiction or drug abuse discourses. He sought to create an understanding from within the local understanding of the community member by *orienting towards what was this person's everyday ordinary life*. Thus, he avoided discourses of dysfunction or pathology, even as he talked to a person who was high on drugs. He shared with them how he felt when talking with them; he talked about smoking or drinking, and his dilemmas at work.

In the process of our conversations with clients, when we *make public our inner dialogue* it modifies a hierarchical relationship where the consultants are usually placed as the experts. The action of being public, sharing our reflections, allows us to lay out our pretensions, prejudices, and intentions and transforms the conversation/dialogue into an act of co-construction without the intention to arrive at a particular point or to impose an idea or manner of looking at the dilemma at hand. For instance, Fernando said he combined his own uncertainty with his curiosity to make his inner dialogue public with the "gang guys"/youth. He stated:

Because of the communication we achieved, I proposed that we change the concept of graffiti—that they not paint only lines and scribbles, but that they do something that really communicated something, something that other people could see and admire. That is how the idea emerged of doing murals: filling the walls with what they felt or imagined … . I spoke to Rocío, Director of Social Development. Through her it was authorized that the "gang guys" could paint walls, in my presence and under my supervision, to avoid problems with the police, as usually happened. I got permission and then graffiti painting was an open act, without causing any type of damage, and this contributed to the guys trusting me and the government more.

(Chaveste, 2014, p. 20, translated)

We cannot fully "know" other people's experience. Thus, when we claim that "we know" what the client is saying, it places us as an expert interpreter in the other person's life. From the CDP philosophical stance, *the client is the expert on his or her life* (Anderson & Goolishian, 1992; Levin & Bava, 2012). This stance facilitates our listening and understanding such that clients begin to assume responsibility;

they break with dependence on the therapist/consultant and generate sustainable processes (see Levin & Bava, 2012). Vanilla/Manuel's associates demonstrated their experience of this in reflecting on Fernando's way of listening: "We can finally talk with someone who is interested in what we are doing ... they don't force stuff on us anymore, they're like our buddies, our bros" (Chaveste, 2014, p. 22, translated).

We are the experts in facilitating dialogical processes, but we choose to be *experts in not being experts on people's lives, problems, and solutions.* The idea of the consultant as engaging in a professional practice that is alien to the clients over-looks how the clients are also producers of such practices. Rivière (1985) states that we as subjects are not only produced but also are producers of reality. In the next section, we examine how all of us—therapists, community workers, research-ers, and the persons with whom we work—are producers of the concept of social justice, a lens through which we can make sense of the Vanilla and Fernando's relationship and collaboration.

Epistemological Construction of Social Justice

There is no single take on what constitutes social justice—rather what it "is" is shaped by the very question of how we know what we know. "Justice and injustice are always playing out in social interactions" (Paré, 2014, p. 207). How we under-stand social interactions and, by extension, the construct of social justice can be understood from within a variety of epistemologies. In this section, we approach social justice from the epistemology of social constructionism (Gergen, 1999, 2009; McNamee & Gergen, 1992) wherein the importance of language practices, local knowledge, the process of meaning making, and dialogic action are centered.

Today's social inequalities are embedded in generations of communicative actions and coordination (Anderson & Goolishian, 1988; Gergen, 2009; Pearce, 2007) which, over time and tradition, have become reified moral orders (McNamee, 2008) and formulated into social practices, laws, and policies—that is, codified (cf. Madrigal, 2014 for how housing policies promote racism). To address these social inequities, one has to address the ways people continue to perpetuate them via communicative action, in the process of organizing our everyday lives. According to Pearce (2007), communicative action is the "social construction" model of com-munication. In contrast to communication as the transfer of information from one person to another, the communicative action perspective focuses on communica-tion as "making of our social worlds" (Pearce, 2007, p. 30) with one another. The emphasis is on what we make together with our words, gestures, and in dialogue. And a communicative action perspective draws attention to the process of relating and co-creating that occurs in dialogue. This discursive process of generating and coordinating meaning and the making of our identities, relationships, and realities occurs in dialogic action (Anderson, 2007a, 2007c; Bava, 2016, 2017; Gergen, 2009; McNamee, 2008; Pearce, 2007). Our daily communicative activities of language use and meaning-making are among the mechanisms that reproduce and maintain the very injustices we seek to fight, for example, using the term "people at risk" versus "people with courage," or speaking of "resistance" as a clinical challenge rather than seeing it as a source of strength. Language gets its meaning in communicative action and through use within a community of practice (Anderson, 1997; Anderson & Goolishian, 1988; Bava, 2014; Gergen, 2009). By adopting the perspective of communicative action, we pay particular attention to our language practices as makers of just and unjust practices.

Language, Discourse, and Reality

In language we create reality. Freedman and Combs (1996, p. 16) state:

> (T)he beliefs, values, institutions, customs, labels, laws, division of labor, and the like that make up our social realities are constructed by the members of a culture as they interact with one another from generation to generation and day to day. That is, societies construct the "lenses" through which their members interpret the world. The realities that each of us take for granted are the realities that our societies have surrounded us with since birth.

The realities that Freeman and Combs refer to are embedded in discourses—worldviews that inform our values and beliefs, directing how we act, think, and feel. Discourse is taken for granted and travels invisibly through our participation in communities of practice (Bava, 2014). It both shapes, and is shaped by, the language we use.

From a social constructionist perspective, language gains its meaning in use and constitutes the worlds of meaning we inhabit. Such a view of language is not representational, that is language does not mirror reality. Instead, language is a social activity by which we construct our identities and what is accepted as reality. For instance, while "love is central to marriage" is a current day, dominant discourse in the West, historically love and marriage didn't go hand in hand (Coontz, 2006). And now, the reality of love-based marriage is growing beyond Western cultures.

Institutionalized practices are maintained by language use that is fixed and representational, rather than fluid and constitutive (Anderson, 1997; Gergen, 2009). And this can happen when we reify social justice discourses as well. For instance, prevalent views of social justice speak in terms of the oppressor and the oppressed (Cudd, 2006; David, 2013; Harvey, 2015; Nakamura, 2007; Ratner, 2011). The use of language such as references to the system of oppression or dominance (Cudd, 2006; David, 2013) is a prevalent way of doing power analysis at the societal level, which is helpful for advocacy and making structural changes. However, what might be a useful language practice at the societal level can be problematic at the interpersonal level by offering a narrow account of a person that does not do justice to the complexity of their experiences. Further, depending on how one constructs reality, there is no single description or system of oppression that defines each person's identity. Our identities are multiple; our selves are narratives created in dialogue and relationships (Anderson, 1997; Gergen, 2009; Paré, 2014). Each of our identities are shaped and mediated by a number of different isms—racism, sexism, heterosexism, classism, ableism, ageism, intellectualism, ethnocentrism, anthropocentrism, and so forth—and by other social discourses and interactions. Thus, when we use the language of systems of oppression/dominance to identify people, we set into motion two practices. First, we focus on the notion of structure and system rather than the fluidity of communicative action and/or local language (Anderson & Goolishian, 1988; Pearce, 2007). Second, the phrase "system of oppression/dominance" shifts from one form of reification—the duality of oppressor and oppressed—to a different form of reification, that is the reification of a system. As a consequence it fails to engage the person's preferred story about themselves. We instead view the person through the reified lens of systems. How is this reification, based on our language practices, helping people get out of "oppression?" Reifications prevent people from shifting their language practices in their everyday interactions thus privileging a binary frame over an interaction of multi-storied identities.

The activity of making meaning of one's experience requires us to categorize and name, but when we reify these categories and the labels (names) they have very real effects. For instance, the way categorization and labeling are often practiced in social services repeatedly seems to us to further subjugate people. The complex question is who gets to label whom, when, where, and how? From a CDP stance we believe this is best negotiated with our clients, as it is at this intersection that our everyday—therapeutic and community—conversations can be just.

From a social constructionist view, we see a complex dynamic unfolding in the Vanilla/Manuel story. We believe there is no single story of his identity, rather his identity is fluid and storied depending on the context (Bava, 2016; Gergen, 2009). Vanilla/Manuel's identity continued to transform in conversations and relationships with Fernando and other people in his life. His identity transformation was further facilitated by the community members' responsiveness to his transformation. In not acknowledging these complex coordinated actions, we are in danger of creating "a single story," as Nigerian novelist and TED speaker Chimamanda Adichie (2009) cautions. For instance, in our story, if we view the community members as "oppressed people," we are creating a single story. Our use of the word "oppressed" positions such individuals into a single category, which makes their agency invisible, and doing so shifts all the power to the gang and its members. Further, such a way of talking fails to highlight gang members' multiple identities. Epistemologies that are individualizing or structural (Dickerson, 2010) do not attend to how our language use is instrumental in the creation and promotion of those single stories. In the case of Vanilla/Manuel's story, an individualizing or structural view fails to attend to the local language and relationships among gang members and the community, and neglects to capture the plurality of "privileged" and "subjugated" identities that constitute a person. On the other hand, a CDP practitioner, while being oriented to context, does not conflate context with identity. He/she/they adopts a stance that promotes social justice by staying in synch, and being public and curious, with people about their language and stories that are relevant to them, as summarized below.

Collaborative-Dialogic Orientation Promotes Socially Just Practices

The Collaborative-Dialogical Practices are considered a philosophical stance rather than a theory or a model with pre-structured steps. Anderson (2012, p. 137) states:

> I use the phrase "philosophical stance" to highlight a sensitivity toward a particular kind of attitude from which a therapist's words and actions emerge in response to the other, and to highlight a move away from the notion of "guiding."

Such a philosophical stance emphasizes a way of being with clients rather than focusing on a prescriptive way of practicing. Traditionally, theories provide conceptualizations of problem, strategies, and interventions. Conceptualization is a form of practice; it is embedded within a theoretical discourse aimed to guide action. However, from a CDP perspective, therapy is a creative activity (Bava, 2017), "a human art" of participation in exchanges with others (Anderson, 2012, p. 137). Thus, instead of techniques and types of questions to ask, we offer the following five orienting assumptions for a socially just practice, which initially might appear as "abstract," but becomes a practice, like meditation, when adopted as a way of being in the world. And by extension it becomes a way of being a therapist, a community organizer, and/or a consultant. How this way of being emerges in practice depends on the context and relationships within which we are embedded.

All Human Acts Are Political

All human acts are inscribed in a cultural/historical context in which each of us might be perceived as located in social categories, such as gender, race, class, ethnicity, etc. Such categorization is an inescapable social and political activity. Thus, even when we do not assume a position, that very act is also political.

The CDP perspective is political. Challenging notions traditional to psychotherapy or community development is political in itself (Anderson, 2012). It means taking a stand and questioning issues that have become a *truth* for mental health or community organizing practices. Most existing models of practice propose a series of techniques or steps to follow in adhering to the model. When we talk about Collaborative-Dialogic Practices, in plural, we are saying that there is not one model or technique to track, neither in therapy/community work nor in the way in which we relate to others in our daily professional acts. Since what is collaborative is discursive and contextually constitutive, there are many ways of being and facilitating processes that can be applied across multiple contexts (Anderson & Gehart, 2007).

Privileging Local Knowledge: History, Culture, and Language

The CDP approach centers the local expertise of clients, diminishing the risk of colonizing their processes of sense-making by offering an alternative to prevailing mental health, social/community development, and/or research viewpoints. By centering the practices of communicative action, we not only understand the historical processes of making structural inequities from the client's perspectives but also focus on being spontaneously responsive (Shotter, 2006) to clients, from within the relationships with them, about the kind of futures we are co-creating. Such a positionality shifts our gaze to *power with* our clients, but we are not blind to the *power over* the client built into the "system" of mental health or community development practices. For instance, we might ask the clients how they want us to report on the therapeutic process to an agency that has mandated them for therapy. By inviting the clients' participation in the reporting process, we flip the script on whose expertise counts when reporting to a mandating agency.

Suspending Our Pre-Knowing

A CDP stance also means that there is no pre-designated method with any population based on their social location, diagnosis, or symptoms, since all practices of classification or categorization are themselves social, political processes (Kutchins & Kirk, 1997; McNamee, 2008; Szasz, 1997). Andersen (2007) states "the problem with methods are that they are pre-planned in another context and at another point in time than where the practice happens" (p. 82). Further, we propose checking our prejudices or pre-understanding about why I have a client in front of me. This includes taking care with the language we use to identify the person who seeks our "help" by not assuming that our language is their language. In the example of Vanilla/Manuel, this involved listening carefully to how the youth saw themselves. Over time, the "gang guys"/youth were invited to paint a mural at the Merida airport. Murals convey something positive; more youth joined the project. The youth gave graffiti an identity and made a community conversation with them: a conversation filled with color.

Attending to the Relational Processes

The CDP view explores understanding the dynamic relational processes of making socially just realities, rather than understanding our social realities as structurally fixed entities. Not to be limited to righting historical wrongs, social justice is additionally understood as a process that we are all currently engaged in shaping and being shaped by.

An understanding of discursive processes—therapy, community work, research, etc.—requires a grasp of both structural inequalities and communicative action. How we engage in conversations with our clients can further the structural inequalities or help us notice our role as co-creators of the larger processes that promote justice and make us agentic change makers through the everyday activities of our professional lives. For instance, how do I position myself as a practitioner with a client who has been mandated for therapy? An activity of sense-making can be used intentionally for making and organizing power over or power with our clients. How we go about doing our practice is a political activity. For instance, in therapy, there is a distinction between locating problems in people's neuropsychology and/or cognition versus in local language and social communication (discourses); each is a political activity that has the potential to create different lived realities.

Reflecting on the Processes of Co-Creating

We inquire with our clients about what we are co-creating through our dialogue and seek to make sense of it, asking who it serves and how. Being curious about these processes shifts our attention to how we are relating and what is being constructed within the consulting or therapeutic interaction. This expands our consideration beyond the construct of power, to a focus on the activities of meaning-making, categorizing, and naming, which are all political activities. A not-knowing, reflective stance with our clients about what is being created, by whom, and how, helps open up space for an egalitarian relationship thus promoting a socially just practice. For instance, when my (Rocío's) team inquired with Vanilla/Manuel about his transformation process, we did not presume to know how he would define his process. Because it eschews categorizing people and searching for preferred outcomes, CDP anticipates that each person will have a unique story to be understood on his or her own terms (Anderson, 2012). Though CDP does not view people in terms of categories, it recognizes there can be a role for the making of categories and labels as part of the meaning-making process, while recognizing that any category or label is only one of the many possible ways to characterize a person's life. Thus, as practitioners we steer clear from categorizing "our clients" (such as abusers or victims or narcissists, etc.) while tentatively holding the categories and labels clients apply to themselves, remaining open to emergence and generativity.

The CDP approach shifts the gaze from a label or a category to the process of relating and co-creating (Anderson, 2007a; Bava, 2017; McNamee & Gergen, 1999). It locates the focus of practice in dialogue and being responsible from within the relationship—that is, relational responsibility rather than focusing on individual responsibility (McNamee, 2009; McNamee & Gergen, 1999). The focus on relational responsibility also acknowledges that our professional practices are historically and relationally situated (McNamee, 2008). So not only are "structural inequalities" part of the contextual dialogue but also how one talks with local participants about inequities—and the meanings created within both the client's and the practitioner's local context—becomes part of the discursive practices. Such a stance is one way to practice what Reynolds refers to as "an ethic of justice-doing" (Reynolds & Hammoud-Beckett, 2012, p. 57) where the focus is on a way of being as a way of "doing."

How such a stance is put into practice is wide open and depends on the interlocutors and the context of their participations. In adopting these above orienting assumptions, a challenge that arises is how to avoid constructing other "oppressive systems" as we use alternative practices that make up new realities? If we cannot control the result of what is created, then how can we avoid re-perpetuating injustice? Anderson (2012, p. 133) offers us one way to respond to the above questions when she states:

> Collaborative practice also calls for shifts in our actions including: setting aside taking on the role of helper; moving from "aboutness" thinking to "withness" thinking and being; maintaining coherence in our ways of being in our professional and personal worlds; and being visible as a person; all of which, in one way or another, contribute to the creation of an alternative view of language and meaning, in which one human being is in relationship with another human being.

Conclusion

The Collaborative-Dialogic Practices approach to social justice focuses on promoting dialogue among divergent voices while attending to the local context, language, and history, considering who is in conversation—with whom, when, where, and how—and attending to emergent relationships and meanings that are jointly created. It is a way of being where one is cognizant of the multiple discourses at hand—any one of which has the potential of being reified in our discursive practices. It is a way of being in relationships that open up possibilities in the ways we listen, hear, and speak (Anderson, 2003). The focus is on creating language that is local to that particular social interaction without imposing a singular language that risks privileging an expert's interpretation. It is a perspective focused on creating and allowing space for innovative practices, new ways of meaning to emerge by engaging the unknown and uncertain.

The practitioner focuses on the communicative action, which invites one into a responsive dialogical practice where fluidity and reflexivity with one's interlocutors are valued. Our purpose is to avoid drilling down into a single story and instead to promote multiple possibilities with open-ended questions.

Eight years after the original work with Vanilla/Manuel, we come back to his story. His words describe the process of his transformation, a process that continues as he engages in other conversations and relationships. When the work started, the people at the Department of Social Development did not set a goal or a preferred outcome for Vanilla/Manuel or any others. The aim was to engage with the community in conversations that were going to bring about transformations. However, they did not know what type of transformations such dialogues would bring about. Relating a small part of the Vanilla/Manuel's story does not mean that we are presenting a guide to working with gang members. This is his story as he described it at that moment in time.

> My mom didn't like them to call me Vanilla. If they called the house asking for Vanilla, she would say that nobody by that name lived there. She has always called me Manuel. Now I introduce myself with a first and last name, Manuel Pérez. With this bit of Manuel, I've gotten to many places raising my face high and saying "Good afternoon, I am Manuel Pérez," I stand up and talk to them, I tell them what it's about, I try to channel my words, making sure they're not vulgar. I haven't been in jail for a long time, I see everyone landing in there, getting out, and being sent back. I go there too, I'm not letting anyone fuck them, but I stay out of trouble, I learned to relate in a different way. The way I dress has a lot to do with it, I learned how to dress. Before just standing in the street dressed like the "clika," the police would stop and shake me down. A while ago I was standing in the street. Some patrolmen saw me, stopped for a minute, and it made me nervous; they looked me up and down, but nothing happened. They stepped on the gas and left.

Reflection Questions

1.   What are our intentions when we "work for social justice?"
2.   Who decides what "social justice" is?
3.   What are we creating together when we are working for "social justice" and who does it serve?
4.   Who decides how these questions should be responded to?

Notes

1 We all contributed equally to this article. Writing our names in alphabetical order constitutes a political decision.
2 Spanglish word that emerges from the English term "clique."
3 Name of the gang he used to belong to. It means "The group of 13."
4 The "full" story of Vanilla/Manuel that we cite throughout the paper can be read in Chaveste (2014).
5 The International Summer Institute, held annually since 1997 in Mexico for practitioners, researchers and teachers/trainers interested in CDP, is organized by Harlene Anderson and Grupo Campos Eliseos.

6 The term tentativity, created in translation within the context of training in Mexico, refers to the notion of tentativeness. We choose to use it as is, rather than to make a grammatical correction, because this is how it emerged in local use and is an example of Spanglish in use.

References

Adichie, C. (2009). *Chimamanda Adichie: The danger of a single story* [Video file]. Retrieved from www.ted.com/talks/chimamanda_adichie_the_danger_of_a_single_story.html

Andersen, T. (2007). Human participating: Human "being" is the step for human becoming in the next step. In H. Anderson & D. Gehart, (Eds.), *Collaborative therapy: Relationships and conversations that make a difference* (pp. 81–93). New York, NY: Routledge.

Anderson, H. (1997). *Conversation, language, and possibilities: A postmodern approach to therapy*. New York, NY: Basic Books.

Anderson, H. (2003). Some notes on listening, hearing and speaking and the relationship to dialogue. Paper presented at the Eighth Annual Open Dialogue Conference: What Is Helpful in Treatment Dialogue? Tornio, Finland. Retrieved from http://harleneanderson.org

Anderson, H. (2007a). A postmodern umbrella: Language and knowledge as relational and generative, and inherently transforming. In H. Anderson & D. Gehart, (Eds.), *Collaborative therapy: Relationships and conversations that make a difference* (pp. 7–19). New York, NY: Routledge.

Anderson, H. (2007b). Historical influences. In H. Anderson & D. Gehart, (Eds.), *Collaborative therapy: Relationships and conversations that make a difference* (pp. 21–31). New York, NY: Routledge.

Anderson, H. (2007c). The heart and spirit of collaborative therapy: The philosophical stance—"A way of being" in relationship and conversation. In H. Anderson & D. Gehart, (Eds.), *Collaborative therapy: Relationships and conversations that make a difference* (pp. 43–59). New York, NY: Routledge.

Anderson, H. (2012). Collaborative practice: A way of being "with." *Psychotherapy and Politics International, 10*(2): 130–145. doi: 10.1002/ppi.1261

Anderson, H., & Gehart, D. (Eds.) (2007). *Collaborative therapy: Relationships and conversations that make a difference*. New York, NY: Routledge.

Anderson, H., & Goolishian, H. (1988). Human systems as linguistic systems: Preliminary and evolving ideas about the implications for clinical theory. *Family Process, 27*, 157–163. doi: 10.1111/j.1545-5300.1988.00371.x

Anderson, H., & Goolishian, H. (1992). The client is the expert: A not-knowing approach to therapy. In. S. McNamee & K. Gergen (Eds.), *Social construction and the therapeutic process* (pp. 25–39). Newbury Park, CA: Sage.

Bava, S. (2014). Performative practices, performative relationships—in and as emergent research. In G. Simon & A. Chard (Eds.), *Systemic inquiry: Innovation in reflexive practice research* (pp. 155–173). Farnhill, UK: Everything is Connected Press.

Bava, S. (2016). Making of a spiritual/religious hyperlinked identity. In D. Bidwell (Ed.). *Spirituality, social construction and social processes: Essays and reflections* (pp. 1–17). OH: Taos Institute.

Bava, S. (2017). Creativity in couple and family therapy. In J. L. Lebow, A. L. Chambers, & D. Breunlin (Eds.), *Encyclopaedia of couple and family therapy*. New York: Springer. doi: 10.1007/978-3-319-15877-8_226-1

Bava, S., McDonough, M., Chaveste, R., & Molina, P. (2013). Is collaborative practice politically and socially just? If so, how? *International Journal of Collaborative-Dialogic Practices, 3.* Retrieved from https://collaborative-practices.com/archived/volume-4-archives-2/faq-4/

Chaveste, R. (2014). *Identidades y Relaciones: Una mirada desde el Socioconstruccionismo y las prácticas colaborativas y dialógicas.* México: Instituto Kanankil, Investigación y Construcción Social, A.C.

Coontz, S. (2006). *Marriage, a history: How love conquered marriage.* New York, NY: Viking.

Cudd, A. (2006). *Analyzing oppression.* New York, NY: Oxford University Press.

David, E. J. B. (2013). *Internalized oppression: The psychology of marginalized groups.* New York, NY: Springer.

Dickerson, V. (2010). Positioning oneself within an epistemology: Refining our thinking about integrative approaches. *Family Process, 49,* 349–368. doi: 10.1111/j.1545-5300.2010.01327.x

Freedman, J., & Combs, J. (1996). *Narrative therapy: The social construction of preferred realities.* New York, NY: Norton.

Gergen, K. J. (1999). *An invitation to social construction.* Thousand Oaks, CA: Sage.

Gergen, K. J. (2009). *Relational being: Beyond self and community.* New York, NY: Oxford University Press.

Harvey, J. (2015). *Civilized oppression and moral relations: Victims, fallibility, and the moral community.* New York, NY: Palgrave Macmillan.

Kutchins, H., & Kirk, (1997). *Making us crazy: DSM: The psychiatric bible and the creation of mental disorders.* New York, NY: Free Press.

Levin, S., & Bava, S. (2012). Collaborative therapy: Performing reflective and dialogic relationships. In A. Lock & T. Strong (Eds.), *Discursive perspectives in therapeutic practice* (pp. 127–142). Oxford, UK: Oxford University Press.

McNamee, S. (2004). Therapy as social construction. In T. Strong and D. Pare (Eds.), *Furthering talk: Advances in the discursive therapies.* New York, NY: Kluwer Academic/Plenum Press.

McNamee, S. (2008). Transformative dialogue: Coordinating conflicting moralities. The Lindberg Lecture 2008. Retrieved from https://pubpages.unh.edu/~smcnamee/dialogue_and_transformation/

McNamee, S. (2009). Postmodern psychotherapeutic ethics: Relational responsibility in practice. *Human Systems, 20*(1), 57–71.

McNamee, S., & Gergen, K. J. (1992). *Therapy as a social construction.* London: Sage.

McNamee, S., & Gergen, K. J. (1999). *Relational responsibility: Resources for sustainable dialogue.* Thousand Oaks, CA: Sage.

Madrigal, A. (2014, May 22). The racist housing policy that made your neighborhood. *The Atlantic.* Retrieved from www.theatlantic.com/

Nakamura, N. (2007). *The relationship between social oppression, internalized homonegativity, substance use during sex and risky sexual behavior in Latino gay and bisexual men.* Washington, DC: George Washington University.

Paré, D. (2014). Social justice and the word: Keeping diversity alive in therapeutic conversations. *Canadian Journal of Counselling and Psychotherapy, 48*(3), 206–217. Retrieved from http://cjc-rcc.ucalgary.ca

Pearce, B. (2007). *Making social worlds: A communication perspective.* Malden, MA: Blackwell.

Ratner, C. (2011). *Macro cultural psychology: A political philosophy of mind.* New York, NY: Oxford University Press.

Reynolds, V., & Hammoud-Beckett, S. (2012). Bridging the worlds of therapy and activism: Intersections, tensions & affinities. *The International Journal of Narrative Therapy and Community Work, 4,* 57–61. Retrieved from http://dulwichcentre.com.au/international-journal-of-narrative-therapy-and-community-work

Rivière, E. P. (1985). *El proceso grupal. Del psicoanálisis a la psicología social (I),* Nueva Visión: Buenos Aires.

Shotter, J. (2006). Understanding process from within: An argument for "withness"-thinking. *Organization Studies, 27*(4), 585–604. doi: 10.1177/0170840606062105

Szasz, T. (1997). *Insanity: The idea and its consequences.* Syracuse, NY: Syracuse University Press.

PART IV

Justice and Gender

Among the various social locations to which the term intersectionality refers, gender has long been a site of struggle for justice. In counseling and psychotherapy, feminism in its various waves has contributed hugely to the evolution of thought and practice with its fine-tuned attention to power relations and discourse, among the many issues impinging on identity. Despite this movement, however, gender inequities persist within the wider culture, and indeed the debate has become more complex and multi-faceted as growing attention is paid to the intersections between gender and other identity dimensions such as race and sexual orientation. The chapters in this section illustrate that diversity, highlighting different aspects of the politics of gender as they play out in therapeutic conversations.

In Chapter 11, Reimagining the Intersection of Gender, Knowledge, and Power in Therapeutic Conversations with Women and Eating Disorders and Men Who Use Violence, Catrina Brown and Tod Augusta-Scott use the phrase positioned therapies as an umbrella term to designate a range of therapeutic approaches that manifest a commitment to social justice concerns by attending to the interplay of language, social discourse, and power in people's lives. Their chapter is devoted to exploring how social justice is enacted in relation to gender in their practice. In some respects, Catrina and Tod's work can be seen as centered on opposite sides of a coin—hers working with women subject to patriarchy and more specifically eating disorders, his working with men who use abuse in intimate relationships. However, the very tendency to dichotomize, which so frequently shows up in this work (client vs. therapist expertise, personal agency/resistance vs. constraining cultural discourses, feelings of power vs. powerlessness, etc.) is unpacked and critiqued for failing to do justice to the complexity of lived experience and thus shutting down fruitful therapeutic possibilities. Catrina uses the term "body talk" to foreground women's agency in the face of disordered eating. She speaks of how women "resource" their bodies to gain a greater sense of control, a practice that can be understood both as the reproduction of and resistance to dominant social scripts. Tod examines men's actions in relation to social discourses—more particularly, discourses associated with dominant masculinity—in which they are immersed. His work also examines hard-edged dichotomies; rather than assuming

141

ill-intent, he seeks to make space for the multiplicity of men's experience. This involves drawing attention to both their desires for controlling relationships and their desire for caring, fair relationships. Ultimately both authors explore ways that dominant discourses are complicit in provoking unjust practice towards self and others, while offering examples of practice that encourages acts of resistance.

Chapter 12, Queer Informed Narrative Therapy: Radical Approaches to Counseling with Transgender Persons, by David Nylund and Annie Temple, addresses the widespread misunderstandings about the experience of transgendered persons and the injustices perpetuated against them, even within the realm of counseling and psychotherapy. The authors review the historical pathologizing of non-dominant sexual orientations and gender identities. This includes the designation of "homosexuality" as a mental disorder in the *Diagnostic and Statistical Manual* (DSM) until 1973, to the diagnosis of Gender Identity Disorder, changed to Gender Dysphoria in the DSM-5. The authors outline the critical need for more trans-informed practitioners, while sharing key facets of their own practices informed by queer theory and narrative therapy. Queer theory challenges entrenched binaries as they relate to identity, embracing a multiplicity of sexualities and genders. Narrative therapy makes a shift to a relational orientation from the individualistic perspective that dominates the field. Rather than regarding problems as expressions of intra-psychic dysfunction, narrative therapy separates persons from problems, and construes many of the challenges transgender clients experience as the effects of transphobia. The chapter presents several case studies to illustrate how Queer Informed clinicians can help to expose the socially constructed nature of gender and assist clients in consolidating self-honoring identities closely aligned with their values and purposes.

The final chapter in this section, Chapter 13, Coming Out: Implications for Sexual Minority Immigrants and Newcomers, problematizes simplistic responses to the phenomenon of "coming out," examining how the phrase is associated with culture-bound assumptions and practices that frequently do not fit for sexual minorities whose origins are not in North America. Mego Nerses and David Paré remind us that while the notion of "gay pride" appeals to many practitioners as a bold statement of one's identity in the face of unjust discrimination and homophobia, the phrase is not universally embraced. For some, disclosure of their sexual orientation may be life-threatening to themselves, friends, and loved ones, or could lead to a profound disconnection from family members. After outlining the complexity of the coming out phenomenon for immigrants and newcomers, the chapter features a case study to illustrate a culturally responsive approach to working with immigrants and newcomers in the context of coming out.

CHAPTER 11

Reimagining the Intersection of Gender, Knowledge, and Power in Collaborative Therapeutic Conversations with Women and Eating Disorders and Men Who Use Violence

Catrina Brown and Tod Augusta-Scott

In recent years, a range of related therapeutic approaches have emerged that place concerns of social justice at the forefront with their emphasis on the interplay of language, social discourse, and power in people's lives. These approaches draw on a variety of traditions, including social constructionism, feminism, and narrative. Some approaches key in on the construction of meaning, utterance by utterance, in therapeutic conversations (cf. Anderson, 1997; Anderson & Goolishian, 1993). Some extend that finely attuned attention to language beyond the consulting room, looking at how dominant social discourses impinge on people's identities (cf. Freedman & Combs, 1996; White, 2007; White & Epston, 1990). Others combine constructionist, narrative, and feminist ideas (cf. Brown & Augusta-Scott, 2007; Madsen, 1999; Paré, 2013; Paré & Larner, 2004; Strong & Paré, 2004) in ways that celebrate the constructive potential of talk while acknowledging the constraining influence of cultural meanings.

These therapies trace some of their ancestry to family therapy, always preoccupied with the pragmatic potential of turns of phrase, while also mindful of the systems that contribute to individual experience. Their commitments can also be seen in the empowerment- and strengths-based approaches of 1970s feminist and anti-oppressive practice. At present these social justice-oriented therapies are more often associated with postmodern and post-structuralist thought. For the purposes of shorthand, we will refer here to these various approaches as "positioned therapies," because of their attention to power relations and the emphasis they put on both (a) the positioning of the therapist in relation to the client and (b) the positioning of clients within the wider discursive contexts of their lives.

In this chapter, we will describe our version of positioned therapy through the gendered examples of women's use of their bodies and men's use of violence, relating the practices to social justice concerns. In describing this approach, we will simultaneously point to overlaps with other positioned therapies, while also clarifying what we consider to be some key distinctions from related approaches in wide circulation. A strong thread running through the chapter is our critique of the many sharp-edged dichotomies that have been proposed to distinguish anti-oppressive from oppressive practices. On closer analysis, we believe this "either/or" impulse shuts down options for therapists and the persons who consult them. Among the dichotomies we will explore are: client expertise vs. therapist expertise; personal agency/resistance vs. constraining cultural discourses; feelings of power vs. powerlessness; disordered eating as speaking vs. hiding; and listening to the voices of women vs. listening to the voices of men.

We believe a therapy concerned with social justice must be attuned to the social discourses and practices that impinge on people's lives, and must be vigilant of the possibility of inadvertently re-enacting those in the practice of therapy. At the same time, to be useful, a therapy must do more than acknowledge constraints; it must create space for identifying and expanding on persons' initiatives and acts of resistance. To accomplish these tasks involves adopting a "both/and" or multiple perspectives (Andersen, 1993; Augusta-Scott, 2003) orientation that we will illustrate through descriptions of our work with women and eating disorders and men who use violence.

Knowing and Not Knowing

We adopt a critical postmodern orientation to our work, viewing therapeutic conversations as exchanges of ideas whereby each person has only "partial knowledge" (Haraway, 1988). This approach is a departure from the notion of an "expert" knowledge position in therapy. However, note this position is different from *either* the therapist as expert position typically associated with mainstream, modernist-influenced approaches, *or* the attempt to redress the deficiencies of the therapist-as-expert position by ascribing ultimate expertise to the client—a stance often associated with certain feminist and anti-oppressive practices.

The elevation of client to expert status is sometimes accompanied by the notion of the "not-knowing" therapist (Anderson, 1997). While we respect what is in effect a social justice-oriented effort to respect and center the clients' knowledge, we prefer to adopt Haraway's (1988) position that knowledge can only ever be partial—there is no total or absolute knowledge—and White's (2007) view that all stories have multiple authors. We believe this stance recognizes the therapist and client as both knowing and not knowing at any given time. This escapes a binary or either/or-based expert approach to knowledge that constrains the constructive back and forth of collaborative conversations. We agree with Anderson (1997) that meaning is influenced through what both the client and therapist bring to the conversation. Acknowledging that neither therapist nor clients are, or can be, absolute knowers moves away from limiting binary approaches where people either have knowledge and power or they don't (Brown, 2007a, 2007b, 2012).

Although the notion of not knowing has understandably been intended to challenge the powerful all-knowing stance of the therapist and to adopt a position of humility, it may unwittingly tie knowledge and power together in an unhelpful way. It is not necessary for the therapist to *not* know in order for the client to know. To acknowledge that the therapist brings something to the conversation does not imply a claim to objective, absolute, or authoritative knowledge. One has to stand somewhere, as White (1997, 2001) reminds us in saying the therapist is always positioned—whether simply listening, asking questions, or inviting people to consider various ideas and practices. This is therefore not a neutral positioning because all knowledge is positioned (Foucault, 1980; White, 2001). What emerges from therapeutic conversations is a product of the meeting of these knowledges, and includes both therapists' and clients' interpretations and narratives of experience (E. Bruner, 1986a, 1986b; J. Bruner, 2002; Scott, 1992). We therefore favor the view of clients and therapists as subjects negotiating knowledge and power through collaborative dialogue.

Shared Stories

Another corollary of the concept of not knowing is the admonition to distrust the conclusion that therapist and client may share some "common ground." Anderson and Goolishian (1993) advise collaborative therapists to focus on the uniqueness of each person's narrative, rather than "search for regularities and common meaning that may validate the therapist's theory but invalidate the uniqueness of the clients' stories and thus their very identity" (p. 30). This rests on the dichotomizing assumption that there can be no overlap in experience between client and therapist. We prefer to honor each person's uniqueness while *also* anticipating common meaning; this is a feature of a politicized, positioned therapy that acknowledges that we are collectively subject to cultural discourses. It recognizes, for example, that women often share common aspects of their experiences by way of the patriarchal structures in which they arise. It is our view that experience and the meaning attached to it are socially constructed within particular social conditions. While meaning varies across persons, it is *also* inter-subjective, and there are often shared understandings.

Understanding people's experience in a social context allows therapists to move away from pathologizing and blaming interpretations that are blind to contextual barriers and pin problems on individuals. Both self-critical and preferred interpretations of experience are part of the marketplace of meanings available to persons. A contextual view reminds us that even our words are permeated with the knowledges of others. This deviates somewhat from Anderson and Goolishian's (1993) claim that "A socio-cultural system is the product of social communication, rather than communication being a product of structural organization" (p. 27). Intriguing as this idea is, we believe it further dichotomizes by characterizing persons as authors who are never "authored," as it were. As we will describe in more detail below, this shuts down perspectives and options that might be useful in therapeutic dialogue. Our view is that neither a socio-cultural system nor social communication are the unilateral products of the other; rather there is a complex dialectic between social structures, social discourses, and human interaction. In this process, human beings are both creators of and created by society.

This more complex view calls for holding what at first glance are contradictory claims—that we author our experience through language while also being subject to the imposition of meanings from dominant social structures. White's (2001) externalizing narrative process, which involves separating persons from problems through language to make space for the authoring of preferred narratives, reflects this view. Externalizing locates stories within a social and political context, and recognizes stories are not neutral. Thus therapists wishing to advance social justice are inescapably positioned in their work (Augusta-Scott, 2007, 2009; Brown, 2014, in press; Brown & Augusta-Scott, 2007; White, 1997). As a result, the conversations that unfold are an interplay of multiple positions—not neutral, not outside power. All positions are social and discursive. There are multiple authors involved in the creation of identity stories; some versions are congruent with persons' cherished values and intentions while others reflect patriarchal and other oppressive discourses to which we are jointly subjected.

This is the setting for the social justice-oriented work we do; a storied realm inhabited by both therapists and clients, in which both can only know what they know within socially constructed and complex discursive contexts. In both of the domains of our practice—eating disorders and men's use of violence—sociocultural discourses, and more specifically gendered norms, are strongly implicated. We believe a positioned therapy that acknowledges this discursive backdrop can encourage the development of counterstories on the side of social justice. We begin this work with the idea that women may get to a place where they do not need to use their bodies to speak the unspoken (Brown, 2007b), and that men will stop using violence, confront any sense of patriarchal entitlement, and find ways to address their hurt, pain, powerlessness, and rage in less hurtful ways. In the next sections, we will describe some of the work we do in these areas to address the unjust and oppressive effects of patriarchal discourse.

Eating Disorders: Talking Body Talk

I (CB) work in private practice as a feminist narrative therapist, primarily with women around issues of health and mental health. I teach at the social justice-based School of Social Work at Dalhousie University with a focus on developing a critical clinical curriculum and I am cross-appointed to Gender and Women's Studies. My research has centered on women, depression, substance use, trauma and sexual violence, and eating disorders.

A positioned approach with women allows them to explore the meaning of the eating disorder in their lives, that is, what their bodies communicate through their eating disorders. I am positioned as I do this, drawing upon ideas I hold about eating disorders. I use the term "body talk" to depict culturally specific ways women speak or communicate through their bodies (Brown, 2001; Ussher, 1997, 2011). As a site for struggle, the body can tell stories of undeniable anguish. "Eating disorders"[1] are embodied performances of gender and provide women a way to simultaneously "speak and hide." In other words, women's body talk may both reproduce *and* resist dominant social scripts (Brown, 2007b, 2014). Gremillion (2003) has suggested that women often "resource" or use their bodies to gain a greater sense of control. Through the body, women may speak the unspoken struggles and resistance they may have yet to fully acknowledge to themselves or others.

Lawrence describes the "control paradox" of eating disorders (1979), which acknowledges eating "disorders" as an expression of power, control, and agency, as well as feeling powerlessness and out of control. It is therefore critical to avoid reifying women as passive victims and instead to assist in creating empowering collaborative conversations. While it is important to address the ongoing social pressure to be thin, the acknowledgment of women's agency, power, and participation in resourcing their bodies through eating "disorders" is pivotal.

My focus is to explore what the body is saying, rather than focusing on weight/eating (Brown, 1993a); directing attention to what makes sense about women's experiences, rather than pathologizing them. Women's body talk expresses not only veiled protests but also the subjective struggles that women experience in the world, by simultaneously *speaking and not speaking*; or speaking without appearing to speak and thus controlling the risk associated with speaking (Bordo, 1993; Brown, 2007b, 2014; Orbach, 1986).

Rather than understanding women simply as victims of culture, we need to encourage them to become more aware of how they actively participate in body surveillance and self-management. Keeping women's agency at the forefront prevents therapy from serving as a mechanism to heighten regulation of the self (Brown, 1993a, 1993b; Lawrence, 1979, 1984). While it may appear paradoxical at first glance, a woman's commitment to an eating disorder can be taken up as a "unique outcome" (White & Epston, 1990), or an instance of defying a problem-saturated story, of a woman defending and privileging her own immediate emotional needs before those of others even if doing so causes conflict (Brown, 2014). In this regard, a woman's actions are a powerful form of resistance to socially constructed dominant expectations of gender performance for women. I have often heard women say that control over their body is the "only thing I have for myself" as they hold even tighter to it.

On the other side of the both/and divide, it is important to not only celebrate a woman's initiative and choice, but to acknowledge the social constraints she is perpetually up against. By externalizing body talk in conversations with women, space is opened to look at how feelings are tied to gendered discourses of thinness and self-management. We need to distinguish socially imposed self-management discourses from individually initiated body talk. This makes it possible to create alternative stories of living less constrained by the discourse of thinness and the cultural imperative of self-management and self-mastery (Brown, 2007c, 2014).

Some positioned therapies construe eating disorders as the victimization of women by social prescriptions for thinness (Maisel, Epston, & Borden, 2004; Nylund, 2002; White, 1991). This sensibility is reflected in the "anti-anorexia" or "anti-bulimia" leagues initiated by David Epston (2000). In that approach, anorexia or bulimia is externalized by turning the "disorder" into an active subject. The emphasis is on women resisting or "waging war against a deadly disorder" (Barton, 2006). In the "anti" approach, therapists bring into the therapeutic discourse a dominant cultural idea that totalizes anorexia and bulimia as bad, as "monsters" destroying women's lives (Maisel et al., 2004). Eating disorders are depicted as abusing women and thus women are encouraged to fight against them. This position suggests that anorexia and bulimia employ "twisted logic" (p. 327) and are a "discursive parasite" (p. 322). The anti-anorexia and bulimia movement construes eating disorders as "ersatz" rather than genuine resistances (Lock, Epston, Maisel, & deFaria, 2005, p. 329), suggesting that genuine acts of resistance require conscious critical reflection. As a result, women's efforts at power and control through the eating disorder are rendered invisible; women's resourcing of their bodies and their resistance through the body tend to go unheard. The gendered strategy of both speaking and hiding through the body talk remains unacknowledged.

Rather than totalizing eating disorders as "bad," I believe conversations need to focus on the both/and of how eating disorders both work and do not work for women to achieve power and control. I use questions to explore how meanings have been organized and what has influenced that process. For the purpose of illustration, I will share a few of the many questions I employ; however, space limitations preclude a detailed breakdown of this work, which embraces complexity in order to do full justice to women's experience.

Women with eating disorders overwhelmingly identify feeling thin with feeling good and in control and feeling fat with feeling bad and out of control. To address this, I help them to unpack the meaning of fatness and thinness in their lives, acknowledging that in dominant Western culture, fatness is considered bad and thinness is good. I might ask:

- You have told me you "feel too fat." Can we focus on those feelings for a bit? Can you tell me what it feels like to you when you feel fat?
- When you feel thin, what do you feel this says about you?
- What does it take to feel thin? Why is this important to you?

These questions explore how women often connect feeling thin with a sense of self-mastery and accomplishment and with feeling socially valuable, acceptable, and desirable (Bordo, 1993; Brown, 2007d, 2014; Brown & Jasper, 1993; Lawrence, 1979, 1984). In accordance with Bordo (1993), I further unpack Lawrence's (1979) control paradox, the self-management discourse that constructs thinness as good and in control.

- Does feeling thin make you feel more in control?
- Can you tell me more about feeling out of control?
- Does feeling fat make you feel more out of control? Can you tell me about that?

- What do you feel you have to do to get to that thin feeling?
- What happens when that thin feeling goes away?
- So it is really hard sometimes to restrict your eating, but you feel strong when you do. How does it make you feel strong and in control?

These questions explore the both/and experience of both feeling out of control while also establishing a sense of control through exercising and restricting eating. At the more extreme end of the continuum, women sometimes report feeling that the level of control they need to assert over their eating and their bodies to achieve thinness can make them feel like "robots" (Brown, 1993a). This provides an opening for expanding on preferences to identify alternative modes of control:

- Does it ever feel too hard to keep restricting? What does that feel like? What is hard about it?
- You told me you are sick of feeling like a robot. What is it like to feel like a robot?
- It sounds like you feel really strong and in control when you are restricting, but sometimes almost too much like a robot. Other times you feel mad at yourself for not being able to hold onto that control and that makes you feel out of control. Can you tell me more about what feeling out of control is like for you?

Some of my questions externalize the self-management behavior as "the robot":

- When did you first notice the robot?
- How does the robot react to the bingeing and purging?
- If you were having a conversation with the robot, what do you think it would say?
- What would you say to the robot?

Many women are caught in a painful back and forth between rigid control and the loss of control associated with bingeing and purging. I deliberately connect the word "choice" with bingeing as women often describe bingeing as feeling out of control, as though it just happens and they have no say over whether they will binge eat or not. I find that when women can give themselves permission to binge eat they actually do feel more in control of the process.

In the spirit of both/and, body talk is characterized by an ambivalence on the part of women. It is important to respect that it is usually too difficult to simply give up an eating disorder. I often ask:

- What part of you would prefer not to have an eating disorder? What part of you prefers to have an eating disorder?
- How hard would it be to give up controlling your body and eating? If people were to see you bingeing and purging, what would they learn about you that they are not usually aware of?
- How is your eating disorder important to you?
- What makes it really hard to give up?

Women often say, when asked about what people would learn about them if they were to see them bingeing and purging, that people would be surprised by how much they are struggling and that things are not perfect; things are not okay. This is one aspect of a woman's experience being spoken through the body. Rather than seeing body talk in terms of a "resistant client," I prefer to acknowledge how self-management efforts may be both useful and harmful to a woman, that eating disorders may be a way to *speak and hide*. I usually say to women that if the eating disorder did not make sense, if it was not meaningful at some level, it probably would not exist. It is my position that women need to listen to the body talk and attend to what it means before they will choose to let it go.

A woman's indirect speech through body talk can be a woman's way to stand up for herself. I therefore want to "double listen" (White, 2004), hearing how the woman is moving outside a dominant identity story by doing something that part of her wants, even though it goes against someone else and causes conflict. This is very significant. I often say to women, asking some variation of the question "You've told me the eating disorder is precious to you; how does it feel when people ask you to give up something important to you?" Most often the women acknowledge it makes them mad when people respond this way, and it distresses them that others are mad at them as well. I avoid engaging in a power struggle over the woman's body; this to avoid exacerbating the control paradox (Brown, 1993b; Lawrence, 1979). Nevertheless, this inquiry makes possible an exploration of ambivalence around the eating disorder:

- It sounds kind of hard, because it sounds like while an eating disorder intends to help you out, sometimes what happens instead is it causes you some trouble. Does that sound right?
- If the eating disorder was not useful to you in some way you probably would not have it. Does it feel like it would be like giving up a friend in some way? What's that like?

Women frequently report that giving up an eating disorder would be giving up a part of themselves; they describe letting go of the only control they feel as terrifying. These conversations provide a glimpse of how fragile the control they have established through controlling their bodies is. It is hard for the women to talk about how their tenacious control of their bodies obscures the lack of control they feel otherwise. However this realization often marks a loosening of the compelling grip of the self-discipline and self-management. It provides an opening to imagining the possibility of living without the eating disorder:

- Can you imagine other ways you might cope than through dieting, bingeing, and purging?
- What difference will it make to your life if you can find a way to feel in control without feeling like the "robot"?

These limited examples of more protracted work demonstrate the complexity of conversations with women about eating disorders—the challenge of simultaneously unpacking the ways that gendered discourses recruit women into actions with negative repercussions, while also understanding and even celebrating those actions as defiant expressions of agency. This approach departs somewhat from approaches that also fit among what we are calling "positioned therapies" but that are more inclined to dichotomize in a manner that we believe reduces options for clients and therapists. This same impulse towards a both/and orientation is evident in our work with men who use violence, which we will explore in the next section.

Men's Use of Violence

I (TA-S) work in a community organization to help men take responsibility to both stop abuse and restore safety and respect. Part of my political commitment is to work within the context of the women's shelter movement. I am inspired by the many men I work with who demonstrate their commitment to taking responsibility. My practice draws on feminism, restorative justice and narrative therapy. In working with men who use violence, I position myself in a manner that both acknowledges that the men are influenced by patriarchal discourses while I simultaneously orient to expressions of value more aligned with respect, gender equity, and non-violence. While I am positioned in my belief that patriarchy influences men to want power and control in relationships, I also ask men *what else* is important to them and what they value in relationships.

Men often identify valuing social justice. They begin the conversations with a story of injustice, either from their present or the past. Through this story, men are invited to articulate the values informing their negative evaluation of incidents when they have been treated unfairly. For example, men often talk about the pain of being abused and, as a result, I inquire about the values they have that lead them to think that this behavior was abusive and wrong. Men often articulate their value of fairness, safety, the importance of listening to various perspectives, and respect. While they start the conversations in a reticent manner, my interest in them and their ideas engage them in the conversation. Then I begin to invite men to consider these values in relation to how they want to be with their families (Augusta-Scott, 2008). I ask them:

- What do you value in a relationship? What type of relationships would you prefer?
- Some men say that respect is important to them; is that important to you?
- What does respect mean to you? What do you want your children to learn from you? What kind of role model do you want to be for them? What do you want to learn about "taking responsibility"?

The conversation continues and men eventually speak about wanting fairness and respect, wanting to take responsibility rather than blaming others for their choices. They express a preference for being caring in their relationships, rather than abusive and having controlling behavior.

In discussions about wanting fairness and respect in relationships, I use questions to help men re-author their identities according to values consistent with stopping abuse and building respect (Augusta-Scott, 2008). This includes asking where they learned these values, and about examples of when they may have lived up to these values. Men often relay incidents of standing up against injustices and abuse in their childhood. As a result, I ask, "How is the child that you were who stood against abuse connected with the man I am talking with now who is trying to take a stand against his own violence?" When men re-story their experience in this manner, they are able to begin to identify more with their own history of standing for respect and fairness and, as result, become better able to do so in the present and future.

The conversation about what is important to men in relationships and the values they would prefer to live up to set the stage for the men to assess the effects of violence on what is really important to them. Men get to assess how patriarchal ideas have influenced their choices to use violence, and have led them away from creating the long-term, caring, loving relationships many men prefer.

This process involves an open, nonjudgmental, and collaborative stance on the part of the therapist, making space for the multiplicity of men's experience: drawing their attention to *both* their desires for controlling relationships *and* their desire for caring, fair relationships. That openness to the multiplicity of their experience builds a foundation for collaborating with men to confront and study their violence, the ideas that support it, its effects, and what they might need to do to address the harms of the abuse. I am politically positioned as I engage in this inquiry; my curiosity is clearly influenced by the idea that men's violence is informed, in part, by notions of dominant masculinity. In effect, I externalize dominant masculinity through the way we speak of its influence on the men. This is a departure from the traditional power and control story (Pence & Paymar, 1993) that essentializes men as wanting, seeking, and using power and control through violence against their partners, a narrative supported by patriarchy.

Rather than imposing the power and control story on men, I work collaboratively with them to investigate their relationship with the expectations of dominant masculinity. I do not assume I know men's relationships with dominant masculinity (i.e., that they like and, as a result, fully want to participate in it). I allow for a more complex view, inquiring about how men concurrently participate in, reinforce, and resist notions of dominant masculinity.

Externalizing conversations make it possible to separate men's identities from patriarchal norms and values that often support the use of violence. We talk about sexist ideas that circulate in society; I interview them about their participation in these ideas (Augusta-Scott, 2009). Through these externalizing conversations, I resist defining men as the problem. Instead, we focus on defining the sexist ideas and men's participation in these ideas as the problem. For example, I often ask men:

• If a man was influenced by these ideas of dominant masculinity (e.g., a man has to be in control), how might this affect him over time? How might this idea affect his partner? His relationship with his partner?

These questions support a man in considering the possible influence of the ideas of dominant masculinity on others and, in turn, privately consider the possible influence of these ideas on himself. I avoid assuming this connection is *necessarily* the case for any particular man; my holding to uncertainty reduces defensiveness on the men's part. They can choose to share the connections they make between the two when they feel enough safety and respect in their relationship with me. Further, my position or politics in these conversations are not imposed, although they are evident in the questions and curiosity I bring to the conversations (Augusta-Scott, 2007).

My curiosity extends beyond the ideas of dominant masculinity to other areas of men's lives that may also be influencing their choices to perpetrate violence in relationships. Often men's decisions to abuse are influenced by their own past experiences of violence (Augusta-Scott & Maetz, 2017). I invite men to tell me about their experiences of close relationships in the past and how these may be influencing their present relationships. Men often report being traumatized in childhood and being required to protect themselves from others by using violence. For many of these men, close relationships have been unsafe and, as a result, they often presume their relationships with their partners are unsafe, even when this may not be the case. I often invite men to consider how they may separate the past from the present, that is, they may consider how they want to stop themselves from confusing their partner with people who have hurt them in the past. For example, I ask men:

• Do you think your experiences in past relationships might be influencing how you feel in your current relationship?
• What did you learn about the nature of close relationships in the past?
• What are the warning signs that you might be confusing your relationship with your partner with hostile relationships from the past?
• If you start confusing the past with the present, what would you have to remind yourself about the differences between the two experiences?

Similar to women's experience of eating disorders, men's violence is often an expression of experiences of both power and powerlessness in their lives. Just as acknowledging both experiences is helpful for women in the therapeutic process, acknowledging both these experiences is important in the process of men stopping their violence. Just as women's body talk is often a way to establish a greater sense of control in their lives, men often use abuse in a misguided belief that to achieve control over their lives they need to control their female partners. This desire is often fueled further by their actual experiences of feeling out of control and powerless in their lives created by being subjected to poverty, racism, and trauma for example. The power and control achieved is only temporary, as they often return to experiences of powerlessness and marginalization. Throughout this process, I keep my positioning visible. While I validate their desire to feel empowered and in control of their lives, I also challenge the recipe they learn from society about how to achieve this power and control through violence (Jenkins, 1990, 2009). I invite them to examine the difference between what violence against their female partner promises and what it actually delivers over the short and long term.

When men abuse their female partners they often act with a sense of entitlement, supported by patriarchal expectations of men. There is a significant gendered difference in how women and men deal with these issues of power and control. In the case of women and eating disorders, their struggles are often turned inwards toward themselves. With men, their struggles frequently manifest outwardly as violence toward their partners.

Feminist therapists working with women and eating disorders have focused on what eating disorders mean to women and, similar to feminist work with violence against women, have helped women to find their voices. In contrast, there has been little attention to exploring the voices of men who use violence. Dichotomous thinking leads us to believe we either have to listen to women or to men; either support women or support men; either respect women or respect men. This leads to a silencing of men's voices on behalf of hearing women. Related to this, gender essentialist assumptions in intimate partner violence work have further silenced men's voices because they are premised on a totalizing view of men as irresponsible, untrustworthy, and only wanting power and control. We believe this dichotomous outlook is counterproductive; we need to hear the voices of both men and women to effectively stop men's violence against their female partners.

When I began working in this area, these gender essentialist assumptions led me to adopt an expert posture with the men, wherein I assumed they had few valuable contributions to make to the conversation beyond confirming the power and control narrative. Further, the influence of dominant masculinity on my own interactions led me to adopt an expert posture of engaging in oppositional practices with men—confronting them every time they engaged in minimizing the seriousness of the abuse, blamed it on external factors, or denied it. When men would try to tell their stories of oppression and marginalization, I, like others, would assume they were just making excuses. As a man, I adopted the traditional gendered position when I closed down men's expressions of shame and vulnerability (Augusta-Scott, 2003, 2006). Like the work with women dealing with eating disorders described above, I now adopt a more complex positioning, remaining open to the multiplicity of men's experience while being transparent about the knowledges and biases that I bring to the conversation.

Conclusion

In this chapter, we have shared our versions of positioned therapy with women and eating disorders and men who use violence. Our approach embraces the complexity of experience. We are transparent in our challenge of the gender discourses that support eating disorders and violence against women. At the same time, we acknowledge that men and women sometimes engage in actions with hurtful consequences in an effort to gain control of what feels like an out-of-control situation, or to protest against and resist injustice done to them. Both women and men conform to *and* resist aspects of the gender scripts they are presented with in culture. Women's resistance is often tentative, veiled, and indirect—spoken through the body. They speak without speaking. For men, it is dangerous to share their shame and vulnerability. They often struggle to express the powerlessness, trauma, and marginalization they experience in the wake of using violence against women.

In this work, both women and men find it risky to speak. Acknowledging this, we attempt to explore the hidden, disqualified, and subjugated aspects of stories in order to develop thicker more helpful or preferred stories (Speedy, 2000; White, 2001, 2007). The stories that emerge emphasize women's and men's agency and resistance. For us, tapping into the stories and supporting the actions that accompany them are all about keeping social justice at the centre of our practice.

Reflection Questions

1. How does this chapter re-imagine collaborative relationships through politicizing knowledge and experience?
2. How is the concept of "expert" unpacked through the idea that knowledge is always partial?
3. In the areas of eating disorders among women and men's use of violence, how is the therapist on the side of social justice seen as positioned?
4. How are the women's and men's stories of power and control gendered in this chapter?
5. How do we externalize the dominant social discourses that often shape client's stories of eating disorders and use of violence?

Note

1 While I use the term eating disorders, I am not supporting a diagnostic, medical model, or pathologizing approach. I am invoking the term in its common everyday use.

References

Andersen, T. (1993). See and hear, and be seen and heard. In S. Friedman (Ed.), *The new language of change* (pp. 303–322). New York, NY: Guilford Press.

Anderson, H. (1997). *Conversation, language and possibilities: A postmodern approach to therapy*. New York, NY: Basic Books.

Anderson, H., & Goolishian, H. (1993). The client is the expert: A not-knowing approach to therapy. In K. Gergen & S. McNamee (Eds.), *Therapy as social construction* (pp. 25–39). London: Sage.

Augusta-Scott, T. (2003). Dichotomies in the power and control story: Exploring multiple stories about men who choose abuse in intimate relationships. In Dulwich Centre Publications, *Responding to violence: A collection of papers relating to child sexual abuse and violence in intimate relationships* (pp. 203–224). Adelaide, Australia: Dulwich Centre Publications.

Augusta-Scott, T. (2006). Talking with men who have used violence in intimate relationships: An interview with Tod Augusta-Scott. *International Journal of Narrative Therapy and Community Work, 4*, 23–30. Retrieved from http://dulwichcentre.com.au/international-journal-of-narrative-therapy-and-community-work

Augusta-Scott, T. (2007). Conversations with men about women's violence: Ending men's violence by challenging gender essentialism. In C. Brown & T. Augusta-Scott (Eds.), *Narrative therapy: Making meaning, making lives* (pp. 197–210). Thousand Oaks, CA: Sage.

Augusta-Scott, T. (2008). *Narrative therapy: A group manual for men who have perpetrated abuse*. Truro, NS: Bridges Institute.

Augusta-Scott, T. (2009). A narrative therapy approach to conversations with men about perpetrating abuse. In P. Lehmann & C. Simmons (Eds.), *Strengths-based batterer intervention: A new paradigm in ending family violence* (pp. 113–135). New York, NY: Springer.

Augusta-Scott, T., & Maetz, L. (2017). Complex Trauma and Dominant Masculinity: A Trauma-Informed, Narrative Therapy Approach with Men who Abuse Their Female Partners. In T. Augusta-Scott, K. Scott, & L. Tutty (Eds.), *Innovations in interventions to address intimate partner violence: Research and practice* (pp. 77–92). London: Routledge.

Barton, C. (2006, February 3). Waging war against a deadly disorder. *NZ Herald*. Retrieved from www.nzherald.co.nz

Bordo, S. (1993). *Unbearable weight: Feminism, western culture, and the body*. Berkeley, CA: University of California Press.

Brown, C. (1993a). The continuum: Anorexia, bulimia and weight preoccupation. In C. Brown & K. Jasper (Eds.), *Consuming passions: Feminist approaches to weight preoccupation and eating disorders* (pp. 53–68). Toronto, ON: Second Story Press.

Brown, C. (1993b). Feminist therapy: Power, ethics, and control. In C. Brown & K. Jasper (Eds.), *Consuming passions: Feminist approaches to weight preoccupation and eating disorders* (pp. 120–136). Toronto, ON: Second Story Press.

Brown, C. (2001). Talking body talk. An analysis of feminist therapy epistemology. Unpublished PhD dissertation, University of Toronto, Canada.

Brown, C. (2007a). Dethroning the suppressed voice: Unpacking experience as story. In C. Brown & T. Augusta-Scott (Eds.), *Narrative therapy: Making meaning, making lives* (pp. 177–196). Thousand Oaks, CA: Sage.

Brown, C. (2007b). Talking body talk: Blending feminist and narrative approaches to practice. In C. Brown & T. Augusta-Scott (Eds.), *Narrative therapy: Making meaning, making lives* (pp. 269–302). Thousand Oaks, CA: Sage.

Brown, C. (2007c). Situating knowledge and power in the therapeutic alliance. In C. Brown & T. Augusta-Scott (Eds.), *Narrative therapy: Making meaning, making lives* (pp. 3–22). Thousand Oaks, CA: Sage.

Brown, C. (2007d). Discipline and desire: Regulating the body/self. In C. Brown & T. Augusta-Scott (Eds.), *Narrative therapy: Making meaning, making lives* (pp. 105–131). Thousand Oaks, CA: Sage.

Brown, C. (2012). Anti-oppression through a postmodern lens: Dismantling the master's tools. *Critical Social Work, 3*(1), 34–65.

Brown, C. (2014). Untangling emotional threads and self-management discourse in women's body talk. In S. McKenzie-Mohr & M. Lafrance (Eds.), *Women voicing resistance: Discursive and narrative explorations* (pp. 174–190). New York, NY: Routledge.

Brown, C. (in press). Critical clinical practice: Creating counterstories through feminist narrative therapy. In D. Baines (Ed.), *Doing anti-oppressive practice: Social Justice Social Work* (3rd ed.). Black Point, NS: Brunswick Books.

Brown, C., & Augusta-Scott, T. (2007). Introduction: Postmodernism, reflexivity, and narrative therapy. In C. Brown & T. Augusta-Scott (Eds.), *Narrative therapy: Making meaning, making lives* (pp. ix–xliii). Thousand Oaks, CA: Sage.

Brown, C., & Jasper, K. (1993). Why weight? Why women? Why now? In C. Brown & K. Jasper (Eds.), *Consuming passions: Feminist approaches to weight preoccupation and eating disorders* (pp. 16–35). Toronto, ON: Second Story Press.

Bruner, E. (1986a). Ethnography as narrative. In V. Turner & E. Bruner (Eds.), *The anthropology of experience* (pp. 139–155). Chicago, IL: University of Illinois Press.

Bruner, E. (1986b). Experience and its expressions. In V. Turner & E. Bruner (Eds.), *The anthropology of experience* (pp. 3–30). Chicago, IL: University of Illinois Press.

Bruner, J. (2002). *Making stories: Law, literature, life*. Cambridge, MA: Harvard University Press.

Epston, D. (2000). The history of the archives of resistance: Anti-anorexia/anti-bulimia. Retrieved from www.narrativeapproaches.com

Foucault, M. (1980). The incitement to discourse. In *The history of sexuality. An introduction, volume 1* (pp. 17–35). New York, NY: Vintage.

Freedman, J., & Combs, G. (1996). *Narrative therapy: The social construction of preferred realities*. New York, NY: Norton.

Gremillion, H. (2003). *Feeding anorexia: Gender and power at a treatment center*. Durham, NC: Duke University Press.

Haraway, D. (1988). Situated knowledges: The since question in feminism and the privilege of partial perspective. *Feminist Studies, 14*(3), 575–599. doi: 10.2307/3178066

Jenkins, A. (1990). *Invitations to responsibility*. Adelaide, Australia: Dulwich Centre Publications.

Jenkins, A. (2009). *Becoming ethical: A parallel, political journey with men who have abused*. London: Russell House.

Lawrence, M. (1979). Anorexia nervosa: The control paradox. *Women's Studies International, 2*, 93–101. doi: 10.1016/S0148-0685(79)93118-X

Lawrence, M. (1984). *The anorexic experience*. London: The Women's Press.

Lock, A., Epston, D., Maisel, R., & deFaria, N. (2005). Resisting anorexia/bulimia: Foucauldian perspectives in narrative therapy. *British Journal of Guidance & Counselling, 33*(3), 315–332. doi: 10.1080/03069880500179459

Madsen, W. (1999). *Collaborative therapy with multi-stressed families*. New York, NY: Guilford.

Maisel, R., Epston, D., & Borden, A. (2004). *Biting the hand that starves you*. New York, NY: Norton.

Nylund, D. (2002). Poetic means to anti-anorexic ends. *Journal of Systemic Therapy, 21*(4), 18–34. doi: 10.1521/jsyt.21.4.18.23323

Orbach, S. (1986). *Hunger strike: The anorectic's struggle as a metaphor for our age.* New York, NY: Norton.

Paré, D. (2013). *The practice of collaborative counseling & psychotherapy. Developing skills in culturally mindful helping.* Thousand Oaks, CA: Sage.

Paré, D. A., & Larner, G. (Eds.) (2004). *Collaborative practice in psychology and therapy.* Binghamton, NY: Haworth Press.

Pence, E., & Paymar, M. (1993). *Education groups for men who batter.* New York, NY: Springer.

Scott, J. (1992). Experience. In J. Butler & J. Scott (Eds.), *Feminists theorize the political* (pp. 22–40). New York, NY: Routledge.

Speedy, J. (2000). The "storied" helper: narrative ideas and practices in counselling and psychotherapy. *European Journal of Psychotherapy, Counselling & Health, 3*(3), 361–374. doi: 10.1080/13642530010012011

Strong, T., & Paré, D. A. (Eds.) (2004). *Furthering talk: Advances in the discursive therapies.* New York, NY: Kluwer Academic/Plenum.

Ussher, J. (Ed.) (1997). *Body talk: the material and discursive regulation of sexuality, madness and reproduction.* New York, NY: Routledge.

Ussher, J. (2011). *The madness of women: Myth and experience.* New York, NY: Routledge.

White, M. (1991). Deconstruction and therapy. *Dulwich Centre Newsletter, 3*, 21–40.

White, M. (1997). *Narratives of therapists' lives.* Adelaide, Australia: Dulwich Centre Publications.

White, M. (2001). Narrative practice and the unpacking of identity conclusions. *Gecko: A Journal of Deconstruction and Narrative Ideas in Therapeutic Practice, 1*, 28–55.

White, M. (2004). Working with people who are suffering the consequences of multiple trauma: A narrative perspective. *The International Journal of Narrative Therapy and Community Work, 1*, 45–76. Retrieved from http://dulwichcentre.com.au/international-journal-of-narrative-therapy-and-community-work

White, M. (2007). *Maps of narrative practice.* New York, NY: Norton.

White, M., & Epston, D. (1990). *Narrative means to therapeutic ends.* New York, NY: Norton.

CHAPTER 12

Queer Informed Narrative Therapy: Radical Approaches to Counseling with Transgender Persons

David Nylund and Annie Temple

While there is increased public awareness of transgender issues in contemporary times, a great deal of misunderstanding still exists. For example, the public often does not understand the definition of transgender, which reinforces misperceptions. Transgender is a term used to describe persons whose self-declared gender identity is incongruent with their assigned sex at birth. Typically, transgender is an umbrella term with many different identities existing under it. Some of these identities are gender variant, transsexual, and genderqueer (discussed later in this chapter). Transsexual is often seen as a dated term; however, people do still use it at times to describe themselves. Transsexual refers to a person who undergoes hormone replacement therapy and/or surgery to attain the physical characteristics of a sex other than the one they were assigned at birth. Transgender may include transsexual persons, but the term also includes many more gender identities.

Despite their increased visibility, transgender persons are subjected to many forms of marginalization, including discrimination in the workplace and schools, lack of access to health care, and transphobic violence (Benson, 2013). Even within the field of counseling and mental health there is a lack of awareness of transgender issues. This chapter will draw attention to some of the experiences of transgender clients in therapy. We will then discuss a social justice oriented approach that is responsive to transphobic oppression—*Queer Informed Narrative Therapy*. Next, we will underscore the philosophical assumptions and therapeutic practices of Queer Informed Narrative Therapy along with case illustrations.

Transgender Oppression in Therapy

It is safe to say that there has been progress with mental health professionals' awareness of the issues confronting gay and lesbian persons. Marriage equality, richer representations of gays and lesbian in the media, the repeal of "Don't Ask Don't Tell" (US), and the passage of anti-discrimination laws are signposts of the recent advancement of gay and lesbian rights. However, this is not necessarily the case in relation to transgender persons (Alderson, 2015). Transgender persons are a highly stigmatized and oppressed community who have not benefited from the recent gay rights movement. For instance, transgender persons cannot serve openly in the US military. Transgender oppression can range from unwanted attention, verbal harassment and ridicule, discrimination in employment, access to health care, education and other services, up to physical attack, sexual assault and murder (Sennott, 2011). Without careful consideration, many well-meaning therapists may inadvertently further the marginalization of transgender clients (Korell & Lorah, 2007; Shelton & Delgado-Romero, 2011) without an understanding of the effects of transphobia. Historically, transgender individuals have been mistreated by mental health professionals (Lombardi, 2001).

Pervasive pathologizing of transgender identities within mental health communities and psychology discourse create unsafe environments for transgender clients. Many transgender individuals fear seeking physical and mental health care and avoid seeking both, due to fear of judgment and prejudice (Alegria, 2011). For transgender individuals who do try to find appropriate counseling services, they are often left to work with clinicians who are not skilled in gender issues (Benson, 2013).

Whereas "homosexuality" as a mental disorder was removed from the *Diagnostic and Statistical Manual* (DSM) in 1973, transgender individuals have continued to be pathologized by mental health professionals (Sennott, 2011). From 1980, when the American Psychiatric Association first coined the diagnosis "Gender Identity Disorder," until 2013, when the "disorder" or label changed to Gender Dysphoria in the DSM-5 (American Psychiatric Association, 2013), transgender individuals have been labeled as having a mental disorder (Byne et al., 2012). This pathological view of transgender identities sets the stage for therapy to increase shame as, by definition, this diagnosis labels transgender people as deviant (Sennot, 2011). Even though Gender Dysphoria is potentially less pathologizing, as it attributes a client's distress to an incongruence between one's gender and biological sex, once something becomes a disorder in our society, it immediately becomes stigmatized (Nagoshi & Brzuzy, 2010).

Many mental health professionals lack education in regards to the challenges transgender individuals face and how pervasive transphobia and societal stigma impacts mental health. For instance, therapists often do not know the correct language to use when working with transgender clients, including utilizing preferred pronouns (Alegria, 2011). In a study done at a large American university with MSW students (n = 197), results showed that MSW students had high rates of transphobia that could be attributed to a lack of education (Logie, Bridge, & Bridge, 2007). The effectiveness of mental health interventions with transgender clients is directly linked to clinicians who are trans-affirming. A study conducted with transgender individuals who were currently receiving psychotherapy services showed a strong correlation between satisfaction with their treatment and the cultural competence of the therapist with whom they were working (Bockting, 2009).

Although the American Psychological Association (APA) recommends that mental health professionals receive cultural competency training in treating transgender individuals, many graduate programs ignore the subject entirely (Sanger, 2008). Diversity training in graduate programs is fundamental to becoming a successful therapist and it is imperative that graduate programs begin to implement training on gender identity as well as education about the social, relational, and psychological needs of transgender clients (Benson, 2013). Furthermore, most current therapy models readily accept the idea of the gender binary and, in doing so, exclude transgender identities. Due to lack of education, insufficient training on transgender issues, and a general acceptance of an essentialist model of the gender binary, there are very few mental health professionals who are knowledgeable in working with transgender individuals (Byne et al., 2012; Sanger, 2008).

In a survey conducted with transgender clients receiving therapy from The Gender Center (an agency based in Sacramento, California serving the needs of the transgender and queer communities where we work), responses from participants illustrated that the solution to creating more trans-informed clinicians is both formal education as well as direct experience working with and around transgender clients. When asked what can be done to better address issues transgender clients face, participants cited more community agencies specializing in transgender issues as well as more education for doctors and providers (Temple, 2013). Without proper training, therapists who might feel uncomfortable or simply unprepared to work with transgender clients may unintentionally create a "null environment" where they ignore or are neutral to issues directly related to the client's transgender identity. Therapists may ignore or not ask about a client's gender identity, or they may rely on the client to educate them on specific subjects related to being transgender. Many participants stated that they detested having to educate ignorant therapists about their transgender identity. It is imperative for mental health professionals to receive education surrounding the psychosocial needs of transgender clients, the socially constructed nature of gender, as well as the specific challenges transphobia creates for transgender individuals.

Queer Informed Narrative Therapy

The clinical work described here was conducted at the Gender Health Center (GHC) in Sacramento, California. The GHC opened up in July 2010, with the intent of addressing the mental health care disparities discussed above and reversing the stigma of transgender individuals. The mission of the GHC, stated on its website, is to "provide education, advocacy, mental health and other health services to underserved and marginalized populations as an act of social justice with a specialization in gender and sexual identities" (retrieved from thegenderhealthcenter.org). Counselors who work at the GHC are committed to an anti-oppressive clinical practice, which includes providing culturally responsive therapy to transgender persons. All of the counselors are trained in Queer Informed Narrative Therapy—a social justice counseling approach influenced by queer theory and narrative therapy.

Queer Theory

Queer theory is a range of post-structuralist critical practices that challenges public sensibilities towards the relationship between sex, gender, and sexuality in the social context with the intent of changing hegemonic understandings of gender and sexual identities (Butler, 1990; Warner, 2000). Queer theory argues against the notion of fixed identities, claiming instead that identity is constructed, multiple, and fluid. Queer theorists have taken the lead in critiquing normative discourses of gender and sexual identities, rejecting binary categories such as male/female or heterosexual/homosexual.

Judith Butler, a key queer theorist, suggests that gender and sexual identities are in constant flux and therefore cannot be delineated with clear boundaries set in binary opposition to one another. Premised on Michel Foucault's (1980) work, Butler (1990) posits that binary understandings of sex and gender identities are regulatory and constraining and work to reinforce heteronormativity. For example, a person who does not identify exclusively as male or female is forced to pick one gender to represent themselves on a driver's license. In *Gender Trouble*, Butler (1990) writes that gender is not natural but performative, that it is what you do at particular times rather than universally who you are. All gender is a performance; it is just that certain expressions of gender have seized a hegemonic hold and appear to be natural.

Butler's vision is to denaturalize and subvert dominant understandings of gender and sexuality that are based on binary understandings of masculinity and femininity. This project encourages a proliferation of genders and sexualities. Envisioning a multiplicity of sexualities and genders allows space for the experiences of individuals who fall outside the binary, including transgender individuals. In a sense, transgender persons are lived, corporeal challenges to gender and sexual binaries. Queer theory is brought to the forefront by people whose bodies and experiences challenge the very notion of stable identities and sexualities. Transgender persons illustrate the limitations of such binary systems, and their experiences provide some of the foundation for queer theory.

Narrative Therapy

Narrative therapy (Freedman & Combs, 1996; Madigan, 2011; White & Epston, 1990) shares a great deal in common with queer theory as both draw from post-structuralism for their philosophical underpinnings. The key narrative therapy tenet is "the person is not the problem, the problem is the problem." Separating the problem from the person, known as externalizing, is achieved by a discursive shift where problems become nouns. Externalizing, developed by Michael White and David Epston (1990), allows persons to separate from problems that have been located in their identity reinforcing a problem-saturated story. Through an externalizing conversation, the client develops a relationship with the problems, which creates space to attend to alternative stories that contradict the dominant problem story. The problem no longer speaks to the truth of their identity.

Most therapy models privatize problems and de-emphasize the role of social structures, unfittingly attributing sociopolitical problems to the individual. Narrative therapy addresses this by reorienting the focus from an individualistic to a relational orientation. Using this framework, many of the problems that transgender clients experience are conceptualized not as manifestations of intrapsychic processes, but as the effects of transphobia. Externalizing conversations invite transgender persons to become more conscious of how their lives and their view of themselves are shaped by the reality of transgender oppression, thereby allowing them to separate and take an active social stand against these discourses and practices.

An important facet of narrative therapy is counselors' self-reflexivity about their social locations. We, the authors of this chapter, are both cisgender persons (a term to describe persons whose gender identity matches the sex they were assigned at birth) who have a great deal of unearned privilege. Some examples of cisgender privilege includes using public washrooms without fear of verbal or physical abuse, being referred to by the correct gender pronouns in day-to-day activity and not being misgendered, and not being denied medical care based on gender identity. A Queer Informed therapy requires counselors to be aware of how wide-ranging cisgender privilege is and how it influences their work with transgender clients. Cisgender is not synonymous with "straight"; it is a gender identity rather than a sexual orientation. Naming cisgender privilege can work to flatten the hierarchical power relations between a cisgender therapist and a transgender client. In addition, being aware of cisgender privilege can help counselors to more fully appreciate the obstacles transgender clients face in a cisnormative society. This appreciation can be brought into therapeutic conversations with transgender clients, creating space for noticing resistances to cisnormativity and transphobia. Conversations about these resistances can lead to an exploration of alternative and preferred stories and practices of the self. Below are some case illustrations based on our work at the Gender Health Center (all names are changed to preserve confidentiality).

Drew

A significant aspect of culturally responsive work is familiarization with health and mental health care standards of care (SOC) for professionals working with transgender clients. The most widespread and recognized SOC is set forth by the World Professional Association for Transgender Health (WPATH). The overall goal of the SOC is to provide guidelines for health care professionals and counselors to help transgender persons achieve "lasting personal comfort with the gendered self in order to maximize overall psychological well-being and self-fulfillment" (Coleman et al., 2011, p. 166). The WPATH-SOC are periodically updated and revised with the latest modification (the seventh version) being released in 2011.

The SOC recommend very specific minimum requirements as prerequisites to hormone replacement therapy (HRT) and sex reassignment surgery. WPATH suggests that transgender persons meet with a mental health clinician to be assessed for eligibility and readiness criteria to receive medical interventions. Numerous criticisms have been made of the SOC; the requirements are quite strict and the language is pathologizing. Many transgender persons state that their right to proper medical care and treatment is unjustly and unduly withheld or even denied based on the SOC. I (DN) agree with the critique: one of my roles at the GHC is to assess clients' readiness according to the SOC criteria. I am very uneasy with this role as it positions me as a gatekeeper who wields power by diagnosing transgender clients and deciding who can medically transition or not.

The seventh and latest revision of WPATH-SOC (2011) has some significant and encouraging changes. For example, the document clearly states that transgender is not a pathology. The standards are much more flexible, for instance no longer requiring a psychotherapist in certain situations such as recommending hormone therapy. These changes have had significantly positive effects on many of my (DN) clients including Drew, a 34-year-old Latinx person who identifies as genderqueer. Genderqueer is used to describe individuals who fit under the broad category of transgender identity who do not conform to a binary understanding of gender as limited to the categories of man or woman, male or female. Some genderqueer persons view themselves as both man and woman, others as neither man nor woman, and yet others as moving between two or more genders (gender fluid).

Drew was assigned male at birth but was never comfortable being perceived as male, and never as female either. In college, Drew came out as genderqueer and requested that people use a gender neutral pronoun, "they." After a great deal of personal contemplation and distress, Drew came to see me at the GHC because of a decision to take female hormones; *they* needed a letter of recommendation to give to the doctor to begin HRT. Even though Drew is gender fluid, *they* wanted the hormones (estrogen) to make particular changes to the body, such as increased breast size and decreased body hair—changes that are connected to a more feminine presentation. Given the choice between being read as male or female, Drew would choose female, but *they* did not want to choose. As Drew shared with me, "I like my in-between-ness."

A concern for Drew is that an MD would not understand Drew's genderqueer identity and expression and would therefore deny HRT. Drew told me in our first meeting [verbatim quote]:

> *I'm searching for a doctor who can hopefully help me in my semi-transition. But I worry that if I go see a doctor and say I don't fit with the binary but would like my body to match the "in-between-ness," will they outright deny me them*

because I'm not a "real" transgender person … Maybe I should go in there and try and play the "type one trans card" and try and convince them that I've felt like a "woman trapped inside a male" my whole life. I've heard stories of other genderqueers who have done that in order to get hormones legitimately. I feel stuck almost … it's choosing between lying about my true gender identity in order to obtain safe hormones or staying true to myself but paying lots of money for unsafe hormones from the street dealers.

Drew's experience is quite common for genderqueer persons and other non-binary persons. They tend to be misunderstood by health care professionals and even within the transgender community itself (Tilsen, 2013). Many genderqueer persons have shared with me that they feel excluded and judged by some in the transgender community for being, as one of my clients explained, "not trans enough."

My response to Drew's experiences and worries was to inform them of the changes in the latest revision of the WPATH-SOC (2011). The SOC, seventh version, allows for a broader spectrum of gender identities, including referring to genderqueer and legitimizing non-binary identities. The new SOC could be considered "queer," as they are compatible with Judith Butler's vision of proliferating genders. Informing Drew of these changes relieved some of Drew's concerns. I referred Drew to an MD who was culturally responsive to transgender clients and receptive to learning about gender and queer issues. I wrote a letter to the MD recommending HRT, with particular emphasis on Drew's genderqueer identity being honored (I also sent the MD a copy of the latest SOC). Cultivating working relationships with medical professionals and educating them about transgender issues is key to a Queer Informed and social justice informed therapy. Drew started hormones soon after the MD received the letter.

Jasper

When working with transgender clients, it is imperative that therapists do not individualize problems that clients may be experiencing. In order to avoid individualizing client problems, it is critical to engage clients in discussions about the social construction of gender. In openly examining issues of gender and transphobia in session, therapists can reduce client shame, show greater understanding and empathy, and avoid re-stigmatizing transgender individuals. Additionally, in externalizing (White & Epston, 1990) and locating problems in cultural discourses rather than in clients, therapists can assist clients in separating themselves from problems and opening up new possibilities for alternative client stories.

Jasper was a 20-year-old FTM (female to male) White transgender client who came to the Gender Health Center experiencing depression and anxiety. Jasper began testosterone four months prior to our first session and had frequently expressed his fear of his family finding out that he is a man. Jasper shared that he was influenced by self-hatred, partially believing that he was "flawed" because of his transgender identity. In this transcript (edited for clarity) of one of our early sessions, I (AT) invited Jasper (J) into a discussion about the effects of transphobia in order to illustrate how Jasper's beliefs about himself and his identity are internalized manifestations of much larger societal forces.

J: I'm always feeling bad about myself and afraid, like if anyone finds out that I am trans, they won't think I'm a real man.

AT: I've talked to a lot of people who worry a lot about others finding out that they are transgender. What about our society? How does our society promote the idea that you aren't a real man? What makes a "real" man?

J: Well, I guess the fact that people don't consider you a man unless you're born that way. I fear my family will never see me as a man because I wasn't born that way.

AT: So there's this fraudulent assumption that someone's gender is the same as their biological sex … that someone's identity matters less than their biology and that somehow you have to explain yourself instead of just being you. As someone with cisgender privilege, I never have to explain or justify my gender. Do you think everyone should practice asking for preferred pronouns regardless of whether they are cisgender or transgender?

J: Yes, I do. I've known I was a boy since I was five. It was other people telling me that I was something that I wasn't that made me feel so terrible. My grandparents have always insisted I was a girl but I knew who I was. I'm just afraid now that if people find out, they won't believe me. But yeah, I don't think it's fair that cispeople are treated like their gender is more valid than mine is.

AT: So it seems like transphobia has wreaked havoc in your life. It recruited your grandparents to be unsupportive of you and tries to tell you that you aren't a "real" man and leads you into self-hate. Do you think it's fair that transphobia has produced a lot of pain for you and your family?

J: It's not fair. People don't understand at all. They think if you're born a girl, then you're a girl and that's that.

AT: Can I assume that you value justice and see a need for increased education about issues of gender identity?

J: Exactly. There needs to be more education out there about people like me. People don't understand and are fearful of things they don't understand. I shouldn't have to hide who I am. I've been this way forever.

AT: It's kind of absurd isn't it, that people who don't conform to arbitrary social norms are feeling depressed and ashamed of who they are. How have you committed to being yourself, going to school and living your life in spite of the effects of transphobia?

J: I won't let it bring me down. I am who I am. It's other people who need to be educated. There's so much misinformation out there. I've spent too much time hiding in fear, at school with my friends and at home with my grandparents.

AT: Does transphobia lose its grip when you refuse to let fear dictate to you?

J: Yes.

AT: In spite of fear, transphobia, and self-hatred, you've decided to medically transition and continue to go to school and hang out with your friends. How have you kept fear and its ally, transphobia, from enforcing its rule and keeping you from honoring your gender identity?

J: I won't let it control me.

AT: What quality are you able to tap into to keep fear and transphobia from controlling you?

J: Persistence.

AT: Is persistence an antidote to transphobia?

J: Yeah!

This de-privatizing conversation was a significant turning point for Jasper as he began to step more into a preferred story. Soon after the meeting, Jasper "came out" to his family who were supportive. We worked on ways that Jasper's entire family could stand up to transphobia.

Zack

Zack, a 16-year-old White person assigned female at birth who identified as male, was referred to me by his therapist, Debi, to assess readiness to start hormones (testosterone). Zack saw Debi for three sessions prior to my interview with him. Gender was not the focal point in therapy; he was very clear about his male identity. Zack "passed" as a male completely including using the men's washroom in school and other public places. He had been living full time as a male since age 11 with complete support of his family, friends, and school. This is an important point for therapists to understand in their work with transgender clients: not all problems are related to gender issues.

In my (DN) meeting with Zack (Z), I felt no need to ascertain his readiness for hormones. Rather, I was drawn to what he had learned and come to value about himself in his transition process. Zack and I explored and deconstructed Zack's ideas about masculinity, a common practice in narrative therapy. I had a sense that Zack had some valuable insights into the social construction of manhood. Below is an excerpt taken directly from our conversation:

DN: As you continue to transition towards your preferred identity, is there an idea of how you want to perform and/or express your masculinity?

Z: You mean the kind of man I want to be?

DN: Yes.

Z: I've seen all different versions of masculinity, kind of my father's version—construction worker, sort of tough. And more "feminine" men—not afraid to wear designer shoes and carry a "man" bag or whatever you all call it …

[both Zack and I laugh] … they're both as masculine, just a different version of masculinity … I kind of want to take parts of all the different kinds of masculinity and all the different ways of expressing manhood and kind of combine those. I want to pick and choose what will work best for me.

DN: I'm hearing that you are taking up a version of masculinities that is different from a more traditional masculinity. Do I have that right? [Zack nods yes] … Do you know what effect traditional masculinity has on men?

Z: I think it's very mentally and physically draining. You're constantly measuring yourself up to that kind of manhood … you're never happy where you are. You're constantly stressing yourself rather than appreciating where you are. To me, you have to measure up to what you want, not what the society says.

[Later in the conversation]

DN: Are there any types of masculinity that you want to distance yourself from?

Z: Abuse towards women and being just blatantly sexist. Things like that … I don't think of that kind of masculinity as manhood. I think of it as a bad habit. I don't really see that as manhood but more about men stuck as immature boys.

Zack eloquently critiques traditional masculinity in our conversation. He illustrates in an embodied way, the central queer theory tenet of gender as a "performance." Furthermore, he is elucidating that manhood is not the private monopoly of cisgender men; that a transgender masculinity is just as "real" and credible. What's more, Zack's form of masculinity, a feminist and social justice version, might offer some useful ideas for many cisgender, white, able-bodied, straight men.

Conclusion

Due to a lack of education about gender and sexuality in most graduate programs, many transgender clients are unable to find culturally responsive clinicians. In adopting a Queer Informed approach, cisgender clinicians can work to flatten power hierarchies through openly examining their privilege. In addition, Queer Informed clinicians can help clients expose the socially constructed nature of gender and assist clients in externalizing and locating problems in transphobia and other social discourses. Several transgender clients at the Gender Health Center who were interviewed for a graduate research project felt that the solution to the deficiency in quality mental health care for transgender clients is creating more community clinics that address the needs of the transgender community (Temple, 2013). This chapter has not only described ways to provide excellent care for transgender clients, but is also a call to action for creation of more social service agencies that specialize in this area. With the development of agencies that practice Queer Informed Narrative Therapy, more transgender clients can receive help from social justice informed counselors committed to undermining transgender oppression.

Reflection Questions

1. In what specific ways might a deeper awareness of cisgender privilege impact your practice?
2. How might you integrate queer theory in your work with your clients— including those who identify as heterosexual?
3. Is it possible to conduct assessments with transgender clients who need medical services (hormones and surgery) while staying congruent with a "non-expert" stance? If so, what would it take?
4. What specifically might your practice and/or agency do to be welcoming to non-binary clients?

References

Alderson, K. G. (2015). Working with clients seeking support for gay, lesbian, bisexual, transgender, two-spirited, and questioning experiences. In L. Martin (Ed.), *Canadian counselling and psychotherapy experience: Ethics-based issues and cases* (pp. 357–382). Ottawa, ON: Canadian Counselling and Psychotherapy Association.

Alegria, C. (2011). Transgender identity and health care: Implications for psychosocial and physical evaluation. *Journal of the American Academy of Nurse Practitioners, 23*(4), 175–182. doi: 10.1111/j.1745-7599.2010.00595.x

American Psychiatric Association. (2013). *Diagnostic and statistical manual of mental disorders* (5th ed.). Washington, DC: Author.

Benson, K. (2013). Seeking support: Transgender client experiences with mental health services. *Journal of Feminist Family Therapy, 25*(1), 17–40. doi: 10.1080/08952833. 2013.755081

Bockting, W. O. (2009). Transforming the paradigm of transgender health: A field in transition. *Sexual & Relationship Therapy, 24*(2), 103–107. doi: 10.1080/14681990903037660

Butler, J. (1990). *Gender trouble: Feminism and the subversion of identity*. New York, NY: Routledge.

Byne, W., Bradley, S., Coleman, E., Eyler, A., Green, R., Menvielle, E. J., ... Tompkins, D. A. (2012). Report of the American Psychiatric Association task force on treatment of gender identity disorder. *Archives of Sexual Behavior, 14*, 759–796. doi: 10.1007/s10508-012-9975-x

Coleman, E., Bockting, W., Botzer, M., Cohen-Kettenis, P., DeCuypere, G., Feldman, J., ... Zucker, K. (2011). Standards of care for the health of transsexual, transgender, and gender non-conforming people: Version 7. *International Journal of Transgenderism, 13*, 165–232. doi: 10.1080/15532739.2011.700873

Foucault, M. (1980). *The history of sexuality: An introduction*. New York, NY: Vintage.

Freedman, J., & Combs, G. (1996). *Narrative therapy: The social construction of preferred realities*. New York, NY: Norton.

Korell, S. C., & Lorah, P. (2007). An overview of affirmative psychotherapy and counseling with transgender clients. In K. Bieschke, R. Perez, & K. DeBord (Eds.), *Handbook of counseling and psychotherapy with lesbian, gay, bisexual, and transgender clients* (pp. 271–288). Washington, DC: American Psychological Association. doi: 10.1037/11482-011

Logie, C., Bridge, T. J., & Bridge, P. D. (2007). Evaluating the phobias, attitudes, and cultural competence of Master of Social Work students toward the LGBT populations. *Journal of Homosexuality, 53*(4), 201– 221. doi: 10.1080/00918360802103472

Lombardi, E. (2001). Enhancing transgender healthcare. *American Journal of Public Health, 91*, 869–870. doi: 10.2105/AJPH.91.6.869

Madigan, S. (2011). *Narrative therapy*. Washington, DC: APA Press.

Nagoshi, J., & Brzuzy, S. (2010). Transgender theory: Embodying research and practice. *Affilia, 25*, 431–445. doi: 10.1177/0886109910384068

Sanger, T. (2008). Queer(y)ing gender and sexuality: Transpeople's lived experiences and intimate partnerships. In L. Moon (Ed.), *Feeling queer or queer feelings? Radical approaches to counseling sex, sexualities and genders* (pp. 72–88). New York, NY: Taylor & Francis.

Sennott, S. (2011). Gender disorder as gender oppression: A transfeminist approach to rethinking the pathologization of gender non-conformity. *Women & Therapy, 34*(1–2), 93–113. doi: 10.1080/02703149.2010.532683

Shelton, K., & Delgado-Romero, E. (2011). Sexual orientation microaggressions: The experience of lesbian, gay, bisexual, and queer clients in psychotherapy. *Journal of Counseling Psychology, 58*(2), 210–221. doi: 10.1037/a0022251

Temple, A. (2013). Breaking the binary: Addressing healthcare disparities within Sacramento's transgender community. Unpublished master's thesis, California State University, Sacramento.

Tilsen, J. (2013). *Therapeutic conversations with queer youth: Transcending homonormativity and constructing preferred identities*. Lanham, MD: Jason Aronson.

Warner, M. (2000). *The trouble with normal*. Cambridge: Harvard University Press.

White, M., & Epston, D. (1990). *Narrative means to therapeutic ends*. New York, NY: Norton.

CHAPTER 13

Coming Out: Implications for Sexual and Gender Non-Conforming Immigrants and Newcomers

Mego Nerses and David Paré

The construct of "coming out" refers to the announcement of one's identity in the public domain, an act generally regarded as a key developmental process among people of non-dominant sexual orientation. A simplistic view of this process, however, depicts coming out as a universally prescribed, celebratory, self-liberating milestone of psychological maturation and a bold gesture in the face of widespread homophobia and transphobia. In this chapter, we will unpack discourses associated with "coming out," acknowledging the construct's utility while also pointing to some very real limitations of the metaphor. While the notion of coming out provides a context for acts of self-determination, it can also inadvertently oppress by imposing a prescriptive normative template for expressions of sexuality and gender, with damaging consequences for people who do not locate themselves within dominant social frames.

The discussion will begin with a reminder that the notion and practice of coming out is not a universal process, but can be located within certain cultural contexts. This includes broad contexts ("the West") but also subcultural contexts among people who identify as non-heterosexual and gender non-conforming. Having considered the ways that coming out is not a metaphor for all, the chapter will delve into existing coming out models in order to illustrate how they fail to capture the experience of sexual minority and gender non-conforming immigrants and newcomers.

In a chapter devoted to attending to fine distinctions in identity, we think it is particularly important to situate ourselves as authors. I (MN) am an immigrant, gay, middle-class, cisgender male psychotherapist who is in private practice and works with marginalized populations focused on sexual issues. I (DP) am a white, straight, cisgender male psychologist who has taught graduate courses on diversity for 17 years as a professor in a Counselling Psychology masters program at the University of Ottawa.

This chapter offers a culturally sensitive approach to coming out that integrates newcomer sexual minority and gender non-conforming migration and cultural experiences to create equal opportunities and accessibility to mental health services within the larger context.

For the purpose of this chapter, newcomers are defined as people who have experienced migration across national borders individually or with family members. A practice-based scenario will be provided to paint a picture of the challenges faced by sexual minority and gender non-conforming newcomers, and to provide illustrations of culturally appropriate interventions with sexual minority and gender non-conforming newcomer populations.

The complexity of newcomer sexual and gender minority experience precludes a detailed account of the scope of challenges faced by this population, including sexism, transphobia, heterosexism, and gender politics. These will be touched upon but not addressed in detail. For the purpose of inclusiveness, we will speak of sexual minority and gender non-conforming[1] people instead of LGBTQ+[2] (lesbian, gay, bisexual, trans[3], queer[4]) as well as kink and BDSM (bondage and discipline, sadism and masochism) practitioners, to encompass as many identities as possible. This concern for the inclusionary quality of our vocabulary reflects a central theme of this chapter, which is the way that entrenched modes of thinking/speaking about sexual minorities inadvertently exclude a significant range of people who so identify. Here, the focus is on a particular subgroup—newcomers who, among the many challenges they face, often find themselves interacting with practitioners unfamiliar with the idiosyncratic challenges associated with the intersection of sexual orientation, gender identity, ethnicity, nationality, and language. This is a matter of social justice because it relates to access to services and the politics of identity.

Coming Out as a Cultural Construction

The coming out process is typically a central focus of writings on therapy with sexual minorities (Hill, 2009; Hunter, 2007). Certainly, the concealing of such a key aspect of identity as sexual orientation from loved ones, friends, the wider public, even oneself, is a substantial and complex concern that begs attention. But amid efforts to address that concern by articulating detailed developmental stage models, the constructed nature of coming out, and indeed of "homosexuality" itself, is quickly forgotten.

When one surveys various cultural contexts, what are now understood as non-dominant sexual orientations are seen to be characterized in various manners. In various contemporary societies, males often have sexual relations with men without this activity reflecting on their heterosexual identities (Ward, 2015). In many Aboriginal societies, gender-variant persons are characterized as "two-spirited" (Gilley, 2006), and frequently prized for the unique qualities they are seen to possess including clairvoyance, healing abilities, and the unique capacity to provide advice on marital issues (Brown, 1997).

In contrast with North America, where gender is typically seen in dichotomous terms and as a person's key identifying feature, cross-cultural data and ethnographic studies show that many cultures practice institutionalized variations of same-sex sexuality (Bullough & Bullough, 1993; Herdt, 1997). Within these cultures, people's sexual roles and acts have greater importance than their gender (Nichols, 2013), and sexualities are used to maintain the power of kinship and the social relationship of the entire community (Herdt, 1997).

These views of gender and sexuality differ in striking ways from the Eurocentric view that dominates in North America—a view that has, nevertheless, seen some transformation over recent decades. In the twentieth century, "homosexuality" was originally characterized as a sociopathic personality disturbance in the *American Psychiatric Association's Diagnostic and Statistical Manual of Mental Disorders* (DSM) (American Psychiatric Association, 1952), and was still included in the DSM-II (American Psychiatric Association, 1974) as late as 1974. Distressingly, the DSM-5 (American Psychiatric Association, 2013) still lists paraphilias (non-conventional sexuality) such as BDSM and fetish and gender variance experiences as mental disorders. While recent years have seen some dramatic shifts in social policy, such as the enshrinement of same-sex marriage within many provincial and state jurisdictions, the psychiatric community has been slower to revise its characterization of performances of sexuality and gender that fall outside the population norm.

The point we want to highlight is that the notion of homosexuality itself is a social construct that manifests in a variety of ways in different social and historic contexts, and one that continues to evolve within dominant contemporary cultural institutions such as psychiatry and psychology. When it is not being employed to pathologize significant numbers of people, the distinction of heterosexual from non-heterosexual helps to organize practices for providing support to people of non-dominant sexual orientations. But that does not mean that it speaks to fundamental truth. The same can be said of the construct of coming out.

Just as the construction of homosexuality rests on frequently unquestioned assumptions taken to be universally applicable, the notion of coming out presupposes a fundamentally binary distinction around both sexual orientation and gender identity. To "come out" is to reveal or announce to self or others that, whereas one has been previously identified as heterosexual, one is "in fact" homosexual. The implicit assumption is that one is *either* straight *or* gay, with no space for identity descriptions that do not fit the neat duality (Tilsen, 2013). This is problematic for the many people who identify as queer or transgender ("trans") and eschew the notion of organizing their identities based on group membership altogether (McPhail, 2004). The dichotomous gay/straight distinction is limited in its utility for painting a rich portrait of people. It excludes nuances of sexual orientation and gender identity, and also overlooks consideration of other identity dimensions that could contribute to a more complex view.

Besides reifying sexual orientation in a manner that does not fit for many people, the construct of coming out also reifies gender. According to the dominant sense of the term, a person who comes out is *either* a male *or* female who expresses a "same sex" preference. For people who identify as queer or trans rather than male or female, the practice of coming out is a social ritual that by definition is unavailable to them (Nylund & Temple, 2017).

This is problematic. While they have their uses, social constructions around gender and sexual orientation also serve the purpose of inclusion and exclusion and inevitably have real consequences in the world. As Butler and Byrne (2008) point out, when we institutionalize gender and sexuality, we produce "knowledges that have served to reinforce the normalizing of heterosexuality and gender dichotomy and the oppression of other practices and identities" (p. 90). With this in mind, it is no large leap to the conclusion that "resisting and disrupting any regulating and limiting discourses is an act of social justice" (Tilsen, 2013, p. 24).

And so we return to the topic of coming out. The construct is clearly not without its limitations; and yet it does describe a process that for many represents a seminal milestone, a profound act of self-acceptance leading from a place of isolation to connection and community (Matthews, 2007). Because this process—whether named "coming out" or not—is so central to the experience of many people of non-dominant sexual orientation, it has been much studied, with attempts to capture its salient features by ways of models.

These aggregated personal accounts of coming out provide a preview of possible signposts along the journey for those entering it (Rust, 2003). In the realm of counseling, this is potentially useful for both clients and practitioners; it facilitates preparation for unfolding events, and anticipates conceivable emotional ups and downs on the horizon. Accounts of the psychological and social aspects of coming out provide a potentially normalizing, and thus reassuring, picture for those engaged in the process. Most models portray a temporal and progressive unfolding, sometimes characterized in stages, offering hope for those mired in doubt or fearful of events to come. In addition, these portraits of coming out offer a glimpse of potential issues to be confronted and the emotional responses associated with these (Rust, 2003).

If accounts of coming out are held lightly—on the understanding that the process is never quite the "same" for two people—they can provide a useful reference point against which people might differentiate themselves and celebrate that which is unique in their own experience. But the story becomes more complex when people are contending with social marginalization in additional dimensions of their experience. This is where the vocabulary of "intersectionality" comes in (cf. Cheshire, 2013; Parks, Hughes, & Matthews, 2004; Tilsen, 2013). As Tilsen (2013) writes, "When organizing around the single identity of 'gay' or 'lesbian,' sexual orientation effectively becomes the sole defining characteristic at the expense of other significant sites of identity production, especially race, ethnicity, and class" (p. 31). For newcomers who define themselves as sexual minorities or gender non-conforming, there is a lot more going on—social pressures crucial to their mental health and well-being—than is touched upon by the various models of coming out.

Our intention here, then, is to hold a both/and position in relation to coming out models, acknowledging *both* their shortcomings *and* their potential usefulness, en route to offering suggestions for revisions to accommodate the experience of newcomers who identify as sexual minorities or gender non-conforming. In the next section, we will provide a brief overview of some of the dominant coming out models by way of illustrating the ways they overlook the complexity of newcomers' lives.

Coming Out Models

Coming out is a lifelong process of identifying and disclosing oneself as gay, lesbian, bisexual, trans, or queer (LGBTQ) (Reynolds & Hanjorgiris, 2000). This process involves a new understanding of the self and self in relation with others— including society more broadly—based on a newly formed identity. Furthermore, integrating and accepting this identity is a difficult process because of the stigmatized and unconventional nature of same-sex sexualities within many societies. Even in North America, which is considered a sexually progressive society, variations of sexuality that fall beyond heterosexual traditions or vaginal sex are typically frowned upon and therefore rejected by the larger culture (Kleinplatz, 2012). A rejection of sexual minorities and gender non-conforming individuals, such as members of LGBTQ+ and kinky sex communities, becomes a slippery slope for exposure to further injustices involving the denial of access to human rights, dignity, employment, housing, health care, and legal recognition of marriage. Thus, coming out is typically a psychologically distressful process for many sexual minority individuals (Cox, Dewaele, van Houtte, & Vincke, 2010; Rust, 2003). In order to capture a picture of this process, several coming out models have been proposed in recent years (e.g., Cass, 1979; Coleman, 1982; McCarn & Fassinger, 1996). The models attempt to break this process into a sequence of stages while acknowledging the complexity of the coming out journey. Processes such as identity integration and disclosure are depicted as unfolding incrementally, accompanied by emotional, cognitive, and behavioral features. The stages typically depict a movement starting with individual awareness, followed by disclosure, eventually culminating in stabilization and active involvement in the gay communities (e.g., Coleman, 1982). The process is not smooth and seamless, however; for example, a person may originally deny same-sex attraction prior to coming out, and will often experience a period of turbulence as they experiment with an altered lifestyle en route to consolidating an integrated new identity (Bilodeau & Renn, 2005).

A key shortcoming of current coming out models—one that provided the impetus for this chapter—is their uni-dimensionality. By treating sexual orientation as a monolithic feature of identity, they fail to provide an intersectional view of people as "multiply cultured" (Paré, 2013), characterized not just by sexual orientation or gender identity but by a range of other social categories crucial to their overall experience. The singular focus on sexual orientations obscures how cultural dimensions associated with immigration (e.g., race, ethnicity, language, etc.) complicate the process. Coming out is greatly complicated by cultural considerations, which need attention given the rapid growth of the multicultural population among sexual minority and gender non-conforming communities. Failing to address the issues and obstacles faced by ethnic and sexually diverse individuals makes it impossible to understand the coming out experience for sexual minority and gender non-conforming newcomers in counseling settings.

Cultural literacy is an ethical obligation of practitioners (Ribner, 2012) and vital for anticipating the experience of newcomers who identify as sexual minorities or gender non-conforming. Attention to these issues is critical for three key reasons. First, the therapeutic alliance is at stake: counselors and therapists who overlook the specificity of cultural experiences are at risk of failing to join effectively with sexual minority and gender non-conforming clients dealing with coming out. Second, a failure to attend to cultural considerations beyond sexual orientation obscures significant challenges and injustices, and leads to an overly simplistic view of the process with immigrant and newcomer clients. And third, a thin reading of sexual minority and gender non-conforming newcomer experiences could result in the pathologizing of what might otherwise be understood as adaptive actions, thoughts, and emotions.

The removal of homosexuality from the *Diagnostic and Statistical Manual of Mental Disorders* (DSM) of the American Psychiatric Association in the 1970s and the de-pathologizing of homosexuality led to a flourishing of research into the experience of gay and lesbian individuals (Rust, 2003). Some of the emergent models focus on women only (cf. Chapman & Brannock, 1987); however, the majority (cf. Cass, 1979; Coleman 1982; Milton & MacDonald, 1984; Sophie, 1986; Troiden, 1989) are the product of ongoing and extensive interviews with older gay men of White, middle-class, Euro-American backgrounds (Reynolds & Hanjorgiris, 2000). These represent well-intentioned attempts to support practitioners in anticipating the experience of persons who are going public with their sexual orientation and gender identities. Unfortunately, the models are handicapped by the narrowness of their focus; they fail to accommodate an intersectional view of identity and tend to individualize a process that happens in a social context subject to systemic discrimination, oppression, and racism.

Reflections on Coming Out: The Problem with "Pride"

The term "pride," closely associated with coming out, has become a "buzzword" in recent years. However, it is of limited relevance to many LGBTQ+ immigrants and newcomers. It implies that until they take overt steps to publicly announce their sexual orientations or gender identities, they are somehow diminishing themselves, demeaning their natures, failing to claim what is rightfully theirs. Coming out, flamboyantly manifested in pride parades through the streets of major cities, has a powerful history in North America. The practice of coming out has helped individuals and communities gain personal and family acceptance, allies in the community, as well as access to civil and human rights. This is a progressive trajectory for mainstream LGBTQ+, but a regressive one for many LGBTQ+ immigrants and newcomers because it encourages a break with family and ethnic communities—both of which typically play key emotional and adaptive roles in their lives. Increasingly, LGBTQ+ immigrants and newcomers are accessing rights taken for granted by other Canadians, but these social advancements sadly do not imply acceptance of self, family, religion, and ethnic community.

The process of coming out is socially located. In North America's individualist-focused culture, differentiation is regarded as fundamental to the family life cycle, and coming out is therefore regarded as a key and healthy step in that process. But the landscape is vastly different for LGBTQ+ immigrants and newcomers, who are expected to navigate through and prioritize cultural, religious, familial, and ethnic considerations over their individual needs and desires. Thus coming out and the pride associated with it are privileges available to mainstream North Americans but not to many LGBTQ+ newcomers.

It is impossible to understand the coming out process for immigrants and newcomers without appreciating the complex web of experiences that includes migration, multiple oppressions, and collective cultural and familial sexual values. Without this intersectionality informed perspective, there is the risk of "Disney-fying" the coming out process, imbuing it with societal, clinical, and community expectations, seeing it as an emblem of pride, satisfaction, and personal celebration. Many LGBTQ+ immigrants and newcomers may not have access to the celebratory variation of coming out due to lifelong experiences of internalized cultural shame, guilt, and oppression. The application of a monolithic coming out lens therefore risks injustice and harm when applied to LGBTQ+ immigrants and newcomers. In the next section, we will present a composite case study based on my (MN) work to highlight some of those risks, and to demonstrate alternate possibilities for engaging with sexual minority and gender non-conforming people contending with identity issues in a counseling context.

Case Scenario: Hamad

Hamad[5] looks distinctly nervous when I greet him in my waiting area. A 30-year-old who identifies as genderqueer, he's been referred to me by a walk-in clinic he recently visited. He told a counselor there he was feeling sad and anxious, struggling to settle into the city he had arrived in as a refugee nine months ago after fleeing his home in the Middle East.

As I wave him into my office, Hamad glances around blankly and tentatively takes a seat in the corner. On noticing his strained look and halting answers to my opening questions, I slow my speech down. I learn that Hamad is enrolled in an English as a Second Language (ESL) course. He says the classes and trips to the supermarket make up the majority of his outings beyond the small subsidized apartment he rents in a government-sponsored housing complex. He has one friend, Juanita, who also attends ESL classes. He sees her occasionally outside of class, but their conversations are limited due to the language barrier. Hamad's family is still back in his country of origin. He texts them from time to time using Juanita's phone, but the contact is limited and he says he feels very lonely.

Hamad is very clear he has no desire to go home, despite his isolation and the challenges of adapting to his new country. The neighborhood where his parents and three siblings live is overrun by government forces and rebel militia, subjected to regular foreign-directed air strikes, a hollow husk of the community it once was. But the conflict aside, Hamad says it isn't safe back home; he was physically and sexually abused there and his life was threatened. "Because of who I am," he says when I ask why this happened, and he explains that he "loves men," glancing at the rainbow flag on my wall to punctuate his point.

Hamad has not disclosed his sexual orientation to his family for a variety of reasons. He feels ashamed and guilty, and says he is a failed Muslim. He fears his parents will see him as rejecting the faith that knits their family together and connects them to their community. He worries about how they would deal with his disclosure emotionally, possibly cutting him off in trying to reconcile their own fundamentalist beliefs and actions. But most of all, he is afraid for their safety, a fear based on stark events that continue to traumatize Hamad. His partner Ahmed was arrested at an underground club, imprisoned, beaten, and eventually executed for his sexual orientation. Hamad's departure for Canada was sudden and desperate, ultimately incomprehensible to his own family. He carries his secret furtively, terrified of the explosive ramifications for the people he loves most if his sexual orientation were to be revealed, bringing shame and dishonor to his family and releasing further violence.

The same trepidation that leads him to conceal his experience from his family lives on here in his new home. He sees his own ethnic community as threatening—populated with compatriots of contrasting political leanings, prone to wildfire rumours that could leap the ocean in the click of a mouse, igniting trouble overseas. Similar fears keep him away from the local gay community. He sees himself surrounded by threats, and he has the lived experience to substantiate his fears.

For Hamad, the notion of "gay pride" is clearly remote. His sexual orientation is cause for shame, a source of tragedy in his life. Similarly, the idea of coming out and embracing his sexuality is more than incongruous—more than merely unnecessary, it is recklessly nonsensical. All of these considerations are before me, as I listen to his story, and inform the gentle and cautious path forward.

For starters, I work hard to acknowledge Hamad's concerns from an intersectionality perspective and validate his experiences. His fears are well founded and he clearly is committed to taking care of his own safety and the safety of his family. I make a point of contrasting the social and legal climate here in Canada with regards to being gay, queer, or bisexual, while acknowledging that homophobia persists—though on a scale and with repercussions that pale in comparison to what he experienced back home. All of this helps to reassure him somewhat, to sort genuine from imagined threats. His shoulders drop and he leans into the conversation. We discuss refugee phobia and Islamophobia, something he has experienced overtly and covertly at various times since his arrival. Again, I help to put these in context and reassure him that while they do endure, neither homophobia nor racism are state-sanctioned, and the city is teeming with people committed to helping him and making his adjustment easier.

I inquire into Hamad's views on religion and learn that he sees himself as a believer, though he has not attended a mosque since his arrival. On the subject of Islam's views of being gay, Hamad is less certain and expresses an interest in exploring further. As to his ambitions for acculturation or integration into North American society, the topic is premature. For now, he wants to deal with his anxiety and attain some peace with himself; where that goes later is an open question.

I am curious about how Hamad has managed to cope with such substantial challenges. Initially, he falters in answering. To help out, I ask him "Who do you know who would predict that you would manage to cope and move forward, despite these major challenges you face? What would they say that would explain where their prediction came from?" Hamad mentions a cherished aunt, who since died in the conflict at home. From her point of view, he tells me stories about his ability to keep hoping in the face of despair, and of his knack for noting and celebrating the small things that point to possibilities. This draws me in and I learn more about those beacons: his friendship with Juanita, the kindness of his ESL teacher, the relative peace and stability of his neighborhood, and of the country more broadly. As our session draws to a close, I check in with Hamad: how is this going; how is his anxiety? He says he feels a little better and that he would like to talk again.

In further conversations with Hamad, I support him in taking small steps to expand the boundaries of his life in Ottawa, while the two of us keep a vigilant eye on potential risks to himself and to his family. I suggest he meet with an LGBTQ+-friendly Muslim cleric to learn more about Islam's compassion with regards to sexuality. We talked about ways he might embrace his sexuality without going public, exercising discretion—not out of shame but a sensible caution.

Hamad's journey, like all of our journeys, is *both* personal *and* cultural. In his case, he lives at a crossroads where two distinct sets of traditions and beliefs meet. He is tasked with negotiating a way forward that acknowledges his new realities while honoring deeply held cultural values, all the while taking steps and making decisions to preserve his safety. The choices he makes are multifaceted and complex, and should not be judged against any Western templates for "healthy sexuality."

While Hamad's example sheds light on dimensions of the coming out construct overlooked by mainstream models, we make no claims to it serving as a template for working with sexual minority and gender non-conforming immigrants and newcomers. This is precisely the point: an intersectional view of identity reveals the complexity and variability of experience, illustrating how it takes place within contexts that can be alternately liberating or oppressive. When experience is seen as unfolding at the intersection of not just sexual orientation or gender, but race, class, ethnicity—to name a few key identity dimensions—North American coming out models begin to look culture-bound in their privileging of individualism and their downplaying of constraining social contingencies. The answer to this is not the construction of an alternate "model," but rather expanded cultural literacy in service of social justice, to ensure that counseling practice does not inadvertently extend the oppression that many sexual minority and gender non-conforming immigrants and new-comers are attempting to leave behind in their fragile engagement with a new social context.

Reflection Questions

1. What are some of the complicating factors that make "coming out" more than a simple, self-affirming celebration as it is often identified in the literature?
2. Why might the construct of "gay pride" not fit for many newcomers?
3. Why is the precision of vocabulary so critical in working with LGBTQ+ clients?
4. Why is the notion of intersectionality critical to capturing the complexity of experience of LGBTQ+ clients?
5. Why is it important to have cultural literacy and competency while working with LGBTQ+ newcomers?
6. How might culture influence coming out processes for LGBTQ+ newcomers?
7. Why is it important to incorporate a social justice perspective into therapy with LGBTQ+ newcomers?

Notes

1 This term refers to people who do not conform to society's expectations for their gen-der roles or gender expression. Some people prefer the term "gender variant" among other terms.
2 LGBTQ+ (with the plus) in this writing indicates variation of identities that fall out of heteronormative and cisgender identities.
3 Umbrella term that includes diverse gender identities.
4 A term becoming more widely used among LGBT communities because of its inclusive-ness. "Queer" can be used to refer to the range of non-heterosexual and non-cisgender people and provides a convenient shorthand for "LGBT." It is important to note that this is a reclaimed term.
5 This scenario is a composite drawn from a number of practice encounters. Names and details have been change to protect anonymity.

References

American Psychiatric Association. (1952). *Diagnostic and statistical manual of mental disorders* (1st ed.). Washington, DC: Author.

American Psychiatric Association. (1974). *Diagnostic and statistical manual of mental disorders* (2nd ed.). Washington, DC: Author.

American Psychiatric Association. (2013). *Diagnostic and statistical manual of mental disorders* (5th ed.). Washington, DC: Author.

Bilodeau, B. L., & Renn, K. A. (2005). Analysis of LGBT identity development models and implications for practice. In R. L. Sanlo (Ed.), *Gender identity and sexual orientation: Research, policy, and personal development. New Directions for Student Services* (No. 111; pp. 25–39). San Francisco, CA: Jossey-Bass.

Brown, L. B. (1997). Women and men, not-men and not-women, lesbians and gays: American Indian gender style alternatives. *Journal of Gay & Lesbian Social Services, 6*(2), 5–20. doi: 10.1300/J041v06n02_02

Bullough, V. L., & Bullough, B. (1993). *Cross dressing, sex, and gender.* Philadelphia, PA: University of Pennsylvania Press.

Butler, J., & Byrne, A. (2008). Queer in practice: Therapy and queer theory. In L. Moon (Ed.), *Feeling queer of queer feelings?* (pp. 89–105). London: Routledge.

Cass, V. C. (1979). Homosexuality identity formation: A theoretical model. *Journal of Homosexuality, 4*(3), 219–235. doi: 10.1300/J082v04n03_01

Chapman, B. E., & Brannock, J. C. (1987). Proposed model of lesbian identity development: An empirical examination. *Journal of Homosexuality, 14*(3–4), 69–80. doi: 10.1300/J082v14n03_05

Cheshire, L. C. (2013). Reconsidering sexual identities: Intersectionality theory and the implications for educating counsellors. *Canadian Journal of Counselling and Psychotherapy, 47*(1), 4–13. Retrieved from http://cjc-rcc.ucalgary.ca

Coleman, E. (1982). Developmental stages of the coming out process. *Journal of Homosexuality, 7*(2–3), 31–43. doi: 10.1300/J082v07n02_06

Cox, N., Dewaele, A., van Houtte, M., & Vincke, J. (2010). Stress-related growth, coming out, and internalized homonegativity in lesbian, gay, and bisexual youth: An examination of stress-related growth within the minority stress model. *Journal of Homosexuality, 58*(1), 117–137. doi: 10.1080/00918369.2011.533631

Gilley, J. B. (2006). *Becoming two-spirit: Gay identity and social acceptance in Indian country.* Lincoln, NE: University of Nebraska Press.

Herdt, G. H. (1997). *Same sex, different cultures: Gays and lesbians across cultures.* Boulder, CO: Westview Press.

Hill, N. L. (2009). Affirmative practice and alternative sexual orientations: Helping clients navigate the coming out process. *Clinical Social Work Journal, 37*(4), 346–356. doi: 10.1007/s10615-009-0240-2

Hunter, S. (2007). *Coming out and disclosures: LGBT persons across the life span.* Binghamton, NY: The Haworth Press.

Kleinplatz, P. J. (2012). Is that all there is? A new critique of the goals of sex therapy. In P. J. Kleinplatz (Ed.), *New directions in sex therapy* (pp. 101–118). New York, NY: Taylor & Francis.

McCarn, S. R., & Fassinger, R. E. (1996). Revisioning sexual minority identity formation a new model of lesbian identity and its implications for counseling and research. *The Counseling Psychologist, 24*(3), 508–534. doi: 10.1177/0011000096243011

McPhail, B. A. (2004). Questioning gender and sexuality boundaries: What queer theorists, transgendered individuals, and sex researchers can teach social work. *Journal of Gay and Lesbian Social Services*, *17*(1), 3–21. doi: 10.1300/J041v17n01_02

Matthews, C. (2007). Affirmative lesbian, gay, and bisexual counselling with all clients. In K. J. Bieschke, R. M. Perez, & K. A. Debord (Eds.), *Handbook of counselling and psychotherapy with lesbian, gay, bisexual and transgender clients* (2nd ed., pp. 201–219). Washington, DC: American Psychological Association.

Milton, H. L., & MacDonald, G. J. (1984). Homosexual identity formation as a developmental process. *Journal of Homosexuality*, *9*(2–3), 91–104. doi: 10.1300/J082v09n02_06

Nichols, M. (2013). Same-sex sexuality from a global perspective. In K. S. K. Hall & C. A. Graham (Eds.), *The cultural context of sexual pleasure and problems: Psychotherapy with diverse clients* (pp. 22–46). New York, NY: Routledge.

Nylund, D., & Temple, A. (2017). Queer informed therapy: Radical approaches to counseling with transgender persons. In C. Audet & D. Paré (Eds.), *Social Justice and Counseling: Discourse in Practice* (pp. 159–170). New York, NY: Routledge.

Paré, D. (2013). *The practice of collaborative counseling and psychotherapy: Developing skills in culturally mindful helping*. Thousand Oaks, CA: Sage.

Parks, C. A., Hughes, T. L., & Matthews, A. K. (2004). Race/ethnicity and sexual orientation: Intersecting identities. *Cultural Diversity and Ethnic Minority Psychology*, *10*(3), 241–254. doi: 10.1037/1099-9809.10.3.241

Reynolds, A. L., & Hanjorgiris, W. F. (2000). Coming out: Lesbian, gay, and bisexual identity development. In R. M. Perez, K. A. DeBord, & K. J. Bieschke (Eds.), *Handbook of counseling and psychotherapy with lesbian, gay, and bisexual clients* (pp. 35–56). Washington, DC: American Psychological Association.

Ribner, D. (2012). Cultural diversity and sensitivity in sex therapy. In P. J. Kleinplatz (Ed.), *New directions in sex therapy: Innovations and alternatives* (2nd ed., pp. 161–174). New York, NY: Routledge.

Rust, P. (2003). Finding a sexual identity and community: Therapeutic implications and cultural assumptions in scientific models of coming out. In T. Castle, L. Gross, L. Garnets, & D. Kimmel (Eds.), *Psychological perspectives on lesbian, gay, and bisexual experiences* (pp. 227–269). New York, NY: Columbia University Press.

Sophie J. (1986). A critical examination of stage theories of lesbian identity development. *Journal of Homosexuality*, *12*(2), 39–51. doi: 10.1300/J082v12n02_03

Tilsen, J. (2013). *Therapeutic conversations with queer youth: Transcending homonormativity and constructing preferred identities*. New York, NY: Jason Aronson.

Troiden, R. R. (1989). The formation of homosexual identities. *Journal of Homosexuality*, *17*(1–2), 43–73. doi: 10.1300/J082v17n01_02

Ward, E. J. (2015). *Not gay: Sex between straight white men*. New York, NY: University Press.

PART V

Anti-Pathologizing: The Politics of Practice

If there is a single thread woven through every chapter in this volume, it may be the critique of the dominant practice of characterizing persons by their deficits, otherwise known as "pathologizing." The definition of problems in relation to official nosological categories is a mainstay of medicine and is sometimes useful in counseling and psychotherapy—for instance, in matching persons up with medications that may provide some relief from distress. However, although it is informed by one discourse among many for describing people's experience, this practice exerts a dominant influence in the mental health professions. In many instances, diagnoses are required for accessing services or insurance, for example, whether the person in question prefers to make sense of their concerns in diagnostic terms or not. And the proliferation of mental disorder categories over recent decades is arguably mirrored in the tendency of many people to frame their own experience in terms of deficit in meeting with therapists, offering up identity descriptions that foreground shortcomings and overlook personal achievements in the face of challenges. This is fundamentally a social justice issue because it pertains to which vocabularies for self-description are mandated and which are marginalized. When personal experience is understood in social and contextual terms, it becomes clear that the politics of identity are ubiquitous. And they play out not only in the public arena where particular modes of description are sanctioned and funded, but in the consulting room as well, where identities are co-constructed utterance by utterance in therapeutic conversations. The chapters in this section examine the politics of identity in a variety of ways, offering useful alternatives for speaking to and about people that escape the vocabulary of deficit.

Chapter 14, Social Justice for Young People in the Youth Justice System, outlines the ways that a pervasive individualistic focus lays the blame for criminal activity entirely at the feet of incarcerated youth, overlooking the myriad social injustices contributing to their life situations. Providing a view from inside the youth correctional system, Donald Baker reminds readers that poverty, addictions, learning disabilities, mental health issues, violence, abuse, racial discrimination, and many other challenges provide barriers that deserve acknowledgment in supporting youth to step towards new ways of being outside of the problems that dominate them. The chapter offers a range of ideas for conversations with youth that keep these challenges in full view while exploring constructive possibilities for moving forward.

The section's next chapter picks up a related thread, arguing that a single-minded reliance on a diagnostic outlook renders invisible the many systemic inequities that are the backdrops of many people's lives. In Chapter 15, DSM Diagnosis and Social Justice: Inviting Counselor Reflexivity, Joaquín Gaete, Olga Smoliak, Shari Couture, and Tom Strong acknowledge the place for diagnostic inquiry while sounding a cautionary note, reminding readers of the long-term ramifications in the lives of the persons to whom diagnoses are assigned. The authors characterize counseling conversations as sites of identity construction, and demonstrate how this process may unfold in detrimental ways through their discursive analysis of assessment-focused exchanges. Their research outlines four key ways in which a conversation intent on assessment can individualize problems, obscuring contextual concerns and reinforcing a narrative focused on personal deficit. As a counterbalance to this insidious and often inadvertent pathologizing, the authors advocate for a stance of what they call dialogical reflexivity, which involves joining clients to vigilantly monitor what is being constructed or overlooked as the assessment process unfolds.

In Chapter 16, Narrative Practice and the De-Pathologizing of Children's Lives at a Walk-In Therapy Clinic: An Opportunity for Socially Just Conversations, Karen Young offers hope-inspiring alternatives to the epidemic of pathologizing practices in children's mental health services. Drawing on stories from Karen's work, the chapter outlines an approach to walk-in therapy clinics that eschews an assessment of deficit in favor of therapeutic exchanges that foreground the knowledges of children and their families. The conversational practices outlined include: collaborating on the session agenda, getting to know the person "away from" the problem, externalizing, and collaborative documentation. Based on a social and relational view of problems, this approach makes it possible to address labels and diagnoses in ways that are respectful of people's current understandings and preferences, while providing alternatives to the limiting descriptions of the child that have developed. The chapter includes reflections and feedback from children and their parents about their experiences of these practices in a walk-in therapy clinic.

Chapter 17, Rosie Had Wings They Could Not See: A Consultation with Michael White and a Woman Labeled with a Dual Diagnosis, offers a critique of coercive confinement practices at the core of the custodial model of care while demonstrating the possibilities inherent in competence-focused conversations with persons too often subjected to institutional control and containment. The chapter reviews a session by the late Michael White, an originator of narrative therapy, to show how social justice can play out utterance by utterance in the conversations therapists have with those consulting them. Authors Jim Duvall and Caroline Tremblay analyze a transcribed therapeutic conversation in which Michael White provides a platform for a woman with an intellectual disability to articulate her experience of confinement. His abiding faith in her ability to articulate her experience reaps a rich account of her continued resistance to indignities visited upon her. The exchange proves eye-opening for the mental health workers accompanying Rosie, who share their insights into the real effects of deficit-focused assumptions about people and change.

The book's final section rounds out with a look at response-based approaches to violence against women in Canada's North. Chapter 18, Creating Safety and Social Justice for Women in the Yukon, is authored by four Indigenous scholars, activists, and community workers deeply familiar with the challenges faced by women in Yukon, the smallest of Canada's territories and one where consequences of a colonizing and patriarchal pioneer history persist. Catherine Richardson/Kinewesquao, Ann Maje Raider, Barbara McInerney, and Renée-Claude Carrier observe that the safety and rights of Indigenous women are compromised by a culture of impunity where male perpetrators are often not held responsible for their crimes due to unhelpful state responses, and where women's responses to violence are often judged and pathologized. The authors document a response-based approach to practice that empowers women by construing their responses as resistance in the face of historical misogyny and oppression. After situating violence and the evolution of response-based practice, a powerful vignette demonstrates social justice-focused responses to victims of male violence. The chapter concludes with accounts of the authors' advocacy efforts in contesting victim-blaming and developing safer and respectful communities for women across Yukon.

CHAPTER 14

Social Justice for Young People in the Youth Justice System

Donald Baker

> When we move away from an individualistic view of clients, and understand personal experience as always strongly influenced by cultural context, we bump into the relationship between mental health and social justice.
>
> (Paré, 2013, p. 19)

Young people involved in Canada's Youth Justice System often receive services that individualize their responsibility for the crimes they have committed. Many of the clients I come into contact with have already been assigned a diagnosis that has been given to them by a professional. Similarly, they will have reports from the education and justice systems outlining learning disabilities and behavioral problems that have hindered their progress. If the clients don't have this information in their file, people like myself and other professionals seek to get assessments completed to assist in helping clients move forward in a positive fashion. While these glimpses into a client's life can be helpful, I feel they are limited due to their narrow focus. They are founded on the notion that responsibility and change is an individual endeavor, with very little focus placed on the contexts these young people have inhabited, are currently living in, and will be moving back to when released.

Multiple forces have impacted these youth while growing up. Systems, institutions, and cultural practices that, for the most part, are outside their control have had powerful influence over what is available to them (Dunbar, 2013). Poverty, addictions, learning disabilities, mental health issues, violence, abuse, racial discrimination, and many other factors need to be uncovered and contextualized if youth are to have a chance at stepping towards new ways of being outside of the problems that dominate them. All these social forces, along with life circumstances, play a huge role in giving people ideas about what they can be. I believe that taking all of these factors into consideration, making them more transparent for clients, is the socially just way to be of assistance.

There are other facets to the work I am undertaking with these youth that are vital to making sure the practice is carried out in a socially just fashion. For instance, attending to clients' basic needs is critically important to giving these individuals a chance at getting some semblance of equal footing with peers who have enjoyed more privilege in life. Szalavitz and Perry (2010) note "high inequality is correlated with high crime rates" (p. 281). In the same manner, Dunbar (2013) cites studies from the US, UK, and Canada that characterize "systemic inequalities, ineffective support systems, experiences of victimization and feelings of hopelessness to make money, gain status, obtain protection and acquire a sense of belonging" (p. 1) as prime factors contributing to youth deciding to be involved with crime. Socially just interventions with clients need to take these factors into account when providing assistance. If housing, finances, job preparation, education, and life skills are not attended to, the impact of counseling interventions will likely be reduced. Working collaboratively with other service providers who have the mandate to be of assistance in helping youth is an important consideration for counselors. Helping them acquire more equal footing with others who have enjoyed privilege growing up starts to address social injustices that have often hindered their ability to succeed in life.

In this chapter, I will outline aspects of the work I do with young offenders residing in young offender facilities and within community settings in Ottawa, Ontario, Canada. This work is a collaborative, client-centered approach that seeks to uncover people's strengths, skills, and abilities. I will talk about some aspects of the counseling work that I feel highlight a socially just way to help people. Many aspects of this counseling work are based in narrative therapy (White & Epston, 1990). I come to this work having grown up in a working-class family of nine in small town Ontario. Both of my parents were immigrants who managed to live through World War II. We were a blended family. I currently live in a family of four and would consider us to be middle class. My ideals tend to gravitate to the left of the political spectrum. I also associate with many activist ideals without necessarily classifying myself as an activist.

I will use examples to bring this work to life and demonstrate how addressing people's social context is the socially just way to provide assistance to young offenders. This approach moves away from individualizing problems and places them in the environments that clients live in.

Counseling, Power, and Social Justice

> [A]cknowledge that people are more than the worst thing they have ever done, and work diligently to find the honourable self of the person. That is a core capacity of our work—to be able to recognize honour in people who are struggling at the margins of our society.
>
> (Reynolds, 2008, p. 14)

Social justice is inextricable from the issue of power as it plays out in counseling relationships. Therapeutic conversations always occur across a cultural divide, a discrepancy in the social location of the participants. In the case of young offenders, that discrepancy includes the counselor/client divide, a power differential heightened by the clients' incarceration. In addition, the social location of young offenders frequently features contexts of poverty, violence, and racism—histories of marginalization that cannot be ignored.

Power

Having a socially just orientation to working with people is more than utilizing a particular method of counseling. For me it is about always taking power into consideration. Who has power? Who has been denied power? Who has the power to set the rules? Are the rules fair? Who has the power to name problems? Where are problems located? These questions, and many others, are constantly present when I work with clients. People's identities are defined by what is available to them in life, and many cultural practices and institutions end up being the mediators regarding who and what they believe they can be. Considering a person's cultural context is vitally important in helping them to get out from under problems that have kept them away from realizing their hopes and dreams in life. In considering the cultural context that people live in, social justice-oriented counselors must be open to the idea that they are now part of a system that is having influence over the very person who has come for a consultation. It is important to constantly check in with individuals regarding what they want from the service and ask if what is being delivered is in line with their wants and needs. I also always offer clients open access to my notes and documentation that is being compiled with the assurance that they have editorial rights to remove things they don't want written down.

Narrative therapy puts forward the idea that people's lives are multi-storied (Madigan, 2011; Morgan, 2000; White & Epston, 1990). People struggling with problems are understood as attached to problematic story lines of their lived experiences. When their lived experiences have been mediated by unjust social conditions like poverty, racism, and a variety of other factors, the stories they have available to them are not on equal footing with those who enjoy privilege. These negative story lines often end up defining people.

Separating Persons and Problems

Youth in trouble with the law can be dominated by problem stories about themselves. These stories often obscure their strengths, skills, and abilities. It is my job to uncover problems through the use of questions. I hope to "externalize" problems and separate them from people's identities (White & Epston, 1990). I regularly experience clients who have been totalized (White & Epston, 1990) by problems and actually attach their identities to the problems. Examples include young people naming themselves as ADHD, pot heads, conduct disordered, or oppositional defiant. Professionals involved in their lives have often been responsible for this labeling, with little thought put towards the social conditions the young people have been subject to. Similarly, assessments and other documents are often circulated from one system to the next defining these individuals as problems. When youth return to their previous social circumstances with an individually focused diagnosis, it fails to help them address the very conditions that brought the various systems' attention on them.

Externalizing a problem involves separating the problem from the person's identity. This is accomplished by using very specific questions and language. I have, for example, worked with clients who have been assessed as being "drug users." They suggest to me that people see them as being "potheads." Often times, they don't necessarily disagree with this totalizing assessment of themselves, regularly stating that they love doing drugs. My work with them, from the first time that we meet, involves using language to externalize drugs. I ask questions like "When weed comes on the scene what kind of influence does it have on you?" or "Are there times in your life when drugs are not present?" They often find this line of inquiry amusing at first because drugs are talked about like they are a living entity with the power to influence. Typically this bemusement recedes as we do more work together.

As the youths' custody time nears completion, I might present a scenario that drugs are "waiting for them just outside the facility's walls." I ask them, "What plans do you think drugs might have for you?" On more than one occasion I have received rich accounts of how drugs might want them to have a "getting out of custody party" or to miss school and not be concerned about work. Once they are able to talk about the problem as separate from themselves, we are able to discuss how they could change their relationship with drugs. We can then find out how drugs came to have influence over them and trace how drugs had become so established in their lives. Alice Morgan (2000) refers to this sort of questioning as an "exploration of the personification of the problem" (p. 25). Speaking about their challenges in this way, these clients have been able to make a shift from being people who are totalized by drugs to seeing themselves as being influenced by them.

The separation of persons from problems through language is something I have also found helpful in working with young people facing anxiety. Typical scenarios involve them having been in state care or having periods of time when they lived on the streets. When I first meet them, these young people may have trouble making eye contact, appear agitated, or generally present in a way that indicates they are uncomfortable and not ready to trust me or the counseling process. In these cases, I always ask permission to have conversations with the youth. I start off by asking them if they are alright. They often wonder why I ask them this question, and I make them aware of my observations and the idea that being in custody can be intimidating. In my experience, in these circumstances, clients are more likely to talk openly about what is troubling them. It is not unusual for them to speak of anxiety, worries, or being agitated. Because of the opportunity presented for separating persons from problems, I prefer to find a problem early in our conversations and to rely whenever possible on the language that the young person uses to describe it (White & Epston, 1990).

Having a name for the problem allows me to ask questions to help unpack a lot of information about its presence in their lives. My questions include: "When were you first aware that anxiety was present in your life?," "Have there been times when anxiety has had a stronger influence over you?," "What kind of things has anxiety been able to make you think about yourself?" Naming and externalizing anxiety allows us to work on its effects and provides ideas about how clients can deal with it in the future. When they are able to see its origins in experiences and situations that were outside their control, it gives individuals a new way to orient themselves to their circumstances.

The effects of poverty, violence, abuse, and unaddressed learning disabilities can be made more transparent when externalized. This externalizing of problems allows me to place them in the context of social justice issues as opposed to having pathologizing conversations about the person as the problem. We can then have conversations about the trauma involved in being placed in care and how it has impacted on them. Foster care and group home placements intended to keep clients safe often fail them in a big way. Addressing the problems with group homes and foster placements, Contenta, Monsebraaten, and Rankin (2015) indicated that in 2013 there were 1,200 serious occurrence reports sent to the Ministry of Children and Youth Services by Toronto Group Homes and the Children's Aid Society of Toronto. These include errors, mismanagement, and acts of abuse mostly occurring in publically funded group homes run by private operators. Through our work together, I join young offenders in examining their experience in the context of events like these, rather than placing all responsibility on their individual choices. Eventually they can start to see redeeming things about themselves and how they have dealt with their life circumstances.

Externalizing and Personal Agency

This may be a good place to talk about one of the major critiques of utilizing an externalizing dialogue with clients. It has been suggested that by externalizing problems, therapists run the risk of absolving clients of responsibility for their actions. This is a particularly salient point when dealing with clients who have committed offences that, in many instances, have harmed other people. However, this is not how I see externalizing.

When a person's identity is collapsed into a problem, they have ready-made excuses to explain behavior. Someone can explain away acts of violence by suggesting that they are Conduct Disordered or inflicted with Reactive Attachment Disorder. Similarly a person identified as a drug addict may feel they have no choice but to submit to drugs being in their lives.

Once problems are externalized, therapists can ask questions to clients that invite them to take responsibility for their actions (Jenkins, 1990). An externalized problem can actually be quite beneficial in helping clients recognize that they have agency outside of diagnoses and assessments that collapse a problem into their identity.

Counterviewing and Deconstruction

Externalizing allows clients to disentangle themselves from problems defining who they are. Social justice-oriented conversations can then start to place more focus on the social conditions that have had a huge influence over their lives. As noted by Paré (2013), considering cultural locations prevents counselors from individualizing responsibility for clients' mental health issues. Stephen Madigan (2011) uses the term "counterviewing" (p. 94) to characterize thera-peutic conversations that achieve a similar purpose. Counterviewing involves placing a critical focus on the naming practices of therapeutic models and insti-tutions that have the power to individualize problems. This critique is offered to individuals as a way to escape being labeled, stigmatized, and in some instances totalized by culturally legitimized practices. Clients who have lived through oppressive life circumstances can consequently get assigned labels and diagno-ses that are taken as "truth."

When they come into contact with systems that have the power to name men-tal health problems, it is helpful for young people to have access to an alternative view that takes their lived context into account. Counterviewing achieves this by helping them to notice that mental health is impacted by social practices, includ-ing the practice of assigning mental illness labels, as opposed to it being inher-ently present inside the individual. A social justice-informed therapist takes an interest in discovering, acknowledging, and taking apart the beliefs, ideas, and practices of the broader culture in which a person lives that are serving to assist the problem story.

A large number of the clients I deal with have multiple labels attached to them, which are confirmed in the documentation constructed by professionals that chronicles their lives. Labels like Conduct Disordered and Oppositional Defiant Disordered indicate individual deficits with little attention directed towards persons' social circumstances. Uncovering contextual challenges and asking questions that can help a client challenge these labels is important to a socially just counseling practice. In narrative therapy, this exploration of the social forces contributing to personal experience is known as deconstruction (White & Epston 1990). Counselors can use questions to help clients develop alternative views regarding themselves and the labels that are applied to them. These questions can focus on social context as opposed to locating problems in the individual. They look at the conditions that these youth have had to endure. Questions like "What was it like to live in such chaotic circumstances?" and "How did the area you lived in influence how you responded?" start to open up a dialogue that places problems in context.

Shedding the Weight of Systems and Social Conditions

Many institutions that have the mandate to help individuals ultimately contribute to those individuals having more problems to deal with. In his insightful book

Asylums, Erving Goffman (1961) made the observation that many institutions put forward the notion that they are there to help individuals when in fact their rules and practices are designed to maintain order within them. Many of the clients I am privileged to work with have experienced being taken into state care because they were deemed to be at risk in the family home. Placed in chaotic group home environments, they lived with other individuals recently removed from their homes. Often these homes are staffed by relatively inexperienced workers with little training in caring for traumatized youth. It is not unusual for conflict and violence to erupt in these group living quarters. It is also not uncommon in these settings for police to be called in to intervene in situations that are out of control. Young people who, for safety reasons, were removed from their family to be placed in state care may end up coming into contact with the Youth Justice System as a result of violence occurring in the group home. This is an example of how a system set up for the protection of young people does not seem to be accomplishing what it hoped to do in the first place.

These institutional interventions can have long-term repercussions in the lives of young people. I commonly work with youth who have experienced well over 10 foster/group home placements in their lives. These youth are often assigned responsibility for the necessity of moving when placements don't work. Each move typically requires new school placements and the challenges of developing new social networks. In working with clients who have been caught up in systems and impacted by forces like poverty, racism, and learning disabilities, the conversational practices of counterviewing and deconstruction can help them get out from under individualizing practices that have defined them as the problem.

Asking questions to give clients alternative angles on their experience is really important. Often these questions are simple and to the point. Questions like "Was money an issue for your family?" or "How many different group homes have you lived in?" can be first steps in clients getting the idea that their circumstances are not merely a function of "something wrong in their heads." Other questions like "What was it like to be moved so much?" or "How did not having money impact you?" start getting clients thinking about how their social conditions have contributed to their problems. The conversational practices I have been describing not only separate persons from problems; in doing so, they enter into new territories that feature more helpful, alternative accounts of youths' lives.

When a therapist externalizes, counterviews, and deconstructs aspects of clients' lives, new stories featuring their strengths, skills, and abilities have a chance to emerge. These positive stories are always present and are connected to positive assessments of the self, but can easily be obscured or minimized by oppressive social conditions and assessments from well-meaning professionals. I see it as my job to use questions to uncover strengths, skills, and abilities in the form of alternative story lines (Madsen, 2007). When persons' strengths aren't highlighted, they have no way to hope, dream, and plan for the future. Crenshaw and Garbarino (2007) suggest that counselors should engage in a "relentless pursuit of strengths, talents and redeeming qualities, the buried treasure to be found" (p. 170). Rubin (1992) talks about the concept of looking for "badges of ability"—strengths that youth can take pride in. People who get to grow up in affluence, positive educational environments, and stable neighborhoods and homes typically have positive validation readily available for them regarding their strengths, skills, and abilities. Poverty and unstable living conditions often result in young people having much reduced availability of positive validation in their lives (Hardy & Laszloffy, 2005).

Many of the youth I have worked with have had interrupted school careers where factors like poverty, hunger, racism, unaddressed learning disabilities, and frequent moves have made it very difficult for them to feel good about their academic abilities. It is amazing to see many of these youth connect with the idea that they are good students. The educators in the detention facilities I work in help them find success and do so in an expedient fashion. Young and Gonzalez (2013) and Dunbar (2013) point out that it is important for youth in detention facilities to experience success fast. Incarceration ironically offers an opportunity for some youth to catch up educationally. To me this highlights the harshness of the social conditions in the daily lives of some young offenders.

Grounding Questions and Comments to Avoid Hollow Praise

While it is helpful to highlight positive developments in the process of moving away from "problem-saturated stories" (White & Epston, 1990), care needs to be taken in avoiding "cheerleading" when working with these young people. I always seek to get them to describe and confirm their stories in their own words. Statements like "You're doing great" or "You have a lot of potential to do well" feel hollow to me because they are disembodied, and they privilege my judgment over theirs. I prefer to use questions to invite young people to uncover and name positives that have been obscured by oppression and social injustices. Questions like "What went into you being able to resist the influence of the problem?" or "How did you manage to accomplish so much despite (the problem's) presence in your life?" offer the person the opportunity to reflect and comment on positive things they have been doing. The therapist can then attempt to get to positive value and meaning with questions like, "What does it say about you that you were able to stand up to the influence of (the problem)?" or "If people were able to see what you have been able to accomplish in dealing with (the problem), what would they come to know about you?"

Beyond Custody

While uncovering clients' strengths, skills, and abilities that have been hidden from clients by the contexts in which they have lived prior to incarceration, it is equally important to recognize that youth are still likely to have to contend with oppressive conditions when they leave custody. Poverty, racism, unaddressed learning disabilities, mental health, addictions, and multiple other factors don't just leave clients' lives because they have connected to positive assessments of themselves. Socially just services need to do much more than uncover injustice. While it is beyond the scope of this chapter to detail the many interventions that can be offered post-custody, it is worth mentioning that ongoing support must be available to help clients address injustices—including the deficits in basic needs referenced earlier. Helpers need to follow clients to the locations they live in and be available to work with them in facing challenges as they arise. This involves advocacy, counseling support, and collaboration with the client and other service providers. Dealing with injustice is indeed not an individual endeavor.

Conclusion

In this chapter, I have attempted to highlight social justice informed aspects of my work with youth who consult with me after having entered into detention facilities. I highlighted aspects of this work that rely on a social justice orientation to engaging with the problems these clients deal with. The examples I have provided here are not meant to be a comprehensive overview of any particular therapeutic model, but a brief snapshot of a social justice-influenced practice.

I have explored the importance of social justice in working with young offenders, and shared some specific counseling practices I utilize in my work. Among the practices covered are externalizing, acknowledging power, deconstructing, and counterviewing. In addition to providing examples of how questions are constructed and used in my work, I also emphasized the need to help clients connect with their strengths, skills, and abilities to assist them in navigating the complex contexts in which they live.

I am grateful to my many colleagues who try to make a difference every day in the lives of youth faced with innumerable challenges. It is a privilege to work with the young men and families I come into contact with on a daily basis. Connecting with their resilience, strength, and hopes for their future is a constant inspiration.

Reflection Questions

1. Has an institution ever impacted on your life in a negative way and left you feeling like you didn't measure up? How did this affect you?
2. Have you ever had to move and establish yourself in a new community? What was this like for you?
3. Has there ever been a time in life where you did not have enough to eat and had no resources to rectify the situation?
4. Have you ever been in a situation where your cultural identity was different than the dominant culture? What impact did this have on your view of yourself?
5. Has anyone ever labeled you in a way that did not fit with how you saw yourself? What was that like for you?

References

Crenshaw, D. A., & Garbarino, J. (2007). The hidden dimensions: Profound sorrow and buried potential in violent youth. *Journal of Humanistic Psychology, 47*(2), 160–174. doi: 10.1177/0022167806293310

Contenta, S., Monsebraaten, L., & Rankin, J. (2015, July 3). Shedding light on the troubles facing kids in group homes. *The Toronto Star*. Retrieved from www.thestar.com

Dunbar, L. (2013). *"Getting out": Youth gang exit strategies and interventions*. (Report for Crime Prevention Ottawa). Retrieved from www.crimepreventionottawa.ca

Goffman, E. (1961). *Asylums: Essays on the social situation of mental patients and other inmates*. New York, NY: Doubleday.

Hardy, K., & Laszloffy, T. A. (2005). *Teens who hurt: Clinical interventions to break the cycle of adolescent violence*. New York, NY: Guilford Press.

Jenkins, A. (1990). *Invitations to responsibility: The therapeutic engagement of men who are violent and abusive*. Adelaide, Australia: Dulwich Centre Publications.

Madigan, S. (2011). *Narrative therapy*. Washington, DC: American Psychological Association.

Madsen, W. (2007). *Collaborative therapy with multi-stressed families* (2nd ed.). New York, NY: Guilford Press.

Morgan, A. (2000). *What is narrative therapy?: An easy-to-read introduction*. Adelaide, Australia: Dulwich Centre Publications.

Paré, D. A. (2013). *The practice of collaborative counseling and psychotherapy: Developing skills in culturally mindful helping*. Thousand Oaks, CA: Sage.

Reynolds, V. (2008, May). Immeasurable outcomes: Underwhelming stories of the unexpected. Keynote address at David Berman Memorial Concurrent Disorders Conference in Vancouver, BC.

Rubin, L. (1992). *Worlds of pain*. New York, NY: Basic Books.

Szalavitz, M., & Perry, B. D. (2010). *Born for love: Why empathy is essential and endangered*. New York, NY: Harper Collins.

White, M., & Epston, D. (1990). *Narrative means to theraputic ends*. New York, NY: Norton.

Young, A. M., & Gonzalez, V. (2013). *Getting out of gangs, staying out of gangs: Gang intervention and desistence strategies*. [National Gang Centre Bulletin No. 8]. Retrieved from www.nationalgangcenter.gov

CHAPTER 15

DSM Diagnosis and Social Justice: Inviting Counselor Reflexivity

Joaquín Gaete, Olga Smoliak, Shari Couture, and Tom Strong

In the 1990s, the American Psychological Association's Clinical Psychology Division took up an evidence-based direction already under way in medicine (Chambless et al., 1996). Needed for this direction were standardized diagnostic terms and interventions to build an evidence-base for counseling. Psychiatry's *Diagnostic and Statistical Manual of Mental Disorders*, in its fifth edition (DSM-5, American Psychiatric Association, hereafter APA, 2013), had been increasingly adopted by psychologists and counselors as the standardized diagnostic language of practice (Grohol, 2013). It is a language of primarily biomedical symptoms and disorders occurring *in* clients. The accompanying development was to identify evidence-based "treatments" for addressing these psychiatric disorders in clients. Such developments have not gone uncontested as concerns have been expressed about narrowing counseling's focus away from other conversations professionals might have with clients (Elkins, 2007; Hansen, 2007). Such concerns extend to counselors' conversations with clients when their presenting concerns can be understood as a function of social inequities or other social justice issues (Eriksen & Kress, 2005).

In this chapter, we reflect on the social justice dimensions of counselors' diagnostic activities. While a client diagnosis is typically central to an evidence-based treatment plan, our sensitivities as discursive scholars draw our attention to what does and does not get talked about in diagnostic interviews and how social justice concerns can be obscured when individual factors and "problems" are overemphasized. Mindful of the reflexivity of counselors' responses to clients, we microanalytically examine the immediacies of their talking together, highlighting how diagnostic interactions occur, and what gets conversationally accomplished in them. We close this chapter with implications from our analyses for professionals' social justice sensitivities and conversational practices with clients.

Social Justice and the DSM-5: Reflexively Creating Room for Both

A DSM-5 diagnosis can help to medically legitimize a client's concerns. For example, a PTSD diagnosis can enable clients who have had traumatic experiences to have their concerns taken seriously or gain access to previously unavailable resources. The logic and terms of the DSM-5 are now part of everyday parlance—accessible via media or participation in online communities—so it should not be surprising that people increasingly self-identify in DSM terms or expect treatment accordingly (Illouz, 2008; Thompson, 2012). Critics counter that the DSM medicalizes formerly normal aspects of the human condition (Frances, 2013; Rapley, Moncrieff, & Dillon, 2011) while obscuring relevant socio-cultural injustices (Rose, 2007).

The so-called neutrality of diagnosing symptoms and disorders "in" individuals might initially seem reassuring to counselors until they consider *what is not responded to* in what clients tell or present to them. Unwittingly, counselors issuing/adopting a diagnosis may de-contextualize clients' distress or misconstrue (e.g., pathologize) culturally marginalized ways of being in the world. Social justice concerns seldom can be located inside our clients; unjust circumstances and relationship problems also need to be named so that they can be addressed (White, 1995). When individual psychopathology is the dominant focus of inquiry, sociopolitical dimensions of clients' lives and experiences can be easily overlooked (Fox, Prilleltensky, & Austin, 2009). This individual focus diverts attention from structural forces influencing individual behavior and experience (e.g., class hierarchy and oppression, policies that foster social disparity, individualist public attitudes toward poverty that contribute to class inequalities). In working with clients living in poverty, for example, counselors may inadvertently adopt individualist attributions that focus on the role of clients and families in their poverty (e.g., exploring clients' lack of skills or motivation as "barriers" to economic success; Bullock & Limbert, 2009). Alternatively, seeing structural forces as professionally relevant means that counseling interactions, including diagnostic conversations, become potential sites for re-producing and transforming a status quo many find oppressive.

Although we acknowledge that receiving a diagnosis may enhance social justice and equity by increasing access of some individuals to services and resources previously unavailable to them (Burstow, 2005), we have some reservations about professionals primarily relying on the DSM in their assessment of clients. The DSM has been established in many professional and cultural circles in the West as the dominant viewpoint on subjectivity and distress (Horwitz & Wakefield, 2012; Illouz, 2007; Lafrance & McKenzie-Mohr, 2013), which arguably makes it difficult to disregard, supplement, or challenge it, in both professional practice and clients' lived experience. This is particularly relevant in light of the evidence-based movement across professions (cf. Levant, 2005; Strong & Busch, 2013), specifically the notion that treatment is linked to, or a natural outcome of, a diagnosis/assessment, with diagnosis being commonly framed in DSM terms. Once a therapeutic conversation is set on this diagnosis/treatment path (e.g., major depressive disorder/cognitive-behavioral interventions), it may be challenging to depart from it or diversify ways of understanding and addressing clients' distress, to include social justice concerns.

Therefore, it is not the diagnostic framework or treatment manual itself that we problematize, but the "pull" that many professionals and clients may experience to explain clients' distress and experience biomedically due to the cultural prominence of psychiatric diagnoses. While such frameworks and manuals direct the therapist's focus to "internal" dynamics, social justice concerns pertain to "external" or systemic forces (e.g., social differences, relations, and inequalities). In this way, diagnostic and social justice orientations potentially have opposing agendas and foci. While both can co-exist in the same conversation and comprise useful interpretive resources, they may also be contradictory. A diagnostic focus can hinder the contextual analysis and even be implicated in the reproduction of social injustices by overemphasizing the internal processes, locating the problem "within" the client, and diverting attention away from the broader dynamics of dominance and oppression (Lafrance & McKenzie-Mohr, 2013; Marecek & Hare-Mustin, 2009). Likewise, an overemphasis on structural factors may take time and focus away from a comprehensive and systematic diagnostic inquiry concerned with individual symptomology. It is what therapists *may not* have a chance to explore because of their overreliance on the DSM, a potential conversational skew in our view, that warrants consideration. This applies to both therapeutic conversations involving clients who have previously received a diagnosis and conversations focused on issuing a diagnosis.

Dialogical Reflexivity

We propose that diagnostic conversations without critical reflexivity—or attention to how relations of power and privilege, including one's position within these relations, shape everyday action, understanding, and experience—may hinder more socially just ways of understanding and addressing clients' concerns of living. Reflexivity is not a new concept. While there is no uniform definition, it has been predominantly understood as an internal, monological process (as in "self-awareness" or "self-reflection"; see Neden, 2012). Specifically, some conceptualize it as "holding a mirror" (Paré, 2013, p. 66) to the counselor's values and assumptions, as well as to their sociocultural positioning related to class, gender, race, ethnicity, age, sexuality, and other social identity categories, to highlight how broader culture shapes (and is shaped by) what counselors privilege and overlook (e.g., Duvall & Béres, 2011). We are mindful, for instance, that this chapter is shaped by our being counselors and researchers sharing backgrounds in constructionist family therapy (CFT; see e.g., Hoffman, 1992; Tomm, 1987, 2014), with a specific interest in how conversation can be political as people propose and resist meanings on a turn-by-turn basis. We also understand reflexivity in ways that proponents of social constructionist, dialogic, and collaborative approaches to CFT (e.g., Strong & Paré, 2004) highlight as "micro" or dialogical. Dialogical reflexivity involves attentiveness to how counselors, at every conversational turn, negotiate the social positions currently at stake both for clients and for themselves (e.g., "I'm an expert, you are not"). This type of reflexivity, focused on the details of how counselors and their clients conversationally sustain or reject lines of talk, can help counselors discern useful and counterproductive times to pursue a specific agenda in interaction (e.g., sociopolitical, diagnostic).

In our analysis, we highlight how social justice issues can be at stake in counseling interactions informed by individualist and medicalized conceptualizations of clients' concerns. As previously stated, we do not suggest abandoning diagnostic conversations, but advocate reflexive participation in them, in ways mindful of broader socio-historical dynamics and relations of power and privilege. We see talk's immediacies in such conversations as consequential and propose a social justice orientation for such conversations with clients. Joining other authors in this volume, our social justice orientation centers on clients' local knowledge (Geertz, 1983). From this stance, we aim to privilege client-preferred ways of sense-making, acknowledging their social embeddedness, life circumstances, and resourcefulness. Rather than imposing dominant culturally endorsed knowledge (e.g., DSM-5) or unreflectively accepting current client offerings (e.g., "I'm depressive") without unpacking how useful they are in clients' experiences, we join clients in reflexively exploring the utility of alternative understandings.

The Diagnostic Interview as a Conversational Process and Accomplishment

Drawing from a discursive research tradition, we see conversation as both constructed and constructive (e.g., Edwards, 2005). It is *constructed* in the sense that it involves ongoing, situated conversational "work" to perform particular actions. Thus, people's ways of talking (e.g., re-formulating an interviewee's answer in medical terms) are constructed for particular purposes (e.g., as "clinically significant"). In addition, conversation is *constructive* for how ways of talking propose particular interpretations or versions of identity or experience, when there are arguably other versions. Accordingly, making sense of clients' concerns by using a DSM diagnostic category is a conversational accomplishment. Through the back and forth of talk, counselors and clients propose, confirm, negotiate, and generate a particular version of the clients' experience. We (Sutherland, Sametband, Gaete, Couture, & Strong, 2012) see the counseling "process" as inseparable from counseling "outcomes," as co-constructing or conversationally accomplishing such outcomes. Thus, a closer examination of such DSM-informed diagnostic interviews may highlight how socially unjust outcomes are talked into significance over other outcomes in counseling.

Four Conversational Practices that Privilege DSM-Centered Outcomes

What follows are the results of our discursive analysis (Wooffitt, 2005) of DSM-informed assessment interviews showing how diagnoses were

Table 15.1 Four conversational practices that privilege DSM-centered outcomes

#	Practice	Accomplishment or outcome
1	Medicalizing	Portraying a client's experience as indicative of a mental disorder or pathology (e.g., as "symptoms" making up a "syndrome")
2	Checklisting	Efficiently gathering relevant information for the purposes of establishing a DSM-informed diagnosis, avoiding potential deviations (e.g., initiated by clients) to explore "less relevant" areas
3	Individualizing	Formulating experience as determined exclusively by individual factors
4	Pathologizing	Co-constructing pathology and problem-focused descriptions and overlooking alternative developments

interactionally *produced* rather than *discovered* in clients. We examined four psychiatric-oriented interviews accessible on the internet (jessygrl2121, 2012; Jill HD, 2010 [examples 1–3]; PsychScene Hub, 2010; University of Nottingham, 2012 [examples 4–5]) and identified four conversational *practices*, summarized in Table 15.1.

These practices foregrounded a medical framing of clients' concerns, identities, and experiences, and closed off opportunities for developing and exploring other social justice and contextual perspectives in counseling. Our use of "practices" avoids ascribing deliberate intentions to therapists, focusing instead on how their talking privileges the accomplishment of institutionally preferred outcomes. When accepted (or deferred to) by clients, these practices become discursive methods for therapists to accomplish particular institutional agendas—here, to attribute clients' concerns to a diagnosable DSM disorder.

Practice 1: Medicalizing

This practice refers to constructing clients' experiences in ways consistent with an underlying mental disorder, such as by using a medical vocabulary (e.g., "symptoms"). By medicalizing, participants in DSM-informed diagnostic interviews (counselors *and* clients) may focus on medical symptoms, potentially bypassing social justice considerations. For example, by introducing a medicalized term to describe a client's mood, counselors might constrain such descriptions within a medical framework. In Example 1, the counselor (Co) initially uses nontechnical language ("things that have been making you feel kind of down"). She subsequently introduces more technical (medical) vocabulary, initiating a more systematic diagnostic inquiry. Our **bold text** in Example 1 (as in examples that follow) helps us highlight the "conversational evidence" we consider relevant to our analysis.

Example 1

Co: So as we talked about before I wanted to ask you some questions about the types of problems you have been having lately and the things that have been making you **feel kind of down**. Is that okay?

Cl: That's okay.

Co: Okay, so I'm wondering if you would say that you have been feeling notably down **or depressed** most days during the last two weeks.

Cl: That's true. It has been hard for me to get out of bed and I just feel disinterested in my job, friends stuff like that.

Co: Okay and I'll ask you about some of those things in just a minute. But have you been feeling **emotionally down, sad, depressed, these sorts of things**?

Cl: **Yes.**

Co: **Okay. And for more than** half the time in the last couple of weeks?

Cl: (Nods)

Co: **Okay. What about** has it been hard for you to find pleasure in the things that used to be fun to you over the last couple of weeks?

Cl: Yes.

Co: What types of things aren't as fun as they may have been in the past for you?

Cl: I don't enjoy spending time with friends as much. Um spending time with my kid. It has just been really hard and I feel like being alone.

Co: **Okay.** I am so sorry to hear that. **What about** things like your sleep?

Medicalizing is evident in Co's replacing and upgrading an everyday expression ("feeling down") with a medical term ("depressed"). This lexical substitution reformulates Cl's original understanding of her experience. Embedding "depressed" alongside everyday descriptions of distress may enhance Cl's likelihood of endorsing such symptom language (if in lay terms it "fits" better). Cl's "yes" confirms Co's depiction of distress (down, sad, depressed) and marks this medical framing of her distress as mutually endorsed. In other words, Cl is now "on board" with the medical description of her troubles.

Medicalizing can also occur through how counselors conversationally *syndromize* or formulate clients' "symptoms" as part of a known "syndrome," or as a set of associated symptoms or symptoms that consistently co-occur. In the DSM-5 (APA, 2013), syndromes are equated with mental disorders. Consistent with this medical narrative, a professional diagnostic interview has to not only ensure that a client's experience can be captured under specific symptoms but also demonstrate the existence of a pattern of symptoms. In our analysis, we noticed counselors presenting an initially identified symptom (e.g., "hard to sleep") as an aspect of a presumably known broader syndrome. Through this syndromizing practice, the client's sleep disturbances purportedly *reveal* the presence of a syndrome (e.g., Major Depressive Disorder). Constructing distress through the medical lens of symptoms and syndromes may focus counselors and clients away from a social justice lens where other influences are considered (e.g., disagreements with superiors at work). Although assessing symptoms does not rule out the possibility of seeing the client's experience as contextually provoked, a continued focus on individual symptomology coupled with a failure to join any contextually centered client offerings will construct an account that symptoms alone may seem sufficient in explaining client distress. Example 2 below builds on Example 1. Co bypasses Cl's talk of not spending time with friends and family and feeling alone, to pursue symptom talk instead.

Example 2

Cl: I don't enjoy spending time with friends as much. Um spending time with my kid. It has just been really hard and I feel like being alone.

Co: Okay. I am so sorry to hear that. What about things like your sleep? You mentioned a minute ago that it has been hard for you to sleep and I am wondering if you can tell me if you have been having trouble sleeping **nearly every night** for the last couple of weeks?

Cl: Ya it has been really hard for me to fall asleep at night.

Co: Okay **so falling asleep** is taking you longer than it normally does?

Cl: Ya.

Co: **Are you able to stay asleep** once you fall asleep?

Cl: I usually just get up and go downstairs and watch TV or something for a couple of hours and doze in and out.

Co: Okay so **how many hours on average** would you say you are sleeping each night recently?

Cl: Probably four or five?

Co: Okay (with a nod) and how many hours were you **usually** sleeping?

Cl: Usually eight hours a night.

Co: Okay so you are sleeping roughly **half the amount of time that you were able to before** you started feeling so badly, is that right?

We observed professionals exploring in depth the nature, severity, longevity, and persistence of specific experiences or symptoms (e.g., difficulty falling asleep). Insomnia or hypersomnia (nearly every day) is one criterion for diagnosing a major depressive episode or major depressive disorder (DSM-5, APA, 2013). As the bolded text above highlights, someone seeking to identify or rule out depression might inquire about changes in sleep, specifically attending to: (a) persistence of sleep disturbance (nearly every night); (b) the nature of the disturbance (e.g., to discriminate between two common forms of insomnia—a more depression-related insomnia of conciliation and an anxiety-related insomnia of maintenance); (c) the severity and direction of sleep changes (sleeps too much or too little); and (d) whether significant changes occurred (e.g., half the amount of time). Therefore, Co's questions seem reasonable for scrutinizing a symptom within a DSM-informed agenda (i.e., gathering DSM-required information to establish a purported underlying syndrome). Both syndromizing and symptom scrutinizing can close off discussing alternative (i.e., non-medical) framings of clients' concerns and experiences. Below, we offer another example of medicalizing.

Example 3

Co: Okay. How has your appetite been lately?

Cl: Hmmm I'm not really interested in food so much just kind of low appetite, feel low energy (shrugging shoulders).

Co: Yeah and surely energy and appetite, food consumption **can go hand in hand**. Um have you noticed that you'd actually lost any weight since you've been feeling down?

Cl: I probably have **I don't really pay much attention but I think maybe I have lost some weight**.

Co: Okay so you haven't been weighing yourself on the scale **so what gives you the impression** that you may have lost a few pounds?

Co reformulates Cl's listing of concerns (low energy, low appetite) as symptoms within a broader diagnosable syndrome. She invites Cl to focus on possible weight loss, to perhaps elicit a measurable response. Cl constructs herself as inattentive to these issues ("don't really pay much attention"), regarding weight issues as seemingly irrelevant to her. Arguably, scrutinizing quantifiable details about Cl's weight might yield "evidence" of an underlying syndrome such as a major depressive episode (e.g., establishing that changes in weight are *clinically significant*, by DSM standards). DSM-oriented counselors might claim such medicalizing talk is needed to understand clients' symptoms, specify a diagnosis, and "treat" them in scientifically warranted ways. Without denying this possibility, clients may find additional foci of conversation empowering and worth exploring, including discussions of how distress is understood and addressed within their local cultures and communities. We wonder about the extent to which "medicalizing," as a meaning-making style, helped center counselor's knowledge while marginalizing other knowledges. We were also curious about what kind of conversation might have unfolded had Co become curious about the relevance of structural forces to the client's sleeping and eating. Questions could be posed to explore if her sleep disturbances were related to unjust internalized demands about her role as a mother at home or at work. Alternative questions could open space for relating clients' concerns to potential social justice considerations. We will later return to this idea, inviting readers to be more reflective with their own conversational practices.

Practice 2: Checklisting

When feeling institutionally obliged to produce a reliable DSM diagnosis, discussing broader issues can seem counterproductive, threatening needed "airtime" for a diagnostic interview. Accordingly, we observed that counselors' ways of questioning and responding to client's answers sometimes worked to keep such threats under control. We categorized this practice favoring the establishment of a known clinical diagnosis as *checklisting*.

Revisiting Example 1 above, one finds four forms of checklisting. First, we noticed Co using *and-prefaced* checklist-type of question (see Heritage & Sorjonen, 1994). Co launched a follow-up question ("Okay. And for more than ... ," bolded in Example 1), after Cl's confirmation of feeling "emotionally down, sad, depressed, these sort of things." And-prefaced questions are often used to adhere to routine medical assessments involving checklists (a symptom of major depressive episode is feeling sad or depressed most days during the last two weeks; DSM-5, APA, 2013). Co's subsequent *what about-prefaced* questions ("Okay. What about ... ," also bolded) exemplifies a variation of and-prefaced questions, as a way to sequence the interaction by following a routine checklist assessment.

Second, Co checklisted by using *Yes/No questions* frequently asked by physicians to efficiently establish a diagnostic agenda (Roter & Hall, 2006). Co's Yes/No questions ("Has it been hard ... ?" "Have you been feeling ... ?") tend to constrain Cl to two response options: confirming or disconfirming the symptom's relevance, with disconfirming being the harder option (Raymond, 2003). Thus, Co's Yes/No questions can be seen to constrain alternative descriptions and discussions helpful in understanding Cl's experience and distress.

A third form of checklisting was Co's use of *confirmation markers* (e.g., "Okay"). Such *Okays* conveyed that minimal (e.g., Yes or No) responses to Co's questions were sufficient, requiring no need to further describe or understand Cl's distress. Similarly, in the last part of Example 1 we observed Co's *polite transition* as a checklisting device to help privilege an institutional agenda. Let us revisit those final speaking turns from Example 1, right after Cl confirmed ("Yes") that finding "pleasure in the things that used to be fun" had been hard for her:

> Co: What types of things aren't as fun as they may have been in the past for you?
> Cl: Ah I don't enjoy spending time with friends as much. Um spending time with my kid. It has just been really hard and **I feel like being alone**.
> Co: Okay. **I am so sorry to hear that.** What about things like your sleep?

The bolded part of Cl's response suggests a potential opening to further explore Cl's subjective experience. Co's display of empathy ("I am so sorry to hear that") may subtly redirect discussion to a more institutionally relevant focus without appearing disaffiliative or uncaring. Artfully, Co's empathetic transition neither fully dismisses Cl's comment nor invites further elaboration, keeping the conversation "on track," perhaps at the expense of discussing alternative (e.g., client-relevant, justice-oriented) matters.

Practice 3: Individualizing

Our experiences are, as hermeneuts suggest (e.g., Taylor, 1989), *about* something *significant* to us. Presumably, Cl's feeling "emotionally down," "sad," or "depressed" is about something significant to her (e.g., something at work, with her children). While discussion could have focused on what Cl sees as significant, Co's talk seems to treat Cl's experience (e.g., sadness, disinterest) as not "telling" something else, but as an object in itself. In other words, rather than exploring Cl's life circumstance, Co *individualized* her talk by inviting Cl to inwardly focus on her experience as an isolated "object" to be contemplated as such.

Co's question had an individualizing direction. Exploring the severity or frequency of Cl's symptoms developed "in" (or "by") her seemed more relevant than exploring the social context or significance of these symptoms for her. In this way, Cl's experience was formulated as unrelated to her current life situation, without any consideration of social justice issues, and perhaps attributable to a DSM mental disorder as an "inner factor."

Earlier we illustrated how Co's checklisting discourse overlooked Cl's openings to discuss the "aboutness" or meaning of Cl's experience. In our next example of individualizing from a different interview, we focus on how Co's (a new counselor) ways of individualizing downplay the subjective significance of Cl's (a new client) experience.

Example 4

Co: What's brought you here today Anna?

Cl: It's just I am just a bit fed up really. My sister said I should come.

Co: Right okay. Has this been going on for some time?

Cl: Yeah, a few months, really.

Co: Okay. Do you want to tell me a bit about what's been going on?

Cl: I just think **things seem to be piling up. I just don't seem to be coping with things … the kids and things.**

Co: Right okay. **Would it be okay Anna for me to ask you a few more detailed questions about how you've been feeling?**

Cl: Uh um

Co: Okay. **What if we start with asking about your mood,** how have been feeling in yourself?

Cl: Um. I'd say a bit fed up [inaudible]. Everything just seems very black. It's like swimming in [inaudible]. I just don't and [inaudible] … and the kids get home and I've been able to have a fairly decent conversation with them but …

Co: Right and can I just check Anna when you say things have been a bit black, do you mean you feel very miserable?

Cl: Fed up, miserable.

Co: Right okay. And what about feeling tearful? Has that been happening?

Depending on Cl's contextual circumstances, her experience may potentially be linked to gender inequality and oppression or other dimensions of her social positioning (e.g., Remer & Hahn, 2012). Instead, this diagnostic interview again subtly and persistently invites a presumably apolitical focus on the "self." Although Co's initial question "what's been going on" invites Cl to narrate her experience in "her own terms," soon after Co's inquiry zeroes in on the "internal" dynamics (e.g., mood, tearfulness, feeling "miserable"). Despite Cl's own reference to her distress as a *response to* structural forces and associated cultural norms and pressures ("things piling up," "not coping with things ... the kids and things"), Co further individualizes her distress. The participants co-construct Cl's concerns as self-afflicted, as biomedically diagnosable rather than an understandable response to possible social inequalities and injustices.

Co's subsequent permission-seeking ("Would it be ok Anna for me to ask you a few more detailed questions about how you've been feeling?") offers another example of polite transition that displays affiliation while bypassing a contextual focus. With Cl's acceptance ("Uh um"), Co launches into checklist-type questions ("What if we start asking about your mood ... ?"). Individualizing focuses the diagnostic inquiry on the intrapsychic dimension of Cl's experience and away from the socio-cultural context, despite Cl seemingly wanting to discuss concerns of being overwhelmed by multiple demands of life (e.g., potentially associated with unequal distribution of domestic labor in the domestic area). Compare Example 4 with Example 5, taken from the same interview, about a minute later.

Example 5

Co: Right, so how have you been managing at work?

Cl: I've not been going in as much, because I just feel so exhausted [inaudible]. The supermarket has been taken over, and **they've cut the wages**, and my **problems with bills** [inaudible] ... **they are writing me letters**. The kids, **they want all these new games and stuff**.

Co: So things are really difficult all around. With all this going on, **how are you sleeping Anna?**

Cl seems to contextualize her experience as possibly related to socio-historic (e.g., gender- and class-related) dynamics of power and privilege (e.g., "they've cut the wages ... they are writing me letters. The kids want all these new games ... "). Still, Co ignores Cl's opening with an unspecific acknowledgment ("So things are really difficult all around") to preface her checklist of questions ("With all this going on, how are you sleeping ... ?"). Throughout the interview, Cl keeps highlighting contextual factors, while Co re-directs the discussion to the DSM's checklist of symptoms (energy, sadness, appetite, concentration).

Practice 4: Pathologizing

Finally, the fourth practice we identified is called *pathologizing* or overemphasizing pathology, deficits, or problems while disregarding clients' strengths, virtues, resilience, or resistance to social injustices. By pathologizing, counselors might privilege an institutional agenda of "finding" individual pathology while overlooking other possible therapeutic developments. For instance, in Example 1 Co could have explored Cl's current experiences of fun and pleasure rather than focusing on Cl's difficulty or inability to experience pleasure ("Has it been hard for you to find pleasure in the things that used to be fun?"). Co could also have reframed decreased desire as an act of resistance to injustices (cf. Wade, 1997). From a conversational perspective, pathology-oriented inquiry can be seen not as merely reflecting an inner inability to experience pleasure but as conversational production. A different conversation around pleasure and fun may have resulted in a different outcome (i.e., a different sense of who Cl is and of her experience). Revisiting Example 4, Co overlooks an opportunity to expand on what may be seen as an exception to Cl's concern:

> Co: Okay. What if we start with asking about your mood, how have been feeling in yourself?
> Cl: Um. I'd say a bit fed up [inaudible]. Everything just seems very black. It's like swimming in [inaudible]. I just don't and [inaudible] ... and the kids get home and **I've been able to have a fairly decent conversation with them** but ...
> Co: Right and can I just check Anna when you say things have been a bit black, do you mean you feel very miserable?

In answering, Cl goes from "Everything just seems very black" to "I've been able to have a fairly decent conversation" with her children. Instead of becoming curious about this seemingly exceptional development, Co ignores exploring this exception (e.g., what made it possible, its meaning and significance for Cl). Co engages in *check-listing* (note the *and-prefaced* question), focuses exclusively on the negative, "very miserable" aspects of Cl's experience (*pathologizing*), and on her objectified, inner feelings and mood (*individualizing*). This final example shows the four conversational practices outlined in this chapter used in conjunction with one another to privilege a particular institutional agenda (i.e., to present Cl as recognizably mentally ill).

Conclusion

Our aim in this chapter was to cultivate an increased awareness of how counselors' actions are implicated in re-producing practices and understandings that may or may not be socially just. Conceivably, the four practices we identified may discourage discussing social justice concerns when conducting DSM-guided diagnostic interviews. While we do not advocate abandoning diagnostic conversations altogether or suggest that medical/DSM and social justice agendas are irreconcilable, our concern is with practitioners prioritizing diagnostic or institutional agendas over clients-living-in-sociopolitical-situations agendas. We focus our critique on potential unjust effects of de-centering clients' preferred, local, experience-near knowledges, when such medicalized or institutional agendas are prioritized. However, we also recognize that clients may benefit from taking medications or having a medical diagnosis; blocking access to such cultural resources could be unjust.

Elsewhere we identify dilemmas faced by many CFT practitioners who adopt a social justice orientation *and* adhere to professional expectations to engage in diagnostic practices (Sutherland et al., 2016). One way to address or overcome such dilemmas is to diversify interpretive frameworks and therapy practices informing counseling, namely broadening the diagnostic, individually focused lens to include structural considerations and more collaborative, dialogic ways of interacting with clients. In practice, such diversification and collaboration may take different forms, for example, manifest as counselors being transparent regarding allocating some portions of conversations to diagnosing. Counselors could voice their intentional exclusion of other explanations and considerations within a specific "diagnostic space" with the understanding that this temporary suspension would be produced within a larger, more inclusive contextualized conversation. Moreover, transparency may be a way to create space for and legitimize alternative ways of understanding and addressing distress and invite negotiation of the therapy process and content from clients.

We join other practitioners in this volume who advocate for a more reflexive professional practice, where a more socially just medically informed practice is desirable and possible. We conceptualize reflexivity interactionally, or as occurring in the back and forth of social interaction in specific contexts, rather than seeing it as a cognitive-perceptual activity divorced from clients' and counselors' larger socio-historical or immediate dialogical contexts. From this perspective, we invite counselors to become more dialogically reflexive as they join conversations with clients (shaping what might be accomplished in them). We proposed that DSM-informed counselors' sense of conversationally being on track needs to be cross-referenced with a social justice stance, extending to how counselors can critically privilege clients' preferred sense-making resources. Such a stance includes actively inviting (but not imposing) joint reflection about clients' as well as counselors' social embeddedness, life circumstances, and resourcefulness. Clients may try to convey that counselors' adherence to institutional protocols are off-target for them, or not aligned with their understandings and preferences in and for counseling. Medicalizing, checklisting, individualizing, and pathologizing—however professionally compelled these practices may seem—can, if single-mindedly pursued, obscure a focus on other important and socially unjust matters clients might want to discuss with counselors. Conversational prudence is required here of course; talking and listening in ways that meet professional and institutional requirements, while not being deaf or mute on our clients' social justice concerns. Heightening awareness of how counselors co-construct versions of client's concerns and solutions to address them, requires focused, responsive, and sometimes inconvenient and uncomfortable dialogues.

Reflection Questions

1. Examine a recording of yourself talking with a client and respond to the following questions: Can you find examples of individualizing, medicalizing, checklisting, or pathologizing practices? Can you identify openings where you could initiate exploration of structural forces? Can you think of a particular question or other response that you would like to try at that juncture?
2. We suggest that a diagnostic agenda can block practitioners from practicing reflexively. At the same time, practitioners often enter therapeutic conversations with some type of agenda. Can you remember a time when a diagnostic agenda was prioritized over another agenda? Can you think of a time when you (or another counselor) engaged reflexively in medically informed dialogue? How can you (or other practitioners) increase awareness of how it may be possible to pursue a specific agenda reflexively (and when such pursuits become non-reflexive) to help cultivate more socially just directions in counseling?
3. Bringing a social justice orientation to conversations with already diagnosed clients need not mean trying to convince them their diagnosis is incorrect. So, how do you invite social justice as an additional discourse where only a symptom-based, psychiatric one has been a focus? Can you and clients resourcefully use multiple discourses for clients' concerns?

References

American Psychiatric Association (2013). *Diagnostic and statistical manual of mental disorders* (5th ed.). Washington, DC: Author.

Bullock, H. E., & Limbert W. M. (2009). Class. In D. Fox, I. Prilleltensky, & S. Austin (Eds.), *Critical psychology: An introduction* (2nd ed., pp. 215–231). London: Sage.

Burstow, B. (2005). A critique of Posttraumatic Stress Disorder and the DSM. *Journal of Humanistic Psychology, 45*(4), 429–445. doi: 10.1177/0022167805280265

Chambless, D. L., Sanderson, W. C., Shoham, V., Bennett Johnson, S., Pope, K. S., Crits-Christoph, P., …McCurry, S. (1996). An update on empirically validated therapies. *The Clinical Psychologist, 49*, 5–18. Retrieved from www.div12.org/publications

Duvall, J., & Béres, L. (2011). *Innovations in narrative therapy: Connecting practice, training, and research.* New York, NY: Norton.

Edwards, D. (2005). Discursive psychology. In K. L. Fitch & R. E. Sanders (Eds.), *Handbook of language and social interaction* (pp. 257–273). London: Erlbaum.

Elkins, D. N. (2007). Empirically supported treatments: The deconstruction of a myth. *Journal of Humanistic Psychology 47*, 474–500. doi: 10.1177/0022167807302003

Eriksen, K., & Kress, V. (2005). *Beyond the DSM story: Ethical quandaries, challenges, and best practices*. Thousand Oaks, CA: Sage.

Fox, D., Prilleltensky, I., & Austin, S. (2009). Critical psychology for social justice: Concerns and dilemmas. In D. Fox, I. Prilleltensky, & S. Austin (Eds.), *Critical psychology: An introduction* (2nd ed., pp. 1–19). London: Sage.

Frances, A. (2013). *Saving normal: An insider's revolt against out-of-control psychiatric diagnosis, DSM-5, big Pharma, and the medicalization of ordinary life*. New York, NY: William Morrow.

Geertz, C. (1983). *Local knowledge*. New York, NY: Basic Books.

Grohol, J. (2013, November 9). Final rules for U.S. Mental Health parity released: No surprises but also no silver bullet. [Blog post]. Retrieved from: http://psychcentral.com/blog/archives/2013/11/09/final-rules-for-u-s-mental-health-parity-released-no-surprises-but-also-no-silver-bullet/

Hansen, J. T. (2007). Should counseling be considered a health care profession? Critical thoughts on the transition to a health care ideology. *Journal of Counseling & Development, 85*, 286–293. doi: 10.1002/j.1556–6678.2007.tb00476.x

Heritage, J., & Sorjonen, M. -L. (1994). Constituting and maintaining activities across sequences: And-prefacing as a feature of question design. *Language in Society, 23*(1), 1–29. doi: 10.1017/S0047404500017656

Hoffman, L. (1992). A reflexive stance for family therapy. In S. McNamee & K. J. Gergen (Eds.), *Therapy as a social construction* (pp. 7–24). London: Sage.

Horwitz, A., & Wakefield, J. C. (2012). *All we have to fear: Psychiatry's transformation of natural anxieties into mental disorders*. New York, NY: Oxford University Press.

Illouz, E. (2007). *Cold intimacies: The making of emotional capitalism*. Malden, MA: Polity.

Illouz, E. (2008). *Saving the modern soul: Therapy, emotions, and the culture of self-help*. Berkeley, CA: University of California Press.

jessygrl2101 (2012, April 19). *DSM-IV-TR multiaxial system* [Video file]. Retrieved from www.youtube.com/watch?v=lDekzlht-JM

Jill HD. (2010, January 27). *SCID interview.mov* [Video file]. Retrieved from www.youtube.com/watch?v=zir1mgEvTL8

Lafrance, M. N., & McKenzie-Mohr, S. (2013). The DSM and its lure of legitimacy. *Feminism and Psychology, 23*, 119–140. doi: 10.1177/0959353512467974

Levant, R. F. (2005, July). *Report of the presidential task force on evidence-based practice*. Washington, DC: American Psychological Association.

Marecek, J., & Hare-Mustin, R. T. (2009). Clinical psychology: The politics of madness. In D. Fox, I. Prilleltensky, & S. Austin (Eds.), *Critical psychology: An introduction* (2nd ed., pp. 75–92). London: Sage.

Neden, J. (2012). Reflexivity dialogues: An inquiry into how reflexivity is constructed in family therapy. Doctoral dissertation. Retrieved from http://nrl.northumbria.ac.uk/8771/

Paré, D. A. (2013). *The practice of collaborative counseling and psychotherapy: Developing skills in culturally mindful helping*. Thousand Oaks, CA: Sage.

PsychScene Hub (2010, June 2). *Psychiatric interview skills—CASC and OSCE videos online.* [Video file]. Retrieved from www.youtube.com/watch?v=fxyf9ILvLAo

Rapley, M., Moncrieff, J., & Dillon, J. (Eds.) (2011). *De-medicalizing misery: Psychiatry, psychology, and the human condition*. New York, NY: Palgrave Macmillan.

Raymond, G. (2003). Grammar and social organization: Yes/no interrogatives and the structure of responding. *American Sociological Review, 68*(6), 939–967. doi: 10.2307/1519752

Remer, P. A., & Hahn, K. (2012). Feminist therapy in counseling psychology. In E. N. Williams & C. Z. Enns (Eds.), *The Oxford handbook of feminist counseling psychology* (pp. 305–325). Oxford, UK: Oxford University Press.

Rose, N. (2007). *The politics of life itself: Biomedicine, power, and subjectivity in the twenty-first century.* Rutgers, NJ: Princeton University Press.

Roter, D., & Hall, J. A. (2006). *Doctors talking with patients/patients talking with doctors: improving communication in medical visits* (2nd ed.). Westport, CT: Praeger.

Strong, T., & Busch, R. (2013). DSM-V and evidence-based family therapy? *Australian and New Zealand Journal of Family Therapy, 34*(2), 90–103. doi: 10.1002/anzf.1009

Strong, T., & Paré, D. (2004). *Furthering talk: Advances in the discursive therapies.* New York, NY: Kluwer Academic/Plenum.

Sutherland, O., Couture, S., Gaete, J., Strong, T., LaMarre, A., & Hardt, L. (2016). Social justice oriented diagnostic discussions: A discursive perspective. *Journal of Feminist Family Therapy, 28*(203), 76–99. doi: 10.1080/08952833.2016.1187532

Sutherland, O., Sametband, I., Gaete, J., Couture, S. J., & Strong, T. (2012). Conversational perspective of therapeutic outcomes: The importance of preference in the development of discourse. *Counseling and Psychotherapy Research, 13*(3), 220–226. doi: 10.1080/1473 3145.2012.742917

Taylor, C. (1989). *Sources of the self: The making of the modern identity.* Cambridge, MA: Harvard University Press.

Tomm, K. (1987). Interventive interviewing: Part II. Reflexive questioning as a means to enable self-healing. *Family Process, 26*, 167–183. doi: 10.1111/j.1545-5300.1987.00167.x

Tomm, K. (2014). Introducing the IPscope: A systemic assessment tool for distinguishing interpersonal patterns. In K. Tomm, S. St. George, D. Wulff, & T. Strong (Eds.), *Patterns in interpersonal interactions: Inviting relational understandings for therapeutic change* (pp. 13–35). New York, NY: Routledge.

Thompson, R. (2012). Screwed up, but working on it: (Dis)ordering the self through e-stories. *Narrative Inquiry, 22*(1), 86–104. doi: 10.1075/ni.22.1.06tho

University of Nottingham (2012, January 31). *Psychiatric interviews for teaching: Depression* [Video file]. Retrieved from www.youtube.com/watch?v=4YhpWZCdiZc

Wade, A. (1997). Small acts of living: Everyday resistance to violence and other forms of oppression. *Contemporary Family Therapy, 19*(1), 23–39. doi: 10.1023/A:1026154215299

White, M. (1995). Naming abuse and breaking from its effects. In M. White, *Re-authoring lives: Interviews and essays* (pp. 82–111). Adelaide, Australia: Dulwich Centre Publications.

Wooffitt, R. (2005). *Conversation analysis and discourse analysis: A comparative and critical introduction.* London: Sage.

CHAPTER 16

Narrative Practice and the De-Pathologizing of Children's Lives at a Walk-In Therapy Clinic: An Opportunity for Socially Just Conversations

Karen Young

In our first contact with children as they step into the children's mental health system we hold a special responsibility. It is a responsibility to see children's identities as precious and unique, and by doing so to stand up for stories of their special knowledge and abilities while standing against categorizing and pathologizing children according to popular diagnostic discourses. This is a socially just response.

We cannot ignore the serious nature of many of the struggles children experience and come to therapists with, and at the same time attending to these does not require constructing their identities within a mental illness discourse. Children's mental health has increasingly modeled itself to mirror the adult mental health system's expansion into psychiatric labeling following the requirements for assessment, diagnosis, and treatment (Duvall, Young, & Kayes-Burden, 2012; Epstein, Wiesner, & Duda, 2013). This treatment increasingly includes pharmacology and a range of manualized treatment approaches. The first contact with children entering the system has been mandated by funders to be a standardized intake assessment with treatment to follow usually after long waits (National Infant, Child, and Youth Mental Health Consortium Advisory, 2010).

I, and many of the children and families I have worked with, would not immediately be seen as oppressed or marginalized—coming from a predominately white, middle-class social location in Ontario, Canada. However, as they enter the children's mental health system, these children are extremely vulnerable. They are vulnerable to contact with professionals that increasingly brings self-descriptions into the conversation that are "heavily laden with psychiatric and psychological terms and jargon" (Epstein et al., 2013, p. 157). An alternative to such pathology-oriented first contacts has been evolving in Ontario—that of the walk-in therapy clinic. There is a groundswell of growth of walk-in therapy clinics across Ontario in many diverse settings since 2001 (Duvall et al., 2012). In this chapter I will explore the approach to walk-in services I have developed with an eye to providing a socially just experience for children and their families.

The "Science-ifying" of the Helping Profession

Children, by definition, are in transition—developing and changing—and are especially affected by and vulnerable to the contexts in which they live. Yet the growing trend within the landscape of children's mental health is toward the establishment of a fixed diagnosis and internalized definition of the problem (Epstein et al., 2013). Children become the problem as they are diagnosed with a range of mental illnesses from the DSM, categorized and labeled: "The DSM localizes so-called psychiatric disorders within the individual and neglects societal, cultural and historical perspectives ... closing down possibilities with respect to our thinking about ourselves, others and the worlds (and realities) in which we live" (Epstein et al., 2013, p. 158). Illness is routinely dispensed to children within this strongly legitimized culture of expert knowledge and master narratives (Danaher, Schirato, & Webb, 2000; Lindemann-Nelson, 2001), overlooking their lived experience and the contexts of their lives. I am not taking the position that diagnosis never has a role, as a name and description to assist in understanding the problem is important in my work. I do, however, strongly prefer not to engage in collapsing the diagnosis with children's identities. Maintaining this perspective can be challenging in the professional culture in which I work, where I am witnessing an ever-increasing trend of constructing mental illness identities.

> For the last 300 years or so, during and after what we refer to as the "scientific revolution," some people began to believe that there are fundamental, unchanging structures, which govern everything. This idea spread through the social sciences influencing people to look for internal "structures" of people, families, culture and so on based on the understanding that people can be studied in the same way that objects are studied.
>
> (Thomas, 2004, p. 93)

We are more and more being required to view children and families through this objectified scientific lens. The emphasis in the field has turned to normativity, disorder, and diagnosis (Batha, 2006, p. 58). As Paré (2013, p. 167) points out,

> Counselors are trained in scientific traditions that adopt rigorous methods to seek answers to fundamental questions about human behavior. A potential downside of this accumulated body of knowledge ... is that it sometimes gets precedence over the process of collaborative conversation and meaning making.

Counselors can become, as Goldstein writes, "numbed by a preoccupation with the mechanics of theory, method and technique" (1992, p. 51). This focus on expert knowledge moves us away from attending to the artfulness of practice conducted collaboratively with clients, a way of working that I see as a more just process.

Walk-In as a Just Alternative

There are practices and service structures that can be put in place to avoid being entirely complicit in the reproduction of the politics of classification and that encourage a more collaborative, artful, and just process. In communities across Canada and internationally, and within Ontario in particular, many organizations have restructured the front door of their services to include walk-in therapy clinics (Duvall et al., 2012). This restructuring moves away from first contact being dominated by the use of assessment tools and toward the first contact being a collaborative, competency-focused therapy conversation (Duvall et al., 2012). Narrative practices are being used quite widely in many walk-in therapy clinics (Duvall et al., 2012) and create the possibility for engaging in "counter-practices" (White, 2011, p. xxviii) to these dominant politics.

Walk-in clinics create an opportunity to fulfill our special responsibility to provide a socially just response to children and their families. The walk-in therapy clinic is a unique way of offering therapeutic conversation to people that is truly client centered as it is there for people to use when they choose, with no more required of them than just to walk in. With a 31-year background in children's mental health with over 25 years of this focused on practicing, teaching, and supervising shaped by narrative practices, my approach to conversations at the clinic inescapably reflect this history.

A Collaborative, Competency-Focused Curiosity

We can respond to the concerns experienced by children and their caregivers in ways that stand within an *ethic* to privilege their voices over "scientific" discourse. Through situating my practice at the walk-in clinic within the philosophical approach of narrative therapy I am able to maintain "a position of ethical curiosity" (Batha, 2006, p. 57). Batha writes, "By declining invitations to engage in these predetermined points-of-view [Western medicalized notions], I hope to invite collaborative curiosity about client's constructions of meaning for her experiences, and by joining in a guided inquiry" (p. 60). Batha's view resonates strongly with my preferred posture in therapeutic conversations, one I describe as "an ethical, collaborative, competency-focused curiosity" (an ECC curiosity). This curiosity is ethical as it privileges the client's voice and is non-pathologizing; it is collaborative because both the therapist and the client become curious together, and it is competency-focused as we listen for knowledge, skill, abilities, values, preferences, and commitments that people have with them. This ECC curiosity informs and shapes how I listen, what I listen to, and therefore the questions I ask right from the very beginning of each therapy session at the walk-in clinic.

This curiosity makes it possible to respond to children's stories in ways that do social justice (Reynolds, 2012) at the micro-level of the therapy room. I am mindful that the words and language I engage in with children and families have very real effects on their stories of identity. As Paré (2014) suggests, "Identities are not merely shared in therapy but also forged there" (p. 209). Therefore my commitment is to co-create language with children and families that illuminates new ways of seeing problems and connects with new versions of who they are. This is social justice unfolding moment-to-moment in the circulation of language (Duvall & Béres, 2011) occurring through therapeutic encounters at the clinic. Practices that are a part of walk-in sessions such as collaborating on the session agenda, getting to know the person "away from" the problem, externalizing conversations, and collaborative documentation are deliberate ways that I attempt to facilitate conversations that do justice. In the Narrative Therapy Re-Visiting Research Project (Young & Cooper, 2008), clients who had attended single sessions of therapy returned to watch their recorded sessions and provide feedback to research assistants regarding what was most meaningful and useful in the sessions. This feedback was transcribed and analyzed for themes by the lead researchers: myself and Scot Cooper. These client participants provided detailed feedback indicating the above practices—described in detail below—were meaningful and impactful in walk-in sessions.

Collaborating On the Session Agenda

In most therapeutic approaches, the beginning of a session involves exploring what the people want to talk about. At a walk-in therapy clinic this is particularly important, as the session may be the only session (Young, 2011). Setting the agenda is one of the first opportunities to hear from children and youth about what they want from the conversation at the walk-in clinic. The posture from this point on is collaborative and respectful of everyone's preferences for the session with an intentional focus on the child's or the youth's voice. I believe that children and youth frequently experience their preferences for the focus and direction of conversations as "taking a back seat" to the agendas of the adults involved. I work to address this concern by checking out which conversations are the ones children and youth want to have.

When Chris, 14, and his mother Tammy (pseudonyms will be used with all client stories to preserve anonymity) joined me for a conversation at the walk-in clinic, Chris's demeanor was quiet and cautious as we explored what to talk about. My guess was that he might have been experiencing some feelings of shame, as his mother described a problem with "lying" and the troubles this had caused at school. I carefully checked in with Chris about his comfort in talking about this, to determine his preferred agenda. In feedback months later to a researcher, Chris said:

> I liked hearing that she was accepting that if I didn't want to answer a question then she would be fine with that, and the fact that she asked if I was … comfortable with talking about it before telling me or asking me about it. That was really impressive, to me.

Asked about the impact of this, he said, "Well, at the time what I was thinking was, 'Wow, this person really cares and I, I can trust them,' and I just sort of, I guess from this point on is when I really opened up." Not assuming that Chris's arrival at the clinic implied permission for any and all questions created a posture that conveyed caring and trustworthiness, making it possible for Chris to speak. This way of beginning therapy collaboratively at the clinic sharply contrasts more medicalized assessment practices focused on an expert professional asking questions to gather information with diagnosis as the sought after outcome.

As I began a conversation with 7-year-old Cameron and his parents at the clinic, I was aware that the meeting was one of several they had recently attended with their doctor, a pediatrician, and then a child psychiatrist. They had been informed that Cameron "has ADHD and ODD" and had written on the walk-in clinic questionnaire (Young et al., 2008) that they are coming today to find out about treatment for these diagnoses. At the young age of 7, Cameron's identity was being shaped by a medicalized, internalized problem description. This expansion of psychiatric labeling has been ever-increasing over my years of working with children's mental health settings. My experience and that of other authors is that clients increasingly bring the language of diagnoses to the therapeutic encounters (Epstein et al., 2013). Cameron's parents arrived expressing this dominant psychiatric language. As I asked about what they want to talk about, Cameron slowly put his head down on the coffee table in front of us, and quietly said, "I just don't want any questions." I took this as a reflection of what his experience had been so far with professionals who mostly ask a lot of information gathering questions. I let him know that I would try to ask interesting, "good" questions, and that he should let me know what he thinks of them. I wondered if I could make some guesses about what he might be happier to talk about. I discovered he was quite willing to give a nod for "yes" and a shake for "no" about my guesses. I took his preference seriously, and wrote his words down on my summary note while reading aloud, "Cameron will give a nod for 'yes' and a shake for 'no' about guesses that Karen makes." This practice reflects my ethical position of privileging of the client's preferences.

Getting to Know the Person "Away From" the Problem

The practice of getting to know the person "away from" the problem is based on an ethical, collaborative, competency-based curiosity that reflects the value of seeing that the person is not the problem, the problem is the problem (White & Epston, 1990) and that the person has many qualities, abilities, values, and commitments. I see it as socially just to maintain this commitment throughout conversations at the walk-in clinic. As the conversation with Cameron and his parents continued, I asked permission to get to know Cameron "away from" the problems so I could learn about the skills and qualities he draws on to contend with the problem. I asked both parents:

> I know there are probably many stories you could tell me about Cameron, stories of the kind of boy he is when the problems are not causing troubles.

What is one story you could tell me that would help me to understand what you appreciate most about him?

As his parents described qualities and filled in the details of these with stories, I wrote up a document that summarized his skills, abilities, and qualities. I checked in with Cameron about each quality and story; did he know this (shook his head), does he agree with this (nodded), does he like to hear about this (nodded), and so on. As his parents and I together brought detail to and thickened these stories, Cameron began to talk, eventually filling in more details about himself "away from" the problem.

This focus on competency stories makes it possible for Cameron to move closer to being able to talk about the problem as he distances from dominant negative self-descriptions. As stories of his preferred identity emerge in the walk-in session, he steps more and more into the conversation. As Cameron, his parents and I looked at the document we created of his skills and qualities, he said, "It is a whole page!" Will knowing these things about himself, and knowing that all of us in the room know these things about him, make it possible to talk about the problem? I enquired, and Cameron suggested I could ask his parents some things about it and he could nod or shake. We agreed that "it" should be called "the outbursts." This was Cameron's language; he decided it was "the best" word for the problem. This description was therefore more meaningful to him than medicalized distant descriptions such as ADHD and ODD. The now strongly built storylines of his skills and qualities gave Cameron a sense of a full identity as a person, not just a problem, and he was then able to approach talking about the problem.

Externalizing Practices

Calling the problem Cameron was experiencing "the outbursts" is an example of externalizing, a practice originally introduced by Michael White and David Epston (1990), which Michael White described as "a faithful friend" (2007, p. 59). Externalizing conversations are central, reliable practices that can be engaged with easily at a walk-in clinic. White has said "it was with children that I first engaged in systematic explorations of externalizing conversations" (White, 2000, p. 5). Children have been my best teachers about the creativity, possibilities, and novelty that externalizing practices can generate. Externalizing practices make it possible to address labels and diagnoses in ways that are respectful of people's current understandings of the problem, and open up new possibilities as the "person away from the problem" and the social context of the problem re-appear. These conversations make space for a more social and relational view of the problem to emerge and seek remedies for the limiting and totalizing descriptions of the child that have often developed. They provide movement away from these dominant identity descriptions of children's lives—distancing from the known and familiar, facilitating or scaffolding new ways of seeing the problem (Ramey, Young, & Tarulli, 2010; White, 2007).

Because they provide a non-pathologizing view of people, privileging their pre-ferred self-descriptions, externalizing thinking and questioning embody an ethi-cal and collaborative curiosity. The therapist engages from a stance or posture that sees persons and problems as separate, collaborating with the child and family to develop language for the problem that makes sense to them. So, for example, "She has an anxiety disorder" becomes a struggle with "the fears" or "the worries." Cameron "is ADHD and ODD" becomes "the struggle with outbursts." The child and problem become separated as we explore the effects of the problem on them and on the family and others. The conversation deconstructs the child's identifica-tion with the problem, separating the problem from the child's identity. Questions create space to understand the ways the social context of a child's life works to create and maintain the problem. This assists the child and family to envision ways they can affect the problem and its context—the problem is no longer "who I am" but is a problem that is "affecting me," so people can now move toward finding ways to respond to the problem and the events, relationships, and experiences that sustain it. This unveiling of context is another social justice practice as it situates problems in the social world rather than inside of the child. This externalizing stance in walk-in sessions "guards against the marginalization that can occur when people's identities are subsumed by pathologizing diagnostic labels" (Combs & Freedman, 2012, p. 1040).

As Cameron's parents began to describe the outbursts, what they look like, and the trouble they cause, Cameron stepped into the conversation with, "Ya, like when I get mad at my sister, and an outburst comes." He described this a bit and then I asked if outbursts ever come and cause trouble at other times or places. Cameron directed me to his parents, who said the outbursts cause trouble in other places, such as school. Cameron then volunteered a story about times at school when things happen that "are not fair," and that this brings on the outburst. The social context of the problem began to appear.

The deconstruction of the problem and separation of Cameron's identity from the problem creates a socially just conversation at the walk-in clinic. With ques-tions shaped by a collaborative curiosity, we are able to understand the problem from Cameron's point of view, including the social contexts in which it emerges ("It comes when things are not fair") and the effects it has on his life and relation-ships ("It ruins the best part of the day … It makes me feel like I'm losing my mind").

As we continued to talk about the outbursts, Cameron took a position on them for the first time, saying that he did not like anything about them and that he wanted to work on controlling them. When I asked how this session had gone for everyone, Cameron said, "Great, 'cause we can take home the list of my skills." His parents said they felt hope and excitement for the first time about this problem as they saw Cameron talk about the outbursts and express that he wanted to do something about "them." They said both they and Cameron himself believe he has lots of skills to do this. The shift to a more hopeful disposition had the effect of orienting them to notice and acknowledge positive developments.

The re-negotiation of the meaning of the problem from a representation of Cameron as having a "mental illness identity" to a view of Cameron as a child with skills and knowledge, and with a preference to change his relationship with a problem, opened up many new possibilities for this family to move forward together. It moved Cameron into a position of agency, as shame and blame subsided and knowledge, skill, and preferences came to the foreground.

> In children's lives, the negotiation of meaning is a highly visible achievement …. . For young children there is so much about the world that is novel, so many new experiences to be negotiated, so many gaps to be filled in their understandings of life. Nowhere is recourse to narrative structures in achieving all of this more manifestly apparent than it is in children's efforts to understand their experiences of life. Nowhere are the social processes of the negotiation of meaning more conspicuous than in children's culture.
>
> (White, 2000, p. 10)

Children and their parents have told us much about externalizing practices that argue for the use of these conversations in my work at the walk-in clinic. I engage children in many different ways to deconstruct the problem, to uncover details about the problem that have not yet been known. I sometimes suggest that we could "investigate the problem like a detective." In our research, 8-year-old Tom told us: "Well, she asked me … . to try to find out things, like to kind of … " and his mother clarified "like being a detective?" to which Tom said, "Yeah, like she tried to get me in the kind of mood for being ok with saying things about it." It is interesting that Tom is saying that this approach helped him to get "in the kind of mood" to talk about the problem as earlier in the session and with his mother prior to the session, he had been quite reluctant to talk about the problem of "worry." In fact he later said: "Sort of seems like I wouldn't say all the things I said on the day, like, some of the things I wouldn't always say in there, but I did." My sense is that this was also very true for Cameron, who had his head on the table prior to his engagement with practices that rendered a view of him separate from the externalized problem.

Collaborative Documentation Practices

At the walk-in clinic we create summary notes and other therapy documents during the session. This is a transparent and collaborative process aligned with a social justice agenda, as it departs from other traditions of documentation that produce files dominated by expert knowledge, interpretation, and diagnosis. We complete a summary report along with other therapeutic documents such as lists, declarations, and drawings within the session, engaging participants in the process, archiving their own words and understandings. Verbal summaries throughout the session serve as a way to check in, giving the families a chance to evaluate on an ongoing basis the therapist's understanding of their situation, ideas, and words.

These summaries are derived from the notes taken during the conversation and are read back to people throughout the conversation. This holds up their words like a mirror, allowing for corrections, but also for the persons involved to reflect further on their own words and to possibly expand on them. Summarizing in this way slows the pace of the conversation and creates a place from which the next question may be asked. In taking away a summary report and other documents, persons are provided with a record and a reminder of their own words, knowledge, and understandings that emerged within the conversation. People often share these documents with others who are not present such as family members, friends, and schoolteachers or principals. This impacts the context of people's lives, engaging a potential audience and support team to assist in sustaining new ideas and commitments.

The collaborative documentation we employ at the walk-in clinic has been strongly influenced by longstanding narrative practices of creating letters and a wide range of therapeutic documents (Freedman & Combs, 1996; White, 2007; White & Epston, 1990). We develop documents in sessions, such as Cameron's document of his skills and qualities, and another document (separate, by his choice, from the page on his skills) of what we learned about the outbursts. These documents travel home with clients, offering reminders of important discoveries and knowledge developed in the session. This creates "stickablility" (Duvall & Young, 2009) for taking what happened in the walk-in session into the various contexts of people's lives.

Sara, age 11, told a researcher that it was "really important how [the therapist] wrote down what I said and read it out to me," because, "it put what I said back into my brain so I could remember it all." She continued, "I could take the papers with me to camp and remember about 'doing determination' [her words] and that I could show the papers to some of my friends so they know." This is just one example of what I have heard from children about documentation.

In-session documentation practices at walk-in clinics offer a range of creative opportunities for engaging others in efforts toward social change (Young, 2008; Young, 2011). Letters and documents can be co-developed with clients in walk-in sessions and used to impact the social environment outside of the session. This can be a simple, gentle, and yet effective way to bring about change in the child's social context. It is important that the therapeutic stance continue to be shaped by collaboration and ethical curiosity, and documents should be developed with careful attention to what the child wants to communicate and have happen.

When Maria, age 6, and her mother, Carmen, arrived at the walk-in clinic, Carmen was visibly distressed and Maria appeared apprehensive as she hid behind her mother. As the story unfolded I learned that Carmen, her husband, and Maria came to Canada from Brazil 4 years ago, settled initially in Toronto and then moved to their current home last summer. It was now late October, and there was a growing number of significant complaints from school about Maria, described in notes home as having "anger management" problems, trouble with "emotional regulation," along with some suggestions she be taken to a psychiatrist for an "evaluation for possible

Oppositional Defiance Disorder" (American Psychiatric Association, 2013). On this day, her mother was called to the school, and Maria was suspended for two days for being unsafe with others, as she yelled, tipped over chairs and ran from the classroom. Carmen appeared confused as she described Maria as usually a happy girl, who generally liked school and had had no prior problems until starting at this school in September. Though initially quiet, with support from her mother and myself, Maria increasingly stepped into an externalizing conversation about what she called the "big booms" at school. She described them as crying, sad, then mad, yelling, and sometimes throwing things. Big booms were happening now most days after the recess break. With such a generous "clue," I asked questions about recess and discovered that Maria was "lonely, sad, all by myself" at recess and that no one played with her. After recess "I feel sad, and mad too, and I just want to go home." This had been the situation for almost 2 months. Carmen was surprised, as she had not heard this from Maria. I asked Maria if any of the teachers or other adults at school knew this, and she didn't think so. I wondered who, if they knew, might want to help? The following is a reconstruction of our conversation about this.

> M: I don't know …
>
> K: Well, is there a teacher or a grown up, one that you like, and seems nice, who might help if they knew about this?
>
> M: (After some time thinking) I think Mr. Toms would.
>
> K: What is it about Mr. Toms that makes you think he would want to help?
>
> M: He's nice, he smiles nice, sometimes he talks to me in the hall or at nutrition break.
>
> K: (repeating Maria's words and writing them down … . He's nice, he has a nice smile, he talks to me …) I wonder how we could let him know about what is happening?
>
> M: I don't know.
>
> K: What do you think Carmen, any ideas?
>
> C: Well, maybe we could talk to him, I'm not sure … .
>
> K: I heard from you that the school has been sending home notes?
>
> C: Yes, lots of notes.
>
> K: I wonder if we should write them a note … write a note to Mr. Toms maybe?
>
> M: (big smile) I like that.
>
> K: (I reach for paper and pencil crayons) Ok, what should we say? *Dear Mr. Toms … . (writing) Maria and her mother have been here at the walk-in clinic at ROCK talking with me today about a problem with "big booms" of sad and mad feelings at school after recesses. The "big booms" have been causing trouble for Maria.* How's that?
>
> M: Good.
>
> K: Now what?
>
> M: Tell about recess …
>
> K: Okay. *Maria has told us that at recess no one plays with her and so she is very sad, lonely and always all by herself.*

M: Ya!

K: So, should we tell him why you are asking him for help?

M: Ya.

K: (writing) *Mr. Toms, Maria thinks that you would want to help her with this because you are nice, have a nice smile, and sometimes come and talk to her.* (Maria nods)

K: Ok, so now we might want to tell how he could help? (Maria and Carmen nod) I wonder how he can help ... .?

At this point Carmen and I ask Maria questions, and Carmen has a few ideas too. The result is:

K: *Mr. Toms, Maria says that you could help by: coming over to where she is at recess and taking her over to where the other girls are playing, telling the other girls who Maria is, and saying names, and helping them to know each other so they can play together.* Is this right?

M: Yes!

K: Ok, so should we sign the letter? (We all sign and Maria decides to draw a picture on it of her playing with other girls at recess.) How should this letter get to Mr. Toms?

Carmen and Maria look at each other, and then Maria says:

M: I want to give it to him.

We make a plan for this and then talk about Maria and Carmen coming back to the walk-in clinic in a couple of weeks to let me know how things are going. At this next session, I greeted a very different looking Maria who smiled and gave me a little hug. Maria and Carmen let me know that Maria gave the note to Mr. Toms the very first day she was back at school. Mr. Toms helped exactly how he was asked to (who wouldn't?). Carmen has had no more notes or calls from school, Maria says she is playing with some girls now, and both tell me that the big booms have disappeared.

Conclusion

We have choices about how to structure mental health services and how we provide the therapy within these services. These services can be shaped by dominant psychiatric discourses and result in the construction of mental illness identities for children such as Maria and Cameron, or we can create therapeutic encounters that maintain an ethical, collaborative, competency-focused curiosity that separates children's identities from the problems they are experiencing, privileges their knowledge and experience, and looks for and creates opportunities for their skills and abilities to emerge. Practices that are a part of walk-in sessions such as collaborating on the session agenda, getting to know the person "away from" the problem, externalizing conversations, and collaborative documentation are deliberate ways that therapists can facilitate conversations that do justice. Walk-in therapy clinics are a newly emerging way to offer quick access to therapy without the requirement of a diagnostic assessment prior to receiving help. These clinics offer an opportunity for socially just conversations for children and their families and provide therapists such as myself with a practice context that makes space for working in ways that are congruent with cherished values.

Reflection Questions

1. What effects on your work and therapeutic conversations are you noticing due to the increasing pressure to engage with people around diagnoses and labels?
2. What does it mean to embrace externalizing as an ethical stance rather than just as a technique?
3. What words would you use to describe the kind of curiosity that you would prefer to have shape your conversations and questions with people? Where would that curiosity direct you?
4. What are some ways you might increase space for the ideas and preferences of children and youth in your therapeutic conversations?

References

American Psychiatric Association. (2013). *Diagnostic and statistical manual of mental disorders* (5th ed.). Washington, DC: Author.

Batha, K. (2006). Ethical curiosity and poststructuralism. *The International Journal of Narrative Therapy and Community Work, 1*, 57–64. Retrieved from http://dulwichcentre.com.au/international-journal-of-narrative-therapy-and-community-work

Combs, G., & Freedman, J. (2012). Narrative, poststructuralism, and social justice: Current practices in narrative therapy. *The Counselling Psychologist, 40*(7), 1033–1060. doi: 10.1177/0011000012460662

Danaher, G., Schirato, T., & Webb, J. (2000). *Understanding Foucault.* Thousand Oaks, CA: Sage.

Duvall, J., & Béres, L. (2011). *Innovations in narrative therapy: Connecting practice, training, and research.* New York, NY: Norton.

Duvall, J., & Young, K. (2009). Keeping the faith: A conversation with Michael White. *Journal of Systemic Therapies, 28*(1), 1–18. doi: 10.1521/jsyt.2009.28.1.1

Duvall, J., Young, K., & Kayes-Burden, A. (2012). *No more, no less: Brief mental health services for children and youth.* Retrieved from Ontario Centre of Excellence for Child and Youth Mental Health website: www.excellenceforchildandyouth.ca/sites/default/files/policy_brief_mental_health_services_executive_summary.pdf

Epstein, E., Wiesner, M., & Duda, L. (2013). DSM and the diagnosis-MacGuffin: Implications for the self and society. *Australian and New Zealand Journal of Family Therapy, 34*, 156–167. doi: 10.1002/anzf.1012

Freedman, J., & Combs, G. (1996). *Narrative therapy: The social construction of preferred realities*. New York, NY: Norton.

Goldstein, H. (1992). If social work hasn't made progress as a science, might it be an art? *Families in Society: The Journal of Contemporary Human Services, 73*(1), 48–55. Retrieved from http://alliance1.org/fis

Lindemann-Nelson, H. (2001). *Damaged identities, narrative repair*. Ithaca, NY: Cornell University Press.

National Infant, Child, and Youth Mental Health Consortium Advisory, The Provincial Centre of Excellence for Child and Youth Mental Health at CHEO, Canadian Association of Paediatric Health Centres (2010). Access and wait times in child and youth mental health: A background paper. Retrieved from www.excellenceforchildandyouth.ca/sites/default/files/policy_access_and_wait_times.pdf

Paré, D. A. (2013). *The practice of collaborative counselling & psychotherapy: Developing skills in culturally mindful helping*. Thousand Oaks, CA: Sage.

Paré, D. A. (2014). Social justice and the word: Keeping diversity alive in therapeutic conversations. *Canadian Journal of Counselling and Psychotherapy, 48*(3), 206–217. Retrieved from http://cjc-rcc.ucalgary.ca

Ramey, H. L., Young, K., & Tarulli, D. (2010). Scaffolding and concept formation in narrative therapy: A qualitative research report. *Journal of Systemic Therapies, 29*(4), 74–91. doi: 10.1521/jsyt.2010.29.4.74

Reynolds, V. (2012). An ethical stance for justice-doing in community work and therapy. *Journal of Systemic Therapies, 31*(4), 18–33. doi: 10.1521/jsyt.2012.31.4.18

Thomas, L. (2004). Poststructuralism and therapy—what's it all about? In S. Russell & M. Carey (Eds.), *Narrative Therapy: Responding to your questions* (pp. 91–99). Adelaide, Australia: Dulwich Centre Publications.

White, M. (2000). *Reflections on narrative practice: Interviews and essays*. Adelaide, Australia: Dulwich Centre Publications.

White, M. (2007). *Maps of narrative practice*. New York, NY: Norton.

White, M. (2011). *Narrative practice: Continuing the conversations*. New York, NY: Norton.

White, M., & Epston, D. (1990). *Narrative means to therapeutic ends*. New York, NY: Norton.

Young, K. (2008). Narrative practice at a walk-in therapy: Developing children's worry wisdom. *Journal of Systemic Therapies, 27*(4), 54–74. doi: 10.1521/jsyt.2008.27.4.54

Young, K. (2011). When all the time you have is now: Re-visiting practices and narrative therapy in a walk-in clinic. In J. Duvall & L. Béres, *Innovations in narrative therapy: Connecting practice, training, and research* (pp. 147–166). New York, NY: Norton.

Young, K., & Cooper, S. (2008). Toward co-composing an evidence base: The narrative therapy re-visiting project. *Journal of Systemic Therapies, 27*(1), 67–83. doi: 10.1521/jsyt.2008.27.1.67

Young, K., Dick, M., Herring, K., & Lee, J. (2008). From waiting lists to walk-in: Stories from a walk-in therapy clinic. *Journal of Systemic Therapies, 27*(4), 23–39. doi: 10.1521/jsyt.2008.27.4.23

Rosie Had Wings They Could Not See: A Consultation with Michael White and a Woman Labeled with a Dual Diagnosis

Jim Duvall and Caroline Tremblay

Individuals labeled with a dual diagnosis of developmental delay and co-occurring mental illness have historically been cared for through institutions. Discourses about what defines a developmental delay or intellectual disability have rested on historical concepts, which, at their core, defined it as a flaw (McDonagh, 1998). In that context, people with intellectual disabilities were seen as representing the embodiment of social and moral degeneration. Granted, the discourses characterizing intellectual disability have gone through significant changes over the last 200 years (Owen & MacFarland, 2002), influenced by changing cultural ideologies. However, professionals' understanding of clients' identities have continued to be embedded in the legacies of institutionalized discourses (Foucault & Khalfa, 2006; Goffman, 1959, 1974, 1986; Laing, 1965, 1970; McDonagh, 1998; Rooke, 2003; Szasz, 1961, 1970). At the heart of these ideological developments lies the foundation of what it is to be human—or not human (Goodey, 1994)—and, as such, these culturally determined identities have impacted on the rights of people with intellectual disability, "treating them as fundamentally less human than others" (McDonagh, 1998, p. 236). This legacy continues to influence institutional practices through structures of oppression, organizing, and subjugating people as the other.

Rosie,[1] the 37-year-old woman assigned a dual-diagnosis who we will introduce in this chapter, was subjected to numerous othering practices, including involuntary confinement. In the institution where Rosie was a patient, the psychiatric care provided was highly medicalized and involved the use of diagnosis (e.g., *Diagnostic and Statistical Manual of Mental Disorders*, DSM-5; American Psychiatric Association, 2013), behavior management plans, psychotropic medication, and segregation (e.g., the seclusion room, which is a locked padded room). When Rosie's behavior was perceived as disruptive, and therapeutic interventions judged to be ineffective, staff would resort to restraint practices. Rosie would be escorted against her will and locked in a room and/or medicated to calm her down.

These coercive and non-voluntary confinement practices are at the core of the custodial model of care, which has been the pillar of the institutionalized model of care provided to individuals (Mah, Hirdes, Heckman, & Stolee, 2015). These control interventions, although commonly used in psychiatric institutions, are less than ideal because, as put by Mah and colleagues, "they counter a patient-centered approach to care and can damage therapeutic relationships while further stigmatizing patients" (Mah et al., 2015, p. 139). As such, it represents social determinism in which one's identity and ability to act is formed and limited by institutional discourses (Szasz, 1970).

The concept of the 'other' is about an identity of difference and is central to understanding the effects of institutionalized oppression. The term, which surfaces in the work of several authors including Michel Foucault, Erving Goffman, R. D. Laing, and Thomas Szasz, serves to place individuals outside of the center, along the margins, where social norms do not exist, robbing othered individuals from the opportunities granted to mainstream society. The characteristic encompasses being different from or unfamiliar to the identity of self or social identities. The other is viewed as dissimilar or opposite to being us or the same. Thomas Szasz, author of *The Myth of Mental Illness* (1961) and *The Manufacture of Madness* (1970), disputed othering through the use of coercive treatments, involuntary confinement, and the use of psychiatric diagnoses in the courts, contending that these practices were unscientific and unethical. He joined Canadian American sociologist Erving Goffman, Scottish psychiatrist R. D. Laing, and French philosopher Michel Foucault in arguing that the process of othering has everything to do with gaining power to achieve a political agenda in its goal of domination. When we "other" another group, we point out their perceived weaknesses to make ourselves look stronger or better. It implies a hierarchy, and it serves to keep power where it already lies.

The reflective position of narrative therapy described in this chapter calls into question these oppressive practices, making it more possible for people to regain control over their own lives. In doing so, therapists' power and control are also called into question, as well as the power of institutions. People's protest against acts of oppression can then be acknowledged as small acts of living (Wade, 1997).

Drawing on the therapeutic conversation with Michael White[2] and Rosie, we will illustrate how the intentional use of non-pathologizing language can serve to counter dominant marginalizing othering discourses. Selected unaltered clinical excerpts[3] will illustrate how the conversation created space for re-considerations about Rosie's life, free from institutionalized, normative judgments and situated in non-pathologizing discourses.

I (JD) was Director of Training at the institute operating the training program in which Michael White interviewed Rosie. I am offering this chapter from the position of a white, university-educated male who grew up in southern Texas in the late 1960s and was involved in the social upheaval resulting from the anti-war movement. This transformative experience left me with a strong appreciation for the effects of social context on people's lives. I have co-authored the book *Innovations in Narrative Therapy: Connecting Practice, Training and Research* (Duvall & Béres, 2011), as well as various articles, interviews, and a book chapter about the theory and practice of narrative therapy. I am dedicated to narrative practices as they make it possible to engage with people while considering the effects of the social, cultural, and political context in which they are situated.

I (CT) was working at the institution where Rosie was a patient and was one of two social workers on the program for people diagnosed with developmental delay and a co-occurring mental illness. My social worker colleague and I both took part in Michael White's consultation with Rosie. I am participating in writing this chapter from the position of a white, French-speaking, middle-age university-educated woman who grew up in a small rural Quebec community within a single-parent, working-class family. My cultural and social heritages have helped shape my views on privilege, oppression, and respect for differences. In my professional life as a social worker, I have become increasingly interested in studying the relationships between personal, professional, and institutional ethics and social justice.

Consultation Setting

The consultation session was situated in the context of a 5-day narrative therapy certificate-training program. As part of the training experience, Michael White provided consultations to mental health professionals and the people who consult them. In narrative practices, the therapeutic process is viewed as consultation and this is connected to the non-expert non-hierarchical position inherent in the therapeutic posture (Duvall & Béres, 2011; White, 2007). I (CT) had proposed to my team that Rosie and the workers involved with her could benefit from attending a consultation session with Michael White since they experienced stuckness in trying to help Rosie with her emotional outbursts and with her frustration at having to live alone instead of in a group home. I had been part of other such consultations with Michael White and had experienced the generative quality of those conversations and how they opened many useful possibilities for change. Rosie was asked if she would be interested in participating in a consultation that would be conducted in the context of training other mental health professionals. She had agreed to attend and had commented: "If it will help you with your learning so that you can help me." In addition to Rosie and myself, the people invited to the consultation included a community support worker (Diane), and the social worker assigned to her from the dual-diagnosis program (Joe).

There was also an outsider witnessing team (White, 2007) comprised of four mental health professionals attending the training program and observing from behind a one-way mirror. They were part of a larger narrative therapy training group of various mental health professionals viewing the session on live feed monitors. In narrative therapy, outsider witnessing teams provide reflections in response to what is heard in the therapeutic conversation. These outsider-witnessing teams do not provide assessments nor do they provide judgment or advice. Reflections express an embodied resonance for the team member and highlight the person's abilities, linking to possibilities that can be further developed into alternative storylines (White, 2007). Selected unaltered excerpts from this therapeutic conversation will be presented to illustrate the overall movements and effects of the consultation and how they contributed to addressing social justice issues, challenging the language and practices of domination and oppression.

Getting to Know Rosie Away from the Problem

Rosie had experienced the effects of living in institutions for most of her life. As a result, she would likely be predisposed to experiencing shame and self-doubt (Rioux & Carbert, 2003; Rooke, 2003). These effects and others would suppress her ability to have a clear voice and express herself without fear of reprisal. Therefore, it was important to begin the therapeutic conversation by acknowledging her initiatives and accomplishments, with an intention to carefully and incrementally scaffold[4] (Duvall & Béres, 2011; Duvall & Young, 2009; White, 2007) the conversation to increase her confidence and engagement while inviting her own voice to come forward.

After introducing himself, Michael White (MW) turned to Rosie and commented:

> MW: Rosie, if it's okay I would like to ask you a few questions. You're wearing a medal. Is that a medal? What is that about?
>
> Rosie: I was in a soccer tournament a couple of weeks ago and we came in first place.
>
> MW: You came in first place. Fantastic! Do you play soccer a lot? Are you big into soccer?
>
> Rosie: Yea, and I also do basketball, floor hockey, and bowling on Wednesday nights.
>
> MW: So, would you say you're a sports person?

After Michael suggested the possible alternative identity conclusion sports person, in order to render her abilities more visible he continued to unpack and thicken Rosie's involvement in sports in great detail, incrementally scaffolding the conversation. This contributed to increasing Rosie's engagement in the conversation and helping her to get in touch with her values and what was important to her. As he did so, her smile widened and she became noticeably more and more engaged in the conversation. When Rosie experienced some difficulties responding to Michael's questions, he used horizontal scaffolding to avoid her experiencing frustration or shame. This horizontal scaffolding involved turning to someone else in the room and continuing to unpack the therapeutic conversation with them, thus placing Rosie in a witnessing position. Michael did so by turning to me (CT) and asked a number of questions, including the following:

> MW: Caroline, can you tell me what it is that you have grown to appreciate most about Rosie and then I'd like to ask you what your thoughts are about coming here today. You've known her for 12 months.
>
> CT: There are a number of things that I got to know about Rosie and that I learned to appreciate. I got to appreciate Rosie's interest in people and social interactions. I also found out that Rosie likes to help people quite a bit. That's very important to her. When I hurt my knee 6 months ago I was

on crutches for many months. When I would come to work in the morning Rosie would see me and rush to my door to open it for me and make it
easier. So, I felt taken care of. I really appreciated that. And, also just having
Rosie around has been nice because of her smile. It's like there's a sense of
sunshine and energy, which is quite pleasant. The days have ups and downs
and it's nice to have someone around who has that quality.

MW: It's good to hear what you have grown to appreciate about Rosie ...
(turns to Rosie) So, Rosie, have you always liked to help people?

From this beginning conversation with me (CT), Michael was able to find out
from Rosie that she had always liked helping people in various ways, and that it
had been important for her to be helpful for a long time, which implied a tradition
to this value of wanting to help people. Michael asked Rosie if he could write these
things down and treat it seriously because he's "getting to know a lot about her." He
then went on to repeat "So it's important to you to help people who are struggling,"
continuing to scaffold the conversation:

MW: Why is that important to you? Do you know? When people are struggling and you like to help out ... do you know why that's important?
Rosie: Because it makes me feel good inside and it probably makes the other
person feel good inside if I help them.
MW: So, it makes you feel good inside and the other person as well ...
(turns to me, CT) ... Is that true? Did it make you feel good inside? (Rosie
smiles)
CT: Yes.
MW: So, that's why you do it, it makes you feel good inside and it makes others feel good inside as well?

This part of the conversation increasingly engaged Rosie in expressing her voice
and making visible her values and abilities such as empathy, as well as verifying
her intentions in helping others; that it makes them feel good inside. My (CT)
response that it made me feel good inside helped to co-construct this now visible
identity conclusion. As stated by Michael White, acknowledging these values, previously known internally, in the outside world, gives them "stick-ability"[5] (Duvall
& Young, 2009, p. 15). Michael then provided a reflecting summary (Duvall &
Béres, 2011; White 2007), which captured the highlights of his conversation with
Rosie so far. As he was doing so, Rosie was smiling widely and seemed clearly
engaged in the conversation. After revisiting with me (CT) the intentions for
bringing Rosie to the session, Michael turned to her and said:

MW: Caroline was wondering if we could have a conversation that might
open up possibilities for you to have more of the kind of life you want. How
does that fit with you for today's meeting? Does that fit for you?
Rosie: Yes.

Rosie Uses Her Voice to Take a Stand

MW: Do you have other thoughts about what you would like to talk about today?

Rosie: Uhmm … I do but I don't know if I'm allowed to say this. (Rosie is leaning forward and looking down at the floor).

MW: Sorry … Will you have a go at it and if I don't understand I could ask you a question, if that's okay?

Rosie: The place where I've been, I just find that it's hard if I go into one room. I find it really hard being there with the door closed.

MW: So, this is the place you are in now, or where you were. And you find it hard being in there by yourself with the door closed? What's it like for you … when you say it's hard being in there with the door closed?

Rosie: It's hard 'cause it gets really hot in there. I just don't want anyone else to be in the same situation.

MW: So, you're concerned for other people?

Rosie: Yes.

MW: Would you say a bit more about the situation, because I don't think I probably understand it. Can you tell me a bit more so I can understand the situation that you don't want other people to be in that you're in?

Rosie: I don't like going in the box. It's no fun being in there because you have no one to talk to.

MW: What is the box? Did you say the box? What is that?

Rosie: It's a room with all mats.

MW: And that's a room you go into sometimes?

Rosie: That's if I have troubles trying to listen.

MW: So, it's something about going into the box. Why do you go into the box?

Rosie: Because I don't listen to what I'm being told.

MW: Oh, I see, okay so … and there's nothing much in the box.

Rosie: No.

MW: You say you don't like being in the box. How does it affect you? Does it make you feel certain things?

Rosie: It's really hard to breathe. There's no air coming in.

MW: Would it be okay with you if I asked Joe and Diane about that? Would that be okay?

Rosie: Yep.

MW: Okay, so I'm gonna ask them a little bit about it and then check that out with you … (shifting attention to Joe and Diane) … So, what are your reflections on what Rosie is saying? I'm not very clear.

Joe: I'm most interested in Rosie's language in calling it the box. What Rosie is referring to is the use of seclusion to control out-of-control behavior. The description certainly is correct, the padding of the room. The purpose being to … it's actually a least restraint type of initiative …

Diane: Yes, Rosie has been able to use it to calm herself. At times she has been on the ward and things have been a little overwhelming for her. She hasn't been able to control herself. Rosie has done very well though at being able to recognize when some of these behaviors are uncontrollable and ask for a PRN[6] to help her settle … would that be true Rosie … do you think? Do you think you've come a long ways that way?

Rosie: (looking down, holding her head in her hands) I don't know.

The above exchange is significant from a social justice perspective. Staff's response to Rosie's expression about the box is a telling illustration of the effects of *power-over* discourse. As stated earlier, language and discourse are mechanisms of oppression. For Rosie to talk about the "box" took significant caution and courage on her part. She clearly chose to bring up that issue in response to Michael's question about what was important for her to talk about. Her expression suggested she was aware of the possible taboo of raising the issue of the "box" when she said, "I do but I don't know if I'm allowed to say this."

The use of rhetorical language in which a power-over practice such as forced confinement is renamed a seclusion room makes invisible its real, lived effects, as experienced and described by Rosie. When Rosie used the word box to describe her experience instead of the institutionally sanctioned seclusion room she exercised her power, which Michael supported by privileging her language. The language of oppression, the box became the language of resistance. Through the respectful scaffolding of the conversation, Michael's questions and Rosie's responses made visible what was absent but implicit (Carey, Walther, & Russell, 2009; Duvall & Béres, 2011) in Rosie's presentation, that she was able to express empathy, discernment, concern for herself and others, and able to clearly articulate her distress.

In the conversation that followed, Rosie spoke of her dissatisfaction at having to live alone in an apartment instead of living with other people in a group home, which she would prefer. That conversation revealed further disjunction and frustrations for Rosie in not being heard. Many times, Rosie looked down and shook her head when comments were made about how much better it was for her to live alone since she often got into arguments with others when she lived in a group home setting. After some time discussing the apartment, Michael revisited the discussion about the box.

MW: Did you want to talk more about the box? I've got some other questions I would like to ask you. But I was just wondering if you want to talk about the box more.

Rosie: I really don't like going in there because I have to lie on the mat. If I don't take my PRNs then I get a needle.

Developing a Subordinate Story Line: Panning for Gold

At this point of the conversation, Michael began to intentionally ask Rosie questions that focused on her ideas and local knowledge about what would work better for her. As he did so, themes and alternative storylines became more richly described and possibilities for action became more visible.

> MW: Do you have any ideas about what would work better for you? You know, if you're getting pretty uptight, do you have the sense of what would work better for you?
>
> Rosie: I could go to my room.
>
> MW: Do you get the sense that you could take yourself to your room when you're feeling uptight?
>
> Rosie: Sometimes I have to ask. I get really upset and have to ask people to bring me down to my room.
>
> MW: You get really upset … you get into a big thing and then have to get people to bring you down to your room.
>
> Rosie: Yes.
>
> MW: … and does your room work, to be taken down to your room?
>
> Rosie: Yes.
>
> MW: That works for you, that works for you better than the box?
>
> Rosie: Yes.
>
> MW: Okay. Can I ask you a couple other questions? Sounds like you've got some ideas about what works when you get into a big thing? What happens when you get into a big thing?
>
> Rosie: I'm not really paying attention and it's hard to be focused on one thing when you've got so many things on the go.

A conversation followed between Michael and Rosie about all the different things that helped her when she was upset. In that conversation, Rosie was able to respond to Michael with a range of ideas about what she could do, within her control, to assist her in managing herself when she was experiencing a big thing. These ideas, such as going to her room or talking to someone, surfaced as viable alternatives to the use of forced containment and/or medication. Michael then turned to myself (CT), Joe, and Diane, and asked questions that led the conversation to the naming of Rosie's abilities. When he turned back to Rosie, he asked "Which of these fit for you?" to which she responded, "They all fit." This was an excellent display of movement on the part of the staff who had been invited to participate in the reconstructing of a more robust identity for Rosie.

> MW: If some of these abilities became more visible to you, would that be useful?
>
> Rosie: Yes, then I wouldn't get so frustrated.

At this point, Michael proceeded to write down specific abilities and preferred identity statements that were expressed and made visible during the consultation, offering those in a letter format.

> MW: I'd like to write a letter about what I'm learning about you and give it to you. This letter is called "Rosie: Who I am."

The details of the letter were verified with Rosie through careful questioning. Each time Rosie would verify a quality about herself, Michael would write it down, adding significance and stick-ability to her emerging sense of "myself."

> Rosie: Reading this letter will make it more possible for me to see my abilities and help me deal with my frustration ... 'Cause then I will do it the right way. And I'll be less likely to be upset 'cause I don't want to be upset.
> MW: How many copies of this would you like? Will this letter be helpful?
> Rosie: One to Joe, Diane, and Caroline and two for myself, one for the behaviorist ...
> MW: Would it be good to have this list to remind yourself about the sort of person you are?
> Rosie: To calm myself down.

The letter shown in Box 17.1, "Rosie: Who I Am," makes Rosie's abilities clearly visible. The letter serves as a public proclamation, announcing the renewal of Rosie's identity away from the problematized identity, such as out-of-control. The distribution of the letter to her friends and to particular staff working in the institution serves to circulate her new story, and works to deconstruct the pathologizing beliefs and assumptions inherent in the institutional discourse.

Box 17.1   A letter entitled "Rosie: Who I Am"

Rosie: Who I am
  I'm a dance person.
  I'm a person who likes to help others when they are struggling.
  I'm a person who can tell when someone is having a rough day.
  I'm a person who can brighten up the day for other people.
  I've learned to calm myself down when I'm upset and this is something I couldn't do so well when I was younger.
  Calming technique, perseverance, respectful ways, maturity.
  All of this says that I am more able to talk to people about it and to use my persistence in ways to get my needs met.

Outsider Witnessing Team

Following the letter exercise, Rosie, myself (CT), Joe, and Diane went behind the one-way mirror, exchanging places with the four outsider witnessing team members. Michael interviewed them, placing us in the audience position. Michael invited the witnessing team members to play a part in rich story development by engaging in re-tellings that were the outcome of close listening and composed of particular aspects of Rosie's story they were drawn to, expressing these retellings in ways that would not be imposing. They were asked to respond personally, speak of their understanding of why they were drawn to these particular aspects and how it affected them. They were also asked to step back from common ways that people respond to stories of other people lives, including from giving opinions or advice, making judgment, and theorizing (White, 2007).

During the conversation with the outsider witnessing team, the team members talked, among other things, about Rosie's ability to care for others and how important it was to bring her voice forward. Following that conversation, the outsider witnessing team went back behind the one-way mirror and Rosie, Joe, Diane, and myself (CT) came back in the room to continue the conversation with Michael.

Post-Outsider Witnessing Team Reflection

MW: What was that like for you?

Rosie: It makes me happy.

MW: One of the team members asked if she could tell her daughter about your story. Would that be okay with you? Someone else said your courage gave them courage.

Rosie: I was happy to hear what they had to say about what I said.

MW: What was it like for the three of you?

Diane: I really liked talking about the positive parts about Rosie. I feel like we always focus on the negative and try to deal with it. It was refreshing to talk about the positive things she brings to the table.

Joe: It was cathartic in some sort of way for me.

MW: So it was cathartic for you in some way … could you say a little bit more about that?

Joe: We are so involved in her life in so many ways about how to get her out of this particular problem or how to get her out of this period of change or whatever it might be. So, to sit back and reflect on her positive characteristics, it was cathartic for me because I realized that Rosie's story has touched us all in such a profound way …

CT: It felt very special to sit behind the mirror beside Rosie and hear other people talk about how it touched them. It's not something that happens a lot. It was special to be part of it. I could see on Rosie's face the more she experienced perhaps joy or happiness, and other times she would be more quiet and watch. The one thing that really stood out for me was the image of opening the door. In terms of what Rosie did for me, she opened the door and made it possible for me to struggle less. I was wondering in Rosie's life ... what does it mean to open doors? When I work with Rosie what does it mean to open doors for her so that she has fewer struggles? The last piece was when someone spoke about courage ... and I was just wondering what Rosie thought about courage ... 'cause we hadn't talked about it yet ... it hadn't come up. So I was just curious.

MW: Thanks Caroline. I appreciated all of those reflections as well ... If it's okay with you Rosie I'll put some of these comments into the letter as well ... the ones that you seem most connected to ... Now would you say that today you were just in the front seat or were you in the driver's seat at this meeting ... ? Well, I thought you were in a bit of a driver's seat this time. I was asking you questions and we were following your lead ... it's been sort of like a front seat day in a way.

Post-Consultation Reflections and Conclusion

The therapeutic conversation with Michael White created space for Rosie to voice her protest, and make evident her knowledge, abilities, hopes, and preferences for living her life. The staff's participation in witnessing and naming of Rosie's abilities represented movement away from social control and transformative movement toward utilizing her ideas and abilities—from *power over* to *power with*.

Rosie had lived a marginalized existence in institutional settings for most of her life. She had minimal influence on important decisions affecting the quality of her life. When her occasional protests to this oppression led to an escalation of her distress, standard institutional control protocols (e.g., medication, physical restraint, or seclusion) were often used to respond to her out of control behavior. Sanctioned by the institution, these responses perpetuate the power-over practices applied to marginalized individuals. An alternative to out of control, the identity letter "Rosie: Who I Am" would be used to circulate her rich identity conclusions into the institution to staff who worked with her and to her friends. As she was showing her identity statement to her friends (which she carried in her back pocket), Joe reported in later discussion that her friends were heard to say, "I want one of those identities too!" The letter served to sustain the changes made in the consultation session and continued a process of deconstruction of the oppressive practices. As language and discourse have the ability to maintain current ideologies and can reinforce inequalities, challenging the language of oppression when it is presented as the norm is essential. As stated by Cudd (2005), "As I will use the term, 'oppression' names a social injustice, which is to say that it is perpetrated through social institutions, practices, and norms on social groups by social groups" (p. 21). Therefore, challenging social justice issues such as the ones illustrated in this chapter requires a willingness to question and expose taken for granted practices, and revisit marginalizing language, beliefs, and assumptions.

The effects of the session on Joe, Diane, and myself (CT) were transformative. Joe spoke of experiencing a catharsis as he witnessed Rosie's moment to moment forthcoming abilities and proposals for action as she responded to Michael White's generative questions. Diane expressed how refreshing it was for her to be able to focus on positive things about Rosie. As for myself (CT), the experience shattered my assumptions regarding what I thought Rosie was capable of expressing and reflecting on with regards to her emotional responses, and her wishes and ideas for her life. What began as shimmers of Rosie's abilities evolved into a very robust identity description.

The effects of the consultation rippled beyond the walls of the room, through the circulation of both Rosie's letter and the transformation experienced by the other people present in the room, on the outsider witnessing team, and as part of the larger trainee audience. Rosie moved us all as we traveled with her through the session, while Michael White helped her to navigate her journey into previously uncharted territories. She moved us through her expression of courage as she shared what was most important for her to speak about, challenging the practices of domination when she had been unwillingly confined. She was able to express her hopes for her life, her concern for others, and her ideas for action that put her in the front seat. All these uplifting possibilities had been hidden in plain view but, through Rosie's conversation with Michael White, they became visible. Now, we can see Rosie's wings.

Reflection Questions

We would like to invite the readers to critically reflect within the context of their practice and the people they work with, on the processes by which social problems are constructed and interpreted, thereby calling into question the claims of institutional structures that contribute to marginalization (othering), domination, and oppression:

1. Can you name particular social institutions that may advertently or inadvertently support oppression in the lives of the people you work with?
2. Can you identify ways that language and terminology used with and applied to persons may maintain those oppressions?
3. What are some institutional discourses that contribute to negative identity conclusions on the parts of the persons the institutions serve?

Notes

1 The names of session participants were changed to protect their identity. Rosie was a woman I (CT) worked with while employed as a social worker at a psychiatric institution.
2 In this chapter, we are expressing our interpretation and understanding of Michael White's work with Rosie and the effects on others who were present in the session. We

are not assuming or claiming to represent his intentions or understandings of his work in this session or those of the other participants.

3 Transcript excerpts reprinted with permission.

4 "Scaffolding" is a conversational structure that makes it possible to traverse the gap between what is known and familiar and what might be possible for people to know about their lives. It can be considered a zone of proximal development (White, 2007).

5 The word "stick-ability" refers to the sustainability of experiences previously known only internally but now known in the external world.

6 (In prescriptions) abbreviation for *pro re nata,* a Latin phrase meaning "as needed." The administration times are determined by the patient's needs. Retrieved from http://medical-dictionary.thefreedictionary.com/p.r.n. When Rosie was admitted at the institution, the PRN had to be dispensed by a nurse.

References

American Psychiatric Association. (2013). *Diagnostic and statistical manual of mental disorders* (5th ed.). Washington, DC: Author.

Carey, M., Walther, S., & Russell, S. (2009). The absent but implicit: A map to support therapeutic inquiry. *Family Process, 48*(3), 319–331. doi: 10.1111/j.1545-5300.2009.01285.x

Cudd, A. E. (2005). How to explain oppression: Criteria of adequacy for normative explanatory theories. *Philosophy of the Social Sciences, 35*(1), 20–49. doi: 10.1177/0048393104271923

Duvall, J., & Béres, L. (2011). *Innovations in narrative practices: Connecting practice, training and research.* New York, NY: Norton.

Duvall, J., & Young, K. (2009). Keeping faith: A conversation with Michael White. *Journal of Systemic Therapies, 28*(1), 1–18. doi: 10.1521/jsyt.2009.28.1.1

Foucault, M., & Khalfa, J. (2006). *History of madness.* Florence, KY: Routledge.

Goffman, E. (1959). *The Presentation of self in everyday life.* New York, NY: Bantam Doubleday Bell.

Goffman, E. (1974). *Frame analysis: an essay on the organization of experience.* New York, NY: Harper & Row.

Goffman, E. (1986). *Stigma: Notes on the management of spoiled identity.* New York, NY: Simon & Schuster.

Goodey, C. F. (1994). John Locke's idiots in the natural history of mind. *History of Psychiatry, 5*(18), 215–250. doi: 10.1177/0957154X9400501804

Laing, R. D. (1965). *The divided self: An existential study in sanity and madness.* New York, NY: Penguin Books.

Laing, R. D. (1970). *Knots.* New York, NY: Random House.

McDonagh, P. (1998). The image of idiocy in nineteenth-century England: A history of cultural representations of intellectual disability. Doctoral dissertation, Concordia University, Quebec, Canada. Retrieved from http://spectrum.library.concordia.ca

Mah, T. M., Hirdes, J. P., Heckman, G., & Stolee, P. (2015). Use of control interventions in adult in-patient mental health services. *Healthcare Management Forum, 28*(4), 139–45. Retrieved from http://healthcaremanagementforum.org

Owen, F., & MacFarland, J. (2002). The nature of developmental disabilities. In D. M. Griffiths, C. Stravakaki, & J. Summer (Eds.), *Dual diagnosis: An introduction to the mental health needs of persons with developmental disabilities* (pp. 15–44). Sudbury, ON: Habilitative Mental Health Resource Network.

Rioux, M., & Carbert, A. (2003). Human rights and disability: The international context. *Journal on Developmental Disabilities, 10*(2), 1–14.

Rooke, J. (2003). Reaching one's potential: A discussion of individual human rights and people with developmental disabilities in Canada. *Journal on Developmental Disabilities, 10*(2), 15–24.

Szasz, T. (1961). *Myth of mental illness.* New York, NY: Harper Collins.

Szasz, T. (1970). *The manufacture of madness.* New York, NY: Harper & Row.

Wade, A. (1997). Small acts of living: Everyday resistance to violence and other forms of oppression. *Contemporary Family Therapy, 19*(1), 23–39. doi: 10.1023/A:1026154215299

White, M. (2007). *Maps of narrative practice.* New York, NY: Norton.

CHAPTER 18

Creating Safety and Social Justice for Women in the Yukon

Catherine Richardson/Kinewesquao, Ann Maje Rader,
Barbara McInerney, and Renée-Claude Carrier

Violence against women is frequent and ubiquitous. This chapter locates response-based informed activist work in one of Canada's northern territories—the Yukon. In this Indigenous Canadian space, infamous for pioneer histories and the Canadian gold rush, many Yukon women are harmed by male violence with relative perpetrator impunity. Structural issues such as a lack of affordable housing means that many women are blocked in finding new homes and living free of violence. Relative isolation and the dearth of services in the Yukon create particular difficulties related to ensuring women's safety. Challenges in the justice system, such as underfunded legal aid and low rates of sentencing, mean that much violence remains unchecked. Here, where Indigenous existence clashes uncomfortably against discourses of brave pioneers conquering a savage land, the safety and rights of Indigenous women are often tenuous and fragile.

This chapter documents a Yukon social justice activism, aligned with response-based practice (RBP), and designed to increase safety for women. We present community work that takes place at the intersection of counseling and social justice activism and share our approach to creating safety and equality for women dealing with male violence in the Yukon. This work reflects a collectivity of counselors, service-providers, and social justice allies[1] influenced by Indigenous holistic approaches respecting the importance of land, relationality, and spirituality. Our work is informed by women's resistance knowledges, feminism, and a respect for the sacred of all beings.

In this chapter we also present the reader with the foundations of RBP, including: the importance of dignity; the ever-presence of resistance; and the belief that violence is social, unilateral, and deliberate. As counselors, activists, and women in various positions of leadership, we share a response-based orientation, founded on a desire to contest the epidemic of victim-blaming and to create safe and respectful communities. In this work, terms such as "victim" and "perpetrator" are contextually and situationally based and do not imply states of identity.[2] We believe that women should not be blamed for the violent actions of men in the community, or targeted with censure, for speaking out against male violence. Often, drawing attention to violence against women is accompanied by more violence in an attempt

Figure 18.1 Photographed: Trina Erin Nolan-Pauls
Souce: Photo by Allan Ogilvie, Photographics. Reprinted with permission.

to silence women's voices. Statistics show that it is more towards the "norm" for women to experience men's violence than an anomaly, particularly for Indigenous women and women of color. After situating violence and the evolution of RBP, a diagram follows that serves as an analytical guide for exploring violence, resistance/responses, and prospects for victim recovery. The response-based practices we will describe are embedded in a social justice-oriented approach. Where social justice is lacking, the counselor/activist addresses the injustices both publicly and privately in therapeutic conversations. The more just and effective the responses to victims of crime, the more likely violence against women will be addressed both as a social issue and as an issue of immediate concern for victims.

Situating Violence and Response-Based Practice

What is social interaction? It is a process of engagement between at least two people in the world. Where violence is concerned, there is a perpetrator and a victim, the first acting against the will and well-being of the other. In studying violence, it is clear that the problem exists in the social world, not in the mind of the victim as so many psychological approaches tell us (Coates & Wade, 2004; Richardson, 2008; Richardson & Wade, 2008, 2012). In RBP, violence and responses to it are the main interest of study, along with an analysis of the situation and the social context. Power relations are of interest, including consideration of who has the most resources at hand to help them when they are accused of being a perpetrator or a victim. This approach was developed through direct service with people who have been targets of violence. Key aspects include contesting the blaming and pathologizing of victims, focusing on accurate representations of interaction, highlighting resistance knowledges, and understanding the actions of victims and perpetrators in context. We work with the understanding that dignity is central to human interaction and that dealing with violence revolves around maintaining and repairing dignity after the humiliation of being violated.

Around 2005, RBP evolved to include an analysis of social responses to victims, linking responses to the recovery processes for victims and becoming actively involved in coordinating positive collective responses to victims. Understanding and evaluating the quality of social responses became important for assessing victim safety and perpetrator accountability/impunity. It further involved understanding the "situational logic" of women's decisions and seeing victim responses as understandable (not sick or dysfunctional) within the specific context.

Categories of Response-Based Contextual Analysis

The conceptual diagram shown in Figure 18.2 may be used for situation analysis in fields such as counseling, clinical supervision, criminology, policing, and for the writing of reports. Due to its circularity, one may begin developing an interactional analysis with any particular category in the diagram. We often begin with a description of the *context/social material conditions* and the situation (*situation interaction*) with answers to questions such as "What is happening and under which conditions could such interaction occur?" For example, certain political moves can make violence against women and children more socially acceptable, such as Russia's move to decriminalize domestic assault (Solomon, 2017) and the election of Donald Trump as president of the United States with his plan to reduce the rights of women (Moore, 2017). Within the socio-political context, one finds the actions, responses, and decisions of individual women.

Exploring the client's experience often begins with the questions "Who is doing what to whom?" and "How is the victim responding?" For example, if we were to see a woman walking down the road wearing two different shoes on her feet, we might wonder why. Typically, without adequate information, we turn to stereotypes or assumptions. In RBP, we would ask ourselves "Under what conditions would a woman wear two different shoes?" We would rely on self-reflection to avoid jumping to conclusions or explanations that lack evidence. We later learn that this woman lives with a man who is violent towards her. In identifying

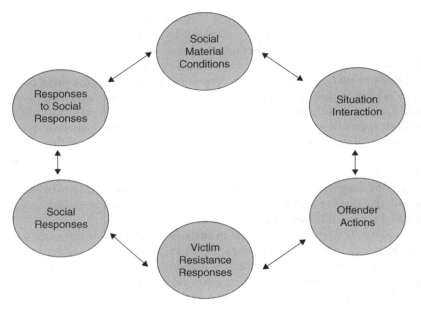

Figure 18.2 Categories of response-based contextual analysis
Source: Bonnah, Coates, Richardson, & Wade, 2014; reprinted with permission.

offender actions, we learn that each morning before he leaves for work, he takes one shoe from each pair and places them in the trunk of his car. He tries to keep her isolated at home. She, in response, wears whatever footwear is available so she can function. We try to *situate the action*, or *interaction*, in the broader context, or the present *social material conditions*, including the status of women in the society. We highlight the patriarchal influences and the conditions leading to impunity for many men who use violence as the backdrop for acts of power, control, and domination. When we consider the lives and situation of many Indigenous women, we consider structural and interpersonal racism and colonial policies in Canada.

Particular situations are placed in context as we gather details about the violence and the responses to it. We understand many of these responses as "acts of resistance" or what have been called "small acts of living" (Wade, 1997, p. 25). As such, we become students or "detectives" of human interaction, understanding that "whenever people are mistreated, they resist in some way" (Wade, 1997, p. 23). In RPB, we assume that: (1) resistance is ever-present (though often mistaken for a symptom or erratic behavior without interactive details); (2) resistance is one response and it seldom stops violence due to power imbalances, but is oriented towards preserving dignity; and (3) providing positive social responses aids victim recovery (Coates & Wade, 2016).

Victims' resistance responses, or acts of resistance, are responses to rather than effects or impacts of violence (Richardson, 2008; Richardson & Wade, 2008). If we focus on how a victim is *affected by* violence, we will conceptualize a person who is unwell, symptomatic, and sick, and we provoke no change in the system. If we focus on the person's *responses to* violence, there are political implications and calls to increase social safety for women. A person's responses to violence and oppression unfold in alignment with a situational logic, and reflect the options open to them as well as their deeply embedded, moment by moment analysis of violence and safety in context. Sometimes people resist in a manner that increases the violence towards them, but serves to reassert their dignity. A victim's actions and responses are often situated in prior experience and knowledge about what to do under certain violent conditions: we refer to these responses as resistance knowledges. Resistance can come in many forms, as described by Wade (1997, p. 25):

> Any mental or behavioral act through which a person attempts to expose, withstand, repel, stop, prevent, abstain from, strive against, impede, refuse to comply with, or oppose any form of violence or oppression (including any type of disrespect), or the conditions that make such acts possible, may be understood as a form of resistance.

Acts of resistance often relate in some thematic way to the violence perpetrated and tend to be fueled by similar energy and force; the more dangerous a perpetrator, the more prudent and thoughtful the resistance tends to be. Self-respect is typically at stake and, while victims can seldom stop violence, they will often respond to their disrupted sense of dignity.

In analyzing victims' resistance responses, we create intervention strategies to help stop the violence and promote victim recovery for this woman as well as for women in general. The approach involves documenting resistance strategies that can be formalized into a safety and social justice plan. After examining acts of resistance, we explore the next category of the response-based analysis, which is the quality of the social responses received by the victim.

Social response refers to what people do and say in response to the disclosure of violence. Research has shown that many people receive negative social responses from family, friends, and professionals (Andrews, Brewin, & Rose, 2003). Women and marginalized groups are more likely to receive negative social responses. These types of responses (e.g., being blamed, being criticized for not reporting, receiving unsolicited advice) are more likely to lead to longer-term suffering, depression, diagnosis with a mental illness, and even thoughts of suicide (Reynolds, 2016). In the final phase of response-based analysis—*responses to social responses*—we pay attention to the ways in which the victim responds to the variety of social responses received after violence. While left to "manage" the responses of others, she often attempts to preserve her dignity (and that of her children), her reputation, her privacy, and her safety. If someone reports to authorities that a mother has been assaulted by her partner, very soon this woman will be dealing not only with the violence but with a number of professionals such as police, child protection, victim services, lawyers, medical doctors, therapists or psychologists, and staff from the children's school. During this interaction, and perhaps in a traumatized state, this woman will often put on a brave face, treat each professional in a particular way while trying to demonstrate her competency, her pre-existing ability, her intelligence, simultaneously trying to preserve her dignity and often the dignity of the professional. To protect herself in an interview with a "helper," the mom might offer a problem for discussion while holding private a different problem that is potentially more embarrassing or distressing. Each response can be understood in relation to events and the aspects of the response-based contextual analysis.

An Example of Response-Based Analysis

We offer the following scenario to provide an example for the type of analysis used in considering events and interaction *in context*.

There was a Yukon couple in which the young mother (B) had two kids and was pregnant with the third. B's partner was considered to be an attractive man. He was charismatic, romantic, and attentive. People liked him and women especially found him to be "a catch." After a period of time, he started to become controlling, surveilling her and demanding to know her constant whereabouts. He would ask her to report who she had spoken to, what they talked about, and why. As well, he started to insult her regularly and to punish her for her perceived infractions. He told her that her friends were "idiots" and that her family was after him. He told her to not let her family into their home. He would monitor her phone calls and texts.

In response, B would secretly go to her neighbors and use their phone to call her mom. She and her mom learned how to block him from being able to monitor her phone.

He started staying out late at night and sometimes wouldn't return home until early morning. When he came home he demanded sex for which he would give her money, both to demean her and to lessen his guilt. Sometimes he had a lot of money. She would stash money in a bag in the pantry with a spare set of keys. He would tell her she was ugly and that everyone hated her, and that she would never find anyone else.

She would argue with him and tell him "this shit was hurting the kids." He would drag her into the bedroom where he threw her on the bed and choked her. Sometimes he would cover her mouth with his hand and rape her. She would stay quiet so the kids wouldn't wake up: she would think about the beach.

One night when he was assaulting her, the neighbors called the police. The police called child protection services. When they arrived, she was angry. Her partner had been choking her; she was screaming and spat at him. He presented himself calmly and talked in a peaceful manner to the police and child protection professionals. The social workers were concerned about her ability to care for her children. They told her she should leave her home and go to a shelter or else they would apprehend the children. They blamed her, at least partially, for the situation.

When B arrived at the shelter, she was quiet and "scoped out" the workers. The staff at the shelter supported B and she got a lawyer. B submitted a statement to police about her partner's ongoing violence and abuse. She received a threat from child protection authorities that they were planning to remove her children because she was not protecting them from witnessing violence. B reconnected with her family and friends. She stayed at the shelter and was required to meet with a child protection worker several times a week. B was angry at this and voiced how unfair she found this to be. She told them this was "shit" saying: "He can go off, drink, and schmooze with other women and I'm stuck in a shelter with lots of rules." He got to stay in the house and she had to relocate with the children, leaving mostly everything behind. B continued working with her lawyer to get custody of her children. Child protection services never eased up their threat of child removal. On the day of the court process, B was victorious and was granted custody of her children. She got on a plane and moved to another province. Her message for the system … "Fuck all of you!"

In this passage, we can observe some of the context and what we might already understand about the rights of battered women in Canada, in the Yukon specifically. One receives basic information about the situation and the interaction between the parties. When considering the actions of the perpetrator, one is made aware of violent acts, such as hitting, controlling, insults, surveillance, rape, and degradation. One can also see that this man is upheld and admired for his charm and attractiveness based on his appearance and outer demeanor. When gathering information about the interaction, we would then ask about what B did and how she responded to each of these violations of her dignity, her body, and her being. We would ask her to tell us more about what brought her to certain safety practices and how she knew what to do in order to maximize her safety and that of her children.

Another critical aspect of our analysis and information gathering is to understand as fully as possible the social responses directed at B. Here, we see her experiencing the shelter as a place that obstructed her freedom with its many rules. She received a negative social response from child protection, and from police who called them. Even though police are obliged to call child protection, there are ways of discussing this with the mother and walking her through a process so that she doesn't feel ambushed by the process.

We can also assess whether police were helpful to B by acting as advocates and letting child protection workers know that the children are now safe and that they have addressed any safety concerns by dealing with the perpetrator. While B doesn't elaborate, one might predict that the social responses of her family and friends are mixed, many being supportive and some involving unsolicited advice-giving or judgment.

The final aspect of the analysis involves understanding how the victim responded to the social responses. As such, B's pre-existing ability becomes apparent as she "manages" numerous professionals, the state, as well as the needs of her children. While there are cases where the actions of the mother create danger to the child, these types of cases are the minority and should not be confused with those where both mother and children are victim of a perpetrator (Strega, 2006; Strega et al., 2013).

As this mother makes a choice to leave the community where numerous social injustices have been directed at her, she is protesting with her feet (e.g., leaving), as well as with her words. Her indignation is clear at having been accused of being a danger to her children when she was actually working hard to manage her partner's violence. As workers, we can align with the preferences and resistance of the mother to offer support in the moment, support that goes a long way towards assisting in the personal recovery from violence and injustice.

Activism within Response-Based Practice

Activism is designed to create social change and can include activities ranging from contesting injustice, advocating for those being harmed/exploited, working on sensitization campaigns, lobbying, as well as more "behind the scenes" activities drawing attention to injustice. A key focus of the response-based work featured in this chapter is our ongoing challenge to contest inequities in service delivery for Aboriginal women, such as unequal access to the law and the justice system due to poverty and racism. While these issues may exist across the board, they become more pronounced the more one has to deal with the system, such as post-assault. Several key issues need to be addressed in order to increase safety and justice for Aboriginal women in the Yukon. These include continuing to support improved RCMP (Royal Canadian Mounted Police), child welfare, health care, and social service practices. Many of these reforms relate to addressing racism. Analyzing the situation in context elucidates what Aboriginal women are facing and how they are already attempting to deal with the situation.

Context and Background

The particular history and social geography of the Yukon are pertinent for understanding some of the risks and the opportunities for women activists. The Yukon is a place of contrast: breath-taking scenery, upscale bistros, trendy bakeries, and a brutal history of violence against women and Indigenous peoples. A recent report showed that violence against women in the Yukon is four times the national average at 1,900 victims per 100,000 and that the severity of violence, and the fear for life, is disproportionately higher in the Canadian territories (Wohlberg, 2013). Colonialism and male-driven enterprises such as the gold rush (1897–1899), the long-term presence of the US military who built the Alaska Highway in 1942,[3] and the mining industry have created a particular landscape where there are few repercussions for perpetrators of violence and many challenges for women. The situation of unmarried men, far from home and with disposable income, can sometimes lead to women being sought and then exploited in various ways. Findings from a 2014 study conducted by The Ending Violence Association indicate a link between extraction industries in British Columbia and domestic abuse (Wood, 2014). Mi'kmaw lawyer Pamela Palmater has recently discussed links between mining and violence against women (Porter, 2016). There are particular social factors at work in the Yukon that need to be addressed to create more safety and justice for Indigenous women in the territory. The colonial history of Canada has left many injustices in place. While there are too many to mention here, Appendix 18.1 demonstrates some of the inequities related to funding disparities as well as the extent to which Indigenous suffering and "management" has become a top industry in Canada. Response-based practice is oriented towards contesting such social injustice, as reflected in the example that follows.

The RCMP have recently been called upon to address inadequate services to women who report violence (Richardson, 2013, 2016). Yukon Member of the Legislative Assembly, Lois Moorecroft, published the report *If My Life Depended On It* (2011) documenting improper RCMP responses to women and why women, especially Aboriginal women, would not report violence. Historically, the RCMP were primarily concerned with gathering enough information for charges to "stick," rather than creating immediate and longer-term safety. Many women who are being harmed will not call police because they know police will contact child protection services and that they run the risk of having their children removed from them permanently (Moorecroft 2011; Strega et al., 2013). The RCMP express frustration that battered women often change their mind about reporting; women have been criticized for this safety-related decision. This has created a "practice tension" between Indigenous people/women and the RCMP. The consequences of an unhappy process are events that move from spousal assault to child removal, to a self-medicating mother who ends up on the streets, often in Edmonton (Alberta) or in Vancouver's Downtown Eastside (British Columbia). The over 3,000 missing and murdered Aboriginal women in Canada is a devastating outcome of suffering, poverty, homelessness, drug addiction, and broken-heartedness (Reynolds 2014, 2016; Richardson & Dolan-Cake, 2016). This is precisely the kind of structural violence that social justice activists are trying to prevent. Concerns about RCMP treatment extend much further, however. Historically, the RCMP enforced the removal and surveillance of Indigenous children as they were interned in "residential schools" (V. Boldo, personal communication, March 14, 2016; Wollmann, 2014).

Reconceptualizing Offender Actions

The actions of violent perpetrators are often explained by linking them in the present to a distressing dynamic from the past (e.g., an unhappy childhood, psychological or anger issues, or just being misunderstood), or to anger or alcohol (Coates & Wade,

2004).[4] While it may be natural for people to try to find the cause, this type of inquiry tends to result in minimizing offender responsibility and increasing the blaming of victims (e.g., How could she report her husband to the police?). Some acts of unilateral violence are re-cast as mutual in what are called "he said/she said" accounts. Perpetrators are seldom referred to as having a "violence problem," but more so as having "anger issues," or issues of self-control or alcoholism. If we mislabel the problem, it is more likely the perpetrator will be sent to a treatment intervention that does not address violence against women directly. Readers may be interested in a analytic tool, the Four Operations of Language, that Coates and Wade (2007) developed to reveal how perpetrators are excused from their actions and how, subsequently, the responsibility/blame is passed onto the victim. It is important to understand that individuals are more likely to perpetuate violence in cultures where impunity for perpetrators exists. Supporting this view, Reynolds applies a social justice-based critique of the absence of justice in cultures of rape (Reynolds, 2014) and UN Special Representative on Sexual Violence in Conflict, Margo Wallström, condemns what she calls cultures of impunity, where male perpetrators are often not held responsible for their crimes due to state inaction (UN News Centre, 2010).

Creating a Positive Social Response for Women in the Yukon

Commanding Officer Peter Clark of the Yukon Royal Canadian Mounted Police was interested in addressing some of the issues in the RCMP and improving the relationship between police and community members. In 2012, I (AM-R), former chief of the Liard First Nation and founding Executive Director of the Liard Aboriginal Women's Society in Watson Lake, approached CO Clark to secure funding for a joint project to address violence, particularly against Indigenous women, to increase safety and to improve the police response to women facing violence. Although the goals of the police and the Kaska women of the Liard First Nation came from different cardinal points, there was sufficient shared concern about violence against Indigenous women that we made progress. This kick-started the Together for Justice project—one of a number of community initiatives through which the Liard Aboriginal Women's Society (LAWS) and the Yukon Women's Transition Home Society representatives became allies. For example, I and LAWS members might advocate for a single mother experiencing health issues so that she could obtain medical treatment, and have support to travel for care and have assistance for her children. Kaska members living with disabilities, combined with poverty issues, often need community support for basic quality of life. I hold male leaders accountable for taking care of citizens and creating safety in the community.

Our team has also developed a number of safety interventions designed to work systemically with families while promoting systems and practice-change in organizations. These interventions include Islands of Safety (in child protection settings), "Together for Justice" (working with RCMP and community/women's groups), and "Telling It Like It Is" (contesting the sexualizing of child rape/abuse). Response-based interventions are also prevalent in the approach of the Yukon Women's Transition Home Society and the Liard Aboriginal Women's Society. LAWS has also brought this approach into the schools, doing anti-violence work with youth. These initiatives involve a noticeable re-adjusting of power relations and new commitments to fairness, collaboration, dignity, and improved outcomes for women, families, and service users.

Conclusion

This chapter has highlighted the perspective of four women activists who have engaged in social change in Canada's Yukon. We have provided examples of how we conceptualize, approach, and problematize male violence, and the tools we use to dismantle violence against women and bring accountability to perpetrators. Much of this learning has been hard-earned, at personal cost, and while attacks on feminist and Indigenous organizers continue. Canada is a colonial country where Indigenous land has been taken, and continues to be taken, by force (Harris, 2002; Todd & Wade, 1994) and where economic and industrial interests take precedent over women's safety. Yet the activist and community development work being undertaken by women continues to produce a powerful counter-narrative to many of the more patriarchal, sexist, and racist influences described in this chapter. The field of counseling and professional helping has an important role to play in violence prevention and recovery, as well as in decolonizing social institutions. While personal and social transformation are parallel processes, the shifting of a powerful group of individuals—violence survivors—can accelerate social justice change in communities. One main aspect of this transformation is the personal releasing of guilt and shame associated with victimization. Once a victim understands "It was not my fault," both the violence and the responses/resistance can be recontextualized into a social justice problem in the community, rather than as individual deficit. Just as rape victims are not responsible for rape, or stopping it, Indigenous survivors of residential school internment are not to blame for the actions of the government. Response-based practice involves an invaluable critique of state and colonial violence, as well as a critique of language use that minimizes and distorts such violence (Coates & Wade, 2007; Richardson & Wade, 2008). Naming violence, and acknowledging and celebrating resistance, can be helpful in this struggle. Indeed, accurate language can be liberatory for victims of violence, and promote justice and accountability for those who use violence. When we clarify violence, as well as resistance to it, we can assist those on the path to recovery and to social justice.

Acknowledgments

We would like to acknowledge all the women activists in the Yukon. There are too many to acknowledge by name but their collective spirit and energy does not go unnoticed. There are women who show up at (uncomfortable) meetings, women who speak up though it is unsafe. There are women who write, document, publish, run for office, work in bureaucracies or from their kitchen table. There are many women who do brave things, who resist indignity and denial, and ask for what all women deserve. We dedicate this chapter to you.

Reflection Questions

1. How can professionals help women when they are blamed for the violence of their male partners?
2. In what ways could you assist "B" (the woman depicted in the scenario described above) if drawing from response-based practice?
3. What differences for clients, community members, and ourselves have we noticed when we do response-based type of work?
4. In what ways can dominant notions of "professional expertise" contribute to negative social responses and the diminishment of client knowledge?
5. What is important about privileging client knowledges, preferences, and pre-existing ability in the work against violence?

Appendix 18.1

Example of Canadian Professionals Profiting from Aboriginal Suffering

The following programs have created opportunities for Canadian professionals, including lawyers, mental health professionals, social workers, prison managers, and guards. Many of these approaches "manage" problems but do not problematize inequality and racism in Canada.

Funding recipient	Amount (source)	Reference
Lawyers overseeing residential school cases	$100 million (federal)	Maclean's www.macleans.ca/news/ canada/white-mans-windfall-a-profile-of-tony-merchant
Aboriginal Affairs to manage reserve, the Indian Act (2016–2021)	$8 billion (federal)	Indigenous and Northern Affairs Canada www.aadnc-aandc.gc.ca/eng/ 1359563865502/1359564020015
BC Child Welfare System* (where 4,450 out of 8,106 children in the system are Aboriginal)	$500 million (federal) $90 million (provincial) and $57 million (federal) annually to Delegated Aboriginal Agencies	The Tyee http://thetyee.ca/News/2013/11/07/ BC-Aboriginal-Child-Welfare

Funding recipient	Amount (source)	Reference
Prisons (2007–2008)	$340 million (federal) (i.e., $117,000 (amount per inmate per year) x 2,906 (23% of total federal inmates being Aboriginal))	Maclean's www.macleans.ca/news/canada/ canadas-prisons-are-the-ne w-residential-schools
Aboriginal Healing Foundation (1998–2014)	$515 million (federal)	Aboriginal Healing Foundation www.ahf.ca/ downloads/september-29- 2014-press-release.pdf

*Note: These funds are for investigation, removal, and foster care, not for family support.

Notes

1 Notable allies include Lois Moorecroft, Allan Wade, Vikki Reynolds, and certain members of the RCMP in the Yukon.
2 We refer to "her" for the specific purposes of this article but acknowledge that men and trans-gendered, two-spirit, gender fluid individuals are also targets of male violence and that response-based practice can be helpful in their recovery from violence.
3 After 1941 and the bombing of Pearl Harbor by the Japanese army, the US decided to build the Alaska Highway as a defense measure. The majority of US soldiers were African-American. Retrieved from http://tc.gov.yk.ca/archives/hiddenhistory/en/highway.html
4 While many people attribute violence to alcohol use, this does not explain why some individuals can use alcohol without hurting others and why sober individuals sometimes use violence.

References

Andrews, B., Brewin, C. R., & Rose, S. (2003). Gender, social support, and PTSD in victims of violent crime. *Journal of Traumatic Stress, 16*(4), 421–427. doi: 10.1023/A:1024478305142

Bonnah, S., Coates, L., Richardson, C., & Wade, A. (2014). Response-based contextual analysis in cases of violence. Unpublished manuscript.

Coates, L., & Wade, A. (2004). Telling it like it isn't: Obscuring perpetrator responsibility for violent crime. *Discourse & Society, 15*(5), 499–526. doi: 10.1177/0957926504045031

Coates, L., & Wade, A. (2007). Language and violence: Analysis of four discursive operations. *Journal of Family Violence, 22*(7), 511–522. doi: 10.1007/s10896-007-9082-2

Coates, L., & Wade, A. (2016). We're in the 21st century after all: Analysis of social responses in individual support and institutional reform. In M. Hydén, D. Gadd, & A. Wade (Eds.), *Response-based approaches to the study of interpersonal violence* (pp. 176–195). London: Palgrave Macmillan.

Harris, C. (2002). *Making native space: Colonialism, resistance, and reserves in British Columbia*. Vancouver, BC: University of British Columbia Press.

Moore, J. (2017, January 23). Here's how Trump's anti-abortion rule will affect women worldwide. BuzzFeed News. Retrieved from www.buzzfeed.com

Moorecroft, L. (2011). If my life depended on it: Yukon women and the RCMP. (Submission to Review of Yukon's police force on behalf of Yukon women's groups 2010). Retrieved from www.womensdirectorate.gov.yk.ca/pdf/rcmp_review_moorcroft.pdf

Porter, J. (2016, August 11). Video represents "all that is really sick about the mining industry," Pam Palmater says. CBC News. Retrieved from www.cbc.ca

Reynolds, V. (2014). Resisting and transforming rape culture: An activist stance for therapeutic work with men who have used violence. *The No to Violence Journal*, 29–49. Retrieved from http://ntv.org.au

Reynolds, V. (2016). Hate kills: A social justice response to "suicide." In J. White, I. Marsh, M. J. Kral, & J. Morris (Eds.), *Critical suicidology: Transforming suicide research and prevention for the 21st century* (pp. 169–187). Vancouver, BC: University of British Columbia Press.

Richardson, C. (2008). A word is worth a thousand pictures: Working with Aboriginal women who have experienced violence. In L. R. Ross (Ed.), *Feminist counselling: Theories, issues, and practice* (pp. 122–143). Toronto, ON: Women's Press.

Richardson, C. (2013). *Indigenous women, RCMP and service providers work together for justice: A response-based safety collaboration in the Yukon. Research to Practice Network, CoreBC, and the Federation of Community Social Services of BC.* Retrieved from http://fcssbc.ca

Richardson, C. (2016). The role of response-based practice in activism. In M. Hydén, D. Gadd, & A. Wade (Eds.), *Response-based approaches to the study of interpersonal violence: New answers to old questions* (pp. 196–215). London: Palgrave Macmillan. doi: 10.1057/9781137409546

Richardson, C., & Dolan-Cake, J. (2016). Invitons la justice et la sécurité pour les femmes autochtones [Justice for the missing and murdered Aboriginal women in Canada]. *Possibles, 411*(1), 25–32. Retrieved from http://redtac.org/possibles/files/2016/03/Richardson-Dolan-Evitons-la-Justice.pdf

Richardson, C., & Wade, A. (2008). Taking resistance seriously: A response-based approach to social work in cases of violence against Indigenous women. In S. Strega & J. Carrière (Eds.), *Walking this path together: Anti-racist and anti-oppressive child welfare practice* (pp. 204–221). Winnipeg, MB: Fernwood.

Richardson, C., & Wade, A. (2012). Creating islands of safety: Contesting failure to protect and mother-blaming in child protection cases of paternal violence against children and mothers. In S. Strega, J. Krane, S. LaPierre, C. Richardson, & R. Carlton (Eds.), *Failure to protect: Moving beyond gendered responses* (pp. 146–165). Winnipeg, MB: Fernwood.

Solomon, F. (2017, January 12). Russia's parliament wants to decriminalize domestic assault. *Time Magazine* online. Retrieved from http://time.com

Strega, S. (2006). Failure to protect: Child welfare interventions when men beat mothers. In R. Alaggia & C. Vine (Eds.), *Cruel but not unusual: Violence in Canadian families* (pp. 237–266). Waterloo, ON: Wilfrid Laurier University Press.

Strega, S., Krane, J., LaPierre, S., Richardson, C., & Carlton, R. (Eds.) (2013). *Failure to protect: Moving beyond gendered responses.* Winnipeg, MB: Fernwood.

Todd, N., & Wade, A. (1994). Domination, deficiency, and psychotherapy. *The Calgary Participator*, 37–46.

UN News Centre. (2010, March 25). Rape must never be minimized as part of cultural traditions, UN envoy says. Retrieved from www.un.org/apps/news/story.asp?NewsID= 34205&Cr=sexual&Cr1

Wade, A. (1997). Small acts of living. *Contemporary Family Therapy, 19*(1), 23–39. doi: 10.1023/A:1026154215299

Wohlberg, M. (2013, March 5). Violence against NWT women nine times national average. *Northern Journal.* Retrieved from https://norj.ca

Wollmann, K. (2014, January 5). Reflection: Elder Gerry Oleman on "healing from colonization." Web blog post. Retrieved from https://askahutterite.com/2014/01/05/reflection-elder-gerry-oleman-on-healing-from-colonization

Wood, A. (2014, July 24). Study shows link between B.C. extraction industries, domestic abuse. *Globe and Mail.* Retrieved from www.theglobeandmail.com

Index

AAMFT (American Association for Marriage and Family Therapy) accreditation standards 47
accessibility of service: for children 115; as core of social justice 29, 46–49, 99; and cultural oppression 32; denial of 17; diagnosis and 197; for disabled people 36; and First nation peoples 246; and private practice 8; walk-in clinics and 223
activism 3–11
Adichie, Chimamanda 131
advocacy 21–22, 29, 33–38, 43–51, 99, 115, 130
affirmative action programs 23
alcohol, drinking 120, 121
Alvarez, A. N. & Miville, M. L. 50
American Association for Marriage and Family Therapy *see* AAMFT
ACA (American Counseling Association), Counselors for Social Justice (CSJ) Code of Ethics 19
American Psychiatric Association (APA), *Diagnostic and Statistical Manual of Mental Disorders* (DSM) 22, 196–209; children 213; dual diagnosis 225;

on homosexuality 142, 173, 176; on transgender 160
American Psychological Association (APA) 160, 161
American Revolution 17, 18
and-prefaced questions 204, 207
Andersen, T. 133
Anderson, H. 6, 126, 132, 135, 144
Anderson, H. & Goolishian, H. 145
anorexia 147, 148
anti-oppressive clinical practice 4, 48, 143, 144, 161
Aotearoa New Zealand, Māori First Nation people 69–79; and colonization 16; hospitality 71–72, 74, 78; knowledge-in-action 78, 79; social justice and social service practice 70
apartheid laws, South Africa 23
Australia, "Stolen Generations" 6

Bakhtin, M. 126
Ball State University 49
Barry, B. 16
Barton, C. 148
Batha, K. 214
beneficence 33, 34, 35

binary categories, rejection of 131, 144
Bishop, R. & Glynn, T. 78
"body talk" 146–150, 153, 155
Bordo, S. 148
Boston College 49
boundaries, re-definition of 35, 36–37
Bracho, A. 113
Brown, E. L. 51
bulimia 148
burdens 116, 117
Butler, J. 75, 78, 165; *Gender Trouble* 162
Butler, J. and Byrne, A. 174

CACREP (Council for Accreditation of Counseling and Related Educational Programs) 47, 48
Canada: European and Anglo-colonialism 6; oppression of Indigenous peoples 6, 32; profit from Aboriginal suffering 250–251app; refugee experience 178; Truth and Reconciliation process 6; walk-in clinics 215; women's safety 239–251; Youth Justice System 186–194
capitalism: and competition 9, 24; and exploitation 20
Caputo, J. 73
Carroll, M. 60
CBT (cognitive behavioral therapy) 104, 105, 106
CDP (Collaborative-Dialogic Practices) 124–136; co-creation 134–135; local knowledge as privileged 133; no pre-designated method 133; *not-knowing* position 127; philosophical stance 126–129; as political 132, 133; "relational hermeneutics" view 125; relational processes 133, 134; tentativity 127
CFT (constructionist family therapy) 198, 208
Chaveste, R. 124, 127, 128, 129
checklisting 200t, 204, 205, 207
children: child protection and male violence 244–247; *Collaborative Documentation Practices* 219, 220–222; education 119; externalizing practices 217–219; Indigenous 6, 247; parental control 113, 114; physical abuse of 6, 241; psychiatric labeling 216; and "Science-ifying" 213; session agenda 215–216; sexual abuse of 6, 20; *sibling rivalry* 118; walk-in therapy 212–224
Chinese Revolution 18
cisgender privilege 163
"Citizens United" Supreme Court decision, United States 23
Clark, P. 248
clinical supervision 57–66; case examples 64–66; as "deliberate practice" 58; self reflexivity 59–62; social justice praxis 61–62; therapy and activism 62–64
Coates, L. & Wade, A. 248
cognitive behavioral therapy *see* CBT
Coleman, E. et al. (2011) 163
Collaborative-Dialogic Practices *see* CDP
colonialism: and accountability 7; and Indigenous peoples 3, 6–7, 16, 69–79, 242, 246, 247, 249; non-Indigenous practitioners 7, 33; and privilege 4 *see also* post-colonialism
colonizer-indigene hyphen 70, 71
Combs, G. & Freedman, J. 218
coming out 171–180; binary distinction 173–174; case scenario 177–180; cultural construction 172–174, 175; models 175–176; "pride" 176, 177; stigmatization 175
common ground 145–146
communicative action 129–131, 133, 134, 135
competition and solidarity 3, 5, 9–10
conceptualization of social justice 47, 48, 126, 132
confirmation markers 204
constructionist family therapy *see* CFT
Contenta, S., Monsebraaten, L. & Rankin, J. 190
control: institutional 184, 187, 236; interventions 226; men's experience of 153–154; paradox 147, 150; social 3, 8–9, 62, 88, 236; therapists' 227; through violence 152
conversation and diagnosis 199

Council for Accreditation of Counseling and Related Educational Programs *see* CACREP

counselor education 43–52; critical pedagogy 44; critical perspectives 46–47; critical self-reflexivity 44; "de-centering" 44; diversity 48, 49; intersectionality 45; managing difficult conversations 50, 51; pedagogical position 50; social justice curriculum 49, 50

counterviewing 191–192

Crenshaw, D. A. & Garbarino, J. 192

Crocket, K. 59

CSJ (Counselors for Social Justice) 21; Code of Ethics 22

Cudd, A. E. 235

cultural literacy 176

cultural stereotyping 45, 51, 241

Davies, D. & Neal, C. 22

deconstruction: in children's counseling 218–219; and dual diagnosis 233, 235; and externalization 91; limits of 5, 19; and local knowledge 95; in narrative therapy 167, 191, 192; and social justice 26

Deleuze, G. 17, 19, 24, 25

Denborough, D. 113

depression 22, 63, 91, 165, 166, 201–205

Derrida, J. 17, 19, 24, 101

desubjectivation 25–26

Diagnostic and Statistical Manual of Mental Disorders (APA) *see* DSM

diagnostic reflexivity 198–199

dichotomy: "either-or" 144; gender 174; "us-them" 34

Dickerson, V. 90

disability 23, 36, 89; learning disabilities 183, 184, 186, 190, 192, 225

discourse: dominant 87; gendered 46, 147, 151; institutionalized 226–227; and language 130; pathologizing 26, 128; patriarchal 146, 151; problems located in 91, 96; of professionalism 5; of sexual identity 162–163; societal 116, 118–121; therapists' 148; about therapy 90

diversity: awareness 48, 49; counselor education 48, 49, 51, 52, 57, 161;

in counselor practice 33, 45, 104; professional standards 47, 48; and transgender people 161; within-group 99

DSM (*Diagnostic and Statistical Manual*) (APA) 22, 196–209; children 213; dual diagnosis 225; on homosexuality 142, 173, 176; on transgender 160

dual diagnoses 225–237; consultation setting 227; outsider witnessing team 234–235

Dunbar, L. 187, 193

Durie, Sir Mason 70

eating disorders 146–150, 151; anorexia 147, 148; "anti" approach 147, 148; bingeing and purging 149–150; bulimia 148; women's agency 147

economic recession 22

editorializing 95

education: equality in 17, 36, 57; lack of and transphobia 160; positive validation and 193; privilege and 30, 31, 58; societal discourse of 119, 120; youth justice system 186, 193, 194

empathy 30, 33, 34, 41, 204, 231

empowerment 41, 44, 65, 143, 147, 185, 203; disempowerment 31, 32

The Ending Violence Association 247

English Civil war 18

Enns, C. Z. 20

epistemological construction of social justice 129–131, 132

Epstein, E. et al. (2013) 212

Epston, D. 148

equality, importance of 22, 23

equity 19, 23, 29, 47

essentialism 45, 154, 161

ethics 3–4; collective ethics 10; CSJ Code of Ethics 19, 22; code of ethics 33–34, 47, 70; of collaboration and solidarity 11; of social justice 99; in supervision 64

ethnicity: and gender and sexual minorities 34, 174, 176, 177, 178; and post-colonialism 33, 69–79; and prejudice 35; and privilege 31, 44

ethnocentricity 34, 45, 46, 131

eugenics 20

expert knowledge 50, 90, 128–129, 144
externalization 91, 152, 162, 163, 188, 189–192

feminism: as collective 10; counseling approaches 22, 144; and eating disorders 146–150, 151; and male violence 151–154, 239–250; and power relations 141, 143; unwanted impact of activism 5, 18
fighting 119
Foucault, M. 19, 20, 24, 46, 85, 86, 162, 226
Four Operations of Language tool 248
Freedman, J. & Combs, J. 130
Freire, P. 46
French Revolution 17, 18
funding: and accountability 8–9; children's services 212; competition for 9, 10; Indigenous peoples 247, 248, 250–251app; legal aid system 239; serious occurrence reports and 190

gay rights 159, 160
Geertz, C. 83
gender 141–180; essentialist approach 154; Eurocentric view 173; female eating disorders 146–150, 151; immigrants 171–180; male violence 151–154, 239–251; as performative 162, 173; rejection of binary categories 161, 162, 164–165, 173; transgender people 159–168
The Gender Center (Sacramento, California) 161
Gender Dysphoria 142, 160
gender identity 34, 159–168, 173
"Gender Identity Disorder" 142, 160
genderqueer people 164–165
genocide, Indigenous peoples 6, 18
George Mason University 49
Glendinning, S. 19
Goffman, E. 226; *Asylums* 192
Goldstein, H. 213
Goolishian, H. 126
Gremillion, H. 147
Griffith, J. & Griffith, M. 106
Guattari, F. 22, 24
Guelph, University of 49

Haddad, J. 11
Haraway, D. 144–145
Hare-Mustin, R. 86
heteronormativity 162
heterosexism 63, 131, 172
Hill, G. 6
Hinekahukura Aranui 70, 72
"homosexuality," C20 construction of 173
hooks, b. 10
hospitality 24
housing foreclosure 65, 66
Houston Galveston Institute 124, 126
human rights 30, 34, 38, 175, 176

identity: assigned 25, 159, 191; intersectional 41, 51, 174–180; multiple 34, 51, 90, 130–132, 162
If My Life Depended On It report (2011) 247
immigrants and newcomers 171–180
inclusivity 23, 49, 99, 104, 208
indigene-colonizer hyphen 72, 77, 79
Indigenous peoples: children 6, 247; and colonialism 3, 6–7, 16, 69–79, 242, 246, 247, 249; and funding 247, 248, 250–251app; genocide 6, 18; male violence 239–250; pathologization of 6; gender-variant people 172
individual desires, focus on 119
individualistic approach: DSM diagnosis and 197, 199, 200t, 205–206, 207; and injustice 26, 41, 131; LGBTQ+ and 176, 177, 180; narrative therapy and 142, 163, 165; and personal accountability 112, 113, 114, 119; youth justice system 186, 191, 192
Industrial Revolution 17
information technology, impact of 20
injustice, new forms of 19, 20, 21
institutional systems, impact of 130, 191, 192
internalization 21–23, 26, 166, 177, 203, 213, 216
International Summer Institute (ISI), Mexico 125
intersectionality 41, 51, 174–180
invitational practice 22
Islam and Islamophobia 177–180
Islands of Safety 248
"isms" 118

Jenkins, A. 22
Jim Crow laws 23
Jones, A. & Jenkins, K. 70, 71, 79
Just Therapy 22, 63–64, 70

Kanankil Institute, Yucatan, Mexico 124
Kaushee's Place 249
Kivel, P. 8, 57
knowledge: as dynamic 126; expert 144;
    local 83–136; negotiating 145; partial
    144; positioned 145
Kvale, S. 4

Laing, R. D. 226
language 116, 117, 130–131, 132
Larner, G. 104
Lawrence, M. 147, 148, 149
Lazzarato, M. 22, 24, 25
learning disabilities 183, 184, 186, 190,
    192, 225
Lee, C. C. 47
legal inequality, institutionalization of 23
liberal justice 16, 17
LGBTQ (gay, lesbian, bisexual,
    trans, or queer) 171–180 *see also*
    transgender people
Liard Aboriginal Women's Society (LAWS)
    248, 249
Lorde, A. 38
Loyola University 49
Lyotard, J.-F. 18

Madigan, S. 191
Mah, T. M. et al. (2015) 226
Maniaroa 69
Māori people 69–79; and colonization 16;
    hospitality 71–72, 74, 78; knowledge-in-
    action 78, 79; social justice and social
    service practice 70
marginalization: counselor education
    46, 48, 49, 51, 61, 62, 64; and
    intersectionality 34, 41, 174; and male
    violence 154; non-dominant groups'
    monitoring of 30; and Queer Informed
    Narrative Therapy 161; practices of 85;
    by psychiatric diagnosis 120, 197, 203,
    226, 235; *social response* and 243; of
    transgender people 159, 160; walk-in

clinics 218; and work of counselor 88,
    89, 94, 95; young people 188
Margolin, L. 112
Marquette University 49
Marx, K. 24
Marxism 17
masculinity: and alcohol 120; dominance
    of 141, 152–154; social construction of
    167, 168; and use of violence 113,
    151–154, 239–251
McCarthy, I. 6
McDonagh, P. 225
McDowell, T. et al. (2002) 48, 49
medicalization 197, 199, 200–204, 209, 214,
    216, 217
men: dominant masculinity 152–153;
    experience of control 153–154;
    power 152
Merida, Yucatan 125
modern democratic state, creation of 17
Moorecroft, L. 247
Morgan, A. 189
motherhood and mental illness 65
multiculturalism 36, 44, 47, 49, 61–62,
    69, 175
Munro, A., Reynolds, V. & Plamondon, R.
    113, 114

narrative letter writing 65
Narrative Therapy Re-Visiting Research
    Project (Young & Cooper, 2008) 215
narrative therapy 90, 91–93, 162, 163;
    children's walk-in therapy 212–224;
    deconstruction 191; non-hierarchical
    227; Queer Informed Narrative Therapy
    161–168; social justice as core 22, 86,
    188 *see also* NTSG
National Rifle Association 18
Native Americans, genocide of 18
neoliberalism 9, 21, 24
neutrality 5–6, 33–35, 46, 58, 145,
    146, 198
New Zealand *see* Aotearoa New Zealand
non-conformity to norms 112, 113, 120,
    164, 166, 171–180
non-voluntary confinement 225, 226,
    231, 236
nonmaleficence 35

NTSG (Narrative Therapy Study Group), Ottawa 98–107; evolution of 102–104, 105; "local knowledge" 106–107; origins 100–102; today 105–107

"Occupy" movement 24
O'Connor, M. & MacFarlane, A. 74
Olson, G. & Worsham, L. 75
oppression: ACA Code of Ethics on 19; and colonization 6, 7; counselor education 44, 46, 50, 51, 52, 63; cultural 30, 32–33, 34; and emancipation 18; family therapy 114; and gender 154, 174, 185; institutionalized 225, 226, 235; "internalized" 21; and intersectionality 176, 177, 180; language and 130–131, 231, 235; and psychiatric diagnosis 198, 206; psychotherapy and 62; and resistance to competition 10; and resistance to neutrality 5–6; response to 243; and social change 8; systemic 38; transgender people 159–161, 163, 168; and work of counselor 20, 21, 29, 98
otherness 23, 34, 45, 71, 75, 79, 226
outsider witnessing team 227, 234

Padesky, C. A. & Mooney, K. A. 106
Palmater, P. 247
paraphilias (nonconventional sexuality) 173
Paré, D. 22, 86, 112, 129, 186, 191, 213, 214
pathologization 160, 164, 176, 183–185, 197, 200t, 207
patriarchy 11, 151, 154
Pearce, B. 129
Pedersen, P. 44
Penn State University 49
personal agency 25, 147, 190
"pink therapy" 22
"policing" of dialogue 102–103
polite transition 204, 206
positioned therapy 143–155; eating disorders 146, 147–150, 151; male violence 151–154
post-colonialism 69–79; and accountability 75

postmodernism 18, 143, 144; and NTSG (Narrative Therapy Study Group) 98–107
post-structuralism 16, 74, 75, 90, 143, 162
power: cisgender 163; Collaborative-Dialogic Practices and 127, 133–4; counseling relationship 4–5, 31–33, 35, 37, 41, 44, 87–88, 90, 93, 163, 164, 235, 241; counselor education 46, 49–51, 58, 61–62, 65, 75; and dialogical reflexivity 198–199; and feminism 10; government services 115; and homelessness 114; and intersectionality 143–155; Narrative Therapy Study Group 98–107; and otherness 226; resistance 19, 22; societal 44, 89, 130, 186, 187–188, 206; surveillance 20
"precarious" lives 9, 25
prejudice 30, 35, 93, 133, 160
"pride" 176, 177
Prilleltensky, I. 46
privilege 30–31; and access to resources 114, 115, 118; and children 214; cisgender 163, 166; and colonialization 74, 79; coming out 177; of counselor 29, 32–33, 35, 38, 44, 45–46, 51, 58, 59, 61–63, 93, 99, 111, 166; and dialogic practices 103, 198–207; intersectionality 41; "invisibilized" 45; local knowledge 131; unearned 4, 30, 41, 74, 163; of white privilege 6–7, 10, 18, 30, 31, 32, 45, 48, 85, 93, 176; and youth justice system 188, 189
Probyn, E. 10
professional standards 22, 47–48, 163, 164, 165
psychiatric diagnoses 120 *see also* DSM (*Diagnostic and Statistical Manual*) (APA)
psychotherapy 41, 62, 86, 126, 132, 160

Queer Informed Narrative Therapy 161–168
queer theory 162

race: and inequality 57; and immigration 175; and intersectionality 51, 59, 174, 180
rape culture 8, 10

Ratts, M. J. et al. (2016) 61, 62
Rawls, John 17
RBP (response-based practice) 22, 239–250; activism within 246–249; contextual analysis 241–244; example 244–246
RCMP (Royal Canadian Mounted Police) 247–248
re-authoring 101, 152
redistribution, economic 24–26
Regan, Paulette 6
relational responsibility 134, 135
resistance 19, 22; acts of 144, 148, 243–245
respect: code of ethics 33–34; counselor education 50, 74; externalization and 217; Indigenous beliefs 239; and knowledge 144; and male violence 151–154; Narrative Therapy Study Group and 100, 103–104; self-respect 243
response-based practice *see* RBP
responsibility to others 34, 35
Reynolds, V. 88, 187, 248
Reynolds, V. & Hammoud-Beckett, S. 62, 63, 135
Rich, A. 88
Rivière, E. P. 129
Rochester, University of 59
Rogers, C. 22, 41
Royal Canadian Mounted Police *see* RCMP
Rubin, L. 193
Russia, domestic violence 241
Russian Revolution 18

Said, E. 78
same-sex marriage 18, 173
"scaffolding" 237n4
schizoanalysis 22
self-reflexivity 44, 51, 60, 163
sexual abuse 6, 20
sexual orientation 31, 34–35; disclosure of 142; and gender identity 173; identity feature 172, 175; intersection of 141, 172, 174–177, 178, 180; non-dominant 142, 171–174
Shotter, J. 127
sibling rivalry 118

situating 92, 93
slavery 18
Smith, A. 8
Smith, L. T. 73, 74; *De-Colonizing Methodologies* 5
social change 8–9
social constructionism 86, 98, 102, 111, 129–131, 132
social context 145; analysis of 242–245; of child's life 219; of gender and sexual identities 162; of symptoms 206–208; of young offenders 188–189
social justice: activism 3–11; aims of counseling 16–26; and children 212–223; clinical supervision 57–66; and Collaborative-Dialogic Practices 124–136; in Collaborative Practice Group 98–107; coming out for immigrants 171–180; in counseling practice 29–38; counselor education and 43–52; and dual diagnosis 225–236; gender and power 143–155; and post-colonialism 69–79; and foregrounding client voice 85–96; and psychiatric diagnosis 196–209; as relational talk 111–121; and transgender persons 159–168; and women's safety 239–250; youth and justice system 186–194
social location: Collaborative-Dialogic Practice and 133; counselor education and 41, 44, 51, 58, 63; and oppression 30, 34, 36; Queer Informed Narrative Therapy 163; youth justice system 187, 188
social movements, historical 20
social progress as problematic 18
"social subjection" 25
societal discourses, influence of 118–121
Sontag, S. 4
Speedy, J. 59
St. Joseph's Neighborhood Center 59
"statement of position" 91–92
stealing 118, 119
subjectivication 24, 25–26
Sue, D. W. 45
surveillance and power 8, 20, 25, 248
symptom scrutinizing 203
syndromize 201–203

Szalavitz, M. & Perry, B. D. 187
Szasz, T.: *The Manufacture of Madness* 226; *The Myth of Mental Illness* 226

Take Back the Land (TBTL) 65, 66
taking it back practices 93
"Telling It Like It Is" 248
"terrorist" groups 20
therapeutic conversations 116–121
therapist roles 93, 94–96
Thomas, L. 213
Todd, N. & Wade, A. 6
Together for Justice 248
totalization 188, 189
trade unionism 17
traditional psychotherapy 86
transgender people 159–168; externalization 165; individualization of problems 165; limits of equity 23; oppression in therapy 159, 160–161; pathologization of 160, 164; and pronoun use 160, 163, 164, 166; social exchange 23; standards of care for professionals 163, 164, 165
transphobia 159, 160, 166–167
Trump, President D. 241

uncertainty, importance of 127
United Nations Declaration of Human Rights 17
USA: "Citizens United" Supreme Court decision 23; Constitution 17; income inequality 57; racial segregation 23; women's rights 241

values conflicts 33–35
violence against women 151–154; acceptability of 241; in Yukon 239–251
vocational guidance movement 43

voice 7, 11, 60, 83, 102; of Aboriginal populations 34; client's 215, 231–236; and collaborative practice groups 103; of counselor and client 37; disembodied 93; gender 144, 154; of other 75; student 50; women's 241

Wade, A. 22, 242, 243
Waitangi, Treaty of 70
Waldegrave, C., Tamasese, K., Tuhaka, F. & Campbell, W. 22, 63
walk-in clinics 212–224; benefit of 214, 217–218
Wallström, M. 248
Weingarten, K. 106
what about-prefaced questions 204
Whitaker, R. 20
White, M. 22, 88, 90, 91, 92, 93, 95, 101, 102, 144, 146, 217, 219, 225–237
White, M. & Epston, D. 100, 162, 217
Wilkinson, R. & Pickett, K., *The Spirit Level* 57
Wittgenstein, L. 126
Women of Color Collective 8
World Professional Association for Transgender Health (WPATH) 163, 164, 165

Yes/ No questions 204
Young, A. M. & Gonzalez, V. 193
youth justice system Canada 186–194; social inequality and crime 186–187
Yukon, violence against women 239–251; history of area 246, 247; response-based practice 240, 241–248, 249
Yukon Women's Transition Home Society 248

Zinn, H. 58

Made in the USA
Las Vegas, NV
17 May 2024

90039331R10157